FORGOTTEN LABOUR

Haymaking near All Cannings, circa 1930.

Forgotten Labour

*the Wiltshire agricultural worker
and his environment*

4500 BC – AD 1950

Avice R Wilson

First published in the United Kingdom in 2007 by The Hobnob Press,
PO Box 1838, East Knoyle, Salisbury SP3 6FA.

British Library Cataloguing in Publication Data
A catalogue record for this book is available from the British Library.

ISBN 978-0-946418-32-9

Typeset in 10/12 pt Scala
Typesetting and origination by John Chandler
Printed in Great Britain by Salisbury Printing Company Ltd, Salisbury

Contents

Picture Credits

I am grateful to the following who have given permission to use their photographs, line drawings and other images in this book.

p5 Sue Walker (*per pro* the late Steve Day); p9 Wiltshire Archaeological Service; p11 Society of Landscape Studies; p12 Butser Ancient Farm; p13 Dr Edward Impey; p14 centre, p16 left & centre, p24-6, p27 tools, p36, 172, 185 John H. Tucker; p 14 bottom - Cotswold Farm Park; p19 Prof Mick Aston; p.6, 23 top, Prof Barry Cunliffe; p. 23 coins, Dr Philip de Jersey; p27 sheep shears, p158 Michael Manser; p27 Flint Jack 1863, p217, Salisbury and South Wiltshire museum; p39, p72 Dr Della Hooke; p40 Dr Bryn Walters; p47-83 line drawings Dr David Hill; p64 Val Porter; p108, Hatcher Review Trust; p95 Very Rev the Dean of Exeter; p105 Elsie Gibbs; p133, p171 Adrian Tinniswood; p142 Tony Graham; p193 Museum of English Rural Life: p195, 202 Wiltshire Local Studies Library; p 203 Somerset Archaeological and Natural History Society; p206, 207, 208, 209, 264, 267, 268, 270, 273, 275, 276, 296 Council for the Protection of Rural England; p212 John Kirkaldy; p224 Wiltshire and Swindon Record Office; p225, 235 R. and S. Pope; p281 Daphne Cooper; p282 Benjamin Spreadbury; p 289, 290, 291 Ann Baxter.

Preface

T HE DIVERSITY of geological strata throughout England has produced a tremendous number of soil types, creating differences in the agriculture of almost every county. In consequence, the agricultural labourer of each county varied in character, work and social habits. A detailed knowledge of the highways and byways of Wiltshire and life-long contact with the agricultural community, particularly in the north-west of the county, stood me in good stead as I studied the factors that had produced these labourers of the soil from their beginnings in prehistoric times, to their end in the mid-20th century.

Wiltshire has produced two strongly contrasting agricultural regions – arable and pastoral – making it an excellent focus for any kind of agricultural study. Due to its accessibility and the prehistoric monuments, the county boasts a wealth of information on its early history, having attracted and fascinated not only casual observers, but also serious scholars for many generations; probably making it the most highly investigated county in England. This plethora of information has made my research much easier. However, very little was specifically written on the Wiltshire labourers themselves until the beginning of the 19th century when the social reformer appeared on the literary and political scene. The Wiltshire labourers attracted much attention, as they were by then almost at the bottom of the social ladder, constantly in want, with little hope of gain. A hundred years later, with more writers, newspapers and innumerable parliamentary reports, some economic progress had been made, but very little compared to that accomplished by industrial workers and others. By the 1950s mechanisation was taking over on the Wiltshire farms, so that within a few decades agricultural labourers *per se* had disappeared. Though little was specifically written about the Wiltshire labourers at that time, during the last fifty years writings touching on their lives have emerged in many disciplines. They include sociology, anthropology and economics, for instance, and more specifically, movement and settlement patterns, manorial lore, religion, housing, dress, union activities, sports and pastimes, drinking habits, to name just a few. A chapter-by-chapter bibliography details books and articles that have provided the greatest contributions to this book. In these bibliographies certain authors' names are asterisked, signifying that I have relied heavily on their other writings for background information.

Throughout, I have attempted to determine who the Wiltshire agricultural labourers were, and how they thought. They played many roles in their lifetimes, family man (and woman), small landholder, tenant, shareholder, serf, slave, employee, and in the last three centuries, most were landless employees. All through their history they worked hard and long hours; today society is forgetting how difficult it was for them just to survive. And that is the main reason for writing this book.

I owe a debt to all agricultural labourers I have known, each one has been a source of knowledge and collectively they have taught me to understand attachment to the land, albeit positive or negative. All my farmer friends and acquaintances have contributed to this book, not only by giving me background knowledge on the practicalities of farming, but demonstrating to me, by their attitudes to the farming scene, the frame of mind Wiltshire farmers need these days to function. Their story through the ages has yet to be told with understanding and fairness, and I regret I do not have time left in my lifetime to attempt its recounting.

Historians in various fields are now in much closer touch with each other than ever before, thanks to modern communications, and I am indebted to many who answered my numerous email queries.

Individually, I wish to thank Dr Lorna Haycock and other staff of the Wiltshire Archaeological and Natural History Society. Pamela Slocombe and other personnel at the Wiltshire Building Record provided much information on the agricultural labourers' housing. The staff of the Wiltshire Local Studies Library always showed patience in answering my endless enquiries, while Mike Marshman vigorously hunted down for me photograph sources. My thanks to Dr Florence Keller, Professor Emeritus, Carleton University, Canada, for information on the sociological front. Again, I am in debt to John H. Tucker for his contributions to this book, not only his photographic work, but also for giving me much background information on tools and other aspects of the prehistoric period in Wiltshire. Daphne Cooper I thank for her photographs taken at Bassett Down Farm. Michael Cooper gave me great insight into the modern farming scene in Wiltshire. In addition, I am grateful to him for comments that led me to dive deeper into the agricultural labourers' attitudes to religion and the church.

On the archaeological front, I am indebted to the excellent advice proffered by Dr Michael Allen and Dr Rosamund Cleal. Dr Andrew Lawson kindly allowed me to read the manuscript of his forthcoming book, Chalkland.

Finally my thanks to my family and countless friends, who, over the many years of my writing on the Wiltshire agricultural scene have tolerated my boundless enthusiasm for the subject.

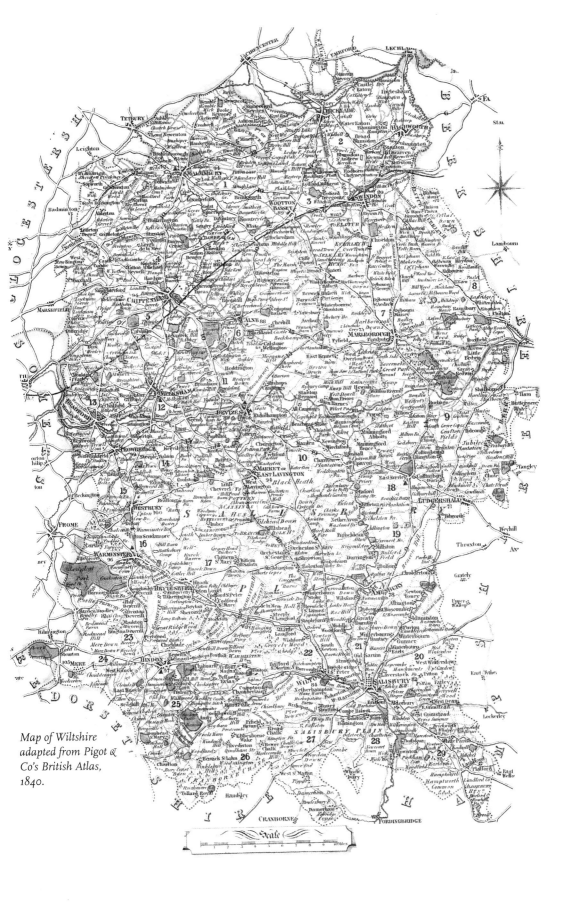

Map of Wiltshire adapted from Pigot & Co's British Atlas, 1840.

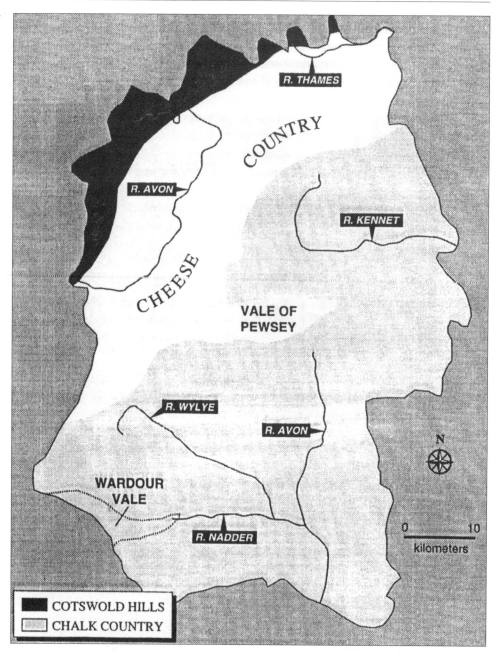

Sketch map of Wiltshire showing the principal agricultural divisions.

1
Prehistoric Man in Wiltshire – the Path to Agriculture

'Do not underestimate the mind of Prehistoric man.' Samuel Johnson

Agriculture is the cultivation of the soil and plants and the husbandry of animals. Man took several thousand years of his history to create agricultural concepts and techniques. On the land now known as Wiltshire, these began to be applied during the Mesolithic, to bring about changes in the Wiltshire landscape still to be seen today. In time, agriculture gave man the ability to live in large communities in peaceful circumstances, to allow him to reach beyond subsistent living, accumulate surpluses and monetary wealth, and to form societies with distinctive characteristics and living patterns. Sadly, the accumulation of surpluses also gave man the knowledge to pursue the arts of warfare on an increasingly damaging scale.

This chapter is a blend of old and new facts, perceptions, ideas. The Prehistoric era in Wiltshire is an exciting period at present. The 1979 Ancient Monuments and Archaeological Areas has provided many opportunities to open up fresh archaeological sites; the knowledge obtained from them has created new facts and hypotheses on man's life in prehistoric Wiltshire. At this particular point in time, new information can be difficult to interpret, sometimes in conflict with previous theses. Many gaps in our learning still exist, and in all likelihood, some of today's hypotheses and ideas presented in this chapter will soon be outdated by new knowledge.

The Palaeolithic (early phase of the Stone Age): Man in Wiltshire

In the immense time span known as the Palaeolithic, at present considered *circa* 750,000-10,000 BC, evidence exists that, on occasion, he came to Wiltshire. This knowledge is gained from the surviving stone tools and a few chewed bones he left behind. From the shaping of the tools, mainly hand axes, through many thousand generations, we can link the various *Homo* species who visited in the Palaeolithic to his ancestors and to those following him.

Southern England underwent many climatic changes during the Palaeolithic. Extremely cold glacial periods alternated with warmer phases. Subsistence and lifting of the land, among other factors, in time formed main drainage patterns, creating rivers and their valleys. These configurations shaped the elements of a landscape we know today. Human occupation in Wiltshire occurred during the warmer phases, when the climate was more hospitable. The first known record of man's presence in southwest England are hand-axes created by ancient man (*Homo heidelbergensis*), as far back as 400,000 years ago. The dearth of lower and middle Palaeolithic find-spots, almost certainly indicates that not only many tools were probably lost through subsequent soil and other deposits, or by movement of water, but that *Homo* numbers were few and widely scattered. Many assumptions are still made about their looks, their social organization, and their ways of life, but most is conjecture. It is even difficult to speculate what sort of shelter they created for themselves. They hunted wild animals, fished, gathered nuts, fruits, vegetables and anything else they found edible. Through the many glacial and inter-glacial phases of the Palaeolithic, *Homo* came, moved on, or died.

Not until 40,000 BC or so, is modern man – *Homo sapiens* – detected in southwest Britain. From tool evidence they continued to evolve slowly. Little alteration occurred in their way of life, they hunted and foraged in small groups, their tools showed only slight evolution from the basic hand axe. But they survived, being able to adjust to their environment when required, or moving on to another.

Knowledge of man in southwest England during the Upper Palaeolithic (circa 40,000-10,000 BC) comes chiefly from tool and bone finds in caves in the Mendips (Somerset). Certainly some of the people who occupied these caves passed through Wiltshire to reach their goals; flint scatters, such as those at Harnham, indicate this.

About 20,000 years ago, the last glaciation to affect southern England began to thaw. Over the next ten millennia, the continuing warmth changed the environment of the area; in Wiltshire, archaeological evidence shows a succession of vegetation changes. The tundra changed to open grassland, and gradually birch and pine forests evolved, forcing the reindeer and other life, needing open spaces and a cold climate, to move away. Freed of ice, the land tilted, sea-levels rose. Rivers settled in their courses, to create fertile floodplains and provide routes for man to utilize; in Wiltshire, particularly in the valleys of the rivers Wylye, Kennet, Salisbury and Bristol Avon. The hospitable climate and forest environment allowed man to begin a new period in his history. From tool finds we know that he thrived, at one with his surroundings, to roam in small bands, still hunting and gathering.

The Mesolithic: (Intermediate New Stone Age – circa 9000-5000 BC) The Path towards agriculture

It is thought that developing agricultural concepts from the Middle East, Macedonia and the Balkans began to spread slowly west across Europe, perhaps as early as 8000 BC, likely carried as one moving band of hunters-gatherers encountered another. One authority has calculated that the basic ideas of agriculture spread across Europe at the rate of 18 kilometres every generation of 25 years. Though a common language to communicate these ideas would have proved helpful, probably it was not necessary, for farming techniques are easily absorbed by observation and practice, especially when the goal of extra food supplies is involved. The success of clearings, corralled hunting, the cultivation of wild plants, doubtless gave the hunters-gatherers enough incentive to try these early techniques.

By *circa* 7500 BC, modification of the environment and some awareness of early agricultural techniques by Mesolithic hunter-gatherers have been demonstrated on a few sites close to Wiltshire, but as yet, none in the county *per se*. Due to its ecological diversity, the Kennet Valley always has been a favourite area for early man, so the chances of finding a site in the Wiltshire upper reaches of the valley are high. Near the county border, in Cranborne Chase (Dorset), a few early sites have been confirmed. A possible site under the parking area at Stonehenge also may later be authenticated, as posthole evidence suggests a dwelling place.

How did awareness of agricultural techniques come about in Britain? Perhaps persons who had crossed the land bridge from the Continent, seeking new territory or looking for trade and barter, influenced the hunter-gathers. Or they devised their own concepts. This is an extremely controversial subject at present; further research may clarify the issue. Early agricultural techniques, such as clearing and corralling, in all likelihood, developed from setting fire to the forest undergrowth to create clearings, and destroying trees, perhaps by fire or by ring-barking. Extra light gained in the newly opened-up areas encouraged the growth of wild grasses and scrub growth. Wild animals also would be attracted to grazing in the cleared areas. While feeding they could be corralled and killed, or, depending on their species, captured for domestication. Mesolithic man may have rounded up the wild pig to root about in a cleared area, to dig up the soil and to rid it of tree stumps. By 5000 BC, pollen records show increased forest clearances, perhaps made easier by the introduction of flint axes. Man did not apparently stay on or near these contrived sites permanently; traces of settled habitation have yet to be found. He may have managed a pattern of sites, each in a certain stage of development, abandoning them after exhausting their usefulness, to move on to more fertile areas. There is much conjecture on this matter present, but definite evidence shows that tilling small plots of land had evolved, a big step forward towards embracing agricultural ideas and concepts.

The acceptance of new ideas has always depended on environmental and human factors – climate, location, topography, natural drainage – and most importantly of all, a flexible mind. New concepts, especially to prehistoric peoples, must always have presented a risk – prudence is called for if starvation may result. This may explain the seemingly long time span in Wessex, at present considered perhaps four thousand years, between first attempts with agriculture techniques, to the point when man felt sure enough to abandon hunting and gathering as the basis for his food supply, to take up a sedentary farming life.

To practise agriculture, the right must exist to use a certain piece of land without interference. As man nudged himself towards an agrarian way of life, it is intriguing to speculate whether, in the late Mesolithic, a sense of land ownership or territory had already started to develop. A particular group of people may have asserted themselves and claimed a right to be at a specific cleared site at a certain time. Strategically-located sites might develop into meeting places, where man brought tools and other items to trade, animals to butcher or exchange for breeding purposes. After these important matters, feasting and other celebrations would have no doubt ensued, perhaps brides and grooms were sought, and if some form of social hierarchy already existed, workers and others moved from one family group to another.

That the gradual change to an agricultural way of life covered a long span of time is confirmed by the contents of a pit discovered adjacent to Coneybury henge monument. Items from the pit, both Mesolithic and Neolithic in character, have been dated as originating towards the beginning of the third millennium (4000-3700 BC). Over 1500 pristine flint artifacts, many pottery sherds, plus burnt cereal remains (probably emmer wheat), together demonstrated a continuity of Mesolithic traditions alongside new Neolithic agricultural practices, suggesting the gradual transition taking place from one lifestyle to another. Noticeably, within the pit, pottery sherds had been carefully placed on the flat base of the pit. Buried debris from some pits in later centuries also shows a formal arrangement of their contents. The arrangements possibly demonstrate a type of ceremonial or special behaviour, perhaps even a sign of territorial possession of the areas around the pits. Pits at Durrington Walls, Windmill Hill, and that section so favoured by early man in Wiltshire, the head of the River Kennet and its drainage area, also indicate this phenomenon. Such evidence is the earliest we have of any kind of sociological behaviour of prehistoric early man in Wiltshire.

Mesolithic tools can be found constantly in most parts of Wiltshire, though, probably due to ancient undisturbed forest growth, comparatively few have turned up on the heaviest clay soils; notably in the Bristol Avon valley area. However from tool distribution, we know bands of hunter-gatherers used the valley as a route-way, traveling on the gravels and open areas bordering the river. A sojourn by one group occurred at Cocklebury, near Chippenham, on a ridge 20 metres from the river. Here was found a cache of tools consisting of small blades, scrapers and flakes left over from trimming. Made from flints similar to those still found today in nearby river gravels, the original flint cores were also present, signifying that a single human group constructed the tools for immediate use. Their abandonment is typical of a short-stay Mesolithic campsite, where tools were fabricated as required and the by-products of the industry left behind. The presence of the tools is a constant reminder that no type of human settlement or social activity is possible without them.

The Neolithic: Last phase of the Stone Age

In Wiltshire, the Neolithic is today considered the time span when the economic and social concepts or bases of agriculture were put into place. But opinion is still divided as to just how long the dual systems of hunting-gathering and agriculture remained in place as a guard against famine. From pollen and fossilized snail studies *circa* 4000 BC, a considerable amount of woodland clearance took place. By 3500 BC, large areas of forest

This is the beginning (or end) of the coppice cycle. This area of Blackmoor Copse has not been touched for about 40 years. There is little or no light reaching the woodland floor, so the ground is bare.

BELOW Ravensroost Wood, in the north of the county, the spring after coppicing. The ground flora is stunning. The cut hazel is already starting to regrow at the rear of the picture.

This area of Blackmoor Copse, near Salisbury, has recently been cut as part of the coppice cycle. The apparent devastation looks shocking, but the light reaching the woodland floor is about to make a dramatic difference.

Photographs showing the stages of coppicing (by Steve Day for Wiltshire Wildlife).

growth in Wiltshire had disappeared, though the west and south of the county retained much of its forest cover. Cultivated plots contributed to a more sedentary life-style, even though grazings for animals may have entailed some journeying on the part of herd-minders. New herd animals (sheep and goat) had arrived from the Continent, and cultivated cereals – such as emmer and einkorn wheat and barley – appear more frequently.

To cultivate these small plots, some form of tilling was devised, a digging stick, antler, a wooden spade or ard-like like tool, or some type of hand-plough, but we have no evidence of any formal ploughing in the Neolithic period, except for the criss-cross disturbance marks in the soil under a barrow at South Street *circa* 2900 BC. An interesting point; one authority, though not doubting the existence of ploughing at the time, claims that those marks may have been made as a ritual gesture before construction of the barrow began and are not representative of actual tilling practices of the time. But some form of cross ploughing had to exist, to ensure full cutting, lifting and turning over of the sod or soil, in preparation towards planting.

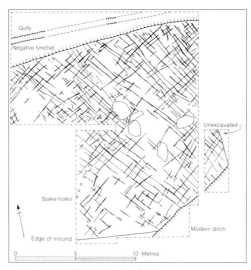

Plough marks profile found intact under South Street long barrow, near Avebury (above); possible form of Neolithic plough (above right).

How the clearances proceeded, we still have little idea. Past archaeological evidence shows that by the end of the Neolithic most of the Wiltshire chalklands had been cleared at one time or another, but so far, the only likely traces of Early Neolithic cultivation may be those located in protected areas of the upper reaches of the river Kennet drainage area. One reason for the lack of finds of Neolithic sites in Wiltshire may be due to erosion. The initial clearings on the thin soil layers covering the chalk made them susceptible to wash-away, destroying their fertility more rapidly than it could be replaced by manuring or resting plots, if either were practiced by the early farmers. So man may have moved on to clear more forested land, exhaust its fertility, and repeat the process. In time the areas left behind regenerated, to be returned to and re-cleared.

Neolithic peoples' familiarity of working with timber is clear from evidence gathered in the Somerset levels, where oak, ash, lime and elm were utilized to created timber tracks in the early third millennium. Willow, alder, poplar, birch, apple, and dogwood also had been worked, and hazel used for coppicing. Wooden artifacts preserved in the levels, bows and a hafted axe, tools such as paddles, spades, a digging stick, a mattock; household artifacts – a toggle, comb, wooden spoon, dish or box – were also found. These tools and artifacts undoubtedly were used by our agriculturists, but not able to survive in the Wiltshire soil environment.

As man trod the road to farming, work assignments in the Neolithic possibly followed the same patterns as those observed in other primitive societies studied in the 20th century. A farming community site delegated the most basic and necessary tasks, even in a unit as small as a family. The nature of agricultural work ensured that it be allocated to the strongest physically, but not necessarily to the cleverest, or the most personable.

Women would have worked on the land too, and to do any type of work for which they had the necessary strength. Certainly they cultivated those essential garden plots lying nearest their dwellings. With their children helping, they hoed and weeded, minded stock, and gathered wild-growing edible greens, fruits, berries, nuts. When working a distance away from the family dwelling, a mother carried her newborn baby on her back in a sling until weaning. Once weaned the child could later be left in the care of an older relative. When homesteads became more permanent, the women are likely to have less time outside and devote more hours within the family habitation, to domestic chores which, beyond the stone-grinding of meal and other food preparation, included the creating or assembling of skin garments and spinning, among numerous other household duties.

How Wiltshire man protected himself from the elements during the Neolithic has yet to be solved. Great difficulty, due mainly to scarcity, still exists regarding the identification of dwellings or any buildings belonging to the period, though a settlement site near Durrington Walls has recently been confirmed. While he continued to move around, Neolithic man undoubtedly built very light structures, now untraceable. Later, an increased sedentary life certainly gave him time to build a more substantial dwelling, with stronger timber supports placed in the ground and a more durable roof, but only posthole or surrounding site evidence would furnish any clues to the existence of such a building, and invariably subsequent soil erosion would eliminate such signs.

From lack of knowledge, the specifics of farming in Wiltshire are really very little known until the Bronze Age. Much research is being done on individual sites, but an overall knowledge of how the farming evolved contains many gaps. For instance, until the Bronze Age, it is problematic as to how much more important was the raising of animals, compared to the cultivation of cereals. But present bone evidence and the absence of field systems seem to support the theory that animals played a much larger role in the diet of man during the Early and Mid-Neolithic times than did cereals. However, finds of grain seeds (sometimes scorched), are frequently found in Early Neolithic pits, and querns (grinding stones), had become an important trade item.

Neolithic monuments

But if our knowledge of the early Neolithic peoples' agricultural activities is still slender, in the past twenty years much has been discovered and discussed regarding their monument building, taking place between *circa* 4000-2000 BC. 'The ceremonial monuments of Wessex . . . are the most remarkable manifestation of human belief and endeavour to be seen in prehistoric Europe. Each one represents high degree of skill and organization, whether voluntary or coerced. Their meaning is beyond recovery . . .' (Cunliffe). As a native of Wiltshire, these monuments, totally overwhelming in their scope and majesty, have left me always at a loss for words.

Causewayed enclosures are among the first monuments left by Neolithic man. Possibly used for nearly a thousand years, the most famous in Wiltshire is located at Windmill Hill, but others survive at Knap Hill, Whitesheet Hill, Rybury, and Robin Hood's Ball. Windmill Hill is also the largest, extending to nearly eight hectares. Others are much smaller, between one and three hectares. The enclosures usually consist of concentric ditches formed by pits separated by narrow causeways. Deposits of valuable artifacts, such as rare pottery and flints, plus bones, both animal and human, in some instances, suggest deliberate placing, which may mean periodic assemblies and rituals occurred among them. For some reason as yet unknown, the causewayed enclosures were positioned near, but not amongst settlement areas, usually slightly on the side of a steep hill, as at Windmill

Hill, perhaps to give space and facilitate trading, for which the sites were ideal.

At the same time as Neolithic man commenced building causewayed enclosures, he had also embarked on erecting long barrows and chambered tombs, of which there are approximately 75 in Wiltshire, a quarter of the total number known in England. These usually contained multiple or family burials. Later in Neolithic and Early Bronze Age, round barrows were built, in which were single burials accompanied by grave-goods, signifying tribute to an important individual, such as a head of a family, or a community group. Dating from the first half of the third millennium, these burial mounds are well known in the Wiltshire landscape, with major clusters in parts of Salisbury Plain and around Avebury. In the course of his daily routine, if the agriculturist worked in sight of a barrow wherein lay his tribal chieftains or family ancestors, it is likely that not only did the structure serve as a constant reminder of their ideals and rules, but instilled in him a sense of belonging and lineage. In addition, if a close relation of a family head or chieftain, he no doubt felt a certain superiority and right to be living so near to the burial site.

Cursuses – massive elongated earthwork enclosures of unknown purpose – followed causewayed enclosures, sometimes sited in areas where Neolithic monuments were rare or non-existent. But the culmination of monument building in Wiltshire is of course, Stonehenge, Avebury and Silbury Hill. Equally complex, but not as visible, are Durrington Walls and Marden. Their construction covers a very long period from approximately 2900 to 2000 BC. These monuments, particularly Stonehenge and Avebury, still have the power to strongly influence us today, and one can only imagine their effect on Neolithic societies. We still have little idea as to how those societies functioned, but historians today suggest that in western Britain, the builders of the monuments shared a similar social organization, beliefs and perhaps rituals. Obviously the societies were not only prosperous and well-enough organised to plan and construct the larger monuments, but they had the ability to seek out extra population to help provide food, shelter, and basic living needs. In addition, building and equipment supplies had to be brought to the sites. At the same time the agriculturist and his family needed to grow their own food and accomplish the work making up their everyday life. It has been shown that centuries passed between the building of some monuments, for instance, Stonehenge took 500 years to erect in totality. Hence society also had to find a means to pass on, from generation to generation, their building skills; or needed to relearn them when building commenced again.

The magnificent sight lines to the monuments signified more or less open countryside around them at the time of conception and initial construction. Between building periods the sight lines seemingly endured, due to the nature of the pastoral farming going on at the time, with its emphasis on cattle-raising. The openness around the monuments, enabled their solstice stones, seasonal and other astronomical sightings, to function unimpeded.

Towards the Bronze Age

Though still with little understanding of how our agriculturist lived his daily life in the Late Neolithic, recent investigation has revealed an apparent crisis by the end of the third millennium. Almost certainly due to the over-exploitation of the land through excessive stock raising, soils became eroded and degraded. Obviously a need existed for better management and, due to a growing population, greater production of food. To remedy this crisis, in Wiltshire, over several centuries, agriculturists began to parcel up the chalklands, resulting in the formation of large complexes of fields and field systems. By the Early Bronze Age, these systems were to dominate agriculture practices, in order to increase productivity.

To execute such changes, an understanding of land ownership or management and some form of tenurial agreements had to exist or be formalized. And before the actual physical work of laying out the fields began, communities had to assent, or be forced, to divide up the landscape, to design and survey the layouts. No traces of defences or defensive structures have been detected, so apparently all was accomplished peacefully, without fighting.

Within the field systems, burial sites were left intact and unploughed, allowing animals to graze round and over them, but access to open grazings were limited, due to the large areas covered by the field systems. In the Salisbury Plain Training Area (SPTA), how far the systems extended has yet to be discovered, though some were as large as 500 hectares, their creation and maintenance an ingenious feat for prehistoric man to undertake and maintain.

In the SPTA, the orientation of the fields was dominantly north-east–south-west, and their layout, illogically, did not always maximise the use of available sunlight. Many

fields tilted away from main light angles, while others were actually built on heavily shaded slopes. Likely yielding little, these fields may have served a symbolic possessive role. On the other hand, they may have been part of a productive farming cycle. This is an example of how little we comprehend the ways of the early agriculturists.

Traces of preliminary layouts of these fields have yet to be found, but ditches and banks have been detected. Those may provide a clue to the presence of hedges, as both banks and ditches make perfect settings for planting effective hedge-making materials, such as hawthorn, sloe and rose briars, not to mention the ubiquitous blackberry thorn. Because of shallow rooting systems, traces of hedges are almost impossible to detect archaeologically, as are sub-divisions of fields. But hedges are likely to have played a large part in the new field

Field systems on the Salisbury Plain Training Area.

systems; they function better than fences to contain cattle. But if fences were used, their traces too, would disappear within decades or be buried under a new system.

Though non-orientated or axial fields are also found, coaxial fields are found in all areas of Salisbury Plain. To maintain these needed a high population. In the SPTA, if all the fields were being farmed at the same time, they would support at least 2000 people. At the end of the 2nd millennium BC, a well-developed mixed farming system had been established on the Wiltshire chalkland and the adjoining river valleys. Sheep, pig, cattle and horse were exploited, while evidence of grazing areas is abundant.

Oddly enough, no habitation sites associated with the fields have so far been detected. If they were sited within or on the edge of each system, traces would be destroyed by later cultivation or more field intakes. And no evidence remains of necessary boundaries and trackways. Were they totally abandoned and obliterated when new field systems came about several hundred years later?

The Bristol Avon valley still calls for more archeological investigation, its intensive cultivation since Saxon times makes the earliest prehistoric settlement sites difficult to find and investigate. Clay soils do not retain imprints of human activity well, but we know that Mesolithic and Neolithic peoples traversed the whole stretch of the river valley in Wiltshire from Malmesbury to Bradford-on-Avon and beyond, as examples of their tools can still be easily found throughout the valley. Aerial photos now confirm complexes on the gravels and other areas near the river, particularly north of Chippenham. They are probably Neolithic and later, but firm evidence of farming sites before 2000 BC has yet to be verified. The chambered tombs at Lugbury, Luckington and Lanhill date from the third millennium. They certainly can be said to link to some form of settlement movement to the valley, perhaps from the Gloucestershire and Somerset Cotswolds, making farming even more probable there by Middle or Late Neolithic. More sites may eventually be found in areas where rubbly limestone deposits at the foot of the Cotswolds intersperse with clay soils, which, at the time, would have provided areas eminently more exploitable than those on heavier clay soils in other parts of the valley. Further investigations possibly will establish a permanent continuity of farming on the edges of the Bristol Avon valley, from Middle Neolithic onwards to the Romano-British period, when the valley began to be opened up in its entirety to farming.

Bronze Age: circa 2000–500 BC

Despite changes in farming techniques in Wiltshire, agrarian organisation apparently changed little until 1400 BC. Efforts were made to produce more crops, curb soil erosion and maintain communities. The open downlands remained, contributing to the importance of the monuments, their structures still dominating many areas. Land clearance continued, to establish farming in or near the river valleys.

It is thought that by the Middle Bronze Age, despite new field systems and cereal cultivation apparently taking a more dominant role in farming, stock continued to remain vitally important in the agrarian economy, not only for production reasons, but for their

Chisenbury Midden

social and ritual uses as well. Farmers thoroughly understood stock management and droving. Two investigations of middens, involving holding areas of cattle at All Cannings and sheep at East Chisenbury around 1000 BC, reveal these animals in goodly numbers, perhaps waiting to be culled, traded, or, at times, used for ritual purposes. Stock moved from their grazings on to droveways, a later example of the latter is one that ran from the Wylye valley to the heart of Salisbury Plain. Flanked by barrows, this way may sometimes have seen stock being moved to sacrifice, for feasting or ceremonial purposes at monument sites.

Iron Age: 500 BC – AD 43

Though a relatively short time period, the Iron Age, *circa* 500 BC to AD 43, saw man in Wiltshire taking many steps towards a more sophisticated and interlocked society. He began the period with a far-reaching understanding of land organisation and had established a social hierarchy from elite leaders to low-level workers. Trading, always important, increased, while society grew more economically oriented. When faced with territorial aggression, man had to reach a greater understanding of the art of warfare, structures, and equipment needed to combat assault. Food production expanded as population grew, so agricultural efficiency obviously continued to increase.

Intensification of agriculture – Domestication of animals

The concept of formal field systems to produce more food started towards the end of the second millennium; adjustments to these systems, in the form of earthen ditches, then began to appear on the Wiltshire landscapes. By the 6th century, these diggings formed elaborate linear systems, enhancing territorial divisions, and apparently in some way not yet understood, yielding more from the land. These new land patterns were served by trackways leading to settlements of dwellings, often circular, with hearths and frequently, small outbuildings. Not dissimilar to the later concept of a farm, they are likely to have functioned as such.

To increase yields, more woodland clearance was needed. Better tools, metal or metal-tipped, undoubtedly contributed to making this work easier and faster. A Wiltshire landscape

Butser Ancient Farm Late Prehistoric dwelling.

began to be created that we would recognize today. This land exploitation obviously was backed up by efficient fertilization, lessening soil erosion, rotation of stock and crops. The Iron Age sealed man's relationship to domestic animals, and pointed to cattle farming as one of the best roads to wealth.

From the Neolithic and before, bone evidence indicates that cattle were long horned, and the practice of dehorning common. By 2000 BC, a smaller animal, now known at the Celtic shorthorn, was also bred in Wiltshire. Always valuable, until field boundaries appeared, constant supervision would have been necessary to prevent them roaming.

The breeding of cattle was easily regulated. Most male cattle are fierce and hard to control, especially if their sexual activities are limited, and they fight amongst themselves, sometimes with serious damage. So it is likely only one or two bulls were kept back for breeding purposes, the remainder routinely castrated and reared for meat and other by-products, or to be worked as oxen. How early man practised any form of selective breeding or some choice in his breeding animals is not yet known. Today's criterion of breeding for flesh is a modern concept; up until the late 18th century, cattle, alive or dead, had many other purposes than just supplying food. It is doubtful that breeding was indiscriminate however. Anyone who has dealt with animals and depends on them for his food and livelihood is going to catch the gist and intent of selective breeding very rapidly.

From traces of dairy residues on pottery sherds, scientific investigation during the past decade has confirmed the use of milk and butter by Early Neolithic peoples onwards in Wiltshire. By the Bronze Age, from bone evidence, dairy farming had become an important economic factor. The milch animals were unlikely to leave the close proximity of a homestead or settlement as they had to be milked at least twice a day. A ready supply of cow, ewe and/or goat milk meant greater use of dairy products – fermented milks, butter, pastes and soft cheeses. But not a long-lasting hard cheese, created by renneting and cooking of the resulting curd; such cheeses were first identified in the Mediterranean around the 1st century AD, and their making is unlikely to have begun in England until after the Roman Conquest.

Not needing so much attention, beef cattle could be grazed further away from a home-stead or settlement, but as their worth increased, it made them more vulnerable to rustling. In all probability, it is likely the cattle were kept within a day's journeying of their home base, especially if herded by youngsters or women, who could not have ably defended them.

By the Iron Age, sheep assumed a much greater role in Wiltshire agriculture. Several factors were responsible for this change. A greater understanding of the principles of running sheep on the higher reaches of the chalklands had evolved, the land's fertility maintained by regular movement of the animals to different grazings, ensuring an even distribution of their droppings. Sheep were more adaptive to surviving on dry pastures, they have a lesser need than cattle for a constant water supply, and damp grazing will supply their requirements for quite long periods. In addition agriculturists had clearly discovered that though sheep supply proportionally less carcass meat than cattle, their yield- versus care-ratio is greater, frequently making them more profitable to farm than cattle, especially on poor grazings.

The original sheep brought from the Continent in the Neolithic had short legs and may have resembled the Soay sheep of today. During the Iron Age, probably due to breeding practices, sheep increased in size (though cattle remained the same, somewhat smaller

Imaginative drawing of Early Iron Age home sited at Cow Down, Longbridge Deverill.

than the modern animal). Sheep breeding was reasonably easy to control. The ram could be kept isolated from the ewes until his breeding services were required, or if isolation was impractical, he could be fitted with a cloth or leather 'apron' to prevent penetration of the female, able to continue running with the flock, albeit with a certain amount of frustration by both sexes!

Sheep provided much more than meat, milk, hair or wool to Neolithic man onwards. After tanning with oak or perhaps by smoking over a slow fire, the resulting leather from the skin could be oiled to provide protective clothing. Lambskins, after being stretched and oiled, become translucent, and therefore when inserted in a wall or door panel could serve as a source of light, while keeping out insects in summertime and cold in the winter. Felted wool would certainly have been used to create tents, or even roofs for short-term dwellings. Wool weaving was understood before looms, as basketry weaving is known in history, long before the first pastoralists. Wool was probably woven in small pieces, perhaps on a wooden frame, and then pieced together. Evidence of the increased use of wool in the Iron Age leading to the making of cloth is verified by such working paraphernalia as combs, spindle whorls and loom weights being found on dwelling sites. The use of earthen dyes and simple or ornamental weaving patterns was understood by the Iron Age and, if used, certainly made a utilitarian cloth piece more decorative. During the Iron Age, as sheep numbers increased, wool no doubt added greatly to the agricultural economy, but man much earlier had depended on his sheep for rugs, bedding, pillows and clothing.

The place of goats in the agricultural life of Neolithic Wiltshire is still little understood. Despite their bones being easily confused with sheep, goat bone finds in Wiltshire are not as numerous as should be expected for such a useful animal; especially so, as the climate in southern England was very comfortable for goats. But large numbers are not needed for high production, and the bone samples are difficult to interpret. Other reasons may exist for the low level of goat bone finds. In all likelihood, the kid was eaten, not the mature animal, and kid bones, due to rapid growth, are porous and disintegrate quickly. If old milch animals or billies were eaten, the amount of cooking needed to tenderize the meat would hasten the deterioration of discarded bones.

Pottery Spindle Whorl. Though Romano-British, prehistoric spindle whorls of baked clay were of similar design.

Early sheep type – Soay.

Goats have many superior advantages and few drawbacks. They domesticate readily, they can even be family animals, as are dogs and cats. Sturdier than either cattle or sheep, they are less susceptible to disease, easily reared in most types of environment, able to graze anywhere. The latter can be a serious fault, for they are more

Rock carving of early Bronze Age 'ship', made of wicker covered with hides, either horse or seal. Able to carry pigs, goats or sheep with legs tied. The Galway curragh depicted is of similar design.

adept at getting out of confinement than are sheep. In addition they are economical providers of large amounts of milk and meat, for their intake- versus product-ratio is high. More easily milked than cows or sheep, they can be readily handled by women or children. Their lactation period can be extended to equal or surpass that of a cow, and able to breed at any time of the year, they can ensure an ever-present supply of dairy products. Finally they are an excellent source for leather, and hair for weaving. It is hard to understand why more evidence of such a useful animal does not exist in Wiltshire's prehistoric times.

All but the squeak is the old Wiltshire description of what could be used of the pig. Bone evidence at most prehistoric sites investigated shows constant consumption of this animal, and that it was bred both large and small. As with cattle and sheep at this and other sites, recent investigations at Durrington Walls confirms previous suspicions that in the Late Neolithic, numerous pigs were utilized for some form of ritual or feasting; the bones and other parts were afterwards disposed of by careful placement in pits.

Pigs love snuffling in woodland, to be able to seek food for themselves, and the forest cover provided them with needed shelter. Before domestication, their ability to uproot soils and destroy tree stumps was almost certainly utilised in early clearance techniques, as pigs are adept at finding areas to root around in. Domestication of wild pigs, likely to have begun taking place in the Neolithic, meant man then chose when or where his pigs made use of their excellent rooting abilities and healthy appetites for a broad spectrum of vegetation. Domesticated pigs were herded in Wiltshire forests until Stuart times, when suitable forest cover finally disappeared. Given good shelter and sufficient pannage, pigs do not stray far away from their home territory, and so needed little herding on open land. But secure confinement is usually necessary to keep them out of a neighbour's land! From the Late Neolithic, a farmer near to woodland where pigs ran, was likely to have taken precautions to confine his sows at breeding time. He then avoided the possibility of interbreeding with the wild boar (present in forests until medieval times), unless a cross-bred litter was desired.

Pigs supplied a fatty meat, easily dried, smoked or salted. Besides curing their tough hides, man no doubt utilised their bristles. If kept around a homestead, pigs consumed household scraps and certainly, when available, whey and buttermilk leftover from the making of dairy products. As field systems began often to separate woodland, pigs always needed to be kept out of pastures and, in the Spring especially, out of coppices, to prevent their rooting up grass, crops and young trees. Perhaps man learnt early on to ring a pig's snout with bone loops or coils, to modify this destructive practice. Finally, pork played an important part in prehistoric eating, a succulent dish always to be regarded highly and looked forward to, as its use for rites and feasting demonstrates.

Other animals, besides cattle and sheep, varied in size from those of today. Ponies and horses tended to be smaller, from 10 to 15 hands. Until Anglo-Saxon times, a horse over 14 hands was a rare occurrence. Wild horses are recorded in Wiltshire through prehistory, but the first evidence of the domesticated horse appears about 2000 BC in Britain. Wild horses, or ponies, are more likely to have provided the original domestic stock, but the possibility exists that young foals were imported from the Continent in the Late Neolithic. Bone studies do not show whether man ate horse to any great extent in prehistoric times, though inhabitants at Tollard Royal in the Iron Age were supplied with horse meat.

Cunliffe has observed that by the Iron Age the number of horse bones found and recorded on prehistoric sites in Wessex approximate 5% of total bone numbers, and were of mainly mature animals. He suggests that young horses ran wild and were rounded up

yearly. Horse teeth usually indicate many animals over 10 years old, indicating a long working life as transport or riding animals. A bronze statuette of the Gallic horse goddess, Epona, found on the Downs, is an early link between Wiltshire man and the horse. In this instance, she is depicted sitting on a throne, with her hands on the heads of two foals. Epona belonged to what is considered today, the Iron Age horse cult.

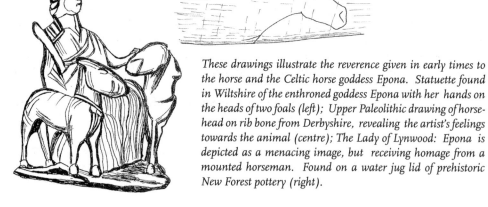

These drawings illustrate the reverence given in early times to the horse and the Celtic horse goddess Epona. Statuette found in Wiltshire of the enthroned goddess Epona with her hands on the heads of two foals (left); Upper Paleolithic drawing of horse-head on rib bone from Derbyshire, revealing the artist's feelings towards the animal (centre); The Lady of Lynwood: Epona is depicted as a menacing image, but receiving homage from a mounted horseman. Found on a water jug lid of prehistoric New Forest pottery (right).

No studies of Prehistoric horse bones found in Wiltshire have reported examination of their teeth for evidence of bit wear, so a conjecture of the time man might have first ridden in the county cannot be made at present. According to Ancient World finds, riding is supposed to have originated around 4000-3500 BC. History has shown that when man and horse occur in near proximity, a long and close relationship between them is invariably the rule. A bond is formed, fruitful and rewarding to both. This is evidenced from very early times, and it could be theorized that riding began much earlier in Wiltshire than the present evidence of 1000 BC demonstrates. The wildest of horses can be domesticated if patiently treated, and horses apparently were for the taking in Wiltshire. For harness, it is feasible to presume bone or leather bits could be used to facilitate riding, fibre or leather used for bridles and reins, and for a saddle, a piece of sheepskin tied on to the beast's back would serve adequately.

As the chalk lands were tamed, the need for more movement by people for trading or social contact would have grown. A group or tribal leader who owned and rode a horse, not only gained in stature and status, but was able to maintain a closer watch on his lands and peoples. Those who had stock would find controlling and moving them very much easier when done on horseback. And if wolves were a menace, they too were far more easily and safely chased away by a person on horseback than several people on foot. Horses could be obtained from the wild, their keep and housing is not likely to have entailed a great expenditure, so it is feasible to assume that man in Wiltshire may have ridden much earlier than 1000 BC. The lack of early evidence of harness does not necessarily defeat this hypothesis.

Archaeological evidence is still not clear as to whether Wiltshire was or was not behind in adapting metal for tools, weapons and harness. Evidence of common usage of metal bits and harness links appears much later than most in other parts of Britain. On the Wiltshire–Dorset border, at Gussage All Saints, a find of broken clay moulds indicates both bronze bits and harness links being manufactured there *circa* 300 BC. The bones of young horses found nearby suggest that horse breeding or capture of wild horses or ponies was being carried out in the area, so near to the New Forest. Whether the harness was used on horses or ponies for riding, chariot pulling or pack-carrying, cannot be ascertained. Horses or ponies in the Iron Age were doubtless attached to chariot-type vehicles by leather or fibre trace lines fastened to a breast plate Except for chariot use, seemingly horses were not used for traction, and did not pull heavy loads until the use of the horse collar appeared in Britain by the AD 1100. This is such a late date for a fairly simple technique to have originated, perhaps up to that time, horses were considered too fine to be used as farm animals.

Donkey, ass, and mule bones do not appear until historic times in Wiltshire, presumably introduced by the Romans. Bone finds of these three animals must be examined with caution, as they can be confused with the remains of ponies. New Forest ponies may date back to prehistoric times, a piece of harness dated 500 BC found at All Cannings Cross perhaps was used for a riding pony. It is possible that until Saxon times wild ponies were not confined to certain geographical areas.

Of the smaller domestic animals, specific information for Wiltshire is slight. Bone evidence in Britain records the presence of dogs as far back as the Mesolithic, cats occasionally after the Neolithic. The dogs, of varying sizes from 24-72 cms high, no doubt were used for working with stock, the cats as rodent catchers.

Poultry and Fowl – Fish – Bees

Very little is known of domesticated poultry and fowl Wiltshire until the Late Iron Age, and the evidence can be conflicting. Julius Caesar, writing in 43 BC, observed that the British kept chicken and geese, but did not eat them! Finds in Britain of duck, goose and woodcock bones originating in the Late Neolithic, may mean that they were also present in Wiltshire, but mallard ducks do not appear until after the Roman invasion. If mallards did breed in the county, the dry chalklands, where most archaeological activity has taken place, is not the most suitable environment to find any traces of them.

Fish and other creatures of fresh waters certainly provided a good source of food for the prehistoric Wiltshireman, but seemingly no evidence has yet come to light as to how he obtained them for his table.

It is likely that man's main contact with bees throughout Wiltshire prehistory happened when he tried to rob a nest constructed by a swarm of bees in a hollow tree. A European rock painting from *circa* 6000 BC depicts such an event, complete with the man climbing the tree, and hauling up a collecting bag into which to put the comb or honey. However, analysis of prehistoric pottery sherds has revealed beeswax and/or honey residues, confirming man's use of bee products. The Romans understood formal beekeeping, and no doubt introduced it to Britain. In the Wiltshire Heritage museum at Devizes are the remains of several pots with clusters of small holes in their sides or base. The indomitable Cunningtons, during their early 20th century excavations at Casterley Camp, found two such pots; they may just predate the Roman occupation. Other pot fragments with similar holes are in the museum and definitely predate AD 43. The holes and the pots themselves seem too small to permit beekeeping efficiently, but they do resemble hives used at a later date in the Mediterranean. A beekeeping expert who viewed these pots, stated that 'they must remain in question.'

Cereals

How large a role cereal growing played in the prehistoric Wiltshire agrarian economy is still somewhat puzzling, the basic grains emerging from the Wessex chalklands in Neolithic times being the emmer(*Triticum dicoccum*)and einkorn (T. *monococcum*) wheats, and the common barley (*Hordeum vulgare*).

By the beginning of the second millennium, cereal growing increased, albeit slowly, our agriculturist finding a greater efficiency in pairing cereal cropping and livestock raising. Experiments at Butser Ancient Farm, near the Wiltshire–Hampshire border, clearly illustrate that cereal cultivation methods by the Iron Age had become highly productive, with emmer

Windmill Hill from the air.

and spelt breadwheat *(T. spelta)* producing similar modern yields to those achieved prior to the use of chemicals. When population pressures increased, emmer wheat may have replaced spelt to a great extent. It grew well in damp soils and shrugged off frosty temperatures, making it suitable for cultivation in areas chosen for agricultural expansion – often less favorable soils off the chalklands. Deeper ploughing, weeding, and the application of fertilizer also seem to have been used in the Iron Age, perhaps creating two cropping systems, one based on spelt wheat and hulled barley *(Hordeum hexasticum)* in shallow-ploughed fields infested with weeds, the other, based on bread/club wheat *(T. aestivum/compactum)*, rye *(Secale cereale)*, wild and cultivated oats *(Avena)*, and beans in deep-ploughed and relatively weed-free fields. Peas *(Pisum sativum)*, and the 'Celtic bean' *(Vicia faba* var *minor)*, the latter an important nitrogen-fixer, were traditional Iron Age crops, and seeds of flax *(Linium usitatissimum)* can be also found at some Iron Age sites. Oats is a cereal abhorring dry soils, so in Wiltshire, it may have been a poor-yielding crop. Rye, with its ability to grow when planted either late in the autumn or in spring, and being a filling grain, may have proved more popular. All these grains provided a more varied diet for the agriculturist; undoubtedly, all were traded.

Archaeologists recognized that well before the Iron Age, the growth of storage facilities for cereals had increased, either in pits or granaries; the latter tentatively identified by holes once containing posts on which storage units were built high enough to bar invasion from rats and mice, and probably to provide ventilation to the grain.

Archaeological remains of storage pits are found on many settlement sites investigated in Wiltshire, and their use continued from the Middle Neolithic to Roman times. The pits were bell-shaped and invariably a metre or a little more in depth. How long a pit functioned for grain storage is an enigma at present, perhaps only a season or two, for pit linings are easily damaged by damp or breakage, hence destroying their function as retainers of the preserving carbon dioxide produced by the grain after their sealing. Most pits apparently ended up as receptacles for household and other rubbish. Seeds, debris and artifacts, shards of pottery, animal and even human bones are found in them. Some pits may only have held seed grain, eliminating the need to access until planting time, whereas grain for food consumption was stored handily in above-ground granaries. Hillforts contained a higher percentage of storage pits than settlement sites and homesteads, so grain may have been brought in from the surrounding area for protective storage or for trading.

In North America, pits were also a comparatively ancient way of storing loose or cobbed maize, and beans, but they also held other dried vegetables, even dried meat, and grease poured into a bladder or other container. The pits were lined with dry grass or other dry vegetable matter, such as twigs and leaves. They were then filled and sealed completely, allowing carbon dioxide to build up and preserve its contents. An elderly North American Indian woman, born in 1839, told of particular patterns her family practiced in the arrangement of the grains and vegetables in the pit, and the careful creation of the cover to seal the pit, keeping carbon dioxide in, oxygen out, mice and other animals at bay. The Indian pits were deeper than those found in Wiltshire, sometimes two metres, their filling traditionally women's work after the men had dug them out. Such storage pits were of great value to be carefully guarded at all times. If robbed or destroyed, much of their food for the harsh unproductive winter and spring months was lost and the threat of famine magnified. One wonders if prehistoric man in Wiltshire used a similar technique as did the North American Indians, not only in the loading and sealing of their pits, but whether they also placed in them other foods besides grains.

Trade

Trading links with the Continent and Wessex are evident from the Bronze Age, due to finds of ornaments, tools, and early weapon types, in Wiltshire, mainly axes. Though its intensity varied, trading continued right on through the Iron Age, when hillfort sites played a prominent role, not only for exchange of goods, but for their storage also.

Pottery, in particular, was a big business in its own right in Wessex by *circa* 1000 BC. Various vessel types with differing patterns make identification sources and destinations of wares easy to identify, by the Lower Bronze Age and Early Iron Age, several distinctive groups of makers scattered about Wiltshire had appeared. Potters made particular types, for instance, at All Cannings Cross, while Latton is considered a juxtaposition of various pottery styles. Sociologically, much can be made of this and other phases of trading. A common lifestyle is implied, held by wide-ranging societies, peacefully interacting, with an acceptance of mutual values, regional coherences, and 'an unprecented economic stability.' (Cunliffe). Hengistbury Head (overlooking Christchurch Harbour, Dorset), had developed into an important trading area by the Iron Age; for several centuries it is likely to have been the major port for goods between Wiltshire and the Continent. Then the Roman Empire extended its continental trading routes, making the eastern ports of Britain more conveniently accessible to trade than the south coast ports had been previously, but any decline in Wiltshire trade is not discernible. The port handled a variety of cargo: bronze, silver gold, salt, Kimmeridge shale, grain, possibly salted meat and hides from cattle brought to the site and slaughtered. And on a less serious note, much wine, judging from numbers of pottery sherds from 'empties', still to be found scattered around the port area.

The Greek geographer Strabo wrote in the 1st century BC of exports from England including corn, cattle, gold, silver, hides, slaves and 'clever hunting dogs.' Slaves, despite present lack of proof of their trading, were obviously an important commodity at the time, but whether they were raised as such, or created from captives of war, cannot be determined. If some traded slaves originated in Wiltshire, one wonders in what part of the Continent are their descendants today.

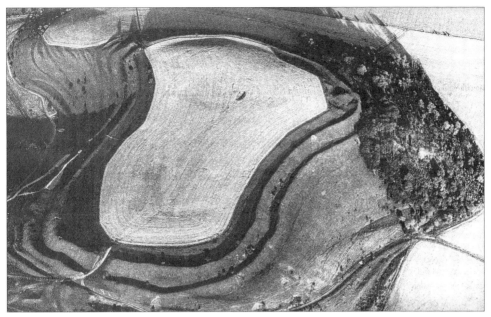

Battlesbury Hillfort.

Hillforts

What are believed to be hillfort sites are dotted all over the southern chalklands, Wiltshire having a goodly share of them. Apparently the earliest known, constructed after 1500 BC were of simple concept, consisting of rudimentary earthworks and perhaps a palisade, but in time they became more sophisticated and may have represented chains of defence systems strategically placed across high ground, adding to earlier resistance measures of fortified homesteads and small earthwork enclosures. By the 5th century BC, the sheer number of hillforts across the Wiltshire landscape suggests that the threat of aggression must have been very extreme indeed during the first millennium, even if not all the forts were in working order through those years. Their presence no doubt provided protection, not to mention reassurance, to the agriculturist during unsettled times as he worked in his fields on the chalklands.

The largest hillforts in Wiltshire are the magnificent structures of Yarnbury and Battlesbury; both to be regarded as the county's earliest and greatest castles they are large enough to encompass a modest village. Five hillforts exist in the SPTA, the largest being Casterley camp. Smaller examples are Martinsell and Knook, with many others too numerous to name. They were invariably situated on promontories, serving as defence sites, but some also began to be used as trading centres. The lives of the agriculturists living nearby could not help but be greatly influenced, perhaps overwhelmed, by these magnificent structures. Though not necessarily continually occupied, many date back to Neolithic times, adding to their already great historical significance.

The hillforts provided many benefits for local people during the Iron Age, particularly a close trading location for grain and other foods, leather and woollen goods made at their homesteads. In return they had easier access to a wider variety of commodities from nearby and far-off places, basics such as salt, slate, the Kimmeridge shale, and manufactured or crafted artifacts – pottery, tools (probably mainly of wood and bone, but by the third century BC bronze and iron tools were beginning to be more common), saddle querns, whetstones, to name only a few items. These marketing places doubtless encouraged agriculturists to produce more, and in turn resulted in an increase in overall trading. Grain storage facilities enabled local farmers to store their cereal crops before trading. The trading forts may also have served as centres for cattle round-ups and culling, a gathering site for socialising, while in time of conflict, control points for tribal leaders and mustering areas for the local male population.

By the 4th century BC, the inner areas of some investigated hillforts show evidence of people living within them or in periodical occupation, with clear-cut tracks leading in and out for easy access. Besides the hillfort links with local agriculture, extensive field systems are often found nearby, suggesting that when inhabited, their occupants used the systems to raise food for themselves. An enormous amount of labour was needed to make the hillforts impregnable to assault, suggesting that some form of forced or slave labour may have been used. If besieged or attacked, were the slaves used for defence, while in more peaceful times, put to agricultural work? If so, this labour might have formed a social class that in later centuries provided the slaves traded to the Continent as a commodity. Certainly the forts would have had an influence on local settlement patterns by their very existence, but also for more complex reasons, such as control of trade. All in all, the presence and use of the hillforts over centuries, suggest an orderly structured society, functioning successfully, but prepared to adjust roles when necessary. Some Wiltshire hillforts possibly continued to function after the Roman conquest, perhaps as garrisons; finds of Romano-British material Sidbury, Casterley Camp and nearby Battlesbury may prove confirmatory of this premise.

Tribal influences in Wiltshire – the last few centuries BC

Fewer hillforts in Wessex functioned between the third and first centuries BC, but those that did were enlarged. Population increased, and tribal groupings apparently grew stronger and more territorial. Definitive boundaries can be recognized from the sixth century BC. Some of these boundaries still existed at the time of the Roman invasion in AD 43, undoubtedly used by more than one tribe. In Wiltshire, three distinct tribal areas can be recognized by 300 BC. Artifacts from the first century, mainly ceramic and numismatic, furnish evidence of settlers from Europe and their approximate tribal territories.

The three tribes associated with Wiltshire at the very end of the Iron Age were the Durotriges, the Atrebates and the Dobunni. The Atrebates inhabited most of the county on

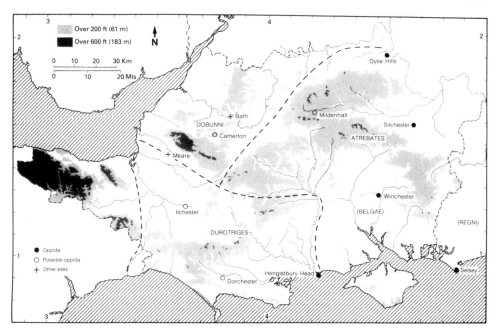

Location of the Durotriges, the Atrebates and the Dobunni tribes in Wiltshire during Middle and late Iron Age. Location based chiefly on coin finds such as those shown below.

the chalklands, the Durotriges, the southwest corner, and the Dobunni, the western periphery of the county. On arrival, the Artrebates may well have inflicted much conflict on the agriculturists in Wiltshire, especially if their invasion was strongly resisted, as the tribe settled in the mostly heavily fortified area of the county. But no evidence is available, and we can only presume that the populace learnt to live with their conquerors and began life anew with fresh leaders and tribal government. But whether as slaves or fellow workers and whether on the same land cannot yet be determined.

By the middle of the last century BC the three tribal areas in Wiltshire had apparently reached stability. The county's agrarian way of life seemingly changed little in this century.

In 55 BC Caesar made a token invasion in southeast Britain, arranged a treaty with regional tribes and returned to Rome. Wiltshire affairs were seemingly little affected by these events, and the county waited for almost a hundred years before the marching feet of Roman legionaries were to be heard across the county.

Tools

Wiltshire people practiced like lifestyles in like times; the thousands of tools found through the prehistoric period convey this message. The toolmakers thoroughly understood their medium, whether stone, flint, bone or wood, and, at the end of the prehistoric period, bronze and iron. Their skills command awe, their expertise respect. After the Mesolithic, we know that some tools were obviously valued for their aesthetic beauty, the earliest art form to be known in Wiltshire.

Even today, few places exist in the Wiltshire countryside where one can go for a walk and not find a prehistoric tool. However, the only tools surviving are those made from flint derived from cobbles or river pebbles. Tool shapes of all ages were influenced to a great extent by the availability of their basic material. If the tool originated from a pebble, it was usually small, if knapped from outcrop flint or other suitable stone, it could be larger when needed. No actual Palaeolithic knapping or camp locations are known in Wiltshire, and find-spots, showing evidence of the use of fire, dating from 200-40,000 BC, are confined to high hilltops. Lower level sites undoubtedly existed, but weather action or burial by solifluction

Early Upper Paleolithic Graver. Found in a gravel seam near the river Avon at Seagry, laying 30 cm above the main gravel and well below the loam which contained Mesolithic finds

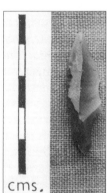

deposits have obliterated them. The earliest tools were made from flint nodules, and shaped by trimming. These are known as core tools, which include hand axes. Butchering was accomplished with handaxes, while sharp flakes cut meat. These flakes were a by-product of handaxe trimming, although at some sites they seem to have been specially made. Some flakes were retouched to form scrapers, used to prepare hides. Edge wear on flakes often indicates that they may have been used to cut bone, wood or leather. But with flake tools, usually it is impossible to determine their precise use. Flint as a material for tool-making has great limitations, therefore tools such as scrapers are similar throughout the prehistoric period

Hand axes continued to evolve during the Middle and Upper Palaeolithic. *Circa* 35,000 BC onwards saw the start of large blades (100mm or longer), and thin flat flakes to make various leaf-shaped points up to 140 mm long. Some of these tools were worked on both sides and are known as laurel leaf points, others long and thin, as willow leaf. Possibly these were used for projectile points or as knives. The only find-spot of leaf tools (bifaces) in Wiltshire is at Fovant. A graver of the same period was found, *in situ*, in river gravel at Seagry.

Lower Paleolithic Hand Axe: From Knowle Farm gravel pit, Great Bedwyn. A fine specimen, only slightly rolled, with some patches of natural 'gloss'

Late Upper Paleolithic pen knife point, from Haywood, Chippenham. Typical of its time, found with a small blade core in similar pristine condition

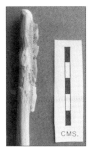
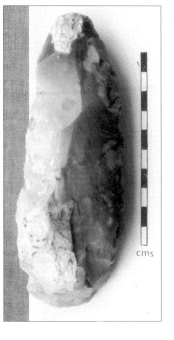

Hafted Mesolihtic microliths assembled to create a harpoon (left); Hafted Mesolithic microliths assembled to create a cutting tool (centre); Mesolithic Tranchet Axe. Found at Free Warren Farm, Wilton. Typical form, sharpened by a transverse removal at the cutting edge (right).

These blade tools were made from nodules which were shaped by controlled knapping, a feat of much skill. In the last few millennium of the Palaeolithic, *circa* 13-10,000 BC, blade tools dominated. Often smaller, they were very well-struck and flaked, some shaped to points undoubtedly served as missiles. Frequently found are larger blades with a sharp edge on one side, the other being blunted by the removal of tiny flakes to serve as a finger-rest, so that the tool could be safely used as a knife. On some English sites, (though not in Wiltshire), bone points and harpoons are found, as were very long blades up to 200mm,with much damaged edges, perhaps used for butchery. Scrapers abounded, made on the end of stout blades or thick flakes. And in this period, tiny Mesolithic-type points appear.

The Mesolithic begins *circa* 10,000 BC, but as regards of tool types, much overlap exists with those of the Upper Palaeolithic. Important is the appearance of axes, certainly to be used for forestry and wood working. As experimentation in cultivation techniques began, a large flint could be used to make a hoeing or weeding tool, to be bound or hafted to a long stick. Later, man can be visualized using a bone stick or blade for digging or seed planting. Wood was no doubt fashioned for spades or shovels, or an ard for preliminary stirring up the soil for cultivation prior to planting.

Blades and microliths also appear during the Mesolithic, made for setting in wooden shafts and functioning as projectiles or cutting tools. Later Mesolithic sites have produced a series of tiny geometric-shaped microliths, again obviously intended for some form of hafting. Site-to-site variations in microliths, no doubt indicate the different needs of their owners who worked with these tools. Placing several microliths in line along a stick created a formidable cutting edge or a primitive saw. During the Mesolithic, man developed a glue formula, consisting of a mix of birch resin, beeswax and clay. The use of this glue added strength to any tool hafted into a piece of wood or stick.

Mesolithic – Neolithic

In Wiltshire, or for that matter, anywhere in Britain, present evidence has yet to demonstrate exactly when or how Mesolithic people began to adopt agriculture techniques

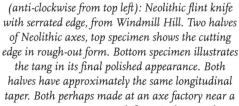

(anti-clockwise from top left): Neolithic flint knife with serrated edge, from Windmill Hill. Two halves of Neolithic axes, top specimen shows the cutting edge in rough-out form. Bottom specimen illustrates the tang in its final polished appearance. Both halves have approximately the same longitudinal taper. Both perhaps made at an axe factory near a track from Avebury to the Ridgeway. Neolithic scrapers from Windmill Hill, including a tiny thumb scraper. Neolithic pounder or miller from Wind-mill Hill.

which in time led to a totally agrarian way of life. As has been shown previously, Mesolithic- and Neolithic-type tools can be found together as late as the beginning of the third millennium (see page 4 above), in all likelihood indicating a long overlap of the two cultures, hunter-gatherers and agriculturists, living side by side. Specific Mesolithic tool types seem to have fallen out of use around 3,500 BC. Microliths were replaced by several more sophisticated forms of arrowheads as missile points, and tranchet axes gave way to more efficient ground and polished versions.

Neolithic

Early Neolithic tool manufacturing tended to follow Mesolithic techniques, producing tools of narrow blade-like proportions, but in time, becoming squatter and thicker with serrated edges. This also applies to re-touched piercing points. Axes and picks are the hallmark of Neolithic tool-making, plus leaf-shaped arrowheads, often slender and finely pointed. By the 4th millennium, man's reverence for axes, beyond their significance as an essential tool, began to be demonstrated. Often, such axes had been traded great distances from their sources.

Appearance of Metal tools

Despite the appearance of metal objects in Wiltshire by 2000 BC, tools created from stone, bone and other materials continued to be used. The adoption of metal tools for agriculture seemingly came very slowly, and the major metal items found in the county which possibly pertain to agrarian practices *circa* 1000 BC onwards, are mainly socketed bronze or iron axes. Because of the value of bronze, and later iron, few discarded tools are found, most were apparently melted down to be re-used. It is impossible to gauge with any

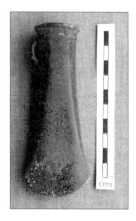
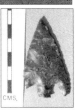

(clockwise from top left) Late Neolithic/ Early Bronze Age flint scrapers. Bronze Age axe found at Sandy Lane, cast from bronze. Medieval sheep shears depicted on Seend church window. They are the exact replica of those found during the Iron Age in Wiltshire. A superb Bronze Age barbed and tanged arrowhead made from black flint. Found at Bayardo Farm, Clench Common, Near Marlborough.

accuracy, just how prevalent was the use of metal tools in Wiltshire in these centuries.

Clipping shears of iron are found after 600 BC. Previously sheep were plucked at Spring moult, a tiresome and time-consuming job; how our labourer must have welcomed this new tool. The clippers consisted of two blades at the end of a circular handle acting as a spring, giving the user leverage on the cutting edges. Clippers of exactly the same pattern were used in Wiltshire for other purposes besides shearing until well into the twentieth century. On the west window of Seend

church is a medieval stone carving of such clippers, recognisable as conforming to the same basic shape as prehistoric clippers.

By the end of the Iron Age, tools discovered in Wiltshire, made from iron and used for agricultural purposes, include axes, large knives, bill-hooks, sickles, saws, hammers. Other iron items that have survived are latch-lifters, possibly indicating dividing doors in dwellings or storage buildings, and iron cleats for boots.

A modern knapper: Edward Simpson, known as Flint Jack, learnt to work flints using the same techniques as did prehistoric man. Sadly, his work was not valued and he turned to burglary for a living.

Chapter 1 Bibliography

Due to the influx of so much new information and theories on prehistoric Wiltshire as of 2007, I have only listed here books or papers published since 1995. A few earlier sources are included in the general bibliography. I wish to take this opportunity to pay tribute to Professor Barry Cunliffe, his perceptive writings have played a most important part in the formation of the early chapters of *Forgotten Labour*.

*BROWN, G., *FIELD, D., & *McOMISH, D., 2005, *The Avebury Landscape*. Oxford: Oxbow Books

CLEAL, R., WALKER, K., & MONTAGUE, R., 1995, *Stonehenge in its landscape*. English Heritage

COPLEY, M., BERSTAN, R., DUDD, S., AILLAUD, S., MUKHERJEE, A., STRAKER, V. and EVERSHED, R., 2005, Processing of milk products in pottery vessels through British prehistory. *Antiquity* 79, 895-908

CUNLIFFE, B., & RENFREW, C., 1999, *Science & Stonehenge*. Oxford University Press

CUNLIFFE, B., 2004, *Iron Age Britain*. Batsford

CUNLIFFE, B., Ed., 2006, *English Landscape – The West*. Collins

*DARVILL, T., 2006, *Stonehenge: Biography of a Landscape*. Stroud: Tempus Publishing

DARK, P., 2000, *The Environment of Britain in the first Millennium AD* Duckworth

*FOWLER, P., 2000, *Landscape Plotted and Pieced*. Society of Antiquaries of London

GINGELL, C., 1992, *The Marlborough Downs: A later Bronze Age Landscape and its Origins*. Devizes: WANHS: Monograph 1

GREEN, M., 2002, *A Landscape Revealed*. Stroud: Tempus Publishing

LAWSON, A., 2007, *Chalkland: an archaeology of Stonehenge and its region*. Hobnob Press

McOMISH, D., FIELD, D., and BROWN, G., 2002, *Field Archaeology of the Salisbury Plain Training Area*. English Heritage

*PRYOR, F., 2006, *Farmers in Prehistoric Britain*. Stroud: Tempus Publishing

WYMER, J., 1999, *Lower Paleolithic Occupation of Britain*, vols 1-2. Wessex Archaeology and English Heritage

2
Into Historic Times – Roman Agricultural Wiltshire

'The population is exceedingly large, the ground thickly studded with homesteads, closely resembling those of the Gauls and the cattle very numerous. . . The climate is more temperate than in Gaul, the cold being less severe. Julius Caesar (*De Bello Gallico*)

The Coming of the Romans

To the Romans, with their empire stretching across Europe to its western edges, the island of Britain presented a logical step of conquest at the end of the last millennium BC. Particularly in the south, Britain was a political and economic plum, with busy trading routes, a strong agriculture, a temperate climate, a vigorous population. In 54 BC Julius Caesar landed and despite the efforts of British charioteers gained a foothold in Kent, but he and his troops returned to Gaul two years later for internal political reasons. The Romans returned to Kent nearly 100 years later to conquer and complete a successful occupation of most of Britain, to last until AD 410.

It is claimed that one of Caesar's purposes in invading Britain was, 'on the pretext of dealing with troublesome tribal princes and druids'. Druids strike a familiar chord to any Wiltshire native because of the long-term association of the priestly caste with Stonehenge, however erroneous the affiliation seems today. According to historians of the time, Druids had an abominable reputation. Strabo accused them of mass human sacrifice, Diodorus Siculus and Tacitus held them responsible for horrible treatment of their victims, including hanging, burning, crucifixion and impaling alive. Tacitus and Dio Cassius both emphasized the importance of sacred groves, particularly of oak, as places of worship, and Pliny emphasized the significance of the sect's identification with white robes and golden sickles. The only good thing said about them concerned their herbal medicines. How strong their influence was on people and whether they had any political power is unknown. Somehow such practices, except perhaps worship in sacred groves, are hard to believe when applied to the prehistoric peoples of Wiltshire who, to the best of our knowledge today, seemed to be dispassionate rather than actively aggressive and hence should have had no need or use for such an extreme sect.

The man-made designation of a new millennium starting in the year AD 1, half way between the two Roman invasions, is a convenient starting point from which to describe the changes in lifestyle encountered by agriculturists in Wiltshire. The last centuries of the prehistoric period in Wessex had firmly established the concept of territorial division, land ownership (of some nature not yet fully understood), and growth of an economy supported by agricultural surpluses. These had allowed for the accumulation of wealth, as indicated by the personal possessions of the upper social ranks. To the small agriculturist and labourer the economic changes had meant more security with greater supplies of food, clothing and shelter with a few more material goods, especially for the farmsteader and his family. But for the employed labourer on the larger farms, it is also likely to have meant a harsh labour division, including involuntary servitude in the form of serfdom or slavery.

Beginning with a landing in Kent in AD 43, 40,000 or so men embarked on a military and political take-over of the south coast from Sussex to Hampshire. The Roman legions moved west and north, where they surrounded the Durotriges, attacked the Atrebates and later made a treaty with the Dobunni and other tribes in the south and west. In doing so, they gained control over the territory later to be named Wiltshire. Unfortunately the historical record is not clear on how these tribes and their territories were eventually overcome. By AD 47, the speedy completion of the great Fosse Way from Exeter to Lincoln ensured a defensive line of forts and a means of supply for occupation troops. Link roads crossed Wiltshire to the Fosse Way from important centres such as London and the areas occupied by the three conquered tribes. Until the withdrawal of troops from the south, Roman troops are likely at this time to have moved constantly back and forth across Wiltshire.

Doubtless the inhabitants of scattered farmsteads and small communities sometimes endured a certain amount of disruption to their lives as troops commandeered food and supplied themselves with other immediate needs, and perhaps fought local skirmishes when Roman troops set up temporary camps. But considering the open nature of the countryside and its sparse population, any resistance to the well-trained Roman troops imposed great risk, except perhaps at the site of those hillforts situated near the major routes. Roman supply bases, forts or military installations have yet to be found in Wiltshire, perhaps an indication that natives withheld their fire, considering discretion the better part of valour. We know nothing of the British frame of mind at this period in history. Because of previous quarrels with the Roman Empire, the Durotriges strongly opposed the Romans and supported Boudicca in her rebellion nearly twenty years later. Were any Wiltshire men among the 60,000 British supporters who defended her in a battle against the Romans somewhere near Watling Street? If so, they would have witnessed her miserable defeat, which caused her to commit suicide a few days later. But much of Wiltshire seemingly remained quiescent, despite nearby disturbances at South Cadbury (Somerset), and destructive fires at Winchester. Roman reprisals against the British in Wiltshire are undocumented, leading to the conclusion that the area remained a quiet backwater. Perhaps the people of the county already possessed what John Aubrey in the 17th century called 'gallipot eyes and phlegmatic character,' therefore presenting little threat to Roman ambitions, and later making easy the county's economic take-over, mainly by administrators.

In AD 71, the Romans consolidated and withdrew their troops from the southwest to combat resistance in southeast Wales. As far as is known at present, only three urban centres evolved within the county, *Durocornovium* (Lower Wanborough), *Sorviodunum* (Old Sarum), and *Cunetio* (Mildenhall). All developed at important road junctions. A few village settlements are known by name, such as *Verlucio* near iron deposits by Sandy Lane. But Wiltshire's mineral resources, some sparse iron deposits and building stone in the northwest, meant its economic development was mainly to come from agriculture. Future settlement patterns never developed urban areas, making it an exceedingly lonely county in Roman times, especially for the agriculturist on the downs and chalklands. The claylands of the Bristol Avon valley seemingly remained somewhat unused, though a few forest dwellers very likely made an adequate living within the dense woodlands of the valley, aided by the grasslands along the riverside. Recently recorded at Chippenham museum however, three possible complex sites on the clay have been identified near the present existing town; additionally, on higher ground immediately above the river in Chippenham itself, three excavations have revealed roofing tiles and Romano-British pottery. It is known that in the 3rd century a few agricultural complexes and villas were established, usually on or near the gravel beds along the Avon. The valley began to be heavily cultivated in Saxon and medieval times, so though more settlement may have existed, these sites later suffered total obliteration due to agricultural activity.

For half a century the chalklands are likely to have continued comparatively empty of anything but a few agricultural settlements, until agrarian expansion began in the 2nd century, in order to produce more foods or revenue for the demanding tax payments *(annona)* instituted by the Roman administration. Where roads crisscrossing the chalk intersected a trading place sometimes would evolve or a temple site be created, demonstrating commerce and people on the move. At Cold Kitchen Hill both developed, at Old Sarum and Badbury small markets evidently supported settlements. Until the 1970s, few if any villas had been discovered on the chalk, but more are now being revealed, particularly on the downs of North Wiltshire, where a concentration of 30 villas, seemingly centred on Mildenhall, stretches from Sandy Lane to Littlecote. Found mainly through aerial photography, some of these are suspected of having uses other than agrarian, perhaps economic or commercial centres; some at the end of the Roman period are believed to have fulfilled an auxiliary religious role.

Scattered over Wiltshire are the sites of Roman military equipment finds, mainly on the chalk and along major routes. Mostly of metalwork – horse harness pieces, iron axes, and small weapons – they perhaps indicate a higher use of cavalry rather than infantry; quite logical when one considers the distances involved in moving from centre to centre in Wiltshire. During the time of Roman administration in Wiltshire, the presence of the army can be seen as carrying out peaceful duties, perhaps more civil than occupational, and assisting with administration and tax collection. It may well be that during the first century of occupation men from the local tribes, the Dobunni, Durotriges and Atrebates, enlisted or otherwise entered the army to receive Roman citizenship after their discharge. Maybe an alternative form of employment had opened up for the agriculture worker.

Thirty years after their arrival in Wiltshire, the Romans began to establish centres known as *civitates,* based on the old tribal areas. Though not in the county itself, the centres at Cirencester, Ilchester, Winchester and Silchester certainly assisted in the government of the area now considered Wiltshire, with a new network of roads and routes linked to these *civitates,* which in turn led further to major centres – London, Bath, Southampton, Exeter and further north. Wiltshire began to be part of an important communication network.

But history records little of the activities of Wiltshire's inhabitants in these early days of Roman administration. The tribesmen remained to be governed, and those at the top of the social hierarchy, the larger landholders and farmstead owners, may have acknowledged the new authority and continued to function as they did before the conquest, directing the cultivation of their land with free and unfree labour. But this social group may have totally lost their lands, and been reduced to smallholders. Other smallholders and those tilling family plots, craftsmen, artisans and labourers made up the remainder of society.

Two hundred years of peace followed, allowing the Romans and the people of Wessex to develop and expand economically. Actually the Roman tax system gave them no choice, as people had to produce and grow more in order to pay their allocations. Under the old system any surplus wealth was apparently distributed downwards through the society system by mechanisms based on patronage and clientage alone, but under the Roman mode, though individual craftsmen and artisans had more of a chance to earn money, the agricultural worker is likely to have been bypassed, to be a paid employee, serf or slave. These years are a blurred period when the top social levels of the labourer and the farmer employing labour cannot be distinguished, and little is understood of the social hierarchy, of Roman officials and land holders. Nor is it understood what position the native British held in Roman society. Estate owners or renting tenants may have continued to work their land and keep their high social position, eventually displaying Roman artifacts and decorations in their later villas. But Saxon law, beginning in the 7th century, ranked the British as inferior, quickly establishing their dominance; but that designation also signified that they held their identity through all the Roman years and the historical dark period before the Saxons established themselves. One wonders if all Romans withdrew, or did some remain, perhaps because of economic or family ties to a British family, to be absorbed over a few generations.

Outside Wiltshire, after the 2nd century began, nearby urban centres – Bath, Silchester and Winchester for instance – began to show evidence of invested Roman capital. The resulting prosperity increased population, both naturally and by immigration; in turn, new markets emerged for rural produce. The extensive tax structure imposed on the British, a property and a land tax based on productivity, settled in place. Officials based in the nearby town centres carried out appropriations and collections fairly but strictly. Besides paying for Roman bureaucratic administration, one of the purposes of this tax was to support the army, which also needed British-produced goods and food. Over most of the next two centuries, to find money to pay their taxes, property owners had to enlarge their farms, intensify their agriculture and increase the output of their workers.

Whether the workers themselves benefitted is a moot point. With the Roman monetary economy in place, employees are likely to have become wage-earners, but doubtless the bartering of goods played an important role in their lives. In time, some families in this category may even have moved from their rural environment to the towns, to enjoy a livelier life-style. For the unfree, they and their families continued to be tied to their employer or master. As the economy grew, the possibility of buying their liberty may have arisen, the ex-slave becoming a free man. A new pattern of life apparently began for the British, far more structured and controlled than in the last centuries of the old millennium, but with a secure economy and more material goods.

That more money was available to earn and spend is shown by artifacts recovered from settlement sites on the Wiltshire chalklands. The quality of the pottery and a greater proportion of artifacts found points directly to a standard of living during the Roman occupation between the 1st and 3rd centuries, higher than that enjoyed by society in the late Iron Age. The land-holding class bettered themselves at the expense of their employees, whose labour was to be absolutely essential for the raising of tax payments and to enable them to furnish the towns and the army with food and other products of the countryside.

From the change in land holdings in Wiltshire after the 2nd second century, large blocks of land seemingly began to be owned by wealthy Romans who came to profit from their new farm or estate. By the 3rd century, many of the larger farmsteads developed into complex settlements. Industry grew, even in Wiltshire, so devoid of many minerals. Pottery kilns set up at Savernake joined many others in Wessex. The new economic growth meant an increase in population in Britain during the Roman era that may have peaked at between two to five million. Numbers began to lessen sometime after the middle of the 4th century as a general economic decline commenced. However, despite the layer of Romanization, judging from the retention of old tribal values, all through the Roman occupation, the rural population of Wiltshire apparently remained loyal to their ancestors rather than their conquerors.

Romano-British Settlement: Patterns in Wiltshire

Roman settlement patterns in Wiltshire evolved around the new and old patterns of roads crisscrossing the county. Settlement numbers increased as the economy thrived, but due to the paucity of the chalk soils and lack of easily accessible water supplies, settlement on parts of Salisbury Plain and the higher downlands remained very scattered. The prehistoric hillfort sites invariably show abandonment by the 2nd century as trading contacts expanded and Roman administration was set in place. Obviously life in the countryside assumed a more peaceful role.

A few fairly extensive settlement sites developed during Roman times. As mentioned before, the largest were situated at Lower Wanborough, Mildenhall and Stratford-sub-Castle (Old Sarum). Smaller sites can often show linkage, though not necessarily continuity, to occupation in the Early Iron Age. These sites, proven by pottery sherds and other artifacts, attracted local population and enhanced agricultural or other employment opportunities. Some sites may symbolize an uninterrupted family line, and many seem to confirm a pattern of reoccupation and often expansion of the site itself.

At White Walls, Easton Grey, settlement spread out due no doubt to such a convenient location half-way between *Aquae Sulis* (Bath) and *Corinium* (Cirencester). In the area around Silbury Hill, much economic growth is perceived during the Roman period, because of the fertile and sheltered land, easy reach of the river Kennet, two nearby major routes, and perhaps accessibility to the ancient ritual site of Silbury Hill. The settlement patterns here are described as 'multi-layered, [and] complex,' perhaps including urban as well as rural communities. In all likelihood, the abundance of buildings so far noted reflect many estate workers and slaves. Coin hoards found in this locality give an indication of its economic importance, not only as settlement sites, but as a cross roads area.

Mystery still envelops the settlements in the area around Sandy Lane and The Ham at Westbury. The presence of iron ore deposits imply both sites had an industrial origin, but obviously agriculturists would have lived nearby to produce food for local workers. Close to Sandy Lane, recent research also has demonstrated several large building complexes, perhaps the site of central offices and dwellings for the tax administration system and its executives. Nettleton Scrubb on the Fosse Way, 17 km or so NE from Bath, may have originated as a quarrying area, later to become the site of an important religious shrine with a temple building. Many other structures surrounded the site, some of agricultural use, including a rare example of a water mill. Broadmead Brook running through the area was possibly partially canalized, an interesting observation when the long distance to a major waterway is considered. (See page 39 below) Obviously this valley area was ideal for mixed farming, with its extensive grazing and grain growing areas to the immediate west. It spawned a bustling community of people of many occupations, quarrying, maintaining the shrine, growing and supplying food and shelter for themselves, travellers and the worshippers of the goddess, Diana.

The site forms of smaller settlements vary. Summarized through the Roman period, nucleated villages are the major pattern, often with planned streets lined with platform houses. At Chisenbury Warren, more than eighty huts on platforms range along a central strip, within an area of six hectares. The settlement grew into a large village with fields attached to the houses. Some villages developed a circular layout. At Hamshill Ditches, a number of hut platforms are ranged within ditched enclosures and include settlement types dating back to the Late Iron Age, indicating probable continuity here through the 1st to the 4th century. The need for defensive ditches and enclosures had ceased, the ditches filled, built over or made into tracks; presumably enclosures were utilized for shelter or torn down.

From particular features noted by investigators a picture of chalkland settlement sites may be drawn. Twelve Romano-British settlements with earthworks excavated on Salisbury Plain, ranged in size from less than one hectare on Compton Down to one of twenty-five hectares on Charlton Down. Nucleated settlements were usually located on a south-facing slope, with properties on each side of a central track or street, sometimes with late Bronze Age linear ditches utilized to form a central course from which houses and fields radiated. Banked enclosures with hurdles or hedging surrounded the compounds of houses. Hollowed out ground areas within compounds are likely to have signified the position of platforms for buildings and outsetts. Frequently field systems are found expanding into the chalk uplands.

Another Romano-British settlement at Chapperton Down, within the Salisbury Plain Training Area, (SPTA: see Glossary), implied a domestic site supported by an agricultural base. Snail counts confirmed the area as open country, shaded by grasses and shrubs. The settlement boasted a central street with house platforms on each side. Building construction indicated flint nodule footings, beam slots and post holes. Quern fragments and household pottery sherds signified an initial occupation between the 1st and 2nd century, with use continuing into mid 3rd to 4th century, the latter confirmed by coin finds. Two of several ubiquitous rubbish pits revealed, besides their usual contents, the remains of several sheep foetuses or newly born lambs, perhaps an indication that disease such as brucellosis had recently struck. A ditch bounded a field system, where cultivation of arable crops took place.

Recent investigations in the SPTA now confirm a well-defined prehistoric agricultural system taken over and expanded during the Romano-British period, especially by the 3rd and 4th centuries. Despite the apparent isolation of the area, a rising population extended cultivation, confirmed by agrarian patterns and expanded field systems found, for instance, at Knook Hill, Church Pits, Sidbury, Weather Hill and Chisenbury Warren. The amount of ploughed land increased, wheat and barley seemingly the main grain crops grown. Vineyards may have existed on southern slopes. Among the animals, milking cattle and sheep predominated. More confirmed settlement patterns included both compact and linear village types, populated predominantly by small communities, obtaining water from cisterns for themselves, their field animals supplied by dams and ponds.

Before recent aerial photography revealed so many more settlements on the chalklands, to explain their apparent paucity researchers proffered theories of exhausted soils, or Salisbury Plain forming a Roman imperial estate. Today investigators recognize an extensive Romano-British landscape emerging across Salisbury Plain, one of dispersed individual settlements sited by their agricultural and economic demands on the land. Where settlements or single farmsteads remained unaltered, whether on the chalklands or surrounding areas, the occupying family, or extended family, may have remained on the same site for several centuries. Retaining the same type of dwellings and buildings over generations, the modestly-living farmers or peasants with family labour continued to cultivate the land. Such situations imply an accepted form of land ownership, but if so, no clues have yet been found to its form. If ownership existed, however, this could be an example of our agricultural labourer in his happiest state, that of self-employment.

Roman Villas and Villa complexes

Both archaeological and other evidence indicate larger Roman farmsteads or villa-type dwellings in Wiltshire beginning to appear at the end of the 2nd century parallel to economic expansion, and so reflecting a delay in investment in the county by Romans

Sherds of Roman pottery and tiles from unexcavated residential site at Bird's Marsh, Chippenham.

themselves. Like the settlements, the number of villa sites discovered has continued to increase during the past twenty-five years in Wiltshire, as has a corresponding need for their investigation.

Pre-1960 investigations into Roman villa complexes took the attitude that they were strictly agricultural units. For instance, North Wraxall villa had suggested a centre for peasantry who cultivated land around it in the 3rd century. In the late 4th century, a reduction in livestock and personnel indicated economic decline. In the same area disaster hit thirteen villas, perhaps by marauders from the Severn area, but six still survived almost to the 5th century.

At present, our knowledge of Roman villa complexes in Wiltshire is in a state of flux. The significance of new complexes revealed in the past twenty years is beginning to change concepts of their economic influence in the county. Unfortunately, from the point of view of this book, the new knowledge gained has yet to provide fresh insight as to how the agriculturist's life may have been affected by the expanded economy. Recent research now tends to imply a rich, powerful elite society dominating the West country by the 4th century, with a considerable financial stake in the countryside, therefore indicating secure property rights of some kind. The complexes reflected a system, which Walters in *Roman Wiltshire and After,* describes as: 'not only of agricultural production, but of the autocracy by which the province of Britannia was governed.' This system also suggests that the largest villas may have controlled lesser villa establishments by installing subordinate tenantry and bailiffs to supervise other secondary landholdings as part of their investments. Perhaps this kind of property management can be compared to that in Wiltshire so common in the

17th and 18th centuries on large estates. Today villas present a chicken /egg problem; were new complexes set up after the 2nd century, or did most of the villas evolve from smaller settlement sites? Enough good, workable land existed in Wiltshire for either or both to have taken place; probably it was a mixture of the two options.

Definitions of a Roman villa abound: 'An agricultural unit whose native owners had adopted a Romanized life-style and were operating within a commercially orientated rural economy. Profits accumulated through the invigorated agricultural system were channelled into Romanized buildings and luxury items, proclaiming . . . wealth and status of the occupants.' Or: 'A rural building complex embodying Roman building techniques, including a residence of rooms and frequently outbuildings devoted to the requirements of agriculture.' By the 4th century it is clear that villa occupants, whether British, Roman or Romano-British, decorated their villas in a style indicating that they wished to be recognized as Roman, at the same time keeping their pagan beliefs, despite the existence of Christianity. Aldbourne Gorse, on clay soils, seems to have specialized in livestock and wool production and is a representative of a wealthy villa, with its mosaics, fine wall paintings and baths. Similarly built in the Roman style, Badbury and Draycot Foliat boasted elaborate artifacts. On lighter soils, both complexes produced large amounts of grain and manifested extensive outbuildings.

At Downton, the villa complex covered twelve acres or more. The scale of actual domestic or family occupation seemed comparatively small, but minor buildings and extensive infrastructure – roads, ditches, drains, ovens and hearths – point to many estate dependants established in modest housing. Barns and granaries revealed the cultivation and storage of various kinds of wheat, barley and vetches, while outbuildings reflected animal husbandry, including pigs. Dairying is likely to have taken place, but at the time of investigation it was not looked for.

Perhaps the Roman villa between the 2nd and 5th centuries can be compared to the development of the Wiltshire dairy farmhouse from the 17th to the 20th centuries, i.e. the growth of a self-contained unit, gradually becoming dependent on exterior economics, then unable to stem the downward drift to breakup or change of form. Unfortunately this is happening to Wiltshire farms today in the span of a few decades.

Surrounding small farmsteads were possibly farmed in conjunction with villa complexes. Individual farming families may have owned the farmsteads, or they were rented out by a villa complex, tenurially independent, the rent paid by cash and/or services. Unfortunately, from outlying buildings found at villa complexes, such as at Castle Copse, evidence of a unit system or labour-sharing cannot be determined. Tenancy may have implied a share basis, as was done in Italy, the estate owner and the tenant dividing the produce according to a written contract, normally on a five-year basis, with the owner supplying implements, working animals, and slaves. Together the villa, farmsteads and settlement sites possibly formed a social and local enclave with obligations and responsibilities on both sides.

The question of serf and slave labour in Roman Britain is still unsolved. Slave-irons found on a Roman farm site near St Albans (Herts) are the only piece of physical evidence so far discovered that may actually indicate formal confinement of slaves in Roman Britain. But slavery existed through the whole era of Roman power, and conceivably in Britain based on labour customs described in Italian agricultural treatises. Or perhaps not. The relationship between a *colonus,* as the lowest level of worker was called, and his *dominus* (master) is still not fully understood. He or she may have been a chattel, or partly free with some obligation to labour and service on his master's behalf. A villa complex may have had a bailiff or other supervisor to work slaves in units, though this was a particularly expensive way of managing labour, especially during times of slack in the farming year. Separate accommodation of labourer and owner is shown to be feasible in some villa layouts, but little research has been done in Wiltshire on this aspect of slavery.

Rather than direct supervision of a slave labour force by a manager on the spot, slaves might have had a small plot of land they could work, and hence lived away from the villa. Alternatively, nearby settlement sites may have housed a villa's labour force, as for example the 200-house settlement close by the villa in Charlton parish in Pewsey Vale. At present, slavery can only be presumed to have formed part of the labour supply in Wiltshire based on time-honoured customs, and evidence of the extensive farming undertaken by the villa complexes.

After the 2nd century, the agricultural labourer in Romano-British Wiltshire is liable to have held either of several positions. At the top of the social labour scale, he might have been a peasant, self employed, working his own smallholding or making a living in the extensive forests Wiltshire then possessed. Or he might have been an employee or somehow tied to a British farmer, a villa complex or large farmstead. Or he could have been a slave, totally owned by his master, whether Roman or Romano-British. While an economy and a society is strong, a slavery structure can be held in place, but it is likely to have weakened considerably in Britain as the economy deteriorated at the end of the 4th century and Romans finally withdrew in the 5th century.

Agricultural characteristics of the Roman Villas

The Roman villa is generally seen today as a centre of rural industry as well as a comfortable country house. Further research may in time reveal the individuality of each villa, its economy and labour structure. However, recent investigations have enlarged our knowledge of the patterns of agriculture practiced by several Wiltshire villa complexes.

The complexes were one response to the need to increase agricultural production in Wiltshire. One way or another they signify growth. The seeming incorporation of nearby farmsteads, expansion of field systems and the appearance of larger stock tallies are all indications of this growth. A large labour force was a necessity. Besides agricultural labour, as was the practice in Italy, and also found on some Wiltshire Iron Age settlement sites, villas employed blacksmiths, and in all likelihood carpenters and potters on their estates.

At Minety, amidst the claylands of the Bristol Avon valley, a brick kiln developed, a link to the appearance of brick structures and field walls. These in turn led to the use of improved animal housing and extended storage facilities, and their arrangement in a complex often demonstrates systematic surveying and the need for water-divining and well-sinking skills. Innovations, such as donkey mills, are likely to have emerged from a constant water supply. The farming economy's expansion increased the reliance on local market-places, and the complexes and farms are likely to have used nearby local centres, Lower Wanborough, Sandy Lane and Mildenhall and other smaller places, to expand direct marketing of perishable foods, while still maintaining their links with traditional distant markets established during the previous century.

New crops appear to have been grown, especially of garden variety, the latter most probably introduced by the Romans, radish, parsnip, pea, cabbage, mustard, onions, leeks, coriander, parsley, dill, fennel, and maybe poppies for seed. The villa complexes exhibit fruit tree cultivation, medlar, figs, an improved cherry and various vines. Sloe, bullace, plum, damson, apple, pear, mulberry, raspberry, all native to Britain but enhanced by cultivation, also show up on villa complexes, as do the use of ornamental trees and other landscaping.

Wheat and barley are the most significant grains grown at the height of the Roman period, as confirmed by the recent investigations in the SPTA. In addition, several Wiltshire villa complexes have shown evidence of high level grain production, so vitally needed for the continental posts of the Roman Empire at the time. To produce and ship large amounts of grain needed large field systems, a highly organized labour force, and cartage to haul the grain to water or other transportation routes. The resulting prosperity meant work for the agriculturalist, labourer and slave, high cash rewards for the villa owners. In north Wiltshire, the grain grown on the edge of the chalklands, such as at Littlecote villa, after warehousing, was possibly loaded into shallow craft and transported on canalized tributaries running into the river Kennet. The grain would then be barged downstream to collection points before continuing down the Thames to the Port of London. At least a dozen other villas could have had similar arrangements for transporting grain; further investigation is likely to show that movement of grain in this manner took place in the same period in other Wiltshire river valleys where villas were situated on or near a major river. Though not proven, Wiltshire may well have supplied part of the British grain used by the Roman army fighting on the Rhine in AD 359.

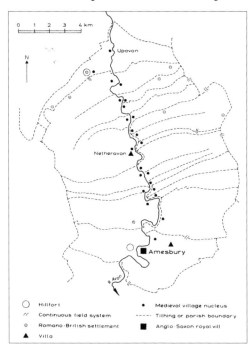

P31 Roman settlements and estate boundaries in the Salisbury Avon valley.

Littlecote villa: boat channels cut from River Kennet.

Several malting furnaces appear at Wiltshire villas during the 3rd-4th centuries, well-documented are those at Atworth, Draycot Foliat and Littlecote. Not big enough to process all the grain grown at these villas, they were obviously used to germinate grain to be used for making beer, the staple drink of the labourer and most others for whom imported wine was beyond their means. Could it be that the concept of the English alehouse and pub originated at this time? Small farmsteads may also have used malthouses. One, discovered at Cockey Down near Salisbury, dates from the late Romano-British period, and is on a site which had known cultivation from the early Iron Age. Though recorded as a corn drier, it is far more likely to have been used as a malthouse.

By the late 4th century, farming activities at the villa complexes begin to slow down. Some villas may have changed their economic direction and become active as religious sites. Littlecote, Tockenham, and Euridge conveniently located near Bath, are examples of such a transformation.

Farmstead agriculture in Roman times

Not all farmsteads, particularly in Wiltshire, were within reach or sight of villas, and those away from the villas at first are likely to have maintained their age-old agrarian and social patterns. The British family owners, after adjusting to Roman rule, seemingly absorbed little Roman culture, unlike those families inhabiting the villas. The often long distances from farmsteads on the chalk to any Roman town and often even villa, may have cut down considerably on the rate of adaptation to the new culture, especially as the pagan faiths continued unabated. Ultimately however, the farmsteads adapted to their conquerors in order to produce enough to pay tax bills. How far they went to increase production is not yet understood, especially as many of these methods were linked to larger scale production beyond the scope of a small agricultural operation. For example, were grain and fleeces collected to be shipped to a central point? And were ploughs and other equipment shared?

Agriculture in Roman Wiltshire, after the 1st century, all points to better tools, organization and exploitation of the land. Field systems expanded into outlying settlement areas. Larger fields and bigger settlements meant greater output. The range of crops increased, while a trend towards greater confinement of cattle appeared, a more economic way of management than roving, whether indiscriminate or discriminate. More bone finds on settlement sights indicate a greater home-consumption of meat, in turn doubtless signifying not only an increase in production and population, but a higher standard of living. The economic growth of Wiltshire agriculture continued until the late 4th century, when a trend of abandonment of the remoter downland and chalk settlements is detected, with a corresponding movement of people to valleys and heavier soil areas. The move to heavier soils is likely to signify that tools and equipment were available to cope with the different farming methods needed in those areas.

How fast the plough evolved in Roman times is still something of an enigma. More and larger fields meant a deeper-cutting plough, with a stronger, larger share, a coulter board (to turn the cut sod), and probably in time the addition of wheels, the whole able to deal with heavier soils beyond the Wiltshire chalklands. A heavier plough betokens a need for a larger, sturdier harrow, towed by an ox team, a substitute for previous hand-labour. The use of a heavy hurdle has been suggested, but Pliny in the 1st century described an improved harrow fitted with iron teeth, a design which may have reached Wiltshire along with the larger plough.

As previously mentioned, the adaptation of metal tools by the Wiltshire agriculturist in the last five hundred years of the prehistoric period, as previously mentioned, is likely to have been slow. Roman ability to exploit iron ore deposits certainly made metal tools more available, both in variety and strength. An assortment of better axes, spades and scythes developed. A general chopping/cutting instrument, similar to a bill-hook or machete, evolved, as did improved hoes, all to become key tools for the agricultural labourer until the middle of the 20th century. At the same time, better means of sharpening these tools materialized. Besides being made in metal with wooden handles, spades also continued to be made from wood and no doubt sheathed with iron. All these tools signify a better utilization of labour and increased production.

The development of farming and its changes in Roman Britain show up when comparisons are made with farming in Wiltshire in the Iron Age and in Saxon times. Besides greater enclosure of stock, and increase in sheep numbers, more elaborate methods of crop cultivation ensued. Square fields, indicate cross-ploughing, and linear earthworks surrounding some of them, no doubt confined sheep and other animals for manuring purposes. (Root crops need twelve tons of manure per acre in a temperate climate to grow well, grain slightly less. The Romans understood well the concept of manuring and in addition practiced marling). Green crops began to be used for winter fodder, possibly grown in a set rotation, such as grass–turnips–beans, or a cycle with grain and vetches (the latter as a nitrogenous soil refresher), plus a fallow year. Perhaps also rape and lucerne were fed to cattle. Grains included not only the all-important bread, wheat and barley, but spelt and emmer wheats, some oats, perhaps for animal feed, and rye. But the latter grain never gained popularity in Wiltshire.

Wells and ponds allowed permanent stocking of animals on higher ground, particularly sheep, whose water requirements are far less than those of cattle. Very large flocks of sheep seem to have been confined to villa complexes, as they only show evidence of large scale wool production. Perhaps the villas' outlying farmsteads participated in a form of sheep sharing. Smaller sheep numbers are evidenced on individual farmsteads. Improved breeding during Roman times produced an animal better fitted to producing wool rather than meat. Pigs, as always, played an important role, and may have been used to consume the whey from cheesemaking on larger farm units or the villa complexes. Depending on the whereabouts of a farm, they might also be put to pannage in woodland or forest. If neither was available nearby, they were somehow enclosed, but no evidence of pigsties in Roman times so far exists. Poultry, ducks and geese seem fixtures on farms, enhanced by the introduction of new breeds by the Romans.

Though it is understood that the expanded agricultural economy in Wiltshire depended on increased water supplies, particularly on the chalk, evidence of the water sources used by chalkland settlements from investigations and at Church Pits, a Romano-British settlement, may have depended partly on a ponded area, with a pre-existing lynchet being used as a dam across a slope. In a remote area of the Plain, a pond, linked by a track to a contemporary field system, was in use until recent times. The pond demonstrates an agricultural continuity of nearly two thousand years, an exciting facet to Wiltshire agricultural history.

The work of the agricultural labourer

It is still difficult to gain any idea of the life the agriculturalist and his labourers led in Roman Wiltshire. What differences in work habits existed between a smallholder, whether owner or tenant, and a paid labourer, serf and slave cannot yet be determined. Obviously the owner or tenant of a villa complex or large farmstead, due to affluence from increased production and seemingly abundant labour, would have relinquished the farm chores himself and, in doing so, created a definitive stratified social layer between him (or her) and the actual toilers of the soil. But until affluent enough, in all likelihood for a century after the Roman invasion, the life on the land may have changed little. Stock had to be tended, grazed or fed, and their breeding, fattening and marketing supervised. The climate through the Roman period was wetter and cooler, no doubt in the coldest months some animals were sheltered, therefore needing to be cleaned out and bedded. In the case of dairy animals, they had to be milked twice daily for part of the year, and their milk made daily into cheese and butter. Newly-born animals needed minding and for some time after their birth, whether calves, lambs and kids, had to carefully watched and protected from marauding animals. The soil had to be prepared for cropping, then seeded, weeded and cared for until harvesting time. However, the extent of haymaking at this time has yet to be understood. After harvest, the grain required threshing, that work held over to do in the winter months. Women are likely to have ground the grain itself on the premises where it was to be consumed. The millstone or quern became more efficient in Roman times, able to grind larger amounts of grain, but the larger stones were probably confined to villas and bigger estates, unless a settlement shared a grinding pair. As the economy grew, the newly introduced green crops meant extra work, with their harvesting carrying through from late autumn to the end of winter.

Social life of the agriculturist

In scttlements, villa complexes and larger farmsteads, some form of social life certainly existed, as people lived closely enough together to create activities, especially in the winter months of long evenings. On isolated farmsteads in winter, families had to rely on themselves to pass their spare time, indulging in the age-old pastimes of story-telling and gossip round the fire. In other seasons, the hours were filled from dawn to dusk to produce food for themselves, for marketing, and to fulfill the Roman tax demands. Of closer details of their social life we have no idea, though through their pagan customs they no doubt celebrated the coming and going of the seasons and followed symbolic forms of worship or ceremony.

A few social factors bearing on the life of the agricultural labourer on the chalklands can be gleaned from cemetery investigations, though it must be borne in mind that findings are based on a minuscule sample of the total population. At Chilmark, continually occupied throughout the Roman period, a small 4th-century rural cemetery held equal numbers of men and women and some children, perhaps eight intact burials, and bones from other skeletons scattered by later disturbances. Possibly the burials represented an extended family who, if they employed labour, buried them apart. Whether bodies were interred in wooden coffins cannot be determined, stone coffins and cists appear at a later date. Adult corpses were buried clothed and shod, but without any accompanying grave goods. Sometime copper coins had been placed in a mouth, while copper alloy stains on the skull or other bones indicated a brooch or hair ornament being buried with its owner. Lying near the body, hob nails from footwear gives a clue that these bodies were likely to be that of the labouring class. At Figheldean cemetery, hobnails were found in all graves excavated, another agricultural continuity link, as the Wiltshire agriculturist wore hobnailed boots regularly until the mid-20th century and for certain jobs still does today.

Also from the cemetery at Chilmark also comes evidence of the state of health of those interred there. Bones and teeth show similar diseases and medical troubles existing in Roman times to those of today. Teeth exhibit calcified plaque, periodontal disease, caries, molar lesions and abscesses. Signs of a sugary diet also appear. On the whole, however, a conclusion was drawn that dental hygiene appears to have been relatively good. From bone evidence, pulmonary infections and blood poisoning could be detected, even vascular disorders such as varicose veins. Damage to bones, besides direct injuries, reflect stress on the neck, left shoulder and right elbow, all signs of manual labour. At Cockey Down, north-east of Salisbury, a cemetery, thought to be associated with a small farmstead settlement, included skeletons demonstrating gum disease, osteoarthritis, sinus infections and possibly a fatal meningeal infection.

If possible population figures for Wiltshire are considered, until the end of Saxon times, a curious dearth of graves, burial sites and cemeteries exists, the significance of which seems to point to casual burial customs and perhaps a plethora of cremations. In Southern Britain up to the Late Iron Age, usually excarnation sufficed as the means of burial, though bodies are found in disused storage pits. In Atrebatic territory, cremation and burial of the ashes in a small urn prevailed, but the Durotriges persisted in inhumation, perhaps in defiance of the Roman custom of cremation. Inhumation continued throughout the Roman period, and the coming of the Anglo-Saxons seemingly made little change to burial procedures in Wiltshire. However, numerically most burial sites from prehistoric to early medieval times pertain to high ranking persons, and for those of lowly social status, relatively few have been discovered.

Decline and end of the Roman occupation in Wiltshire

Well before the Romans left Britain, the decline of their rule can be seen. It commenced in Wiltshire soon after the mid 4th century when the economy showed signs of slowing and villa complexes began to lack farming continuity. Local evidence is confusing, many villa sites in NW Wiltshire show signs of abandonment or change of use to religious purposes, yet at Atworth, farming operations increased after AD 350. Villas in the NW corner of the county were raided; several recovered to continue farming, others did not. Some of the bigger Roman estates may have consolidated at the expense of smaller farmers, changing their social status to employee, increasing the monetary gap between them and villa owners or tenants. The move by settlements from the high chalklands to lower-lying land may have been encouraged by a lack of demand for grain in the last years of the Roman Empire and the ease of running sheep on lower ground, certainly making farming easier.

Population numbers began to fall (as was happening in Roman Gaul) and logically with farming declining, the percentage of coin and artifact finds decrease. Trading slowed, though a few local markets kept their importance, in particular, Old Sarum and Mildenhall. The gradual economic decline was to see a monetary system become redundant by the mid-5th century, the lack of coins apparently heralding a return to bartering. Wiltshire, however, was well equipped to survive these bad times. Fewer urban centres and less mouths to feed meant food could stay in local areas and feed the adjacent population. The structure of the Romano-British society was strong and seemingly remained so, to lean back on its British origins and discard Roman attributes. The disappearance of the Roman settlement patterns, building types and artifacts in the 5th century clearly shows the rejection.

Meanwhile the Roman tax structure continued to unravel and raiding parties appeared more frequently. Towns near Wiltshire, such as Silchester, Winchester and Bath, showed signs of refortification, as did Mildenhall, though the building of its defensive walls c. AD 360 may have been prompted by another reason, to protect money or goods, particularly grain, collected by the tax authorities. Hillforts in Wiltshire may have been re-occupied as the Roman authorities began to feel threatened by the barbarians from the Continent.

These raids became more numerous after AD 410, the year the Romans officially withdrew from Britain. What happened to the people of Wiltshire and their intermingling with Germanic invaders during the rest of the 5th century is still hazy. Very little can yet be deducted from pottery and other artifacts of the time, or changes in burial customs. Undoubtedly Anglo-Saxon settlement began, but a definitive emergence of their influence cannot yet be dated. Local British leaders may have taken over after the Romans left and made efforts to combat the prospective settlers. Their resistance was not unsuccessful, but – certainly in the context of modern times – the settlers slowly gained ground and by the end of the 6th sixth century they had political control over most of Wiltshire. They were to alter the countryside and its people for all time.

Chapter 2 Bibliography

Up-to-date source material for this chapter depended heavily on:

ELLIS, P., 2001, *Roman Wiltshire and After: Papers in honour of Ken Annable*. Devizes: WANHS

HOSTETTER, E. and HOWE, T., 1997, *The Romano-British Villa at Castle Copse, Great Bedwyn*. Indiana University Press

The following articles supplied important archaeological information:

ROBINSON, P., 1997, A Roman Inscription from Charlton Down. *WANHM* 90, 141-3

LOVELL, J., HAMILTON-DYER, S., LOADER, E. and McKINLEY, J., 1999, Further investigations of an Iron Age and Romano-British Farmstead on Cockey Down, near Salisbury. *WANHM*, 92, 33-8

McKINLEY, J., 1999, Further Excavations of an Iron Age and Romano-British Enclosed Settlement at Figheldean, near Netheravon. *WANHM* 92, 7-32

FITZPATRICK, A. and CROCKETT, A., 1998, A Romano-British Settlement and inhumation Cemetery at Eyewell Farm, Chilmark. *WANHM* 91, 11-33

BROWN, G. 1995, Salisbury Plain Training Area (The management of an ancient landscape). *Landscape History* 17, 65-75 gave me my first overview of the work in progress on the SPTA, followed by:

McOMISH, D., FIELD, D., and BROWN, G., 2002, *Field Archaeology of Salisbury Plain Training Area*. English Heritage

For in-depth writing on Roman farming, see WHITE, K.,1970, *Roman Farming*. Thames and Hudson and *A Bibliography of Roman Farming*. (University of Reading 1970)

*R. BRADLEY's *Prehistoric Settlement of Britain*. (Routledge & Paul 1978), gives a good overall view of what settlement in Roman Wiltshire might have been. Comprehensive views of Roman Wiltshire were obtained from GLASSCOCK, R. (ed), 1992, *Historical landscape of Britain from the Air*. Cambridge University Press

W. Ford's unpublished archaeological survey of the Chippenham area, written just after the hot dry summer of 1976, correctly predicted the possibility of finding Romano-British settlements in the Bristol Avon valley.

3
Saxon Wiltshire

' Come south to me, beloved, I am in a rich land,' old Scandinavian sea-song

The withdrawal of the Romans from Britain in 410 AD and the aftermath years until the coming of Saxon settlers is a period of obscurity in British history, so how the Wiltshire people lived in the following two centuries is uncertain. The Roman taxation and monetary systems collapsed, the absence of coin finds and a lessening of economy point towards material poverty for many. Trading diminished, grain exports dropped, slave exports to the Continent were no doubt disorganized. The little that is known about this period points towards many people having to endure a subsistence lifestyle for several generations. Gildas the historian, asserted that until the 6th century the countryside estates continued to function, thereby supplying one of the few clues to what was happening in this period. Farmstead owners and other smaller landholders may also have survived economically; if so, both would have provided employment for the labourer. Presumably slaves continued to be worked, as no evidence exists to show that the institution of slavery faltered at any time during the 5th and 6th centuries.

How law and order were maintained throughout Britain between the Romans leaving and the first Saxon arrivals at the end of the 5th century is little understood. Presumably the Roman codes continued into the next two centuries, until the new Saxon kings began to form their own laws and controlled enough manpower to maintain stability. No evidence of a breakdown in society exists, but the sparsely populated countryside no doubt became very vulnerable to local raiding parties. An estate, if a viable working unit, had the advantage of offering economic protection and a certain amount of security to its workers and their families by numbers and organization alone. But by their very nature, small settlements and individual farmsteads in remoter areas of the chalklands presented an easy target for covetous local raiding bands and are likely to have suffered damage or even displacement.

Coming of the Saxons

In 442, due to the increasing number of raiding attacks suffered, the inhabitants of Britain had appealed to the Roman government for help, but the request was ignored and they were left to fend for themselves. The settlers or invaders, whichever role they played, penetrated slowly into the area which after the 8th century was to be known as Wiltshire. The first evidence of them comes from pottery sherds and a few discarded artifacts on sites in the upper reaches of the Thames valley. Following in the steps of the earliest prehistoric colonists, many more are likely to have arrived via the south coast, up the river valleys, seeking suitable locations in South Wiltshire and on the chalklands. The newcomers stemmed from northern Germany and the frontier region of northern Gaul. Known as the Jutes, Angles and Saxons, of diverse origin, they had the blood of Frisians, Danes, and Huns running in their veins. In time, especially in southern England, they were to be called Anglo-Saxons or Saxons, all to become even more diverse as they presumably assimilated and intermarried with the British. By the 8th century, history records that these people were known as the English.

Few settlement sites of the newcomers can be recognized prior to the 8th century, leaving doubt about their numbers and movements. According to archaeological investigations, of the settlements so far examined none had utilized previous British sites, which seems to indicate that they lived separately to the British. Settlement movements went from east to west and can be trace partially through the writings of Gildas and Bede, and after the 8th century from Anglo-Saxon chronicles, charters and land grants.

By modern standards, the influence of the Wessex Anglo-Saxon kings grew slowly as they waged their battles against kings and tribes from other parts of the adjoining countryside or occasionally engaged in conflict with local inhabitants, to gain and keep control of the area to be known as Wiltshire. From the battle of Mount Baden (thought at present to have taken place at Badbury Hill or Badbury near Swindon) circa 500, through the next two hundred years, the definitive Wessex kingdom would be established. Centred around the future Wiltshire, it extended from what is now known as Berkshire and Oxfordshire, into the southwest as far as Cornwall. The last battle to be waged, in the Bath and Cirencester area, where rivalry between the Saxons and the Mercians had continued, the latter were finally vanquished, and lost control of their territory in 802.

The making of Wiltshire into a Saxon kingdom

From the departure of the Romans to the coming of the Anglo-Saxons, the British apparently managed their own society, using Roman law and, probably for official use, Latin. Celtic continued as the spoken language. The following years of battle and assimilation sorely tried the British in the area later known as Wiltshire, and no doubt many upper class Britons lost status and wealth as their lands were taken over by the Wessex kings and granted away from them. The farmer, smallholder and labourer are likely to have spent some time in a state of preparation for battle or skirmish. Saxon attacks would have destroyed crops and made life bare-boned for many of them. Various types of plague created more affliction, several are recorded, a particularly grievous one striking in 540. The Saxon way of life was to predominate, due to a combination of conquest and co-operation. Undoubtedly intermarriage took place, for no conqueror has ever prevented this happening. But crops had to be planted and animals cared for, so basic routines of life continued on the land. If a homestead was raided and perhaps devastated by the Saxon invaders, its inmates had no choice but to pick up the pieces and work on; the land was their only sustenance.

The inhabitants of the future county of Wiltshire may have lived close to poverty, but they were not culturally poor. Their traditions originating from Europe, pre-dated the Roman conquest, and had remained strong in the county, holding peoples' beliefs together from the prehistoric years until Christianity finally overtook ancient pagan values by the 9th century. The isolation of the chalklands and the absence of towns, the scattered rural population undoubtedly hampered the spread of new ideas, and so intensified their culture and beliefs. People continued their traditional way of inhumation burial in cemeteries away from settlement sites and dwellings. Despite a Roman influence on many sculpture pieces found in the area, the so-called Celtic art and artifacts from the late Iron Age are numerous, testifying to the survival of a rich heritage.

Folklore has long contributed to an assumption that native populations of Wiltshire and other Wessex counties fled further west when the first Saxons arrived. Among the more affluent of the British element, perhaps a wealthy few did grasp the opportunity to move into Cornwall or Wales, but for the agriculturist flight was not a choice, he continued to cultivate his land, finally to be assimilated by the Saxons. Abandonment of the land can also be disproved by the continuation of pagan burial rites and the presence of grave artifacts of the period and after. History, contemporary or later, makes no mention of such a movement of people, neither is there any indication of it in Wessex laws.

The Romans had imposed economic power on the people of Wiltshire, though they left untouched their pagan beliefs and culture. Efforts in the 4th century to promote Christianity, the official religion, were given no Roman support. The Saxon settlers also held on to their pagan credos, though at the beginning of the early 7th century Irish monks had worked in Wiltshire, trying to advance the Christian dogma. Birinus, an Italian monk, came on the Wessex scene in 634 and had more success. Due to his influence the Wessex king, Cynegils, accepted baptism into the Christian church the following year. Birinus was then permitted to create a church administration in Dorchester, later moving it to Winchester, which became the church and state capital of Wessex by 660. Strongly supported by the monarchy, in Ine's reign (688-726) Christianity consolidated and became the official religion. It also became the official culture and the Church was to be economically

favoured by large grants of land, which in turn gave access to great legal powers and wealth derived from land holdings. Thereafter, in conjunction with the Crown, it would use its power to control the agriculturist, from smallholder to slave, in all facets of his lifestyle. However, pagan beliefs held on, as illustrated by a pagan shrine still in place at Hardenhuish, near Chippenham, at the end of the 7th century - 'the open land within the woodland of Thunor,' or Waden Hill, Avebury, both names referring to pagan gods.

The British and the Saxons blended to create the English, but always the British held inferior rank to their English counterparts as the laws created by the Wessex Kings, particularly Ine and Alfred (871-99), well indicated. The concept would remain in effect until the Norman Conquest. In legal documents, the British were referred to as *wealas or weahls*, the Saxon description of a Briton or Welshman. The word also meant serfs or slaves in Old English. So from the British ranks probably came most of the lower status persons, the slaves, the tied labourers, the half-free. But some Britons held land and many were designated free men. Though it is usually accepted that Saxons remained dominant over the British, some settlers surely failed to make a successful transition. They then had to take a drop in status, to change from an independent small landholder to a labourer or even a slave. And perhaps a descendant a few generations later would reverse the progression, gaining economic success and able to achieve a higher rank.

Little is known of how English usurped the British speech. A dual language period must have existed when both British and English were spoken, and the retention of British place-names and words is an indication that the language was not discarded immediately. In Wiltshire, at the remote village of Aldbourne, British was supposedly spoken until the 12th century. But after the 7th century, a sense of Saxon identity begins to be established in the county, suggesting the presence of a significant number of immigrants amongst the indigenous population. It is unfortunate that the combination of place-names plus historical and archaeological records cannot track the rate of settlement by the Saxons through Wiltshire and the various directions it must have taken, besides generally east to west; but so far any correlation has proved difficult.

Formation of Saxon government – effect on the agriculturist and agriculture

The first essentials to conquer and rule are power and revenue. One key to the creation of immense power in Saxon Britain was the presumption that the King owned all the land, to use for his own benefit, or to apportion out as he saw fit. Persuasion and force put this presumption into place. To achieve their goal, Saxon kings began to grant the land out, at first only to the royal families, who were the easiest to control. With their relatives in place, grants and charters were conferred, first to aristocratic families, then the Church, to form a ruling triage, headed by the king. Each land grant was assessed by hidage (originating from 'hid' meaning household), a measure of output of the land, to be paid by money, kind, services or a mix of all three. The pattern of these handouts formed one of the bases which made up the English landscape we know today.

To raise revenue, the first Saxon king, Cerdic, who had begun his rule in 538, possibly followed the previous Roman tax structure until he obtained the necessary legal base and administration divisions to be able to collect his own assessed fees or taxes. Side by side with the land grants, the new tax structure formed a strong foundation for Saxon feudalism. The landholder, whether secular or religious, was expected to keep the peace, endorse the laws of the Crown and carry out local administration of justice. His major investments were his workforce and his own efforts. Over the years, a large landlord turned into a small capitalist, though powered by production rather than money. He kept his holding or holdings in proper cultivation by work services from his tenants, labourers and slaves. A truly feudal society began to emerge with all playing a particular role, from King to slave. In time, however, feudalism gradually grew extremely rigid, too much so for society and individuals to tolerate, with a the trend for wealth to go upwards, creating more poverty downwards. Adjustments had to be made and by the 11th century the manorial structure, eventually so well defined in Wiltshire, emerged.

Taxation laws continued to evolve slowly but surely. All persons received a social classification, so contribution levels could be readily defined. In time the tax structure reached nearly all social strata including the labourer, who often found paying any levy, whether in money or kind, difficult, as he never had any surplus, especially in times of poor harvest. A lord employed a reeve and other officers to organize his estate to create enough goods, rents and moneys for his tax payments, while leaving him a margin to enjoy a comfortable lifestyle. Calculations had to be made to produce enough to pay and house his estate officers, for his tenants to grow enough food for their own use and be able to provide their own shelter, while furnishing food, clothing and shelter for their slaves and house servants alike. This was only a part of the calculation; it was also vital (if feudalism and the triage of power were to remain successful) that the lower levels of society were never to be allowed to amass any moneys and remain subservient, therefore being more easily kept to their particular social strata. In this respect, it was also important to the Wessex kings that the landholders themselves did not become too powerful, or they might threaten the Crown. So the Exchequer diligently calculated the taxes levied on estates, not only for pay for the king's government to function, but also to prevent wealth and power accumulation.

Besides monetary assessments, taxes came in the form of services and other charges: purveyance, public labour, justiciary duties, military service. It was the responsibility of a lord to fulfill them, but they all contributed further burden to the worker, already obligated to assign part of his labour, crops and animals to his lord. Lords were also responsible for the lodging and purveying of unexpected noble guests who demanded it, supplying extra post-horses or escort duties to the kings' men; but the actual work involved is likely to have come from the labourer, interfering with his regular services to the estate and his own cultivation work needs.

The local lord held responsibility for the construction and repair of roads and bridges in his jurisdiction. Later written records demonstrate that it was always a contentious matter as to whose liability it was to fix a certain bridge or road section, and the work

doubtless devolved to the labourer, yet another hardship. Other duties for a lord's workforce provided them with an early introduction to English law, as they were required if necessary to testify in his court and, to perform jury duties. They also had to assist in the pursuit and arrest of thieves, aiding justice to be carried out on the estates. For example, a thief caught had to be conveyed to the nearest 'cyninges tun' (king's tun), then a fundamental unit in the Old English organization of justice and finance. All duties mentioned above were considered basic tenets of feudalism, the work involved to be distributed evenly by landlords.

Royal Estates

Wiltshire was the centre of the kingdom of Wessex, so the Saxon kings knew the county well, constantly crisscrossing it as they travelled throughout their realm. Undoubtedly the kings and their entourages were a familiar site to county residents. Proceeding from estate to estate, he and his entourage needed large amounts of food and supplies as they journeyed, to be obtained as services from landholders and local people. Though often stopping with high-ranking lords, royal residences began to be built at convenient stopping places. In time, the resident sites often materialized into important royal estates, particularly around the larger settlements on major routes and river crossings. Some of these, Chippenham, Malmesbury, Highworth and Marlborough in the north, Amesbury, Downton and Wilton in the south, all with hinterlands of productive agricultural land, developed into vital and vigorous trading centres.

The royal estates at first may have fulfilled the role of collecting centres for renders or feorm (the first tax used to raise the provisions needed for the courts at each stopping place), rather than for agrarian exploitation. By 7th century law, from every 10 hides of land held, a lord was obliged officially to pay dues of 10 vats of honey, 300 loaves, 12 ambers of Welsh ale, 30 ambers of clear ale, 2 full grown cows or 10 wether, 10 geese, 20 hens, 10 cheese, a full amber of butter, 5 salmon, 20lbs in weight of fodder and 100 eels. To regularly organize the delivery of such a variety of goods when the king was due took much skill and many hands, from the reeve down to the slave. At Leominster, a Herefordshire estate, eight reeves, eight bailiffs and eight riding-knights formed a collecting unit, apparently operating in teams of three men, each consisting of three different officials to ensure the delivery of renders. The resulting procedures to make sure that each estate had duly paid its hide assessment must have given both royal and estate accountants nightmares! So much for early bureaucracy.

Church taxes

By the 8th century, the Church began its own tax system, the most far-reaching in the countryside. It took the form of one-tenth tithe to maintain clergy, relief of pilgrims and the poor. This was enforced by secular law in the 10th century, but payment for agriculturists could be in kind. This particular tax resulted in the building of large barns to store these tithe payments of grain and legumes. Other Church demands consisted of Scot payment at Martinmas, the 11th of November, the amount to be determined by a local priest in proportion to the amount of land a man worked, a ruling open to abuse and bribery. All had to pay except slaves. Peter's Pence, a tax raised centrally by the Church for the poor, for oil for lamps and offerings to the Pope, caused much resentment, as the moneys raised went to Rome, so nobody benefitted locally. The first payment of Peter's pence to come from King Alfred and his Wessex subjects was taken to Rome by the Earl of Wiltshire in 877. Another tax demanded by the Church, Soul Scot, valued the goods of a dead man, (a process immediately open to abuse) whose heirs then had to donate a portion of his goods to the parish priest. It is no wonder that the lower levels of society remained poor and burdened, though how rigorous was the enforcement of these Church dues in Saxon times is a moot point. It is human nature to evade tax payments, but in years of bad harvests, these taxes were lowered proportionally. When living was hard, or a famine occurred, possibly a priest starved as much as the labourers, for his dependence on the sustenance of the land was as great as the lord, labourer or slave.

Over the Saxon centuries, wealth gradually accumulated from the land and foundations to English society and the countryside began to be laid. In the 10th century feudalism began to blend with public offices and more power came to those running the machinery of law and order. In turn, to pay for the extra bureaucracy, more pressure to produce was exerted on the labourers, increasing their work loads and services. The successful growth of the Wiltshire estates provided employment and a living for the agricultural labourer. But it happened at the expense of his freedom, for by the end of the Saxon period even the free labourer was tied to his lord's land and could only move with his permission. Half-free peasants and slaves were tied completely. However, the agriculturist, whether tenant, labourer or slave, toiled as always, planting, sowing, reaping and harvesting, to ensure food, shelter and clothing.

Development of local government

Ine, the twelfth Saxon king, (688-726) unified the area formed by the future counties of Somerset, Dorset, Wiltshire, Hampshire and Berkshire into the Kingdom of Wessex. A great lawmaker, he brought about a new legal infrastructure, but it still primarily accommodated the upper classes and church dignitaries, and relegated the British to a lower status than the Saxons, though laws made provision to allow them to hold land in the name of the king. Ine's laws laid the foundations for the origination of shires, i.e. a shorn-off or separated area. Wiltshire as an administrative unit with declared boundaries came into being before the end of the 8th century. (These boundaries remained mostly intact to the end of the 20th century, despite the 1974 sort-out, but in 1997 Wiltshire lost land when the Swindon area was declared a separate unitary authority area from the county.) In time the important royal vill and burh of Wilton gave its name to the county, Wilton deriving from the river Wylye. By 900 a strong indication of political unity in Wessex came when the shires were divided into hundreds, and those subdivided into hides, giving every county a hidage assessment. The hundreds, designated areas, became court and legal administration centres. Villagers or estate officers, with their reeve, met royal officers at the local court, and their decisions on how taxes were to be paid from an estate would filter down to affect the peasant's life. As part of the network and power of feudalism, surety was decreed by his lord for every man, every free man enrolled for tithing, and the shire court became the resort of all from bishop and lord to peasant and serf. But no recourse from the decisions of the courts existed and there was no knowing how often rulings were biased by local influences or interests. However, a legal structure was firmly in place, which although harsh, eventually proved a foundation for moves towards democracy of the common man, besides the aristocrat.

Alfred who succeeded to the throne in 871, though better known as the conqueror of the Danes was, like Ine, another brilliant legal innovator. He added to the foundations of English law created by Ine, and categorized his subjects simply as fighters, prayers and workers. But despite these designations he further refined status, and for those in lower social levels the administration of his laws towards them were to become more rigid.

Social strata in Saxon Wiltshire

As can be seen, the rank of a person was crucial in Saxon law and his or her own life depended entirely on the designation received, to seldom change during a lifetime. Depending on the authority, various terms describe the different levels of society, but in a simplified form top level members of Saxon hierarchy were called *geneat* - companion or retainer of a king or nobleman. A Wessex nobleman was referred to as a *gesitheundmant*. Often involved with execution of the law and judicial matters, an *ealdorman*, was also a companion to a king. A *thegn* acted as a nobleman's servant, and at the bottom of these ranks was the *ceorliux*, often a commoner, sometimes a landowner.

The lower ranks of Wessex society are mostly referred to in legal documents as *ceorls, gebures villiens, bordari* and *cotters*. These too can be confusing, apparently varying in rank names according to regions, duties and privileges differing from estate to estate, so it is best to generalize them. Ceorls seem to have been mainly smallholders or husbandmen tilling a few acres, sometimes a ceorl was a woman who had inherited her land from a father or husband. Ine's laws lay down specific responsibilities: a ceorl had to fence his own land strips, and pay compensation to his neighbours if his cattle obtained access to their crops. He was permitted to share-plough an area with other ceorls and entitled to protection from brawling on his premises, no doubt a status symbol to his rank. If his lord did not provide him with a dwelling, he owed no services to him. If he quit before he harvested his crops, he could not claim any part of them, probably as his lord supplied the seed. But though officially a free man, he was still dependent for most of his lifestyle on his lord.

Later, Alfred's laws defined the ceorl as a tiller of the soil and not fully free. By the end of the Saxon period, ceorls had lost their right of movement and were as liable as geburs to services and rents. Seemingly many agriculturists in Wiltshire held the rank of ceorl and several place-names incorporating Charlton are a reflection of their numbers.

Gebur, often mentioned in Saxon documents, is a rank between ceorl and slave, a labourer tied to an estate, but having a semi-free status which their descendants inherited. A rich lord in possession of multiple estates had the right to move him from one estate to another. His freedoms decreased during the Saxon period. Geburs worked a yard or more of land for which they paid 10d per yard. *Rectitudines singularum personarum,* a document of *c.* 900, described a gebur as an 'outfitted' farmer, granted sown acres of land on his yardland, two oxen, six sheep and a cow, tools for his work and utensils for his house. In return he contributed certain services and paid monetary rent, though not in his first year on an estate. Services were levied at two days a week, increasing to three during ploughing and harvest times. His land likely lay in the estate's demesne (adjoining the lord's) giving him advantages such as better land and the privilege of running his pigs with the lord's, but it also meant he was within easy call to act as shepherd, house a puppy for the lord's hunting pack, or help tend to sick animals or a calving during the night. In these circumstances he resembled the inhabitant of a tied cottage on a Wiltshire farm in more contemporary times, because he was under an obligation to the person who had supplied him with work and housing. Towards the end of the Saxon period, the bottom level of ceorls are sometimes referred to as serfs. Semi-free, the serf had a small piece of land, perhaps five acres or so that he rented from his lord and worked to support himself and family, its surplus paying the rent. Unlike a slave, his lord was not as economically essential to his serf as he was to a slave, who was a total dependent.

From the 8th century onwards labourers had access to small currency, and sometimes were able save enough to buy land or their freedom. A labourer could also buy his freedom to move; two men at Great Bedwyn paid 300d (2.4d pennies equals one pence) to break their tie to the land they lived on and proceed they pleased. When a change of landholder

took place on an estate, geburs had to stay with their land, as happened when nuns at Shaftesbury Abbey in 950 were bequeathed certain lands along with its 'geburs that are tenants of the rented land.' The gift implied that all the labourers, stock and provisions on those lands went with the bequest.

Slavery

Even before Roman law a slave was considered a chattel. In the 5th century St Patrick's father owned slaves in the Severn valley; in contrast British slaves sold in Gaul and Rome won the pity of St Patrick himself. Slavery continued right through the Saxon period, playing a vital economic role in the labour supply for cultivation of the land. The laws of the Wessex kings document slavery in great detail, illustrating its importance, and estate documents later substantiate this. As has been shown previously, Ine's laws refer to Britons as *wealhs*, a word used to mean Welshmen or foreigners, hence accorded a lower status. By the 10th century slaves are often referred to as *wealhs*, an inference that it was mostly Britons who bore the designation of slave status. Several Wiltshire place names, some lost - Walton in Downton, Walecote near Malmesbury, Waledich in Avebury, and Walcot, a part of Swindon - all are thought to indicate places or cots where low status persons lived, Wal deriving from the OE wçalatûn, 'farm of the serfs.'

Many more of Ine's laws related to slavery. The descendants of slaves always inherited slave status. A slave could request freedom if made to work on Sunday by his master, an early illustration of church influence on law making, but could be whipped or fined if he worked for himself. A freeman who worked for himself could also be made a slave, pay a heavy fine or plead his lord's command. In another reverse role, a freeman could be made a slave if he thieved. It was a crime to steal a slave and sell him overseas. These laws were so extreme that they were later modified, no doubt proving unworkable, but the Church's humane influence is likely to have also played a mitigating role.

With clearly defined legal status, the slave, whether Saxon or British, man, woman or child, was owned by his lord or master, who could be Saxon or British, nobleman, churchman or ceorl. But slave-owning by low status persons, small landowners or ceorls, did not apparently convey any symbol of importance or raise their given status. By Saxon law the slave was a nonentity and considered kinless. His owner had the power to transfer, sell or export him anywhere, including to the Continent, but it is doubtful if a family was split up when sold, for such an action would provoke much resentment and even lead to rebellion, the fear of every slave-owner throughout history. As specified by law and later upheld by the church, slaves were to be given a reasonable diet and the bare necessities of clothing and shelter, no doubt just enough to keep them quiescent. However, if a Wiltshire slave-owner did decide to sell a slave, by the 9th century he or she would certainly be sent to Bristol, where the English export trade was well-established.

A slave could be redeemed by purchase or by gift of freedom from his master or mistress, freedom being given at the church door or altar, over the relics of saints or at crossroads. He was also able to buy his freedom if his lord was willing or be acquired for money given by a free relative who would then confer him freedom. A whole slave family could be purchased together. Prices varied, a single person from 24d to 60d, a family from 50d to £4. Sometimes part of the price was paid by the sale of an animal.

By Alfred's reign, Saxon law had defined specific punishments for slaves who committed crimes, the punishments usually harsher than those awarded to persons of higher status. Slaves were often the result of want or poverty; Saxon law permitted people to sell themselves or their children into slavery. Later Church Law decreed that boy slaves could be sold until the age of seven without their permission, with their consent until the age of fourteen, and after by their own choice. A harsh decision to make but perhaps one sometimes inevitable in time of famine. And some slaves sold themselves to pay off a debt.

To justify his or her keep, slaves were usually well-trained, for it cost as much to keep an unskilled person as one who was skilled. In the late Saxon period their work often became more defined, they are recorded as holding specialized jobs, ploughing or stock-keeping. Women slaves, until the advent of watermills, ground corn for bread, looked after small animals and poultry, made cheese, brewed beer or made bread for an estate or Church establishment. In a high-status household, women slaves could be weavers, seamstresses, or needle workers.

Custom and the economy decreed that the Church invariably worked and kept slaves on its estates. However, it quickly recognized slaves as persons with souls and therefore worth saving, able to contribute to the Church and pay for their road to heaven. The Church insisted on a day of rest for slaves, though later ordered compulsory church attendance on that day. A later edict insisted that the day off be Sunday. The Church advocated marriage for slaves. These dictums turned out to be a form of emancipation, as it gave slaves some recorded family status, and a little time to work for himself. They also modified the age-old factors of slaves being considered completely owned, in total command by their owner, with no legal recognition of family or kinship, making the slave even more of a chattel. Though slaves shared only a few of the thirty-seven holy days when freemen were not required to work, on the four Ember Wednesdays slaves might sell anything they had received in alms or had earned when working in their free time.

After the 8th century a slave could accumulate enough currency to buy his freedom, but unless his lord was willing to sell, it is probable that the process was difficult.

As free souls, slaves had the right of sanctuary, which meant if a slave took sanctuary for a crime, the Church then had the advantage over his lord in bargaining for justice or mercy to be shown to him. Landholders had the power to free their slaves, a gesture which was believed to contribute to saving one's soul on the Day of Judgement. In time this became a worthwhile Christian duty; canon law enjoined a bishop, when dying, to free some of his slaves for the good of his soul, and both religious and secular holders, in their wills or on their deathbeds freed slaves from ownership or from debt. In what seems a benevolent gesture, in 902 at Ebbesborne, one of the Wiltshire estates belonging to the Bishops of Winchester, a prospective renter, Beornwulf (probably a thegn) was requested by the Church to allow Lufu and his six children and Lufu and her three children, all born on the estate, to remain there; at the same time, Beornwulf was to be given three penal slaves of peasant birth and three slave-born persons with their off spring. The Church, and other slave-owners with multi-estate holdings, frequently moved their slaves from one estate to another when needed.

By the time of Domesday (1086), when some of the very first statistics in English history were transcribed, 16% of labourers in the West were designated as still being slaves and slavery continued well into the 13th century in Wiltshire, mainly for economic reasons and perhaps also retaining a long tradition. But the Norman feudal system preferred to assign dependent peasants with enough land to support themselves and extracted substantial labour services and rents in return. And again, Christian values and Church influences played their part, eventually making slavery redundant, though a few individual cases are on record as late as the 14th century.

By medieval living standards, it has to be presumed that the slave was generally treated not too unkindly. If he and his family were ill-handled they would not have produced enough labour to pay for their keep and shelter. If kept in prisoner-like conditions, enormous supervisory expenses would have been incurred. So the slave apparently made up the bottom layer of the labouring society. By today's standards, all labourers were slaves to the land and the lord they lived under, as to move without permission was a crime, and from documentation in late Saxon times onward, people who did were sought and returned, even years after their move. Those slaves who suffered disablement or illness, or lived long enough to be too old to work, are never mentioned. In all likelihood, with persons of other status, their families kept them until they died or suffered a pauper's death. But until the 15th century, when poor people became numerous enough to be a social problem and laws had to be made to deal with them, history hardly acknowledges paupers.

These ranks just described are the agriculturists of five centuries of Wiltshire's rural history. As a closing observation, here was the value of a rank as spelt out in law. If a man was killed, his worth, to be paid as a compensatory fine in shillings (s=5 pence) was as follows: a noble 1200s, a geneat 600s, a ceorl 200s. And a slave's worth was only that of his value to his owner.

It can be noted from the above paragraph that no mention is made of the value of a woman. If referred to at all, it is invariably in conjunction with a matter of property or rank. Women of the royal families are well-documented, they had to be to prove any claims to royalty or the throne. Both they and women of the Saxon aristocracy were allowed to be landholders, sometimes granted land on their own account and not through the death of a husband or brother. Royal women were frequently used to form suitable marriage alliances, such as that of King Alfred's sister Ethelswitha, married at Chippenham *circa* 853 to a Mercian king. Or his daughter Ethelflaed, married to another Mercian, Ethelred, who later played a large part in uniting the Mercian kingdom in the Midlands. Alfred left his Chippenham estates for his daughter Alfrith to use during her lifetime. Women shared the status of their family and were considered superior to men of lesser birth, and women landholders performed the public duties that came with their land. Widows possessed more freedom than wives or unmarried women, unless they were abbesses, which then

gave them even more power, bequeathed by Church hierarchy rules. But women needed the support of their family to play these roles and although this is definitely a debatable topic, after the 10th century Church documents seem to give much less consideration to women whatever their class. The status of women in the lower classes is still not understood. As with most patriarchal societies women were judged differently from men, and the double standards in sexual matters were seldom to women's advantage.

It is hard to ascertain what was happening to women of lower social strata in the Saxon period. No doubt many worked on the land at harvest and haymaking, certainly the wife of a working agriculturist took care of poultry, the family cow and other smaller animals. In late Saxon times, particular work was often allotted to women slaves - dairying, brewing, etc. In the close social network of an estate, the abuse of female slaves by their masters or supervisors may or may not have been routine, it would all have depended on the tolerance level of her surrounding workers and their families. Habitual abuse, especially sexual, generally causes much tension. Supposedly the number of male slaves lessened as status and respectability grew, while women slaves took longer to become emancipated as humility, submission and threatened innocence held them back. Church ethics in some cases are likely to have helped women slaves to avoid exploitation, as such behaviour was considered a sin and could soon be exposed in a small community such as a village or estate. In Alfred's laws, if a slave raped another slave he could suffer castration. Unchaste behaviour in a slave might lower the price of a bondswoman, and culprits could be flogged and put in the stocks as well as excommunicated.

The Agriculturist at work

The agriculturist's working life in Saxon times still has to be described through what information we can glean from estate and legal records, which makes for gaps in our knowledge. But that is one of the trials of writing the history of a common man; though his status, from an economical point of view, had begun to attract attention in the late 1700s, society was not really interested in him as a person until well into the 19th century. Until then, he was a labourer, and just a contributory unit to society.

In his work on the land, by Saxon times, the field has assumed the most important element in the labourer's life. Field today describes an enclosed plot of land used for cultivation or pasturing. It is derived from the old Saxon word feld, meaning land free from wood, an open space or downland, a patch of land cultivated or grazed within forest, or a detached meadowland. The latter delineated meadows by rivers or streams, apportioned to parishes that did not possess any within their boundaries. A field system denotes a planned use of a cultivated space, usually made up of field plots adjoining one another, surrounding or within reach of a settlement, or the later- formed Saxon villages and towns. Fields were mainly rectangular, in clusters. Since the early 19th century field systems have been an enormous source of interest to historians. Invariably the perceived fields received the vague designation of Celtic, whatever their date of origin, which in Wiltshire could be from late prehistoric to early modern times. Aerial photography of archaeological subjects pioneered after WWI by Crawford and Joseph (who did much of their original photography work in Wiltshire) began to solve the problem of dating fields and field systems. Now aerial photography has changed our whole perception not only of fields, but of ancient routes and tracks, dwellings of all times and shapes, and sometimes whole farming systems.

By the 10th century, records detail estate lands more definitively and references begin to appear of field systems, the demesne, common land or fields and detached meadowlands, all as separate entities. These clarified further the social strata of the labourers and later, more leases from estate or manor lords to lower levels of tenants perhaps allowed an ambitious hard-working man to work upwards. For instance, the rental of demesne land around the estate or manor house, invariably the most productive land, signified a definite rise in status for the lessee, whereas a man who rented marginal or waste land assumed a lower monetary obligation and hence a lower status.

Field systems dominated the work of any arable labourer. Their location to dwellings, their soils, their water supply, all were crucial, in turn affecting the way they were tilled, fertilized, planted, cultivated and harvested. The further the labourers and their plough teams had to walk to them, and the heavier the soil, the more work and energy needed to cultivate them. In Wiltshire, many field system patterns were inherited from Romano-British times, as the new Saxon settlers apparently did not replace them with systems they had left behind; no trace of European field systems so far have been found in Wiltshire. All through the Saxon period, as estates formed and expanded, by cultivating unused and wooded lands, fields expanded creating the beginning patterns of today's landscape. Ostensibly derived from the 10th century, the large open strip field systems characteristic of medieval farming in some counties, made up in Wiltshire only a small percentage of the total cultivated land of the Saxon period. The crops grown within the fields were protected by fences, ditches, walls or hedges, though of the latter few traces can be found archaeologically until the end of the period. All were necessary, as severe fines were meted out to the labourer if he left untended animals who broke in and ruined crops.

Ploughing information is slender. Later documentary references appear to make the ploughman and his team one of the most important elements of a Saxon land-holding, though this may not have applied on the Wiltshire clay soils, stock may have assumed more importance. Oxen were used rather than horses, as working harness for horses is rarely found and the horse collar not yet invented. The sharing of ox teams by peasants is frequently documented in late medieval times, but if the labourer was too poor to share and not allowed to use his lord's team, or his land allocation was so small it did not warrant the use of a team, it is highly likely that ploughing was still done by humans with a breast plough or an ard. Both methods of ploughing are labourious and time-consuming, but cheap, and the work can be done by women or older boys. The author saw women in Poland using a breast plough as late as 1993 and Portuguese men working with ards in the 1980s. Saxons seem the first people to have tilled the heavy clay soils of northwest Wiltshire, but the question of whether they adapted a plough rig able to tackle the clays, or, because of economic necessity, just worked harder with what they already had, is a conundrum yet to be solved.

Whether cropping and fallow cycles were favoured all through Saxon times is another enigma. By the end of the Saxon period three-crop rotation and probably other crop cycles were known in Britain; by the 12th century crops were known to be cultivated *quolibet anno seminanden* - to be sown in any and every year. What was happening to cropping in Wiltshire in the Saxon period remains a matter for investigation.

The Agriculturist and his animals

Some information on the labourers' and smallholders' relationship with animals can also be studied from documentary evidence, the Chronicles, charters, wills, and law codes. More bone evidence from Saxon sites is gradually turning up, but as mentioned previously, past interpretations of bone finds and their relationship to humans and their activities should be viewed with care.

During the Saxon period the common domesticated farm animals in Wiltshire remained cattle, sheep, pigs, goats, horses, dogs and cats. Horses are seldom alluded to, neither are cows, though they must have been familiar, for they were needed for breeding the oxen for plough teams. The Saxons did not use the cow as a dairy animal, they made their cheese and butter from sheep and goat milk. Constantly referred to, cattle still topped the scale in economic importance and individual worth, making them by far the most valuable farming animal. Sheep and pigs occurred everywhere but it is impossible to get any idea on their actual economic value to either the county's economy or to individuals. Goats are seldom alluded to and their bones hard to distinguish from sheep bones. Dogs were essential for herding cattle and sheep, cats a necessary foil against rodents invading food stores, especially grain stocks. Both dogs and cats are depicted in Saxon art as human companions, besides working animals.

Besides being grazed for meat, cattle were a form of money, used to pay taxes and other obligations. For all the cattle around Wiltshire, only one herd so far is specifically documented; established at Baverstock on a Wylye estate in the 10th century, it undoubtedly grazed the meadowlands lying on the flood plain. From bone finds, cattle in Saxon Wiltshire appeared to be somewhat smaller than present day animals. At least four breeds of cattle known today are recorded in Saxon times, Dexter, Kerry, Ayrshire and Herefords, but whether they grazed in the Wiltshire countryside and whether selective breeding techniques were used cannot be determined.

Bone evidence points towards a large percentage of cattle being raised and killed in their prime on larger estates, particularly in late Saxon times; in parallel, their importance meant that the agriculturist spent a goodly proportion of his time involved with cattle. Alongside the raising of cattle for meat ran the breeding of oxen for plough teams, a very skilled occupation, as a supply had to be constant. A certain number of cows producing sturdy calves always had to be on hand, the number depending on the total ox teams an estate required. Good female calves were retained for further breeding, suitable bull calves underwent castration at an early age, to be pastured until three years old, when they possessed enough strength and stamina to be suitable for the heavy work of ploughing or carting. As their bones firmed up, at about the age of two years, their preparation began with light work. Trained and mature, oxen worked hard, too hard to survive to old age, and had to be replaced at the age of eight years or so. It is calculated that for one working oxen to be put into commission, three breeding females of varying ages existed. Oxen had to be kept fit through the winter, their busiest time. References to extra fodder for working oxen are frequent. In the winter, when grass was scarce and they worked their hardest, they ate oats when available, supplemented or replaced by a mixture of beans, dried legumes, chaff, straw and vetches. Reference to hay is seldom, though certainly supplied if an estate had access to detached meadow lands.

Possibly individual herders, whether slaves or not, were required to sleep alongside their lords' cattle, as shepherds lived with their flocks on open land. If a peasant possessed cattle or other animals, he and his family may have lived under the same roof for warmth. Mention is made of cattle being housed in byres; if a byre was attached to a dwelling, it may or may not have been a type of longhouse. When grass disappeared in harsh winter months, nonworking cattle ate young twigs and leaves of elm, live ash and hazel. In addition, apparently holly and mistletoe too and, perhaps, oak, a custom that continued into the 17th century in Wiltshire. One feels for the cattle, mighty hungry but with no choice other than to consume such poor rough forage. In a long winter, on a farm with little early grass, 18th century cattle are reported ending up as skeletons, and this no doubt applied equally well in Saxon times and the following centuries. Life was uncomfortable for most, both man and beast, until the 20th century.

At Collingbourne Ducis, an investigation of nine Saxon houses revealed undisturbed bone finds, mainly of sheep/goat and cattle. Horse, pig, dog and cat, red and roe deer, fowl, goose and songbirds made up the remainder of the find, except for two bones each of badger and crane. Perhaps a crane was considered as much a delicacy to our labourer as the peacock was to the upper class! Overall, the residents favoured sheep/goat and cattle for meat. They killed the cattle at about three years old, lamb under two years old. Though pig meat (both domestic and wild) was consumed, the percentage compared to that on other Wiltshire sites was low. Certain bones showed axe, cleaver or knife marks, indicating instrument types used for butchering carcasses. Split and broken bones may have indicated a taste for marrow, and butchery techniques demonstrated an ability to create lamb chops! This settlement probably had easier access to grazing animals, rather than pigs on pannage, and enjoyed eating both roe and red deer.

The primitive breeds of sheep in Saxon times were smaller and tougher, able to cope with cold and harsh winters more easily, while still bearing their lambs successfully. From bone finds and later documents, it is thought that shepherds had to cope with rot, scab, red water, the mange and bad joints. Though tails were not docked, primitive breeds were rarely troubled with maggots, a later source of anguish and often loss, as treatment is difficult if maggot infestation is not discovered early. Other diseases are described, but hard to identify.

In Welsh law a good sheep dog was worth the price of an ox, and in Wiltshire was probably just as highly valued, as a dog was essential, not only for rounding up on the broad spaces of the chalklands, but also as a guard dog in case of rustlers. Over the centuries numbers of sheep increased in Saxon Wiltshire and were kept alive longer, no doubt an indication that the wool crop had begun playing a more important economic role. In conjunction, the importance of ewes as milch animals also increased. Cheese is more frequently mentioned towards the end of the period, and an increase in pigs is noticed, perhaps

Eleventh century shepherds .

an indication of their involvement in dairying practices as consumers of leftover whey. It is likely that the age-old position of shepherd in Wiltshire became increasing important during Saxon times, just as it seems dairymaids also assumed more importance.

Goat herdsmen appear in Saxon records and goats are often mentioned along with sheep. The goat population in Somerset is well recorded, but not so in Wiltshire. Such a useful cottage animal may still, however, have been owned on smallholdings or by labourers. They excelled as providers of meat, milk, kids, dung, hair and skins, and their production ratio to intake of food is much higher than that of sheep or cows. Goats are not mentioned in Ine's laws and seemingly not considered a commercial enterprise in Wiltshire. Maybe as with cats and dogs, goats were such an everyday feature around rural households that records ignored them.

Like goats, pigs are animals easily maintained, as they love to scavenge and have a very broad taste in foods. But they are labour-intensive as they cannot be tethered to an object, only by a leash, and unless confined in a building, even in enclosures they need minding for their notorious habit of rooting up everything in sight, which is extremely destructive to good land. The custom of ringing pigs' noses is, in the main, only a slight deterrent. Keeping pigs in sties is not recorded until the 16th century in Wiltshire, when it apparently became common due to the great loss of forested lands and the advent of Enclosures. But the custom may have started much earlier, as the word for 'pig-sty' derives from Old English. *Rectitudunes* states that a slave herdsman if his lord allowed, had a pig in a sty (and every male slave was allowed a strip of land for ploughing).

Pigs in the Saxon period were bristly, long legged, razor-backed and prick-eared, not apparently interbred with wild boars (except by accident!). The Tamworth and Gloucester Old Spot, both primitive breeds until interbred with Chinese pigs in the 8th century, may have resembled them. The Wiltshire agriculturist surely developed a local breed, as until the 19th century every county had its own, which varied over the centuries.

If near enough to a forested area, swineherds, considered a very low rank on the social scale, took their pigs to woods where foraging was permitted, from August 29th until January 1st. Doubtless in the larger expanses of the Wiltshire forests, the herders had assigned areas, the holders charging pannage rights. The timing of this custom coincided with the production of the acorn crop, an important

Pigs at Pannage

element in pig-raising; a calculation cites that if all the acorn crop of a single oak is consumed by pigs, they will produce 100 lbs of meat. Beech nuts would also be used for pannage in Wiltshire. In the forest the pigs were carefully guarded from predators, including human pig-rustlers and wild boars. In early medieval drawings pigs are depicted as being restrained by owner or herder on a leash tethered to a back leg. Spears and dogs provided means of protection and horns were blown to keep herders in touch with one another. Some pigs are likely to have foraged around the settlements, feeding on household scraps, grass, seeds and berries. Where bracken grew, a pig's rooting abilities became an asset, curbing the plant's ever-spreading root system and hence its intrusiveness into grazing areas.

Pigs were used for tax payments to the Kings and they were driven to a collecting point. An invaluable resource for labourer and small holder, for although labour-intensive, they ate relatively anything, and like goats had a good weight/food ratio. They produced huge litters, and were delicious to eat from birth onwards. Invariably slaughtered within two years, they provided the traditional autumn kill. Because of the high ratio of fat, the salted meat preserved well, and the rendered lard helped keep starvation at bay until spring months yielded garden crops.

Fowl, goose and duck bones are found on settlement sites, but like goats, cats and dogs they get little mention in Saxon records. Perhaps all were so familiar they were taken for granted; fowl made a considerable contribution to the food supply of the common man in Wiltshire. Bone evidence has to be carefully interpreted, as bird bones are extremely perishable. Poultry often served as a means of tax payment or obligation, particularly when the Kings travelled and needed supplies for their courtiers and the servants with them. Presumably plenty of wild duck, geese and swans existed in Wiltshire in Saxon times, though nothing is documented until after the 13th century.

Fish certainly contributed an important source of protein for the Wiltshire agriculturist, especially if he lived near a stream or river. Until the 20th century eels travelled overland extensively at certain times of the year and could be easily caught on land as they were predictable in their movements and the times of their appearance. Before landlords had control of all Wiltshire's waterways, fish weirs are likely to have been constructed on bigger streams and rivers to make a catch easier. In addition to catching by rod, line and hook, the labourer was no doubt apt at creating eel and fish traps in suitable places.

It was not illegal to snare hare as a source of food, but no rabbits are mentioned in Saxon times. Eggs undoubtedly formed another protein contribution to a Wiltshireman's diet. To obtain a deer or boar from the forest was an act of poaching, to be done with great care and secrecy. Like peacocks, deer and boar were reserved for aristocrats.

Bee-keeping is known from antiquity, but little mention of it occurs in Saxon times. It was likely to be the prerogative of the lord, rather than of the labourer, though with luck or skill, he would have access to honey made by a wild swarm. Western counties yielded much honey for taxes and mead. A bee *ceorl* was the lowest rank of a freeman. Bee-keepers and honey-gatherers are mentioned by the Domesday book, a mellitari at Westbury, for instance. Two Wiltshire place-names connected to bee-keeping are recorded: *Beoleah* (Bee clearing), and *Beocere Eo* (Bee-keeper's Island).

Vineyard cultivation is likely to have utilized the agriculturist's skills in Wiltshire through the Saxon period, though there is a strange dearth of any mention of vineyards in charters and other documentation. However, they appear later in Domesday.

Finally we come to the question of the role that horses are likely to have played in the life of the Wiltshire agriculturist. By 904 a document, referring to the Taunton (Somerset) area, tells of carts drawn by horses for the conveyance of royal possessions from estate to estate. This is feasible if the horses pulled light loads on dry roads correctly harnessed with a strap across the chest, a substitute for the harness collar, which was not supposed to be known in England until the following century. But oxen were unbearably slow in their work and believed not to be willing to work far from their home area (though this myth was surely disproved during the pioneering days of African Cape Province and North America; probably it depended on their training), so using horses made for a faster journey. However, whereas oxen will pull well in mud, a team of horses, particularly without harness collars cannot, due to their differences in placement of muscles and hoof design. Horses wearing a harness similar to that used when pulling a chariot would be able to move small loads on firm surfaces, either with a wheeled cart or a sled. Packhorses also were undoubtedly utilized. Judging from the plentitude of horseshoe and nail finds, it is likely that a smallholder or well-off peasant kept a horse, especially to go to market, and may have shared its possession with a neighbour.

Religion and the agriculturist

After 634, the political moves of Birinus the monk allowed the Christian church in Wiltshire to thrive, but from the coming of the Saxons to the Norman conquest, only a few clues are available to define the role that religion, and later the Church, played in the Wiltshire agriculturist's life. The Christian faith apparently made little headway amongst the people, although declared the official religion of Wessex by King Ine towards the end of the 7th century. Pagan burials continued until well into the 8th century or later, pagan shrines and markers persisted even longer. Christianity made progress, but slowly. Monastic estates show no evidence of proselytizing, and possibly were more interested in the labourer for what he produced rather than the good of his soul.

In common with other dominant religions of all ages, to replace alien practices, Christianity forbade worship of the devil, pagan or heathen gods, and natural features such as the sun and the moon; doubtless the stones of the Wiltshire henges and the Roman shrines at Nettleton and other places became forbidden territory. Predicting the future, whether for an event or an individual, witchcraft, charms and amulets were to be replaced by the sprinkling of holy water, prayers and the symbol of the cross. Easter was substituted for the pagan celebration of spring solstice, Christmas the winter solstice, both with local customs no doubt being incorporated into the revelries. Christian saints were substituted for pagan symbols. A sharing of beliefs may have hastened the amalgamation of the Saxon and the British, but that is impossible to ascertain.

At first monastical buildings did not necessarily represent the beliefs of the people living in their surrounds. After the Church had established itself and organized the large land grants from the King into the pattern of monastical life, a labour force had to be acquired to till its land, cultivate and bring in the hay and harvest. The labourer's status was controlled by the Kings' laws, which the Church rigorously followed, but their courts administered the same laws often more justly and mercifully than did the secular courts. The influence of the Church on the labourers in the first centuries of Christianity in Wiltshire further defined their status in society, eased the harsh life of the tied and the slave, and perhaps gave them some hope for comfort in the life after death.

Initially small minsters run by communities of priests became established in southern England, often near royal estates, though little evidence of them survives in Wiltshire.

Despite their lack of Saxon fabric, Ramsbury and Amesbury churches started as minsters; their Saxon crosses demonstrate early Christian activity, as does the Saxon cross associated with Codford St Peter. As the minsters continued, the priestly communities acquired property, usually gifts of piety from the royal family or nobles. Their duty was to care for the spiritual life of the population and they travelled to preach at open sites often marked by crosses, at a crossroads, or by a cemetery or burial site. According to pagan belief, the dead were feared, hence cemeteries were located away from settlements, often by roadsides, but Christian belief taught that the dead were not evil and hence there was nothing to fear from burials near settlement sites.

The influence of the travelling clerics declined by the 10th century, perhaps diminished by the devastating local conflicts inflicted on the countryside by the Danes. The decline may have spurred secular landholders to acquire their own priests and subsequently build small places for worship, so gaining even more control over the lives of the people on the estates. The Church benefited also, the priest had closer scrutiny over the fulfillment of church tax payments, and if he so desired, obtained a closer spiritual check on his congregations. In the 10th or 11th centuries, some preaching places may have served as the first location for a village church. Wooden churches do not survive the centuries and sadly, Wiltshire is deficient in Saxon church remains despite early diocese organization in the county. This may be because of few towns and a scattered population, with not enough wealth concentrated in one place to build a substantial stone church. Alton Barnes is an exception that proves the rule, doubtless built with wool money, or St Mary's at Limpley Stoke, probably because high quality building stone lay nearby and a certain amount of luck ensured its survival.

Early estate churches served as a focal point for landlords' tenants and labourers, their families and estate servants. Compulsory church attendance on Sundays and holy days, baptisms, marriages and burials and other spiritual matters may not have proved as

Medieval Priest receiving animal tithes from his parishioners

important as the site itself, which frequently turned into a trading place and no doubt a recreational area. 10th century laws made against Sunday trading show it already as a fact, and in later medieval times, many important Wiltshire market places, both rural and urban, developed alongside churches and crossroads.

The only involvement in charity by the Church, encountered by the author, is £100 left to Aelfsige, bishop of Winchester circa 950, by King Eadred in his Will, to purchase for the people of Wiltshire 'relief from want and from the heathen army.' The concept of the Church or a priest fulfilling the function of spiritual ministering to Christians does not appear in Saxon times, neither does the role of the monks and nuns as healers of the sick and carers of the poor appear in any documentation until after the Norman conquest. Hence the humanity of the Church seemed to take a back seat in its aims and achievements, of which the most important are defined as establishment, power and riches. No agriculturists of whatever rank are documented as receiving religious help and the impression gained is that they are only of importance for laboring or financial purposes, never in a social context.

Estate management and administration

The West Saxon Kings decreed that they owned all land in their kingdom and their laws and actions initially decided the lives of the men and women cultivating the lands of Wiltshire in the Saxon period. Ine's laws ensured a place for all men, resulting in a rigid stratification of society. If a land grant included a small settlement or family farmsteads, it is assumed the grant included them and all the people living there belonged automatically to the new estate, to henceforth farm those lands at their new lord's will. So they remained on the land where they were born, retaining the status held at their birth, working for their lord, or a tenant of the estate, assuring a steady supply of labour. Seemingly families were able to keep together, unless of slave status, when separation may have occurred for financial reasons.

Abundant labour permitted intensive farming, particularly in the river valleys and lowlands. According to Crown records, during the Saxon years estates produced enough tax revenues to make Wiltshire a comparatively rich county. But any attempt to survey the area's growth and cultivation patterns is fraught with difficulty. Few Saxon sites have undergone archaeological investigation in great depth, due mainly to high costs and difficult access. What is known at present from aerial surveys, settlement growth, climate changes, movement of soils, pollen counts and crop husbandry, all still needs to be co-ordinated and studied to obtain a definitive picture of agriculture between the 5th and 11th centuries. Some of the little understanding we have of Saxon farming life in the county is based on 'a handful of texts' including the Charters, and on three major documents surviving from the 10th century, *Rectitudines singularum personarum*, thought to be connected to east Somerset and west Wiltshire; a charter of Hurstbourne Priors, Hampshire; and a survey of property at Tidenham, Gloucestershire, both places near enough to Wiltshire to have relevance.

Estates could be large or small, some of single land grants, others a combination of several grants. Often scattered, away from the lord's home base, they would be difficult to run without efficient reeves and supervisors. On more remote estates, a labourer may have benefited if, to quote Hare: 'administration lines were weak, it may have given a little more freedom in his everyday life, less supervision, less exacting demands on his time and bonds of service.'

Among the laws pertaining to landholdings, provisions were made to preserve existing Wessex estates. If a lord left an estate, he was permitted only to take with him his reeve, smith, children and nurse and had to leave 50-60% of his land tenanted by husbandman, a sure way of keeping together the estate and its social structure. Note that a lord seemingly had no obligation to take his wife; perhaps she was permitted to remain behind to manage the estate! But he was allowed to move half-free or unfree labourers from one estate to another, such as one newly acquired needing more labour to produce greater yields. Unfortunately, finer details of estate administration during late Saxon years are just not known, neither is the specific acreage allocated to the different social levels of tenants and labourers, as when these are defined, they are of unknown measurements.

To allow for the extra work needed at haymaking and harvesting times, and because apparently few itinerant labourers existed in Saxon times, most estates are likely to have carried more labour than was absolutely necessary. And when labour is cheap, as it was in a feudal system, there is usually plenty of it. Work demands on estates would have varied, depending on the strictness of the lord and his administrators. Glastonbury and Malmesbury Abbeys were not particularly efficient in the running of their estates. The Glastonbury estates in Wiltshire were scattered and located far from its home base, resulting in distant lines of communication and the likelihood of laxer administration. The Bishops of Winchester on the other hand always conducted their Wiltshire estates in a most businesslike manner, their written records in late medieval times obviously based on past edicts of rigorous economies and strict estate regulations. They invariably showed a good profit by their accounts.

Life no doubt differed from one estate to another. As more land was brought into production in Wiltshire, chalkland, downland, greensands, the clays, farmwork on these different soils meant work conditions would not be uniform from one estate to another. By modern standards, much of the work was no doubt routine and monotonous, the long hours it took to carry out tiring, but for the Saxon agriculturist, his chief concerns were no doubt to obtain enough to eat, enough to wear, and to enjoy a dry roof over his head each night. And this his lord and the feudal system provided.

In the countryside, rents and taxes were paid in cash or with goods, such as timber, stock grain, food or even ale, produced from an estate. By late Saxon times records show a lord, particularly if a member of the royal family, a churchman or an abbess, began to rent out acreage to freemen. They too paid rent in kind, services and perhaps some cash, obtained from selling a portion of their harvests. Smaller land portions and perhaps a dwelling were assigned to half-free laborers; they contributed all their harvest, gave much service, but were allowed to keep certain amounts of food and produce for themselves. Slaves, who

toiled on the lord's inland or demesne, had either the privilege of a dwelling or a dwelling site, where they built and maintained rude shelter and perhaps had a little land to cultivate for themselves. It has been suggested that buildings on settlement sites showing evidence of shallow sunken floor levels may have been assigned to slaves. Allowances of food and other privileges are cited for certain other levels of labourers.

We have no idea what life on the royal estates was like for the peasant, labourer and slave attached to it. Was it any better or worse than one held by a religious order or by a secular lord? One presumes that a royal estate offered a better life, as theoretically it would be run fairly, according to the laws of the kingdom. Unfortunately, this may not be a logical conclusion.

Development of the Saxon countryside

The earliest written records of the Wiltshire countryside are the Anglo-Saxon charters documenting surviving land grants. A few are kings' grants to their families, particular nobles or thegns, a few refer to kings' estates, but most are derived from the cartularies of monastic orders. All surviving documents are copies of copies made for use as title deeds and ownership claims for many centuries until the Dissolution of the Monasteries. At present, 171 Wiltshire charters are known, granting parcels of land between 675 and 1065, from a few to several hundred acres, a fraction of the countryside. To establish identification of a grant, some charters carry detailed descriptions of the land's topography and its whereabouts can often be determined by routes, water courses, hills, coombes, ditches and balkes, etc. Some landmarks are more descriptive, 'cove of the meads' (a deep cleft in the landscape), 'a steep stoney slope' for instance. Boundary markers of stone and the mention of barrows are numerous; some can be identified today. Leap gates abound, made high enough to prevent sheep or cattle clambering over, but of a height deer could jump.

Burial places are often mentioned, a reminder of the importance attached to them. Some are described as heathen, though recorded a century or more after Christian burials had begun. Types of countryside are distinguished, downland, woodland, open country, arable, and meadowland, 'the sandy lea,' 'the Black marsh.' Glimpses can be caught of human features, how the land was cultivated and wherein lived the labour needed for that purpose. Hedgerows, 'the gate of the hay lea,' 'to the end of the strip of ploughland and headland,' 'the farmsteading,' 'the small wood of ash trees,' 'coombe of the watercress,' 'seven pear trees,' 'the bent apple trees (obviously an old orchard), watering holes and fords, detached meadowlands. Other features are detailed, a sand pit, a path to a stile, roads(often Roman), a 'whiteway' leading up a down, a deep lane, tracks, and finally dwellings – *mansi* and crofts.

The first recorded grant for Wiltshire in 675 from the bishop of the West Saxons to the priest Aldhelm, was the land called 'Malmdumesburg' where he was permitted to live under holy rule. Many grants to Malmesbury and Glastonbury Abbey followed, mainly of land near the Avon or the Thames, implying early Saxon control of this corner of the county. Later charters of Glastonbury included lands at Nettleton and Grittleton, bequeathed by a thegn Wulfric, a holder of much land in Wiltshire. More lands included the Deverills, Mildenhall and one of the Winterbournes. The first recorded acquisition of Wiltshire land by the Minster at Winchester was at Downton; other lands nearby followed, at Bishopstone, Ebbesbourne and Wanborough, among other places.

Like secular landholders, all religious holders had to clear their lands to produce money and goods to pay their taxes and land grants often stated the tax assessment in the form of a hide or hideage, the amount the land should yield. Unfortunately, just how much land each hide represented cannot be determined, as it varied from county to county and depended on the fertility of the land itself.

Royal estates or vills added to the development of the Saxon Wiltshire landscape, their number and extent at any given time impossible to determine; written evidence of royal estates in Wiltshire does not appear until 840. Several clustered near Wiltshire towns and monastic establishments, evidently stopping places for the kings and their entourages when travelling. Sometimes a clue appears, such as King Ethelwulf, whose daughter in 853 married at Chippenham 'from the Villa Regia' Burhred, King of Mercia. Other Villae Regia can be identified at Amesbury, Bedwyn, Bradford, Calne, Ramsbury, Tilshead, Warminster and possibly Westbury. In time, trading places and markets grew up around Villae Regia, and if not important centres today, they have had their time of eminence as important market towns.

We have very little idea what acreage of the county's area was being cultivated when Saxon settlers first came into Wiltshire at the end of the 5th century compared to the amount in the Roman period when the economy was at its peak. From the writings of Gildas and Bede, and later the Anglo-Saxon charters, we can determine to some extent the spread of the Saxon settlement in Wiltshire, mainly from east to west. Gildas mentions that large estates entailed division of land after the Romans had left, which could apply to Wiltshire, with its many estates. Romano-British owners may have obtained even more land after the Romans departed, then increased their labour force by enslavement, hiring local surplus workers or even new Saxon settlers when they arrived in Wiltshire. How long these estates were maintained and whether some or all were split, sold, or commandeered by Saxons, cannot be determined. Then came the conflict years between the Saxons and the British, their later amalgamation and the landholding takeover by the Wessex kings.

What may illustrate a link to Roman or Romano-British estates and the present are the survival of a few early 'minster' parish boundaries and early ecclesiastical boundaries (e.g.hides at Garsdon and at Rodbourne allocated to the Abbot of Malmesbury by King Ine) which later are seemingly identical with hundred boundaries . But no documentation of estate ownership by Britons exists; it is as if they were erased completely. And perhaps they were, by being forced from their land and ending up as labourers.

To the end of the Saxon period, when most of the land in Wiltshire was under cultivation except waste, forests, and marshes, the evolution of the Wiltshire countryside is presumed to have been synonymous with the spread of Saxon settlement. The rate assuredly depended on the nature of the land, the size of the land grants and the growth of population to supply labour. When possible, mixed farming was the general rule, particularly where strips of land running from hilltop to valley bottom gave access to different soils and topography. Many examples, often in very narrow bands, exist in the Nadder, Wylye and the Salisbury Avon valleys, their boundaries still to be discerned today. Agrarian evidence points to these lands being taken over at the beginning of the Saxon period for more intensive cultivation. On higher ground, sparse settlements or farmsteads continued to be the norm. This was remote land and may still have challenged smallholders to make a

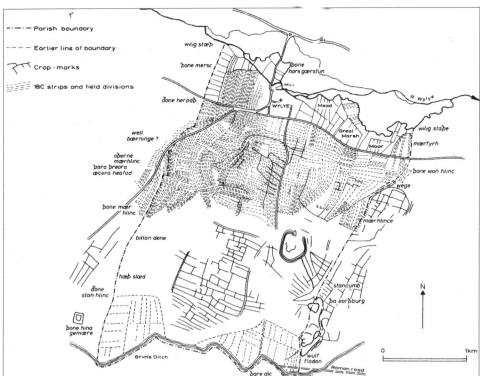

Wylye valley Saxon estate boundaries.

living from it, if they could carry on their farming undisturbed. At the edges of the chalklands, the adjoining river valleys, on the Greensands, the Corallian ridge and by forest borders, settlements and farmsteads were denser. Having shown habitation from prehistoric times, though not necessarily in continuous occupation, these sites offered anew excellent habitat and farming, and still do at the present time. Cherhill is an example of such continued settlement, as are Mildenhall, and Shrewton, to name other locations.

The Bristol Avon valley runs right through the forested lands of northwest Wiltshire. Away from the clays, the valley's lighter soils had attracted cultivation probably as early as the third millennium BC, and settlement continued, albeit sporadically, the pattern proceeding through Roman times. By the end of the Saxon period the valley had undergone a great deal of clearance, particularly around the present Malmesbury, Chippenham, Lacock, Melksham, Staverton and Bradford-on-Avon, all ancient river crossing places. The same period saw the instigation of continuous settlement in the valley and its surrounding higher lands. The distribution of early medieval settlements is dense, particularly in the valley above Chippenham, a fairly well-studied area, and is likely to prove so in other parts of the valley. Many are spring-line settlements originating in early and mid-Saxon times, attracted by water emerging from geological strata divisions. Below Chippenham, Lacock, Bewley, Bowden, Notton and Lackham almost certainly owe their origin to such springs, assuring their inhabitants of an easily accessible and plentiful water supply. In addition, the valley offered good shelter and, apart from its frequent dampness, a more comfortable life than one on the windy open chalklands. Admirable for mixed farming, cattle grazing lands were established on the clays, hay meadows on the river gravels, grain growing on the lighter soils in open fields and sheep runs on the limestone to the west.

Anglo-Saxon charters indicate many valley estates cleared and highly cultivated by the 8th century and the establishment of several royal estates. Towards the end of the Saxon period, fragmentation of these estates began, often resulting in the formation of new manors, and the creation of parishes. These in turn originated villages still in existence today.

Forests

Until the 6th century, the great belts of Wiltshire woodland offered a natural hindrance to settlement. The forests later known as Selwood, Melksham, Chippenham and Braydon, extended from the Somerset border northeast to the start of the Thames valley. The Saxons in the 9th century referred to this wooded area as Sealwudu. Alfred's laws understood the need to protect the forest resources and contained provisions against burning and cutting down of woods, while land charters specified portions to be set aside for the use of tenants, no doubt grazing and pannage rights for ceorls, according to local customs. Though every lord had the right to hunt his warren (in the sense of a game park), only the king and his court hunted in the forests. Travelling through the forests could be dangerous, due to robbers, and laws decreed protection from attack. Though trees were singled out for size and their capacity to cover swine, a large tree covering thirty, it is not possible to be definitive about the Royal forest boundaries for sheer lack of documentation; and forest does not necessarily designate a wooded area, it generally describes the King's hunting area, especially after the 11th century.

Selwood forest lay mainly on the Upper Greensands, where overlying soils are easier to work. The other forests in the northwest grew on heavy Oxford Clays, those soils proving more daunting to settlement, so people came later to them than to Selwood. Other forested areas, Savernake, Chute, Clarendon, presented less deterrent to settlers, due to more easily worked soils, so they received earlier development than those in the west of the county. Significantly the names Savernake, Chute and Melchet are British names, as was the former name of Clarendon - Penchet. All denote the early importance of woodlands.

Leah signifies clearing of woodland, and after the 8th century many Wiltshire place-names contain this element, in the form of lea, ley, leigh, etc. Possibly they first denoted small settlements on what had been previously forest land, and after the mid 10th century began to indicate a place near pasture or meadow. The element *tun,* about the same time, often signified outlying cleared land of an estate, and *ham* an estate centre. Villages as we think of them today can seldom trace their name or boundaries until the 10th or 11th centuries, demonstrating the slow growth of an individual settlement.

By the 11th century, tracts of land at the edges of the forests had yielded to cultivation. An Anglo-Saxon poet spoke of the peasant as the long term destroyer of the forest; he may well have fullfilled the role many times as he felled trees and strove to provide a living and security for his family. At the same time, a lord exploited the forest to produce tax payments. One Wiltshire family can trace the ownership of its lands to an ancestor who gained permission from the Crown to assart on the edge of Chippenham forest near Heddington in the 13th century.

The larger the stretch of forest, the lower was its population density. Parts of the Saxon Sealwu, in the Bristol Avon valley on the heavy clay soils, made any kind of agricultural activity arduous, likely spawning exceptional men and women able to cope with the extra hard work. For those who lived completely within the forest, life may have been even more difficult, but the independent peasant it produced is well documented after the 13th century. The deep forest may have lacked pastures, but it provided timber for houses and fences, animals to hunt (except deer and wild boar; that privilege was only granted to kings and nobles), honey for sweetening, fruits and berries for gathering on its edges, acorns for pigs, even leafage for a cow or two. A peasant perhaps ran a few goats independently, his wife kept fowl, and he may have owned a horse for his journeys to market.

Boundaries

The development of the countryside depended on boundary lines. They have a fascinating history and affect the lives of everyone who has ever lived in Wiltshire. Lines cover the Wiltshire countryside, they are the hedges of the farms, the open spaces of the chalklands, the borders of the few remaining woodlands, the enclosure lines of urban and rural settlements. Research in the past thirty years has pushed boundary origins in Wiltshire

further and further back and, despite some controversy, this work still stands. Due to several workers in the field, particularly Bonney, and more recently Eagles, we are now comfortable with the concept of boundaries seemingly having evolved from Roman times, and it is likely, as Cunliffe suggests, some of these may soon be traced back to prehistoric times. Ellis seems to think that old tribal boundaries of the Iron Age tribes carried over into Roman times, and, linked by the Roman *civitates,* can therefore be extended into Saxon times.

The first boundaries were formed on the basis of the geology and the topography of the landscape, its rivers and valleys, forest and open land. The lines began with routes or trackways that man followed in this travels, and, later on, how he wanted to work the land agriculturally. The first clearances became fields, then systems attached to settlements, so by Roman times land units can be defined. Saxon estate and manorial boundaries frequently influenced the evolvement of parish boundaries. Saxon town and burh boundaries are our first urban boundaries and these, too, can often be easily traced today. Possibly the boundaries used by early Saxon settlers may one day be traced and used to indicate the amalgamation of the British and the Saxons.

Boundaries determined a labourer's location for his lifetime. His work and his dwelling was always within walking distance. His tie to his lord was absolute throughout the medieval period, with the exception of movement from one estate to another, or the purchase of freedom. Few agriculturists are likely to have ever travelled farther than their nearest market until after the 10th century, when the conveyance of agricultural merchandise by cart is recorded, and the carter evolved into a specialized worker, a link between the workers of a manor or estate and the outside world.

Settlement in Saxon times

In Europe, after the fall of the Roman Empire, possibly in the wake of sophisticated villa architecture, new technology produced sturdier, larger buildings and rectangular houses. Perhaps in a trickle-down effect, in time for agriculturists this meant better shelter, though their accommodation may have meant both family and animals under one roof. At about the same time, food production became more efficient, and these changes began to add up to a less austere way of life for people, even though famine and plague always threatened. Similar technological progress apparently came later to England, and in Wiltshire such changes cannot be recognized before 800, though this may be due to lack of archaeological evidence rather than the absence of new ideas.

By mid-Saxon times upper class families were building larger houses, with timbered halls, living and sleeping areas divided, and more than one hearth, allowing the preparation of food to be in separate quarters. Outbuildings began to be sturdier, creating more durable granaries and other food storage quarters. Later, estates built places of worship – wooden chapels or churches. In contrast, a dwelling for a tenant or independent farmer was unlikely to have been more than two or three rooms at the most, one of which may have housed their animals. But the Saxons do not seem to have adopted the European concept of what was known much later in the West country, the longhouse, and evidence of such a dwelling is lacking in Saxon Wiltshire at present. For the labourer, free or non-free, they and their families had to suffice with a one-room dwelling round an open hearth, furnishing little else but shelter. And this would be their standard dwelling form until the late 19th century.

General features of Saxon dwellings show a post-and-hole construction, circular but later rectangular. Walls probably consisted of fired clay/daub, or timber covered with daub, though on the western edge of Wiltshire near the limestone, perhaps stone walls. Doorways were often located on the east-south east side suggesting a preference for facing the rising sun. What provision was made for light to enter a building is still conjecture, the best guess at present is a framed space in a wall, with a stretched transparent skin of a young lamb covering the frame. Internal partitions catered for the different needs of human activities. Roofs still consisted of thatched straw, supported by beams. New roofing and probably major rebuilding took place at least every generation, and this may account for the constant movement so discernable about settlement sites. A well-built foundation and some form of drainage would prolong the life of a house, but evidence of either is seldom found in Saxon Wiltshire.

What seem to be sunken floor levels on some Wiltshire Saxon sites have raised some speculation. Usually of a metre depth or less, the hollow, if very shallow, may have served, after compression, as a dirt floor. If deeper, the hollow may have accommodated a wooden boarded floor above it. Items found in such an area point to its being part of a domestic habitation rather than an auxiliary building.

No village settlements in Wiltshire can yet be traced back farther than the late Saxon period. The terminology of late 7th & 8th century charters gives the impression that villages with well-defined boundaries did not exist, and signs of them only begin to appear by the 10th century.

Present archaeological evidence suggests constant shifting of the settlement nucleus, some large enough to be considered hamlets during the whole medieval period. Some settlement sites showing evidence of frequent movement retained their attachment to the same cemetery site. Other sites may have completely disappeared, their population dispersed to other settlements. Settlement site movement within apportioned boundaries suggests a form of agricultural re-planning, generated by Saxon lords for better productivity from their lands, such as the rearrangement of open strip fields for arable purposes, but this is hard to demonstrate. The deserted village concept, so acclaimed thirty years ago, declared whole villages disappearing in late medieval times. Many seemed abandoned as too small for economical survival, others in later years were re-populated and re-established. But settlement desertion possibly existed in Wiltshire all through the centuries from prehistoric to modern times, until population pressures and economic forces began to force man to utilize new sites, some of which, in pre-modern times, would not have fulfilled the necessary criteria of providing a living for their inhabitants.

The use of space in new settlement areas was still dictated by dwellings forming a nuclear or linear pattern, with adjoining fields or field systems reflecting the importance of having easy access to ploughing and grazing areas. Obviously as population grew, so did settlement size and this holds true all through the Saxon period in Wiltshire. By the 10th century, fragmentation of estates off the chalklands began and, combined with the establishment of parishes and church building, produced stable settlements and hamlets. These in time evolved into villages, the patterns they formed in different locations still recognizable today.

Founding of manors

The present concept of a manor implies a working estate centred on a manor house, villagers living close by and a church contiguous with the manor, the church and priest supported by tithes and other rents and payments. The manor court functioned separately from the central legal system, dealing with queries of estate management, tenure, disputes between unfree tenants and workers, duties and rights of the people living on the estate. Though the origin of Wessex manors can be tracked back to Ine's laws as far as the relationships between lords and dependent peasants are depicted, not until the 10th century does the manorial concept emerge as we think of it today. It rapidly strengthened and continued in much the same form until Norman rule. The earliest evidence of a Wiltshire manor is in a lease given by Denewulf, bishop of Winchester in 902 of a 15 hide estate at Ebbesbourne, the lessee being made responsible for repairs to the local church.

Coming of the Vikings and aftermath

From the end of the 4th century, Germanic people had come slowly into Wiltshire, increasing their numbers until they became dominant. By the 9th century the county achieved peace and Wessex was ruled by a well-respected and effective royal house. The amount of coinage circulating illustrated a steady growth of trade, an efficient tax collection system and a strong government. Unfortunately, nearly a century later this stability was to be upset and the county exposed to assaults by raiders, this time of Scandinavian origin. The raiders, known as Vikings, had spasmodically attacked various parts of England for nearly half a century and reached Wiltshire in 870. Alfred's brother Aethelred, King of Wessex from 865-871, understood the danger. He promptly bought them off and they temporarily withdrew from Salisbury Plain. But they went back on the bargain struck and soon returned. The fighting against them was constant and heavy, no doubt giving the agriculturist and others many worrying days as troop movements disturbed their slow pace of life, not only by their presence, but by the necessity to fight against them, as no standing army in Wiltshire apparently existed. Raiding in surrounding areas continued for several months, and finally, at Ashdown (Berks), Aethelred and Alfred routed the Danes, to achieve peace for several years. In the south at this period, the Vikings became known as Danes, despite their origin from Norway; Denmark at the time was not a settled kingdom.

In 876 the Vikings began fighting again in Wiltshire. They drove Alfred, by then King, to the Somerset marshes, where he is reputed to have burnt the cakes while taking refuge in an old peasant woman's cott. After some guerilla warfare, Alfred regrouped his troops to achieve total victory at Edington. He then arranged the peace treaty of Wedmore, which decreed that the Danish leader Guthrum should convert to Christianity. Prisoners were exchanged and Guthrum marched his army off to Gloucester, leaving Wiltshire in peace for a hundred years.

The accord reached by Alfred's and Guthrum had the eventual result of partitioning England into two regions, much of the south and west, including Wiltshire, remaining in English hands, while the north and the east were governed by the Scandinavians under Danelaw, a fiercer regime. Alfred continued to work hard for peace during the last two decades of his reign, giving his people time to recover from the ravages of the Danish invasion. In the countryside life resumed its quiet pace, but those living near populated areas are likely to have added their labours to aid Alfred's long-term defence plans.

One aspect of these defences was burhs or fortified towns, all within 50 kms of each other. The Wiltshire burhs formed parts of defence chains. Wilton in the south was linked with towns from Taunton (Somerset) to Eashing (Surrey). Chisbury, an old Iron Age hillfort in the east of the county, and Malmesbury and Cricklade in the north, formed links of another chain of burhs from Bristol to Wallingford. To these towns, trained men, perhaps including our agriculturist, were always on call in case of the threat of invasion, a statement to the Danes and the Mercians that a state of alert was always maintained. Alfred had used his Wiltshire victories against the Danes to create this successful fortification system across Wessex and to raise manpower to oppose invaders if subsequently needed. He also divided his army in two, alternating the two halves to service or standby duties. In this way, he always had men working on the land to ensure food supplies. At the same time, Alfred organized the shire as the basic unit for fiscal and military needs. The shire law courts functioned through the hundreds. These arrangements evolved from earlier years, when in all likelihood, estates were grouped together and supervised from a royal vill. Local administration was hence set aside, and Alfred's demands were met with reluctance, especially by the Church. But this was the price to be paid for peace and security. Alfred's strategy turned out to be well worthwhile, considering that in other parts of England the Vikings continued to terrorize the inhabitants. For Wiltshire the end of the Viking threat came after 896 when they withdrew from the south, giving Alfred, one of England's greatest rulers, tranquility in his last three reigning years.

Alfred had helped to lay a firm law-abiding basis for life in the countryside. Despite some harsh laws, the common man's rights to the courts were recognized and given. At a local court, before people who knew him, he could present his case and be heard. This was a recognition of the right of the individual, and its acceptance laid one of the earliest foundations in the building of English democracy. It also led to the Englishman's awareness of political power, his demands for representational rights and, from the 16th century, the rejection of an established Church. History shows that even the lowliest Wiltshire agriculturist made use of these principles through the centuries, as will be shown in later pages of this book.

900-1066

Alfred's successors, all direct descendants, ruled well. Further stability came to Wiltshire in 918 when the kingdoms of Wessex and Mercia united under one king, Edward the Elder. Despite terrible battles for decades in England's north and midlands, Wiltshire remained quiescent. Fear of the Danes may have been ever constant, however, for in the Will of King Eadred (Alfred's grandson who reigned from 946-955) 100 pounds was left to Aelfsige, Bishop of Winchester to purchase for the people of Wiltshire relief from want and from the heathen army.

The culmination of the rule of the Wessex kings came in 973 when Bath saw the crowning of King Edgar under the auspices of the highest Church dignitaries, the Archbishops of Canterbury and York, the actual ceremony containing elements making it a forerunner of the present coronation service. Edgar, Alfred's great-grandson and another lawmaker, helped to merge certain Danish legal procedure into English law, while recognizing the importance of the unity of Crown and Church. He made the first attempts towards the unification of the north and south English kingdoms and also reformed the coinage and its minting codes.

The role of coinage in the lives of the agriculturists until the end of the Saxon period is hard to define. Coin hoards and single finds in Wiltshire confirm their presence from the late Iron Age; circulation of Roman coinage is confirmed not only in and around the few urban centres, but since the advent of the metal detector, many rural finds have emerged. These point to an increase in prosperity in rural Roman Wiltshire, while the number of bronze coins found of lower value (as against silver coins), may indicate that the lower strata of society were able to be involved in a monetary, rather than a barter economy. Coin use in Wiltshire declined by the early 5th century and it is thought the Wiltshire agriculturist returned to the barter system for two or three centuries.

By c. 600 many foreign coins circulated, to be followed by crude silver coins with a localized circulation, for which the Wiltshire peasant may have had little use until the economy began to expand in the 8th century. Two hundred years later a very sophisticated coinage existed in England, stemming from the tradition founded by King Offa (757-96), who had organized mints producing beautiful silver coins. The need for coins grew through the 9th century, particularly when the standby defence forces within Alfred's burh system had to be paid. Then came a further demand, for between 991 and 1018 Saxons in England were forced to pay tribute to the victorious Danes, perhaps as much as £200,000 altogether, requiring an enormous number of coins. Alfred's son founded a mint at Bath and others were sited at Malmesbury and Wilton. By 1005 Bedwyn, Warminster and Old Sarum also boasted mints. With several million coins in circulation and the return of a monetary economy, the Wiltshire peasant is likely to have handled money for small personal transactions, probably mainly silver pennies. Tenants leasing small amounts of land are likely to have paid their annual rent with these coins. But the basis of twelve pennies equalling one shilling and twenty shillings equalling a pound was in place by the 8th century, to remain in Britain and the Continent in the same 12-20-1 sequence until decimalization began in the 18th century, to finally finish in the 20th century.

Peace in Wiltshire ended in 990. A wave of Danish invasions into Wessex commenced, to continue until 1013. The combat was particularly bloody, as the armies were made up of highly trained professionals known for their expertise in fighting and looting. They undoubtedly affected the Wiltshire agriculturist and his lord in various ways, not only from burnt houses and settlements, but in other more indirect ways; by the upsets of market forces affecting the distribution and sale of food and other products; and the disruption of labour supplies, as many slaves were sold to pay *gafol* - silver tribute to the Danes.

In 1006, after a battle in the Kennet valley, slaves were rounded up to be driven in front of the army and marched to the sea via Winchester. Seven years later, Wiltshire bore the brunt of a march from London to Bath, made by the son of a Danish King, Swein Forkbeard , who undoubtedly took prisoners all the way. At Bath, western lords gave him hostages and fealty, but the Danes continued to ravage Wiltshire. At Sherston, an important battle was fought between the forces of Cnut and Edward Ironside. The Danes were bought off with large payments, as had been done in previous campaigns. By 1016, despite vain resistance in Wessex, Swein's son, Cnut, was proclaimed King of all England.

Wessex paid dearly for the Danish conquests. Between 991 and 1014 it paid £158,000 in taxes. After Cnut's final victory in 1017 he demanded and received £82,500. The churches contributed significantly. Malmesbury Abbey had to sell estates or mortgages to meet its commitments. But these payments did not apparently destroy the economy, as Wessex continued to show prosperity, its wealth produced by agriculture and low labour costs.

Cnut turned out to be a great King, the best since Alfred, and until he died in 1035, life in Wiltshire remained comparatively peaceful. The Saxon Godwine is likely to have played a role in keeping the peace. Godwine, one of the King's chief advisers in 1018,was appointed Earl of Wessex. He came from an important wealthy family with considerable amounts of land and buildings in Wessex. In time, he married his daughter Edith to Edward, (later King Edward the Confessor 1042-1066). He also sired Harold, the last English King.

Godwine was wily and astute, wanted power and achieved it after Cnut's death, so the support of the Wessex nobles remained vital. The Danish wars and feudalism had weakened the independence and spirituality of the Church and Godwine prevailed on the rich Bishops of Winchester to act on his behalf. His meddling finally manoeuvered his son-in-law Edward to kingship. Godwine's success went to his head; he became grasping and avaricious, so much so that ten years later he was ordered to hand over his 'commended men in their earldoms,' i.e. his supporters. They and Godwine fled the country, but he brazenly returned and, with the support of the Wessex lords, tried to make his son Harold declared successor to Edward. A year later in 1053, Godwine died, but Wiltshire, unlike other parts of England, apparently remained orderly until the Norman Conquest despite so much factional upheaval and its political church leaders and lords being in disgrace.

The orderliness was no doubt due to a strongly functioning local government and a stable coinage. Sheriffs (*scirgerefa* or shire-reeves) were appointed, one to each county; they helped control the political machinations of the aristocracy and gentry, besides collecting revenues. Edward the Confessor showed more strength in the last few years of his reign and he appointed strong clerics to head the Church, in turn making the three great monastic landholders in Wiltshire, Malmesbury, Glastonbury and Winchester, even stronger in ruling estates and their dependent workers.

Stability and the reorganized manors allowed the old estates and the new manorial lords to raise their production ratios. Their hard-working reeves all played their part, helped by dwindling freedoms to keep tenants and labourers working hard while sharing none of the profits from the their extra production. This meant proportionally lowered labour costs, resulting in further profit, in turn meaning more tax contributions to the King's exchequer. It will be seen that after the 1066 Conquest, the Normans would take full advantage of the resources of the Wiltshire countryside, but our agriculturist was soon to begin seeking what he felt was his share and due of these created riches.

Chapter 3 Bibliography

These books were of major importance for this chapter on the Saxon period in Wiltshire:
*ARNOLD, C. J., 1984, *Roman Britain to Anglo-Saxon England*. University of Indiana Press, and by
    the same author, *An Archaeology of Early Anglo-Saxon Kingdoms*. NY: Routledge (1997)
ESMONDE CLEARY, A., 1990, *Ending of Roman Britain*. Maryland: Barnes & Noble
FAITH, R., 1997, *English Peasantry and the Growth of Lordships*. Leicester University Press
*MINGAY, G., 1990, *Social History of the English Countryside*. New York: Routledge
YORKE, B., 1995, *Wessex in the Early Middle Ages*. Leicester UP.

For specific subjects: development in of government in Wiltshire; royal estates; religious and secular
    estate management; the following proved valuable:
ANDREWS, C., 1892, *Old English Manor*. Baltimore: John Hopkins Press
FINBERG, H., . 1964, *Early Charters of Wessex*. Leicester University Press
HASLAM, J., 1984, *Anglo-Saxon Towns in Southern England*. Phillimore

HINTON, D., 1977, *Alfred's Kingdom*. Dent

For exploring settlement patterns across the county, of great use were:
*HOOKE, D. (ed), 1988, *Anglo-Saxon Settlements*, 59-76 . (New York: Blackwell), particularly the
     included article by M.GELLING, 'Towards a Chronology for English Place-Names.' In addition,
     I referred personally to Dr Gelling regarding use of Wiltshire place-names in this chapter.
ROBERTS, B., 1996, *Landscapes of Settlement: Prehistory to the Present*. New York: Routledge
PINE, J., 2001, The excavations of a Saxon Settlement at Cadley Road, Collingbourne Ducis, Wiltshire.
     WANHM 94, 88-117
WILLIAMSON, T., 1988, Explaining Regional Landscapes: Woodland and Champion in Southern
     and Eastern England. *Landscape History* 10, 5-14
(It should be noted that Wiltshire archaeological excavations of Saxon settlements are not plentiful
     in this period, partly due to so many sites being overlaid by later settlements.)

Though knowledge of medieval slavery has expanded, information of the subject at any period in
     Wiltshire is still very limited. Beside Faith (1997) and Yorke (1995), my major reference was:
PELTERET, D. 1995, *Slavery in Medieval England from the Reign of Alfred until the Twelfth Century*.
     Rochester, NYS: Boydell Press. (Sources quoted in Pelteret's work proved well worth following
     up.)

Delving for information on the Saxon agriculturist at work turned out to be never ending, with
     much of it open to interpretation, resulting in a blending of many facts. Particularly useful in
     this chapter and the next:
DOUGLAS, D. & GREENWAY, G. (eds), 1981, *English Historical Documents 1042-1189*, 2, London:
     Eyre Methuen #172 "Rights and Ranks of People" (*Rectitudines Singularum Personarum*) (*?*1042-
     66); #173 statement in Anglo-Saxon of services rendered at Hurstbourne Priors, Hampshire
     (*c*.1050); #174 survey of an estate at Tidenham, Gloucestershire (*c*.1060) Eyre Methuen. In
     addition, from volume 1 of *English Historical Documents*, c.500-1042, edited by Dorothy Whitelock
     (1955), #503.
For the agriculturists' relationship to their animals, the basic text still remains Trow-Smith (see
     general bibliography).

For food and drink of the period, Ann Hagen's books take precedence: *A Handbook of Anglo-Saxon
     Food Processing and Consumption.* (1992, England: Pinner); published in 1995, *A Second Handbook*

of *Anglo-Saxon Food and Drink: Production and Consumption*. Norfolk; and finally, *Anglo-Saxon Food and Drink: Production, Processing Distribution and Consumption* (2006, Norfolk, Anglo-Saxon Books)

My comments on how the Church may have affected the everyday life of the agrarian worker are based on Jonathan Pitt's unpublished PhD thesis, *Wiltshire Minsters Parochiae and West Saxon ecclesiastical organization*(University of Southampton 1999).

Printed studies of specific early medieval Wiltshire manors are lacking; for general manorial information, the extensive studies of E. Postan and C. Andrews still stand up well.

4
Norman to Tudor Rule

Kings, nobles, churchmen, they come and go, the land stays for ever.

Norman Conquest and aftermath in Wiltshire

History records an easy conquest for the Normans when they arrived at Wiltshire in 1066, with no opposition from the Saxons. An invasion force reached Highworth in the north, but turned back east along the Vale of the White Horse to move south through the county. At the time, Old Sarum, a hillfort site and later Wiltshire's only major castle, saw no fighting. A lack of defensive structures and very little organized resistance implies immediate submission by the Saxons – they accepted the inevitable. One wonders why, after their past fighting history, but stories of fierce conflict had perhaps preceded the Normans' arrival in other parts of England. The sparse chalklands may have been looted, but more populated areas seemingly sustained no damage and the towns remained untouched. However, three years later, Norman forces marched from Salisbury to Dorchester to suppress a local rising. Alongside the route taken, some manors were ostensibly sacked, as the 1086 Domesday Survey later indicated that manors in the county's southwest corner suffered a loss of value after being taken from their Saxon holders. But they were the only manors recording any perceptible setback during these years. Such documentation contributes evidence to the peaceful acquisition of Wiltshire in 1066.

The Normans immediately imposed tax increases all over England and, shortly after, replaced all but a few of the Saxon landholders. Presumably because of the quiet and orderly takeover, the co-operation of both tenants and workers was obtained, but in the existing feudal system they were but servants and had little choice but to comply with their new rulers. Some Norman lords may have created radical changes in work patterns on some estates, others may have changed little from the previous Saxon administrations; much obviously depended on the new lord's character and whether his land was productive enough for him to easily fulfill his obligations to the Crown. An inept administrator or a depleted estate would have forced a lord to be more ruthless with his work force.

By the time of the Norman Conquest, Wiltshire land was already divided up into three groups of holdings, those belonging to the Crown, and those being held either by religious or secular holders as part of a feudal system. The Normans took this system and attempted to make it more rigid, particularly by emphasizing military service obligations and by demanding an inflexible structure of servitude by all those under the jurisdiction of the manorial lords. But, as will be seen, the system proved too exacting. Military service obligations were an example. A tax, scutage, or 'shield-money', was eventually paid instead of a man serving. And slowly over the next four centuries peasants, exchanged their bonds to be free labourers, wage earners, tenants or sometimes small landowners, working for their own benefit, instead of their lords. Some free and independent smallholders prevailed in the open and forest lands of Wiltshire, and until the 16th century may even have increased their numbers.

The Saxons had to adjust to their conqueror's feudal designs, but they kept their own language, though French names remained in Wiltshire until they became Anglicized. Wessex had supplied from its local dialects the standard English that the Normans encountered on their arrival in England and this speech continued after the Conquest. In time, documents began to appear in what is now called Middle English, a case of speech being converted to written forms as scribes began to write what they heard. Interestingly, Norman-French was still spoken by nuns at Lacock Abbey right up to the Dissolution. By Elizabethan times, Modern English had injected itself into local dialects. However, legal documents continued to be written in Latin often until the 18th century. When English began to be used, phonetic spelling was the rule and the grammar tailored by the individual scribe. The advent of Johnson's dictionary and grammatical texts by the end of the 1700s inaugurated standard written English. But habits die hard and even in the 1820s phonetic spelling still occurred and place names in particular still evidenced a multitude of spellings. These hand-written documents, originating in Wiltshire, when read aloud convey the sound of how Wiltshire people spoke in those years and the rule applies to other counties. To the author, especially when reading documents written about Chippenham, her home area, the words sound exactly the same as those spoken by locals in the 1940s, particularly those living in a rural area.

Domesday Survey

As with the Saxons before them, the Normans fully realized that the first matters to deal with after subduing the Saxons was to set up a power structure and provide revenue to keep it in place. The system the Normans had taken over was a sophisticated arrangement of landholding, tax raising and social strata, but remained in some confusion when it came to the role of the landlord and his jurisdiction. The conquerors acted to type and imposed their own rules upon England. They had immediately replaced the Saxon landholders by Norman lords. How this was done so quickly and quietly is not understood, but by 1086 the Domesday Book recorded 99% of Wiltshire landlords as bearing Norman names. Whether these Saxon landholders were removed or demoted to tenants or labourers cannot be determined, but Saxon manorial tenants are later listed and presumably the labourers were not displaced either, as no record exists that the Normans brought in any agricultural settlers.

To extract the highest taxes and obtain more control over the people, Saxon society had to be tightened and a basis created to accomplish this goal. The Domesday Survey, as it would be called in later years, was organized and quickly enacted. Teams of investigators, their results recorded by scribes, surveyed all cultivated land in the kingdom, county by county, manor by manor. The result reshaped society to a Norman image, seemingly to remain for nearly a hundred years, as official records convey little alteration of social status.

In 1086 at Salisbury, as a preliminary to the Wiltshire survey, the King extracted fealty from all the largest landholders. Besides the Crown, which held the most amount of the land in the county, five bishops, five abbots and five abbesses represented the Church holdings; one Count and three Earls, the Sheriff (Edward of Salisbury), twenty-two other gentlemen and last but not least, landholders among the King's serjeants, thegns and 'servants' represented the secular holdings. The manors are likely to have retained the boundaries originally encompassing the areas in Saxon times and an individual's holdings may still have been scattered, but probably some redistribution or consolidation of small manors occurred. Internally, for good farming reasons, estates with inter-dependent areas, e.g. ploughland and grazing areas, wooded and open land, were not likely be fragmented. Retaining the same boundaries also kept the social structure of the estate intact, the labourer had a change of manorial lord from Saxon to Norman, but as far as can be ascertained, he and his family continued to cultivate the same land. Whether he retained the same social position cannot be determined, as some ranks were renamed by the Normans and may have changed their connotation. And Wiltshire apparently continued its established tradition of mixed farming, except on the less fertile areas of the chalk and downland.

To obtain the information needed for a new tax basis, the Crown appointed commissioners to seek 'whether more could be had than was accustomed to be had,' and enumerate all landholdings existing in England, an enormous undertaking, but successfully accomplished within the year 1086. Teresa Webber in her book *Scribes and Scholars at Salisbury Cathedral,* (Oxford 1992), has suggested another local involvement with Domesday, that a scribe at Old Sarum may have written the companion book to the Survey known as the Exon Domesday.

When the commissioners had finished their findings in Wiltshire, the number of land holdings totalled 569. Each was given a tax evaluation calculated in hides, the hide still a measurement of tax yield. Nearly 4,000 hides were recorded in the county. The amount of pasture, woodland, grazing, and if listed, meadow lands, was measured in acres or leagues. What amount of land the hide

Shepherdess in cloak, wimple and veil
circa 1320

represented is unknown. Perhaps 30 acres, but hidage in the Wiltshire Domesday Survey remains a controversial topic. The tax value of arable land was calculated by the number of ploughs, that is, plough teams of oxen and men used on a holding, or ploughlands, the area a team worked yearly. Presumably this did not incorporate small arable pieces ploughed by hand by serfs or other ranks for their own use. The number of mills present on an estate was recorded with their tax value given in pounds, as are some particular estate portions, such as a specific tenant's holding, meadowland or pasture. The numbers of those who laboured on a holding are always provided, listed as slaves, various ranks of labourers and smallholders, sometimes craftsmen.

An old saying labelled the commissioners as 'not missing a pig,' but in such a complicated project, some land was omitted and a few tracts are listed twice. As is to be expected, the great landholders backed the Survey, for not only did it incorporate their rights to the listed landholdings into English law, but to object would certainly have antagonized the powerful and ruthless King William I. Nothing in history indicates that anyone else locally disagreed with the Survey. If any one had, they no doubt would have received short shrift from a Wiltshire sheriff armed with ample powers to maintain law and order.

The Domesday Survey gives for the first time a detailed picture of the Wiltshire landscape. Here are the meadows and pastures, the grazing lands, the arable, woods and forests, and land still unused by the estates. Here too are manors, both prosperous and penurious, differentiated by geological strata, soil, topography and size, the richest in the river valleys, the poorest usually on the chalk, unless extraordinarily large, such as the monastic manors. The most prosperous areas stand out in Domesday by their high manor populations, numbers of plough teams and the location of head manors. The Wylye valley was particularly remunerative to the Crown with its fertile elongated estates running from sheltered river valley to chalk hills, hence allowing the full gamut of mixed farming.

Manor and village coincide to a remarkable degree in Wiltshire. By 1066, the manorial system in the county was in place; manors tended to be large, more than fifty estates are assessed at more than 20 hides and ten of these are over 50 hides each. Though spread throughout the county, they were more concentrated along the major river valleys and quite sparse on the chalk and downland, and in forested areas.

Much less populated was the large amount of forest land in Wiltshire. As with the chalk and downland, few manors are recorded in the areas. The forested areas in Domesday, though larger, match in outline the 13th and 14th century boundaries of the Royal Forests of Braydon, Chippenham, Melksham and Selwood in west Wiltshire and Savernake, Chute, Clarendon, Melchet and Grovely, in the eastern part of the county. These forests remained important to many labourers, particularly if free, for they could eke out a living within, or on the edge of the forest.

Tenants and workers attached to a manor or holding were divided into major categories in Domesday, according to their economic and social ranks. At the top are the *villani*, who rented land from the lord, perhaps five or more acres, but who owed services. The *bordars*, *cottars* and *coscets*, all seemingly implied labourers with dwellings and small holdings. A *colibert* is likely to have been a half-free peasant on a large manor, and at the bottom are the *sevri*, born into slavery or relegated to serfdom by some criminal act. The Normans seemed uncomfortable with slavery and its implication of total possession of a human being; by the 12th century, the term serf connotes the lowest level of manorial labour and little or nothing is heard of slave-trading.

Social category names changed quickly and often. Perhaps with the exception of extremely well-off villeins, the ranked men listed above can be described as peasants for the next three centuries. But about their status many questions, left over from the Saxon period, still remained unanswered in Domesday. What defined one class from another, how clear-cut were the divisions and the specific degree of freedom each enjoyed? Was the rank a man bore always linked to a specific amount of land he worked or rented? Were any particular services incorporated into each rank? (For instance, ploughing is often linked to slaves or servi). Could a slave, or later serf, buy his or her freedom, or had it to be given by the lord? How easy was it for a worker or tenant to move to another manor, purchase land or free himself of services? In later years some answers can be obtained, but usually they pertain to a specific person on a specific manor and it is not safe to apply them generally to the whole county.

The workers and tenants on the 569 Wiltshire estates and manors listed in Domesday merely represented those who were bound to a manor or estate. They numbered 9,735. Their families were not included, nor estate administrators. Craftsmen are occasionally mentioned, but no blacksmiths or others common to the society of the time. Neither are village personnel listed, innkeepers and others who did not work on the land but were always part and parcel of a community's make-up. Some urban populations are recorded along with the holders of town lands, Malmesbury is an example. To calculate the population of Wiltshire in 1086 from information contained in Domesday is obviously impossible, even an attempt to calculate the size of a family unit working on the land is hazardous, though a factor of four or five has been suggested.

Generally applied, the services owed by these men and their families to their lord amounted to so many days a week on the lord's demesne, cultivating, planting, reaping, hedging, carting at the discretion of the lord's reeve. This is the agriculture labourer of the time. On many estates *servi* are described as ploughmen, often of demesne land, but for the other ranks, a worker of the soil and with animals must be presumed, as many manors engaged in mixed farming. Bee-keepers (*mellitarii*) are mentioned once, the King's manor at Westbury having nine. Swine herders (*porcarii*) appear 87 times on four manors owned by the King, all adjoining woodland. Obviously from the mention of meadow and rough pasture land in the valleys and grazing downlands, herders of sheep and cattle were always a necessity. 197 mills are mentioned in a total of 335 places signifying the economic importance of corn-growing and the need for carters to haul the grain and millers to grind it. For some reason, fisheries and dairies are omitted in the Wiltshire survey, though it is known, from other sources, such as custumals or cartularies, that they existed. Marsh and waste land remained untaxed.

Tracts of woodland, sometimes their extents, needing woodsmen to work them, are mentioned for many manors. South Newton and Washern manors each had permission to take 80 cartloads of wood and timber for house and fence repairs. Entries of spinneys and groves suggest coppicing, providing further employment. Most of the woodland mentioned occurs on the claylands and some around the Wardour, Pewsey and Warminister vales.

Oddly, considering the tax potential involved, livestock is seldom recorded. Entries include Sutton Veny 300 sheep, Yarnfield 2 cows, 25 swine and 134 sheep and Kilmington 14 *animalia*, 15 swine and 137 sheep. At Porton, 50 sheep were grazed on pasture, quite a high number. Four vineyards at Lacock, Wilcot, Tollard Royal and Bradford on Avon were noted by the commissioners. For their owners, all sheriffs, hopefully they bore well!

A list of rents paid from Edward the Sheriff's shrievalty are as follows: 130 porkers, 32 bacon-hogs, 3 pecks and 8 sesters of wheat and as much barley, 5 pecks and 4 sesters of oats, 16 sesters of honey, 480 hens, 1600 eggs, 100 cheeses, 12 lambs, 240 fleeces, 162 acres of unreaped corn, signifying highly productive manors on the chalk and other lands. The complexities of a large manor gave room for what today might be referred to as 'fiddling the books' (or should one say today, 'adjusting the spread-sheet'). Set up in supposedly legally rigid organizations, fluctuating social and economic circumstances in the future changed those structures. So settlements and leases were made and unmade, manors accumulated and sold, profits made and lost.

The compilation of the Domesday survey reveals already-established traits in English culture: marriage, property inheritance, agrarian customs and the fundamentals of an active legal system for all. Some historians perceived these fundamentals as the source of the English common man's individualism and unity, already beginning to be formed by the end of the Saxon period. Shire courts before the Conquest applied the English law code created by the Saxon kings and codified by the reign of Edward the Confessor. William the Conqueror in 1066 promised the English people that he would preserve these laws and the only changes he made related to the new feudal system of landholding he introduced. English law continued to develop and unify under the Norman and Plantagenet kings. In time, through statements and decisions of the courts, a body of laws common to the entire kingdom was formed. At the shire level, the courts shed the previous authorities of the earls and bishops, their powers ultimately transferred to the sheriffs.

Labourers digging and pruning 1400-10

Civil law on the other hand, centered on the manorial courts. Their advent is unknown; the Domesday survey refers to them, but no mention of activities by Wiltshire manor courts appears until a century later, due to lack of documentation. The agriculturist gave his loyalty to his manor court, it was the first place he sought for justice, always provided that he had committed no criminal action. Domesday stated certain past rights acknowledged by manor courts, and it also defined new alterations in feudal law. New rules of labour service particularly affected the peasants' everyday life and he apparently objected to and subsequently fought some of them. In time, certain manorial rights and privileges acknowledged in Domesday became custom, then by later generations were to be considered ineradicable and invulnerable, whether legalized or not. These beliefs foresaw the beginning of a faith that all men had the right of access to the law and deserved a fair hearing in court. And our Wiltshire agricultural labourer, to keep his way of life and what he thought were his rights, acted upon that faith, sometimes for the better, sometimes for the worse, until the 18th century, when the odds against him became so daunting that he no longer dared seek his day in court. However, manorial courts in medieval times could well be slanted to the lord, sometimes their jury and trial jury staffed by men from wealthy levels of village society and hence likely to be less favourable to the lower worker. But nevertheless, the tradition of a fair hearing survived.

After Domesday

Judging from Stratton's weather reports, both lord and labourer endured a rough interval after Domesday. Very hard winters, combined with famines, had begun soon after the Conquest. People must have thought the wrath of God was upon the Normans! Twenty years later, pestilence broke out amongst cattle and the following year plague occurred in both cattle and men. Old Sarum cathedral lost its steeple top in 1091, doubtless thought of as another sign of heavenly disapproval. At the end of the century, heavy rains and storms inundated the South, making life on the land harsh and dreary for tillers of the soil; the rains spoilt crops, to create food shortages severe enough to cause famine. Weather and harvest records until the middle of the 13th century were never very optimistic overall, but despite these natural adversities, more cultivated land came into production, trade thrived and population grew.

The Wiltshire manor to 1349

At present little is still understood of the land make-up of any individual Wiltshire manor until at least the 12th century and then many details are missing, particularly on secular manors. Did the tenants holding larger acreage have their land all in one piece, or was the total scattered about the manor, split up into pasture and arable, maybe the latter in strips? Who made land allocation decisions and did a family always retain the same land from generation to generation? Did the smaller holders, who held the rank of bordar, cottar and coscet at Domesday, still hold similar land acreage (scattered or not) in the next three centuries, but under other named ranks such as villeins or villanus?. And when did the term villein begin to apply to the half free tenant? What about the virgater, supposedly a holder of a yardland or about 30 acres? At present such questions still need further research specifically applied to Wiltshire manors and to those of the labouring classes. Difficulties of research in this area exist however, as Wiltshire manor records in the National Archives and other repositories are scattered and many also need transcribing and/or translating.

But the rigid manorial structure laid down by the Normans slowly began to change. A hundred years after Domesday, landlords began to lease portions of their demesne lands for monetary rents, tenants and labourers wanted release from services to substitute money for their service rents and to use the time given in services to further their own life, preferably on monetary rented land. The customary labour obligations to the manor were being challenged, challenges which would continue and, particularly on monastic manors, be resisted until the late 15th century, when service traditions finally died out in Wiltshire.

Economically, the results of the new feudalism, albeit in its altered forms, turned out to be a success story, particularly in Wiltshire. Notwithstanding the definite climate change to colder and wetter weather at the end of the 13th century, famines due to bad harvests and wars to be paid for, until the first round of plague (the Black Death of 1348-9), England enjoyed what today would be called a prolonged economic boom. Export and import dealings expanded, increased food production and population stimulated internal commerce. The issue of several thousand market and fair charters (licences) throughout the country, of which Wiltshire enjoyed its share, confirmed a steady expansion of trade. But there is no question that both tenant and labourer had to work harder for success and continually resist exploitation of their labour. Whether the labourer and his dependents felt more secure or enjoyed a better family life cannot be determined, their happiness was not a consideration of their betters at the time; such a concept was not to emerge until the 20th century. Little active protest against work conditions is recorded until the 14th century, law and order in Wiltshire evidently being maintained without difficulty. The manor unit, the basis of feudalism, stood firm, despite constant change and challenge.

Where records survive of the county's manors and estates, they follow the pattern of more intensive farming and acquisition, or take-in, of land wherever possible. Increased yields from a manor's farming was not only accomplished by management and tenurial changes, it is very plain in Wiltshire from the 12th century until the middle of the 14th century, that the alteration in farming techniques was extremely consequential as well.

Post-Domesday Agriculture

Several changes in post-Domesday agriculture account for the economic gains made in farming during the remainder of the medieval period. Assarts made from forests, fringe and waste lands opened up more land to agricultural use, while greater yields were obtained from those lands already in cultivation.

Tremendous variations existed in the county regarding the use of cultivated land through the late medieval period. A description of the magnitude of variation in Wiltshire extent is nowhere better described than by Richenda Scott writing in volume four of the Victoria History of Wiltshire. Widespread use of communal field systems existed, often depending on complicated systems that had evolved from place and manor, terrain and soils, plus the underlying social organization of the land workers. Cropping cycles and changes in ploughing were attempted, often opposed, as basic changes to life styles are. But the aim of the manor lords, both religious and secular, was to produce more from the land and that they did.

Major crops grown on Wiltshire farms during this period were wheat, barley, oats, a little rye, peas and vetches, the latter two sometimes for added fertility by nitrogen fixation of the soil, or as animal fodder, besides traditional cropping for human consumption. Where records survive, apparently large estates sold one- to two-thirds of their grain crop and held back one third for seed corn. According to custom, tenants usually grew, or provided by other means, their own grain seed. Meadow lands produced the hay crops and were, consequently, far more highly valued than rougher pasture or grazing lands.

Woods and coppices were essential for supplying building wood, fencing, hurdles and other farming needs, firewood and kindling, and in many manors proved an important source of income. Like the pig, every part of the tree had its value, to be listed accordingly down to the smallest twig or 'scroggis.' Marlpits, also, had evolved as another source of income on some manors.

After the Conquest, the Normans governed the extensive Wiltshire forests by their own laws. Though forest administration records survive from the 12th century, little is known of the actual forest boundaries (which could include arable, pasture and meadow lands) until the beginning of the 13th century. The forests provided an income for the exchequer, be it from fines for encroachments of forest lands, taking deer, trespasses of animals or cutting wood illegally, to legal rents for small game hunting, pannnage or pasture rights.

Free forest inhabitants, and some who were seemingly tenants, gained a living as they endured the rules and regulations governing their lives. Deer – red, roe and fallow, their pasture and undergrowth were protected and the few wolves left were considered vermin. Encroachments into forest lands grew steadily as the need for land increased. The establishment of deer parks by the wealthy and clergy made the animals a regular source of food, besides hunting quarry. For example, Alan Basset at Wootton Bassett in 1230, made a deer park within the royal forest of Braydon. These intrusions presumably drove the forest peasant further into the woods to find enough land to live on. Pannage was overwhelmingly important; a 1280 Bishopstrow manor custumal stated that on their distant manor of Heddington, workers 'shall give pannage for their swine . . . [and] give twopence yearly for the pannage'. As will be seen by the 16th century, the Wiltshire forests were being nibbled away, to the detriment of the forest dweller and to the advantage of the new farmer.

Though the later traditional division of agricultural Wiltshire, the Chalk and the Cheese, had not yet appeared in the late medieval period, farming on the chalk and surrounding high dry ground had long been sheep-rearing and grain-growing. At the time of Domesday, sheep were raised as much for their milk as for their fleeces, and meat in the form of lamb, hoggett (one year sheep), and finally mutton, probably very tough, as the

Girl carrying pail of milk and woman breaking sods circa 1340

sheep, if spared, had a lifespan of four years or more.

By the 13th century lord and tenant alike enlarged and acquired greater numbers of sheep and in general, sheep-raising expanded the economy by increasing the amount of cash circulating within the county. An increase in coinage made an impact on the Wiltshire peasant, who wanted his share of the prosperity. One means he used to obtain it was to demand cash for his services and paying his rent in cash, often to save enough to buy sheep. Tenants raised their own sheep and paid dues to the manor lord; at Bishopstone in 1256, payment enacted was 1/4d for one ewe, or a lamb for each ten full-grown sheep. The dues gave the tenants the privilege of grazing their sheep on manorial land. Probably every Wiltshire manor with large sheep flocks had free or tied tenants who were in essence small sheep farmers. Share-holding of flocks is also frequently recorded, as is sheep grazing on common land.

On manors around Salisbury Plain and the Marlborough Downs, shepherds and dairy maids were likely to be the main types of labourers. An Inquest of the Knights Templars of 1185, worded archaically, and so likely to have originated in Saxon times, states that at Rockley manor near Ogbourne St George, where the Knights rented out land, every villein holding five acres or more had to send one woman every day to milk the sheep and make cheese and butter. For her pains she was allowed to keep half the whey and buttermilk resulting from her work. In addition she had to help in the dipping and washing of the sheep and to shear them, operations requiring, like cheese and butter making, a considerable amount of skill and stamina, not to mention strength, especially for the shearing. Whether the women on Rockley manor did all these jobs just because the Inquest stated it is open to discussion, and this question applies not only to Rockley, but to all manors. Many custumals and inquests have survived, composed or copied through four centuries, but how closely they were adhered to is not known. It is best to treat them as a basis for descriptions of services. Subsequent events show constant modification, especially when services were replaced by cash payments or extra rent charges.

Other components of sheep farming also involved a considerable amount of labour. Chalkland manors carried large flocks, often divided into ewes, wethers (castrated males) and yearlings. Each had a separate shepherd in charge, who also maintained the structure of the folds. On smaller manors, villeins and cottars often built hurdles as part of their service dues, or were responsible for moving hurdles to different folding areas.

Both men and women were needed for the yearly sheep dipping procedures and sometimes were hired from other manors as well as the home manor. One manor lord provided ale, bread and meat. A common custumal reward was a sheep's milk cheese, as at Sheldon, a small manor on the clays near Chippenham. The Wiltshire shepherd was one of the first labour categories to be paid totally with money for his services at the end of the 14th century. In addition he received a set amount of wheat and barley, fleece, lambs or milk with which his wife no doubt made cheese. Some manor lords granted him land and had it sown for him if the seed was provided, others allowed him to run his own sheep with the manor flocks. Always in attendance, the shepherd was held responsible for missing sheep, unless he could formally account for them. This ruling prevented stealing or taking sheep to market to sell, but instances of either were not unknown.

On smaller manors, sheep ran on pasture, crofts and small fields. This began to encourage more enclosure, unlike the open downland sheep runs, and enclosure no doubt

Exeter Cathedral pew end carving of 3 Shepherds, circa early 15th century.

increased profits, for, though needing extra labour for pasture care, it allowed more sheep on less land. In time, tenants became small sheep farmers within the manor structure and no doubt achieved a slight measure of independence from their manor lord. The lord in turn benefited from charging higher rents. Several separate pastures at Cherhill in 1265 sustained sheep, an early date for enclosures. More evidence of enclosure comes from manors belonging to Edington Priory. The Priory leased out its demesne arable holdings and turned to sheep, cows and horse-breeding. The sheep flocks numbered between one to two thousand, cattle numbers trebled between the 1390s and 1450s. Despite the closeness of the Priory to the chalklands, much of the demesne existed on the nearby grasslands just off the chalk and the increase in stock warranted enclosure.

Neighbouring small peasant sheep farmers seem to be found on manors in or near the downs and chalklands, causing problems with sheep straying. By the end of the 15th century, the odds began to weigh in favour of the lord, rich graziers and large-scale sheep farmers with resources able to pay more for hay and grazing land than the small man. The peasant's demise begins to show in areas of concentrated sheep farming. To combat such moves, a man had to fight hard to preserve his income, his land and his animals. Numbers in peasant flocks decreased in the 16th century, forcing some tenants to resort to grazing on common lands where they had no rights. An inevitable decline of the Wiltshire peasant and small farmer began. 'On the economic security of the emerging yeoman of the later Middle Ages, our records speak clearly: their prosperity, although impressive, was shortlived, and new men of the Tudor Age supplanted them.' Growing numbers of sheep meant large numbers of fleeces, so shearing time was always important on Wiltshire manors. The increasing decline of services available meant an increase in the cost of producing sheep's milk cheese, and expanding markets meant a greater demand for wool. By the 15th century wool was to be the major crop from sheep farming and the Wiltshire cloth industry continued to increase its export trade. The county had long made its own cloth, a record of a fulling mill at Chippenham dating from 1189, shows most of the cloth was for local consumption and the London market. Exports destined for abroad appear in Bristol and Southampton port records by the 1300s, but apparently large numbers of fleeces were sold to the Continent much earlier.

Away from the chalk and downlands, in north and west Wiltshire and the areas south of Salisbury Plain, custumals suggest that mixed farming prevailed. Grain, legumes and some vetches are likely to have been the main arable crops, small flocks of sheep on areas of dry or high enough ground where foot-rot could be avoided. Where sheep-raising was not possible, cattle were raised. The early 1200s saw the beginning of the Wiltshire dairy industry on the claylands in the northwest of the county, cow's milk cheese beginning to replace sheep cheese. The latter had ceased to be profitable to produce in commercial amounts, so some larger landowners turned to cheesemaking from cow's milk. Dairies were small at first, supporting perhaps seven to ten cows, but their numbers grew on larger manors with enough grazing and capital to set up dairy farms, or vaccaries as they were then called. Lacock Abbey practised dairying and by the end of the 13th century it had spread to farms around the village. Adam de Stratton, with many estates near Swindon, can be considered Wiltshire's first large-scale dairy farmer, his accounts between 1269 and 1288 show his cheesemaking operations to be very similar to methods used on Wiltshire dairy farms three centuries later (For further information see *Forgotten Harvest* pages 29-33).

The small peasant was never in a financial position to set up a vaccary, because of lack of capital to provide enough grazing land, purchase cows, buy cheesemaking equipment and hire the necessary labour. However, in Wiltshire share-milking with cows doubtless became as common as had share-herding and milking sheep. It was a based on very simple principles. A landowner or farmer supplied a man with pregnant cows for hire for one milking season, spring to autumn, then took them back to provide for them for until the following season. The calves born remained the property of the owner, but the hirer milked the cows, looked after them and took the proceeds of the sale of the dairy products made from their milk. His wife made cheese and butter, his family helped with the milking, care of the animals and raising poultry on the farmer's land. Sometimes the hirer kept the calves and reared them. A 1383 report stated that cows with calves were hired out for the season at 5s each, half the monetary value of the cow, according to accounting records. Ewes rented for 6d each. A pig rented for 6s 6d, the sow being returned to its owner after the piglets were weaned on the whey left from cheesemaking. Obviously the piglets provided the profit in the deal, as they were raised and sold by the renter.

Share-milking was a gamble, especially if disease struck, or a damp. cold spring and summer ensued, making it difficult to raise young stock. Presumably in a few successful seasons a man made enough money to rent his own land and start as a dairy farmer if he desired his independence. After the Black Death, the prevailing labour shortage put the share-milker in an even stronger position to obtain and hold land and in time, if he was lucky, to acquire his own dairy operation. Unfortunately, by the 17th century, the Enclosure movement had sent the price of farming land in the cheese country to levels far beyond the pocket of any share-milker. But share-milking continued for generations in Wiltshire, existing until WWII.

Finally, rabbit farming had come into its own. Warrens were established, particularly on the chalkland edges, such as at Warminster, Winterbourne Stoke, Marlborough and Teffont Evias. The most famous and the largest was at Aldbourne warren, where thousands of rabbits were taken over the years, to be sent to distant markets. Henry VI and John of Gaunt are recorded amongst those receiving rabbits from Aldbourne.

Work of the labourer

Much information on this topic is available, as it seems endlessly fascinating to the historian, sociologist and economist. How the Wiltshire agricultural worker may have lived in medieval times can be gleaned from *Inquisitiones Post Mortem*, manorial custumals, account books, monastical documents and the early government and legal records with which England is so richly bestowed. Manorial custumals date mainly from the 12th century, but many are archaically written and obviously based on similar documents of earlier centuries. Records of the manor courts are particularly revealing, for that was the first resort for the agriculturist when any dispute arose, particularly if it involved land.

The basics of the labourer's or anyone's life in the labouring class was always hard physical work, at least twelve hours a day, particularly if he worked with animals. Time off was not permitted during the six working days of the week. If he was not working for his lord, he worked

Threshing with flails circa 1340

for himself, to produce his own food on his own plot. If a freeman with his own free land, he is likely to have laboured from dawn to dusk, just to maintain his few acres, his animals and to feed and house himself and his family. On a manor or estate he was responsible for his own shelter, or at least the maintenance of it. When he worked for his lord, he was performing tasks set in stone from time immemorial, for by the end of medieval times, very few agricultural tasks had basically changed since the beginning of agriculture, albeit aided by better tools and equipment, such as the plough.

Larger crop yields depended on better fertilizing, and manorial accounts and custumals, particularly from monastical estates, confirmed the two major methods used to achieve this goal, dunging and marling. Farming records during the 12th to the 14th centuries show increases in the numbers of sheep and later of cows and cattle, all very able and willing to produce large quantities of manure. Sheep have the added advantage of being their own spreading-machine, cows are not such convenient animals. On arable or grassland sheep were allowed to roam during the day, at night confined on open land by light hurdles which were moved daily to a new area to facilitate manure distribution. Cows, on the other hand, were seemingly confined frequently, so their manure accumulated and had to be moved and spread over the land. At Monkton Deverill, a manor belonging to Glastonbury Abbey, virgaters had to haul at least fifteen cartloads of dung a day from farmyard to field. Lacock Abbey home manor specified each virgater had to spread a row of dung on half an acre of the demesne land. The process by which the author spread dung, while working on a Wiltshire farm in the 1940s (see *Forgotten Harvest*, p.71), is unlikely to have differed one jot from how these labourers did it in medieval times, and they no doubt found the job just as arduous, smelly, and monotonous as did the author. The work was unforgettable, mainly a winter job, often on a rainy day, so once cold, one never warmed up.

Weeding

The other method used for greater fertilizing of the soil, marling, entailed the use of lime, heat treated in a kiln and slaked with water. One does not need much imagination to realize the misery of the job of getting it to the land. At Downton manor, held by the Bishops of Winchester, fourteen acres of land recovered from woodland were marled in 1235 at a cost of four pounds and four shillings. Marling was labour-intensive, five boys with ten horses took forty-three days to marl recovered land held by Glastonbury Abbey in 1252. A virgater at East Knoyle, a manor belonging to the Bishops of Winchester, was excused all his year's services in order to marl his own holding, a newly-given privilege. Though costly, obviously those who ran the farms had convinced the clergy of the worth of marling.

Increased manuring and liming meant extra fertility for weeds besides agricultural crops. Weeding would have become even more essential and possibly more frequent. To be done by hoeing, rather than hand-weeding, it was vital to obtain a good grain crop. Not only did hoeing give the crop room to grow, it also loosened and refined the soil, allowing for better penetration of moisture and worms. Manor custumals illustrate a sound understanding of weeding and laid out their demands for their labourers' services for this work.

Ploughing was the key operation to sound cultivation and keeping the land in good heart. Whether the lord or tenant provided team and plough, ploughing spawned many customs and regulations, even ploughing patterns, according to the lie of the land. The Wiltshire medieval labourer had to deal with improved stronger ploughs and for some, the beginnings of ploughing by horses rather than oxen, as is recorded at South Damerham (now Damerham, Hants) in the mid 13th century. Other labourers had to get accustomed to ploughing three times a year instead of two, a custom sometimes met with by objections to the lord.

Haymaking and harvesting were the most important times of the farming year. The crops ready to be harvested, only a few days' grace existed to take them from the ground to safe storage. The more labour mustered in this period, the better the chance of getting the crops into the rick or barn in good condition, ripe and dry, unless the weather incurred total defeat of this aim. So crucial was the work that higher payments were the norm during haymaking and harvest and manors probably vied with each other to provide the best harvest supper at the end of the season. In Wiltshire, harvest suppers survived on the chalklands until 1914, and gleaning rights, the work of women and children were considered an essential contribution to the food supplies of all rural labouring households until the 1870s or even later.

Some of the oldest manorial customs recorded concern rewards to labourers during and at the completion of haymaking and harvesting. Rewards were often set by a measure of the item being cut. At hay time, mowers could claim a certain amount of grass and hay, the measuring of which in Wiltshire was frequently archaically worded, but consistent from manor to manor in amount and description. The amount a mower could carry under one arm is recorded at Wishford manor in the 1315 custumal. At Priors for the work of raking the drying grass, a cottar received an armful. Ham manor tenants received one haystack to divide amongst themselves, the size of the stack or the meadow not stated, whereas at Winterbourne Monkton, the reeve of the manor was entitled to two cartloads of a certain meadow, each load as much as a horse could pull, so two conditions are included in this perquisite. At Hatherop manor (Glos), belonging to Lacock Abbey, all haymakers were awarded 'the mead-sheep and one cheese together, and each of them shall have one loaf of sixteen inches in breadth. . .' On some manors, the unfortunate sheep was let loose and had to be caught by the haymakers before it could be butchered. Referred to as a 'sporting chance' on some manors, the custom also specified the selection of the sheep, e.g. the second or sixth best in the fold. By the 1280s in Wilts, these rewards for services began to be replaced by money, by the middle of the 14th century such services had become totally replaced by cash awards.

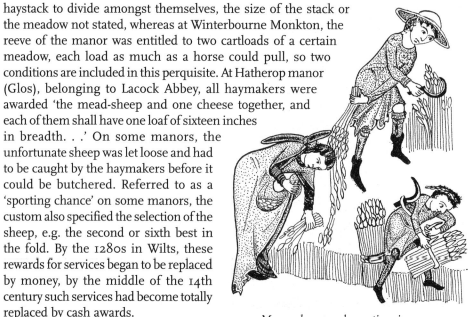

Men and woman harvesting circa 1150

The importance of the grain harvest in southern England is illustrated by the detail contained in the numerous customs it generated. Wiltshire manorial customs were no exception and harvest rewards were often greater than those awarded at haymaking, perhaps because some of the hardest work and the longest work days in the yearly farming cycle were endured at this time. Variations in the rewards occurred, depending on the grain being harvested. The most common award was a sheaf or handful of the grain stalks for each phase of the harvest. In some cases the length of the binder encompassing the stalks was specified, the longer the binder, the larger the sheaf. Sometimes the tightness of the binder round the sheaf was also delineated. A variation was a choice of taking every thirteenth sheaf from each harvested acre, as at Knoyle, whereas at Kingston Deverill a virgater could take the tenth sheaf of each half acre, but limitations existed at both manors on the size and choice of sheaf. A 1250 customal at Stockton manor specified that a cottar could take the sixteenth sheaf after reaping one-half acre of wheat, or the fourteenth sheaf for a similar area of oats.

Other work of harvesting besides the reaping – the binding, stooking, carting and ricking – also had sheaf awards – the wain-sheaf at Longbridge Deverill , obviously a reward for carting. At Wishford Parva in 1315, the carting of sheaves was rewarded by one sheaf for every three cartloads moved in from the fields. In 1265, the Cherhill manor custumal specified that two tenants were allowed to select four of the best sheaves for their day's carting at harvesting time.

At certain Wiltshire manors the worker was allowed the choice of a meal or a sheaf, or sometimes both as his perquisite. Ham manor specified two sheaves or lunch, as did

Patney. At Wroughton a reaper was given one sheaf instead of a meal, the same applied to Tilshead. In time, these awards became simplified, and a gift of grain replaced them. Compulsory labour service at harvest time was paid later by money rather than in kind, as it was for haymaking.

Tenurial changes

Due to so much variation, little is understood regarding the amount of a tenant's holding on an estate. A guess for Wiltshire at the time of the Domesday survey is 30 to 50 acres. But change came fast, 'In 1100 the Lord of the manor was lord of men who held lands of him, in 1200 he was the Lord of lands occupied by tenants.' A holding became more precisely defined, to encompass a greater range of acreage from perhaps 5 to 50 acres, with inheritance rights usually assumed. This was to lead to much exchange of small plots of land between peasants.

The first land to be leased appeared to be from the demesne, the earliest lease in Wiltshire being 1126. Leasing created a chain reaction between manorial tenants and workers; if the lord rented them land, then those who could afford it increased their acreage and moved up a notch in the social hierarchy. At the same time came the demand to commute services. Rent-paying villeins began to pay a few pence instead of giving services or options to work part of the demesne or their own holding, and to pay a cash rent for the holding itself. By the end of the 12th century, demesne rentals in Wiltshire had greatly increased in number, freeing more land for other ranks of peasants, the cottagers and virgaters, for instance.

Similar land transactions had reached monastical lands in the early 13th century and so had subletting. The payments of villein tenants on the Bishop of Winchester's estates, show that parts of their landholdings were sublet. Judging from manorial court records, on secular manors the same applied and no objections seem to have been raised. This was a point in favour for the agricultural labourer at this time, as it paved another way for him to have land to work for himself, becoming a tenant in his own right. This growing freedom continued until the 17th century, by then, any agricultural labourer fortunate to possess the necessary means who tried to better himself by buying or renting land in Wiltshire was sure to evoke disapproval from 'his betters' as he attempted to 'change his station in life.'

Unfortunately, obtaining a landholding by manor tenants was not a certain road to riches. The right of inheritance was not always applied to the new lessees, particularly if they ranked low on the social scale. Landlord-tenant relations probably covered a wide range, from a peaceable easy-going lord to one in constant conflict with his lessees. And the lord usually had the last word, particularly in the question of inheritance by his worker. If he did not want the heir, he felt he could exclude him or the man's widow and chose another tenant. Or, if accepting one he did not like, that incoming tenant might have to pay a hefty entry fine (fee) to enter the manorial structure and till its land. Tenants periodically faced problems of labour shortages, high labour costs, depressed prices, periodic epidemics of animals, the problems prevailing through late medieval tenancies. Wiltshire records so far indicate that a tenant's prosperity was often short-lived, he lived a precarious existence and the tenant in following generations was not always of the same family that had held the land in the past. Lack of capital was no doubt one of the major causes of failure for the peasant tenant. But a tenancy meant hope and perhaps the start of a better life, despite records revealing an ever-fine line between failure and success.

More land rented out meant a relinquishing of control by landlords over their manorial workforce. Service customs diminished or ended, but certain manor traditions, particularly regarding the upkeep of land fertility, maintenance of the infra-structure of the manor lands e.g. hedges, ditches, care of woodland and timber, cropping and field systems, are likely to have continued, to be confirmed by the manor court. (All these factors and more echo down the centuries to be firmly incorporated in Wiltshire farmers' leases by the end of the 18th century.) The new tenant-landlord relationship meant that a new or different set of rights had to be established, often as the result of many years of compromise. When money, not services, became the basis of control, it proved easier to establish rights, but the process was not always smooth. One ever-recurring problem was the maintenance of buildings on both the manor and its holdings. Tenants were reluctant to do more than the minimum and landlords, especially if somewhat distant from their tenanted land, had great difficulty in enforcing repairs or finding labour willing to do it. In the 14th century, especially after the Black Death, this factor was to considerably reduce the value of some manors, as tenants moved elsewhere and shrinkage of income became a permanent factor. A Glastonbury manor, Badbury, with 260 acres of demesne land suffered the loss of houses and other buildings after the Black Death. It also lost population, having 48 landless labourers just before 1348, but less than nine in 1366. Small tenants also declined in number, while holdings became larger, meaning fewer tenants in all.

What happened to those in Wiltshire at the bottom of the hierarchy, the serf or slave, is still not understood. He and his family seemed to be literally lost in the shuffle of labour services, new tenancies and rearrangements of landholdings. They are seldom referred to in manorial records after 1300. The whole family supposedly still belonged to the lord and legally had no right to inherit, let alone move from the manor, but more liberal attitudes to serfdom probably allowed him and his family to gradually shed their social disabilities, to begin to move up to the position of cottar, or similar rank, or enter the main stream of society by their own personal efforts. Surviving manorial records give the impression that serfdom in Wiltshire lingered longer on the chalk than in pastoral areas, though this may be due to the extra study given to monastic manors on the chalk. Their hierarchy, particularly the Bishops of Winchester, kept a very tight rein on their work forces, strongly combating tenancies, regression of service customs and monetary payments to their labourers, so their manors continued to record very low percentages of free tenants up to the 14th century. Secular manors, more numerous in pastoral areas, show many more lessees in the same period.

A now famous but isolated case is that of John Halle, once a serf belonging to Amesbury Abbey. He had somehow left and had achieved the position of merchant in

Salisbury. The abbey in the 15th century made an unsuccessful attempt to retrieve him. The case is so unusual it is obvious there was more to it than ever recorded. Perhaps he ran off with a nun or a very valuable item of Abbey property or otherwise grievously offended the Abbess.

The Black Death obviously had tremendous effects on the interaction between manorial lords, tenants and labourers, the latters' shortage inflicting a major impact on any surviving lord. (And sadly, many Wiltshire lords who survived in 1349 were felled by the plague of 1361, increasing their family's already onerous burden.) Manor custumals, the Ordinance and the Statute of Labourers, all so simply translated into facts, apparently important to the agriculturist's life, intrigued historians through much of the 20th century. What has proved far more difficult to unravel is how the labourer gained more economic freedom, particularly after the Black Death, how long he enjoyed it and how he increased his status and political power for the next three centuries. And how beholden was he to his lord or any other authority?

Wiltshire manors found new tenants harder to control in the atmosphere of change after the Black Death, especially on small manors. Religious manors were more successful, particularly those belonging to the Bishops of Winchester. They continued their authority over their tenants and enacted services from lower level workers, but not without difficulty. At Downton manor, services continued to1453, but this was unusually late in Wiltshire. To mitigate the labour shortage at first, large landholders are likely to have drawn on smaller manors to provide extra labour during ploughing, sowing, haymaking and harvest. Free labourers sold their labour to the highest bidder, as the Statute and Ordinance of Labour indicate.

The trend to renting land to tenants continued on Wiltshire manors, so that by the reign of Henry VII, not even on monastical manors were administrators needed, except to collect rents and supervise tenancies. Gone were the services and other manorial customs. A study of Eastrop manor, Highworth, shows money as the basis of the manorial economy, no barter or payment in kind for services, and only such customs remaining as gleaning and the post-harvest feast. Land transactions disclosed new tenants as likely to be members of families within the manor, rather than from another manor. On some manors villeins began to hold all the demesne lands of a manor, indicating perhaps that the manor lord had died from the plague and new management could not find workers. The larger tenants, and particularly those holding the most profitable land, had definitely left the ranks of the labourers and were in reality small farmers. Here begin the use of the words farm and farmer, as villeins rent payments are recorded as a farm, a fixed payment for their land.

It was to take until the end of the 15th century for Wiltshire manors to regain a normal quota of tenants, some of the delay due to an economic slump from the late 14th to the end of the 15th century. Meanwhile it was a tenants' world, not the landlords'. Then larger tenants began to consolidate and the Enclosure movement came into being, both putting great pressure on the smallholder to give up, forcing him to move back to labouring status. Coercion increased, until a man who tilled just enough acreage to support himself and family, without hiring himself out or having any other source of income, was to become somewhat of a rarity by the late 17th century.

Markets and Fairs

The general increase in the economy benefited the life of the agricultural worker in several ways. Greater output from the land meant more work to do on the manors, while additional money in circulation enlarged existing markets and fairs. All through the medieval period new marketing charters or licences were issued; the Crown granted at least 53 in Wiltshire between 1199 and 1428. Many of these undoubtedly removed those markets and fairs held for several centuries at or near the local place of worship and put them under the jurisdiction of the local manor lord. Certain fairs in Wiltshire remained in place at remote crossroads or on the high points of drove trails. A lord paid the Crown for his licence, which in turn gave him turn the right to exact tolls from market tradesmen and women. The manor's steward organized the marketing, often in favour of the local residents, e.g. they were allowed primary trading privileges. A local court appointed an ale-taster, who also examined the bread for quality and loaf size. The Crown appointed weights and measures officers; also cloth examiners and others who checked on engrossing, forestalling and stale goods. Later, such appointments were made into concessions and farmed out to local landowners, which on occasion opened doorways to deals and intrigue.

Markets and fairs gave people an excuse to congregate and then to enjoy themselves after doing business. Fair days had become a traditional holiday in many places by medieval times, some fairs lasting more than a day. Local markets served both labourer and smallholder alike. Sunday trading was prohibited in the 13th century and hence a market could not be visited after a church service; no manorial conventions have appeared to show how time off was granted in order for a man, wife or family to attend their local market. But to market they went, one way or another. A need to purchase a particular tool, a wife to sell her butter, eggs, poultry, fruit or vegetables and other produce, always a need existed to justify a market visit. Reputedly bargains were made and kept. Verbal contracts guaranteed in advance payment for goods when delivered, small amounts of cash were lent and borrowed between people who met regularly at particular markets. Seldom did the courts have to be resorted to, due to a bad debt or reneged contract, a handshake sealed and completed a deal.

In time, the larger town markets attracted specialist retailers and many market area names reflect them, the cheese and butter crosses, the shambles where animals were slaughtered, the corn market where grain was bought and sold. Suppliers of second-hand clothes, leather goods, chandlers, bakers, fishmongers (in Wiltshire selling the produce of fisheries, not necessarily of the sea), all attracted customers from the countryside. Most of these retailers are presumed to have been men, but women made their own market traditions, not only with small produce, but as brewers and hawkers of ale (ale-wives), and the serving of cooked foods, pies, cakes – anything needing very little capital investment.

These are the services due to the lord by the men of Schuldon for the year 10 Edward 1.

They must plough for the lord twice in a year, if they have oxen, and they must harrow twice if they have horses or mares; and the lord will feed them once in the day.

They must dip and shear the lord's sheep; and they shall have one cream cheese and wool called 'womblokes.'

They must bring the lord's hay homewards as he wants it put into the barn or onto a rick.

Hurdled sheep and shepherd with ploughing and carting illustration.

Early Wiltshire documents make it perfectly clear that Wiltshire had several major animal markets. Cricklade dated back to Saxon days. Deals between manors involved large numbers of beasts, but the prosperous tenant certainly took a few fat animals to market when necessary, and even the peasant with only one or two had to cull at times, or move a sick animal to market to be 'killed to save them.'

The proliferation of available ready cash, meant more trade in items produced or found with little capital. Nuts, honey, eels, rabbits (though the rabbits from the famous Aldbourne warren supposedly went mostly to London), firewood, all are items known to have been sold in markets by the 14th century. Certainly in Wiltshire, markets sold butter and cheese, besides products from the autumnal pig-killings. Small amounts of grain such as wheat, oats or rye were sold. plus malt for ale; perhaps also cider and perry, as the Normans, cider connoisseurs, greatly promoted its production in England, though peculiarly, records of both are absent until three centuries later. Pear and apple orchards in Wiltshire are likely to have continued from prehistoric times to persist until the 20th century, but they seldom are mentioned.

By the 13th century carting had become an important part of the Wiltshire economy, certainly contributing to its expansion. A record of 1171 confirms the movement of wheat in horse-drawn carts for milling and marketing; the transport of grain would become big business, particularly between large manors. All this provided work for peasants, as payment for due services and later for cash wages. A hundred years later the traditional work and trade of a carter was well established. Inter-manor deliveries persisted to the 15th century, particularly between manors owned by the monastic houses. 'Wheat and [some] rye for bread, barley and dredge for malt and ale, oats for riding and working horses, sometimes grain was even transported for threshing.'

Carts moved about the county slowly but ceaselessly; larger, wider wheels allowed their passage through deep mud. Two or more horses began to be used, increasing the amount a cart could carry. A manor reeve (probably on horseback) took the shepherd with him when sheep were driven to markets or fairs, and a carter moved behind with their supplies for the journey. Most of the grain went to markets within ten miles, often to more distant markets in years of high grain prices. For livestock, purchasers and sellers alike went further afield than did grain dealers. Wool moved up to twenty miles, and lengthy journeys could be made to fetch certain items, such as millstones. Much of the manors' trading was informal and involved their own tenants, but on two Glastonbury Abbey manors, Longbridge Deverill and Monkton Deverill, carters carried goods to Glastonbury, Salisbury and Winchester and to private addresses. Inevitably, less grain moved about in times of poor harvest, but generally the amount of grain produced on these two manors steadily increased over the years. However, by the 15th century sheep farming dominated their economies, with sales and exchanges of oxen, horses, pigs and indicating more mixed farming. Often the destinations for these animals were fairs, hopefully work combined with pleasure for the drover or carter.

In 1260, virgaters of Bishopstrow, manor, the property of Lacock Abbey, were expected to cart corn to either Canford, (Dorset), Southampton, or Bristol, entailing three days of service. A peasant carter knew where to avoid tolls and new toll bridges such as the one over the Thames, built in 1416 at Abingdon, which brought trade into the west. Tolls perhaps redirected routes rather than impeded trade.

Some manor tenants had too little land to grow corn and so were forced to buy it from their lord. A common practice on the manors of the Bishops of Winchester, such transactions were a form of control on dependant tenants, as the lord was able to fix the price he obtained for the grain. In 1352/3 their Wiltshire manors carted large amounts of wheat to Southampton for sale at a high price to the King. Carts from their manors not only carried goods to the diocese, but to London and other major regional centres, giving the carter or tenant the opportunity to look around and chat of happenings beyond his own doorstep. Carters were no doubt the medieval equivalent of the newspaper- or letter-carrier, and in later days of discontent and religious protest in Wiltshire, certainly used to 'carry the word.' Holding a position of great trust, the carter was a man of skill and expertise, determined to deliver the goods he carried and look after his horses and his cart , while at the same time keeping his eyes open to further his manor's markets. Not until the 16th century would the Wiltshire carter have his work confined to local journeyings and be replaced by a commercial general carrier.

The Black Death

For the Wiltshire agricultural labourer, the first half of the 14th century was not always an easy time. According to Stratton, he suffered drought, great heat and a smallpox epidemic in 1305. A series of wet harvests ten years later led to four famine years between 1315 and 1318. Luckily their severity was never to be repeated, despite many starvation years between 1375 and 1520 and several famines up to 1600. His cattle and horses were hit by disease, 'murrain ' and 'ffarsine' in 1320. Disasters continued for two more decades, occasionally interspersed by a favourable harvest. In 1348 rain fell continuously from midsummer to Christmas, providing damp conditions which aided the spread of the plague organism, *Yersina pestis,* from the Dorset port of Melcombe in June to reach North Wiltshire via Bristol and Gloucester in February 1349.

The Black Death, as it is now known to history, brought to Wiltshire extreme suffering from February to September, the most important months of the farming year. No-one escaped misery or grief; if they did not lose their lives, they lost their nearest and dearest, and often their living. The death toll in Wiltshire is now reckoned as at least one-third of the population, with monastic inmates and church clergy reaching a 50% mortality. This high figure is accounted for by the deadly combination of their services to the sick and their communal lifestyle.

The Church kept close records of its dead, and the deaths of manorial lords and their families are transcribed for inheritance reasons, but very little information has survived as to how the agriculturist coped. He lived or he sickened and died, to be buried without notice, for parishes kept no written or official records before 1538. Obviously his life was totally disrupted. The fields would have been ploughed and ready for planting, but few persons were left to sow the corn and other crops, or to later cut and carry the hay and

Pipe Roll extract showing effect of Black Death on the rent rolls of Bishop Edington's estates 1348-9, which included his Wiltshire manors.

harvest the corn. Who looked after his animals and those of his lord? Reputedly the plague affected the animals also, and many are likely to have died of neglect during the months following. No doubt a communal effort by the survivors was organized to do as much as possible. A Malmesbury monk noted at the time: 'women and children had to be used to drive ploughs and carts, which was unheard of.'

To mention just a few statistics from around Wiltshire gives an awareness of the immensity of the disaster. At Tidworth, all the tenants of the manor were dead. One freeman only remained in the moiety (a manor half-portion) at Broughton Gifford. Stockton manor lost 50% of its tenants. Everyone had left Cowsfield in Whiteparish by 1350, and at Stockton all old houses were pulled down for lack of tenants. At East Grimstead and West Dean manors, seven tenants had died and tenements, vacant for lack of purchasers, were worth nothing and continued to deteriorate. In addition five bondsmen (half-free) men had died, leaving only three others alive. The immediate fate of family members is never mentioned, illustrating how little worth they represented to a manor. Future records repeatedly document lowered rents as late as 1427, and on the whole for Wiltshire, rents did not return to pre-1348 levels until the end of the 15th century.

Aftermath of the Black Death

Psychologically people undoubtedly remained in a state of shock for many months, as they tried to continue their lives; for some, perhaps depression never lifted. The Church offered little comfort, since it had fervently preached and firmly believed that plagues were caused by the sins of mankind. But when so many were stricken, especially the clergy, it presented a dilemma to the common man; to his knowledge so much accumulated sin had never been evinced before in his world. The first seeds of doubt, regarding the creeds and the worth of the Catholic Curch, began to appear, to influence many a Wiltshireman's relationship and attitude towards religion in future years.

But disaster invariably creates strength and resilience, and so it was in Wiltshire. The first actions for the individual were no doubt the reorganization of what was left of the family and its labour to produce food, a strategy to be applied on any manor from serf to lord. Society seemingly quickly gathered itself up to restart local administration and the law; central government continued making its decrees and King Edward III proceeded with keeping peace at home while warring against France.

The shortage of labour immediately sent up wages, strengthening the worker's position, weakening manorial control over him. The old ways of keeping tenants poor and dependent on their manors, exercising stringent punishment if a man attempted to leave to seek a life elsewhere, could no longer be applied. Suddenly the agriculturist was free to move about, seek better wages and better land, or even just land if he had had none previously. The feudal structure of land-holding no longer held good.

Women's lives changed, too. If widowed, before the Black Death she usually had to allow a son to inherit, or seek remarriage if she wanted to retain the land her late husband had worked. But after 1350 records show a trend for women beginning to hold land in their own right, and sometimes even a daughter who had lost a father and had no brothers was allowed to inherit. Women continued to be mentioned more frequently and held more tenancies in their own right. Remarriage of widows occurred less often – there was less necessity to do so.

The immediate rise in wages caused the Government to pass the 1349 Ordinance of Labourers, clarified and updated after 1351, then called the Statute of Labourers. The Ordinance tried to enforce a vain attempt to hold wages at pre-plague levels and to prevent people from moving from their manor and seeking higher cash earnings. The Statute went further, forbidding men to leave their parish to work, or be imprisoned, and if all other measures failed, to be branded on the forehead with the letter F, standing for fugitive.

A few incidents surviving in the records demonstrate efforts in Wiltshire to enforce the Statute, not only against agricultural labourers but also craftsmen, clerks and household workers, but to little avail. It is recorded that even low-paid clergy demanded and apparently received higher salaries. A surviving Assize Roll of 1352 from northwest Wiltshire, documents several hundred labourers of both sexes who accepted higher wages, ranging in amount from 3d to 3s 4d. Labour payments, according to the Statute, should not have exceeded 1d a day for weeding, hoeing or haymaking, for mowing 5d an acre, reaping from

2d-3d a day. Where meat, drink or other sustenance was traditionally provided, the wages should have been less to reflect these perquisites. But to carry out any punishment, imprisonment or branding, meant an expenditure of much energy, money and labour, none of which was in large supply at the time. Contractual agreements between lord and labourers were particularly difficult to enforce. Often the worker had upped and gone, leaving no trace. Employers continued to be desperate for labour and broke the Statute's regulations, particularly at harvest time, when it was so crucial to get crops gathered. Judging from future developments in the economy, workers remained unpunished, prices and wages rose, landlords continued to offer higher wages and demanded less services. Change was in the air and there was no going back.

Soon, in combination with higher wages, came a rise in commodity prices. Many offenders, who 'took excessively against the Statute' or 'received against the Ordinance' were tradesmen, particularly butchers and brewers and those involved in grain distribution.

Before the Black Death, service demands from manorial lords had decreased and continued to do so after the plague had passed, especially on ecclesiastical manors. To compensate, lords raised monetary rents, but to no avail, prospective tenants balked and sought lower rents in fresh territory. Comparing *Inquisitio Post Mortem* records before and after 1349, and charting name-changes in leaseholders, an indication of tenant movement can be ascertained. The decline in population also caused many family names to disappear from tax lists. The changes continued for the rest of the century, due to at least seven recurrences of the plague. In the 1360s proportionally many more high-ranking people died than in 1349, greatly disrupting the running and administration of manors and the Church.

The Black Death was a turning point in the Wiltshire agricultural labourer's life; now for the next hundred years, if he had enough enterprise, energy and luck, it was possible for him to move upwards socially by acquiring and holding onto land. How many were successful will never be known, but among those who prevailed, a number no doubt became the forebears of Wiltshire's agriculturists, tilling the Wiltshire soil through the centuries, some until present times.

Discontent

In trying to create a picture of the Wiltshire agricultural labourer it is necessary to attempt to envision how he thought about his life and himself. By the 1300s he is likely to have had a slightly wider outlook, as communication had grown with the rest of the county and even further. As more of the outside world revealed itself to him and the feelings of other people in the same situation as himself, doubtless some of the shortcomings of his life were revealed to him. Few examples of discontent are recorded in Wiltshire until the 14th century, when the peasant in other parts of southern England was also protesting, but he may have made his superiors aware of what he considered shortcomings in his life far more often than records reveal. Discontent is a mild word compared to revolt, which often connotes violence. The Wiltshire agricultural labourer throughout his history seldom provoked violence, or showed signs of being prone to making sudden decisions. His renowned phlegmaticism and other similar traits, so aptly recorded in the 17th century by John Aubrey, are likely to already have been in place, acquired from generations of living in the peaceful but humdrum Wiltshire countryside. Did he look to the future as we do today, or was he concerned only with life within his parish or even just his manor, and his immediate family? At this stage of his history it is almost impossible to say.

1185 is the earliest recorded example of discontent. Tenants and labourers at Lockeridge manor, held by the Templars near Ogbourne St George, ' a distinct but spirited community,' protested in common against the introduction of a new Templar ruling regarding their customary payments by service. As so often happens in early records, whether the miscreants were brought to court and punished cannot be determined, but the lack of such a record meant that a peaceful settlement was likely reached.

No more documents recording discontent can be traced until after the Black Death. Poll taxes of 1377, 1379 and 1381 went up from 4d to 12d per head, a contributing cause to the great Peasant's Revolt of 1381, when Wat Tyler and his men marched on London. In Wiltshire urban people demonstrated, but all remained quiet in rural areas, no gatherings and no participation in the Revolt; it was, after all, a long march to London. But events previous to 1381 demonstrate the Wiltshire peasant's lively interest in his own welfare.

Tenants of Great and Little Ogbourne, (now known today as Ogbourne St George and Ogbourne St Andrew) had conspired in 1327 and raised a common purse to push for enforcement of what they thought was the right to claim ancient demesne status. The establishment and gentry found this threatening. Another similar case occurred in 1348 at Badbury. The manor peasants protested against their lord, the Abbot of Glastonbury, by bringing proceedings in the Court of Exchequer. Led by John Stephenes, a tenant with large holdings, also a brewer and one-time reeve of the manor, the matter concerned procedures of the manorial court and again the tenants claimed the right of ancient demesne status, i.e. the manor was an ancient demesne of the Crown and therefore, by bringing the suit to the court, they felt they had acted within their legal right and hence were not engaging in an act of outright defiance. Like the 1327 protest it was a hopeful rather than a realistic gesture, as it was not written into law that the rights and customs recorded in Domesday were legally binding on either lord or tenant. Both protests illustrate reverence to the Domesday book, enhanced by its given biblical name, and faith in the powers of the courts.

The 1377 Poll Tax is likely to have contributed to the tenants' restlessness that year, the tax being felt far more by those in the lower ranks of society. At the same time, most agriculturists were seeking more personal freedoms and some still attempting to throw off vestiges of payments by labour services. Protests began in September on several manors; in the following May tenants on the Abbess of Shaftesbury's manors in Wilts and Dorset all claimed to be exempt from certain services and rents. In all, seventeen Wiltshire places recorded protests. On several ecclesiastical manors, tenants threatened to burn down the foundation building and any monks within it. Strong words, but they came to naught. Special commissions, appointed to look into these protests, were sworn in, to find for the peasants no value or relevance to the question of personal freedom, and that they should continue the service customs as before. No record exists that the commissions actually sat.

The risings illustrate how well the Wiltshire peasant was aware of his rights and willing to protest for them. Historians claim from their considerable study of the Peasants' Revolt that relations after the rising changed irrevocably between the landlord, tenant and peasant. The trend to rent out land accelerated and secular lords began to sell land, though the religious houses in Wiltshire seldom or never did. The idea that all men were free beings in their own right began to gain acceptance much more rapidly than before 1381, and is illustrated by the increased stature men gained from holding tenured land. Church scot and heriot dues were demanded less on many manors, though it is likely that their enforcement continued on the chalklands, where larger estates often meant greater control by a lord over his workers, and the many monastic manors certainly attempted the continuation of any religious dues. On those manors payments probably did not cease until service rents had disappeared and all lands were tenanted.

Due to the Peasant's Revolt, poll taxes were abandoned and attempts to change the social or geographical basis of taxation came to an end. A new system of direct taxes came into being, to remain essentially unchanged until the 16th century. Another consequence of the revolt concerned the accelerated pace of land-leasing by the estate owners, who in doing so, shed the burden of direct administration. By the 15th century leaseholds led to selling land to tenants and the lords sought investments for the proceeds. In Wiltshire this often meant buying into an element of the woollen cloth industry. By the end of the 15th century merchants were again looking to buy more land to create country estates. The only large amounts left, particularly in the pastoral areas of the county, belonged to monastic estates, whose owners did not consider selling any land. Wealthy merchants began to put pressure on the Crown to confiscate monastic land, pressure that contributed in time towards the Dissoultion. So a direct link can be formed between two great events in English history, the Peasants' Revolt and the Reformation.

Discontent and the church

Little definitive information regarding the Catholic Church's contacts with the agriculturist is available until well after the Norman Conquest. A feature of the Wiltshire countryside from Saxon times, the Church did not apparently begin to formally exert its spiritual influence on the agriculturist until the 10th century, when ministering begin to be perceived.

Physically, the Church becomes more evident when most villages achieved houses of worship by the end of the 11th century; in the next two hundred years these, if of wood, were replaced by stone edifices, mostly financed by manors. These churches entailed enormous expenditure in a very short period of time and reflected the wealth of the county, as its economy managed to increase at the same time. In nearby Gloucestershire the parish churches built there during the same period are frequently larger and more elaborate than those in Wiltshire, no doubt reflecting a greater and more extensive economy. In later centuries the same parallel applies to farmhouses. Economically, the Church tithed all, through the manors and the parishes. Churches and monasteries kept separate administrations. Monasteries had a direct line of authority to the Pope, but the Bishops' control of dioceses and hence parishes, was national – later grounds for trouble. Nominations of secular priests to fill Church vacancies were made by the nearby religious house, and confirmed by the Bishop, possibly sometimes bypassing the preferred choice of the local people.

Many French monastic orders received large grants of Wiltshire land and their attached workers from both King and nobles after the Conquest. The orders promptly exploited the lands to the full by forming manors and administering them according to the Norman feudal system. By 1350 they began renting out land, which increased their monetary income. During the prosperous years of the first half of the 13th century, much building and rebuilding of churches took place, church records reflect this by the number of churches the Bishop of Salisbury consecrated in his travels around his Diocese. Help for all this building activity came from the parishioners themselves, the gentry and large tenants contributing money, the poorer adding their pence and labour when possible. Soon, nowhere in Wiltshire was likely to be out of the sound of church bells, a pervading symbol for generations to come.

By the 15th century most churches had acquired rood screens and begun to feature seats and pews, the latter often with elaborately decorated ends. Rental of seats and pews began, but seating in churches was still seldom the lot of the agricultural labourer or his family. Well-to-do parishioners spent money raised by gifts, festivals and other means, on Wiltshire's churches, right up to the Reformation. The actual construction was supervised by churchwardens; sometimes parishioners helped supply stone, scaffolding or timber. But what pastoral duties the clergy carried out for those at the bottom of the social scale cannot be ascertained.

Medieval church attendance by the agricultural labourer, or any other class of person for that matter, is also unknown. Was he compelled to attend, as he was forced to pay tithes and Peter's Pence? Judging from inscriptions on the fonts in Avebury and Stanton Fitzwarren churches, much emphasis was put on the conflict of good and evil in the peasant's life and the Church's role in protecting its parishioner from the forces of the devil and his attacks on the soul. If not resisted, horrible consequences supposedly followed. The churches, by present standards, were cold and damp, but colourful medieval wall paintings instilled a warm atmosphere and gave relevance to the teachings of the Church and the pronouncements of the priest. Often a local person, he was not far removed from a peasant, except for a little understanding of Latin and Church pronouncements. Priests, too, were tillers of the soil, with their glebe lands near or by the side of the church. Sometimes he married and his son succeeded him as parish priest. Besides conducting services and collecting tithes, he presumably ministered to the labourer and his other parishioners. Some churches were poor and carried only a priest, others were extremely well off, employing a large staff. Such an extravagant use of church moneys was later to give rise to much resentment among the working classes, both rural and urban.

After the Black Death, peasants' attitudes to the Church are likely to have started to change as they began to acquire more independence and perhaps became disillusioned from the terrible events of that plague and others in later years. Certainly a change was seen in Wiltshire church architecture. What building there was after a century of plague, illustrated the limited scope of available financial resources, particularly away from towns and villages beginning to prosper from the woollen cloth industry. The sparse Perpendicular style with its sombre walls which finally emerged suggests it may have been reaction to the agonies of the plague years, inferring a starker attitude to life and the prominence of death in everyday living.

It is almost impossible to pin-point the beginning of anti-clerical feeling amongst Wiltshire agricultural labourers and tenants. As the 14th century progressed into the 15th, the prominent roles played by Bishops in political and Crown matters increased and their influence strengthened. The monastic estates made great efforts to control their workforces and succeeded in limiting their freedom to move about and reject service demands to a greater extent than did secular manors. This probably gave rise to a certain amount of discontent on monastic manors.

John Wyclif, in the mid-14th century, had attacked Catholic fundamentals – papal authority, confession, transubstantiation, monasticism, and he believed in the sole authority of Holy Scripture. His views, adopted by Lollards, gave rise to more anti-clericalism and made popular the concept of Bible-reading and acting literally on some scripture precepts. Though Henry V tried to stamp out Lollardy, the ideas continued to spread; their emergence in Wiltshire can be traced from the cloth-workers of Bristol, a tradition of Lollardy extended through the Thames and Kennet valleys and the Pewsey area to reach down to Salisbury, all, it should be noted, linked by good communications. Probably a protest march of Bristol cloth-workers to London in 1414 extended the Lollard influence.

Naturally Lollard beliefs had to be spread in secret, as the Church had declared their ideas as heretical. They varied from group to group, individual to individual, and fed the religious dissatisfaction of both the urban and rural Wiltshireman. Protest broke out in Salisbury in 1431, incited by Berkshire Lollards, some of whom were present and later indicted.

Lollardy undoubtedly influenced a man from Netheravon (never a heretical village), who had appeared before a Sarum Diocesan court in 1441, asserting, among other claims, that money spent on pilgrimages was better spent on ale. He possessed an English book and declared that neither pope, bishop, nor priest had the power to pardon men; furthermore the Church's pardon was of no avail and only God forgave.

A culmination of protest against the Catholic church manifested itself in 1450. A plot to murder the Bishop of Salisbury was conceived by men from the city and other parts of Wiltshire, particularly in the Pewsey Vale. They converged on Edington Priory where the Bishop was conducting a service. He was dragged from the church and stabbed to death, the men observing the rule of altar sanctity. Other protests occurred at the same time in Tilshead, Devizes, Wilton, Biddestone and elsewhere, indicating the strength of the anti-clerical movement.

A known active area of Lollardy existed between Devizes and Bradford-on-Avon. Lollards had a wide network of contacts and in 1514, villagers from Wilsford, Chirton, Pewsey and Marden appeared before courts of the Sarum Diocese. They were accused of the denial of transubstantiation, that pilgrimages and offerings to images were a waste of time, and that it was as good to pray outside a church as inside one. These villagers repented and were believed, but one, John Bent of Chirton, was condemned as relapsed and handed over to the Mayor of Devizes for execution. As in the past, no record can be found of his subsequent fate.

A century after the Reformation, other sects, the Ranters and the Muggletonians played a small but influential role in the religious life of rural Wiltshire. But the Lollards made the greatest impression in the county by their emphasis on a direct approach to God, with no altar and costumed priest between. This concept had furnished the first religious alternative in Wiltshire to conventional Roman Catholicism. In medieval times the church acted as a disciplinarian, an organization attempting to channel parishioners' lives into paths acceptable to the Church's teachings. After the Black Death, Church discipline began to lose its effectiveness, allowing other forms of religious thought to germinate. By 1535, the ideas of the Reformation had found fertile soil in Wiltshire, and would make the path to Protestantism much simpler. Lollardism was the religious path some of the Wiltshire agricultural labourers began to tread, and later its ideas would help towards bypassing the new Anglicanism; in time, furthering the development of Puritanism to lead finally to Wesley's teachings and the chapel movement.

Chapter 4 Bibliography

A thorough background to the Domesday survey was provided by Volume II of the Victoria County History of Wiltshire, supplemented by:
WOOD, M., 1988, *Domesday: A search for the Roots of England*. NY: Facts on File Publications.

A vast range of publications are available on late medieval settlement, manorial practices, tenure and the *famuli* (permanent agricultural manorial servants). The listing below includes my major sources of information:
ASTON, M., AUSTIN, D., DYER, C.1989, *Rural Settlements of Medieval England*, Cambridge, USA: Blackwell
CARUS-WILSON, E. M. 1966, *Essays in Economic History*, ii, 59-84, Oxford University Press
*DYER, C., 1989, *Standards of Living in the Late Middle Ages*. Cambridge University Press. (A most comprehensive study, particularly useful.)
FAITH, R., 1997, *English Peasantry and the Growth of Lordships*. Leicester University Press
FARMER, D., 1996, 'The *famuli* in the later Middle Ages', in R. Britnell and J. Hatcher (eds), *Progress and problems in medieval England: essays in honour of Edward Miller*, Cambridge University Press
FRYDE, E., 1996, *Peasants and Landlords in later Medieval England*. NY: St Martin's Press
*HARE, J., 1992, Lords and their Tenants, Conflict and Stability in 15th century Wiltshire, in B. Stapleton (ed), *Conflict and Community in Southern England*, 16-34, NY: St Martin's Press
HARVEY, P. (ed), 1984, *The Peasant Land Market in Medieval England*. Oxford: Clarendon Press
LEES, B., 1935, *Records of the Templars in England in the Twelfth Century*: Oxford University Press

MULLER, M. and DYER, C. 1999, Archaeological and documentary research on Badbury, Wiltshire, *Medieval Settlement Research Group annual report* 14, 34-6

TITOW, J., 1969, *English Rural Society,* London: Allen Unwin

TITOW, J., 1994, Lost Rents, Vacant Holdings and the Contraction of Peasant Cultivation after the Black Death. *AHR* 42.2, 95-114

Two sources on the Black Death gave a fresh outlook on the plague in Wiltshire:
HARE, J. N., 1998, The Black Death in Wessex. *Hatcher Review* 46,

HORROX, R., 1994, *The Black Death.* Manchester University Press

Specific information on cultivation of the land and agricultural customs in Wiltshire come from a wide range of sources, For information on medieval share-milking, BRAY, W., 1816, An Account of some Customs in Husbandry *Archaeologia* XVIII, 281-6, proved useful, plus: KENDALL, S. G., 1944, *Farming memoirs of a West Country Yeoman 1944.* Faber and Faber. For share-milking in the 19th and 20th centuries I am greatly indebted to Mr George Bailey, whose family have farmed at East Tytherton for several generations. He told me of local customs and several examples of the practice, which ceased during World War II.

For medieval agricultural customs and the life of the labourer I drew heavily on the following publications:
FARMER, D.L., 1989, Two Wiltshire Manors and their Markets. *AHR* 37.1, 1-11

HARVEY, P. D. A. 1993, Rectitudines Singularum Personarum and Gerefa. *EcHR* 108, 1-22

JONES, A., 1977, Harvest Customs and Labourer's Perquisites in Southern England, 1150-1350: the corn harvest, *AHR* 25.1, 14-22

JONES, A., 1977, Harvest Customs and Labourer's Perquisites in Southern England, 1150-1350: the hay harvest, *AHR* 25.1, 98-107

The Wiltshire peasant's discontent is documented in: FAITH, R. 1984, 'Great Rumour of 1377 and Peasant Ideology', in R. Hilton and T. Aston (eds), *The English Rising of 1381.* Cambridge University Press; plus HARE, J. 1982, Wiltshire Risings of 1450, *Southern History,* 4. In order to trace the activities of the early lollards across Wiltshire, for background information THOMPSON, J., 1965, *The Later Lollards 1414-1520.* Oxford University Press, proved useful.

5
The Decline Begins

The cheese country:
'Riding betwixt Malmesbyri and Chippenham al the ground on that sie of the ryver was
chaumpain, fruteful of corne and grasse but little wood [until]Bradenstoke...al the quarters of
the forest of Braden be welle wooddid.' Leland

The chalk country:
'They are the most spacious plaines in Europe, and the greatest remaines that I can heare of of
the smooth primitive world when it all lay under water...The turfe is of a short sweet grasse,
good for the sheep, and delightfull to the eye, for its smoothness like a bowling green, and
pleasant to the traveller.' Aubrey

Introduction

The period 1500-1640 was destined to make a radical change in the life of all involved in the agricultural scene of Wiltshire, from the noblest landlord to the lowest labourer. The first three decades of the 16th century saw a stagnant land market, a slow economy, religious discontent. Then followed the Reformation, causing a real estate boom in farmland, as nobles sold to gentry, gentry sold to the *nouveau-riche,* and they in turn rented or sold to local farmers with the capital to expand. Religious dissension continued for the next century, with an ever-widening gap between the conventional Anglican, usually a supporter of the Crown, and the more aesthetic, newly-categorized Puritan. Actions of King Charles I and central government increased the divisions between the two groups. By the time of the Civil War, Wiltshire had formed two very distinct camps, they roughly followed another new county division to be known as the Chalk and the Cheese Countries.

Momentous changes came from the redistribution of monastic land, which in Wiltshire probably amounted to at least one third of all the cultivated land in the county. New ownership released it from its unproductive tenancies to be exploited and more intensely farmed. Secular manors that remained intact would follow along with the new farming ways, consolidating their tenants and lands, driving out small tenants by raising rents, creating larger but fewer farms.

The population of Wiltshire grew all through this period, advantageously creating a bigger market for food and other agricultural products, but at the same time as farming became more labour intensive, it used fewer workers to produce more. Obviously this affected the life of the agricultural worker in many harsh ways. Prices rose over the same period, creating more hardship as wages failed to keep up with the increasing cost of goods.

During the 16th and 17th centuries in Wiltshire, the cloth and woollen industries continued to grow, but in economic leaps and setbacks. The clothiers and wool merchants survived if they had reasonable reserves of capital, but the industry as a whole cannot be rated as a good steady source of income for the worker, either male and female, or indeed for the clothiers themselves. It did bring more coinage into circulation in the county, and so helped to raise the general level of economy. It also brought extra income to small husbandmen and yeomen farmers, whose families wove cloth pieces in their own homes, if located in cloth manufacturing areas. How many labouring families also wove is difficult to determine; little mention is made of them in such a role.

Prices through this period rose threefold, making it impossible for a worker to provide a living for himself and his family on a few acres and survive; if they wanted to remain independent, money or capital had to be found to rent or purchase enough land to provide for their families. Those few lucky ones moved up the social scale to become husbandmen, yeomen or farmers. Others, fortunate to be able to retain a few acres and enough common grazing to provide partially for their needs, made up their income by part-time labouring, particularly at haymaking and harvest. The rest who lost their land by cancelled leases, enclosure or deprivation of common grazing rights, had two alternatives: to move to a town or find rural work as a wage-earner. Low wages, surplus population and lack of opportunity began to push the agricultural labourer to the bottom levels of society, where, as this book will show, he would always remain.

So, from the end of feudalism in the late 14th century to the Reformation, the agricultural worker had on the whole improved his way of life, either by having access to land for his own use, or as a labourer, enjoying what was, for the times, considered a living wage. Landlords, on the other hand, were not helped by the labour shortages, wars and times of economic slowdown. Both secular and religious owners had resorted as a matter of expediency to mainly leasing out their lands, and in proportion to the rents received, agricultural land was a poor producer. (This situation was to occur again when, in the 1880s, country estates could not meet their expenses from their rents.) While owners lived on rentals, their tenants, many working only on small pieces of scattered land with no access to capital, were not able to farm productively with any degree of efficiency. And so was set the scene for the Dissolution of the Monasteries and the Reformation, in Wiltshire all ultimately to lead to the decline of the agricultural labourer.

The Distribution of monastic land in Wiltshire

The first Tudor King, Henry VII, reigning from 1485 to 1509, led the English to economic and domestic political stability. He ended the Wars of the Roses, united England with

Wales, made peace with Ireland and Scotland and tempered his autocratic rule with justice and respect for the growing influence of English law. His son and successor, Henry VIII, while inheriting his father's intelligence and autocracy, lacked his patience and diplomacy. Unfortunately for England, unlike his father, he was greedy, vain and a spendthrift. These three traits soon led him to make heavy demands on his Exchequer, to institute new and higher taxes and to seek further sources of money. One answer to his search was to sell Crown land to chosen courtiers, thus creating a completely new base from which to raise taxes. The new owners made money by splitting up and selling the lands they had purchased to wealthy merchants, hungry to acquire a house and country estate, particularly in Wiltshire, where some clothiers had prospered greatly. But Henry had no intention of selling all the Crown land, nor did he wish to make his courtiers wealthy enough to put them into position as rivals for his power. The two other major large landowners in England were the aristocracy and the Catholic Church. Neither had any reason or incentive to part from their estates, but the clamour for land continued and by the late 1520s, the situation had become a stalemate.

Henry was very much aware of growing religious unrest and dissatisfaction in England. Urged by his courtiers and ministers, he began to consider the wealth of the Catholic Church a target. He had always preferred ultimate power and never was comfortable with the Church, as he had to answer to a Rome-based pope, the equivalent of being at the beck of a foreign power. He sought excuses to start proceedings against the church and his 'great matter' finally provided it. In 1533 he secretly married Anne Boleyn (whose father, Thomas, received the appointment Earl of Wiltshire in 1529) and separated his life from Queen Catherine of Aragon. The Pope promptly excommunicated him and in the next three years Henry cut all fiscal, legal and spiritual ties with Rome. The Crown commenced making plans to investigate all religious houses, and in 1535 a financial appraisal appeared - *Valor Ecclesiasticus*. Soon after, actual confiscation of the houses began, although some in Wiltshire, despite the haste with which the government acted, were in a greater hurry to surrender. Money came into the treasury quickly, partly from the immediate sale of church artifacts, roof lead, stained glass and even stone, and from parcels of land that were quickly granted to Henry's court officials and other members of his household. From the earliest disbursements, often a week or so after the investigating commissioners had turned in their reports, the complexity of monastic land allocations illustrated carefully planned parcelling out, long before the dissolution had officially begun. (See *Cocklebury* Chapter 5)

Besides gaining wealth, Henry bestowed upon himself all the political power lost by the Catholic Church, by appointing himself head of what was to be called the Church of England. He intended to break the spiritual influence of the Catholic Church and replace it with other authoritarian views, which in Wiltshire did happen for a time, but non-conformity to the new Anglican Church waited in the wings. Despite a scattering of dedicated families, very little Catholic influence remained in the county, except in the extreme southwest, where the devoutly Catholic Arundell family held authority over their estate workers for many generations. Their Catholicism did not spread, mainly due to geographical isolation and acceptance of new religious creeds by others surrounding them. In other parts of Wiltshire, the agricultural labourer apparently conformed to the new worshipping patterns, which, if of a pietistic nature, may have sorely concerned him. History records not the acceptors but the later protestors against the new Anglicanism in Wiltshire history.

For the Crown, the Dissolution of the Monasteries went as planned. In three years, all the Church lands were in the hands of the aristocracy, who with great rapidity resold the land to those wanting to form both large and small estates. These in turn, especially in the Cheese Country, were rapidly divided up into suitable areas to create farms to be rented to tenants. Nearby smallholders who had not been able to expand or obtain a new tenancy, began to be pressured to sell their land to small farmers with enterprise and access to capital, which would enable them to enlarge their farms. Small landholders, who after 1536 no doubt felt that their hopes to obtain more land and financial security in their lifetime were about to be fulfilled, could not foresee their fate - to be swept out of the way by lack of access to capital and larger landholders eager to acquire more. It was a case of too many smallholders and not enough land. Fifty years later appeared another hazard, a smallholder or husbandman not able to produce enough, cheaply enough, to compete with the lower market prices brought on by more goods appearing on the market, due to farming on a larger scale. The Dissolution of the Monasteries, besides affecting the small agriculturist and labourer, has been described as 'An unparalleled secular spoilation of ecclesiastical property,' but from the opposite point of view, the Church had misused its land, satisfied to produce only enough to maintain its structure and hierarchy. It was inevitable in the name of economic progress, that a way had to be found for the land to produce more, and the King's affairs had provided the means.

The Wiltshire agricultural scene

Within a few years of the Reformation, the new landowners began to adapt the old farming practices of both north and south Wiltshire. All the changes were to have a bearing on the life of the agricultural labourer. The reshaped farmland in the 16th and 17th centuries created a landscape that is still with us today, though somewhat mutilated by the expansion of towns and villages and 50 years of hedge removal, particularly in the northwest of the county. (Here a comparison can be made here between 1950 and 1990 when hedges fell into disfavour, as they prevented large machinery from operating in very small fields. Uprooting them saved the expense of hedge and often ditch maintenance. After about 30 years, hedge removal slowed down, and some machinery was modified to operate in smaller areas. At the time of writing, farmers have re-discovered the advantages of hedges, but the tiny fields are unlikely to return, at present seemingly uneconomical.)

From the adaptations emerged two economic and agricultural regions, the Chalk and the Cheese Countries, giving rise to the old adage: 'as different as chalk is from cheese.' In the Cheese Country, consolidation of the farms changed field patterns, creating many small grass stretches edged with hawthorn and blackthorn hedges. New fields gradually nibbled away both large and small forest remnants, as the farms extended wherever fertile

Wiltshire horn breed of sheep, as depicted in Thomas Davis's report on the agriculture of Wiltshire, 1813 edition.

land was available. The Chalk Country saw a great deal of rearranging of the common fields after the mid 16th century, though superficially the landscape changes were perhaps not so noticeable, as the high ground remained almost untouched. The new field areas created out of arable land and the old sheep grazing runs still remained generally without hedges. But their boundaries, both old and new, were to be rigidly observed.

Some strip field systems remained in both the Chalk and Cheese countries, many on the outskirts of towns or large villages. Chippenham kept common fields strips until the end of the 18th century. But particularly in the Cheese Country, the practice of renting them out to small agriculturists began to be discontinued in the mid-1500s, so that the strips were consolidated and discrete farm holdings were created. On the other hand, many Salisbury Plain manors kept their open fields well into the 19th century; some are shown on the 1840s Tithe Award maps. And Stert, probably the last manor to do so, resisted all pressures and retained some open field land until 1928. Again, here is another topic with an important bearing on the history of our agricultural labourer, warranting further investigation.

Farming on the Chalk and Cheese

The merging and extension of sheep runs were to be crucial to farming the chalk lands in the next two centuries, as they were to produce more easily worked grazing, with the least amount of labour. Displacement of settlements, even villages, aided the extension of the runs by both old and new estate owners. A resistant tenant soon found out that his tenancy would be put in jeopardy if he did not agree to his landlord's new arrangements. Estate owners on the chalklands increased the size of their demesne flocks, sending more wool, lamb and mutton to markets, while also providing for manuring of the corn crops grown on the light chalky soils. The farms settled down to a pattern of seemingly using half of the land for sheep runs, the other half being nearly all for corn growing with a little permanent grazing. Smaller farmers shared their sheep, maintaining common flocks and folds, thus eliminating the need for as many shepherds as before. For the small farmer in the Chalk Country, sheep and corn were intertwined, if a man could afford a flock large enough to manure his corn land, he could survive on the chalk as a small tenant. Those who could not were elbowed out of the market and off their land, while the enclosure of arable strips and the extinction of common grazing rights finished off most husbandmen, who had no other alternative than to become labourers.

Sheep were folded all the year round on the chalk, as the land, being well-drained, was always fairly dry. The general stock was always the Old Wiltshire Horn sheep, considered a native breed; and likely to have populated the Wiltshire Downs 'from time immemorial.' The sheep were white-faced, short-fleeced, with high heads, arched white faces, horns in both male and female, long straight back, and long, large-boned legs. Indeed no oil painting! Their chief virtue was their manuring abilities, as their great stamina allowed them to be driven long distances to arable soils, while making good often on only scanty herbage whatever the weather. They were slow to fatten and produced only tolerable mutton. Their wool, of medium length and very fine, produced a fleece weight of little more than 2 lbs. It was woven into a particular type of hard-wearing broadcloth, for which Wiltshire was renowned.

Between Cotswolds and Salisbury Plain, the open-pastured farms began rapidly to specialize in dairying, though Aubrey called much of their land 'sour and woodsere,' as until the 19th century drainage, especially on the heavy clays, was always a perennial problem, expensive to remedy except by larger, more wealthy landholders. Arable crops continued, wheat, barley, peas, oats, rye, vetches and beans in order of production, but grass and hay were the main crops, and gradually dairy and beef cattle became the primary producers on the farms. Farms with fields on drier soils ran sheep. Many of the smaller farms depended on family labour, hence a greater social distinction was to come about between the small tenant, or owner, farmer, and a wage-earning farm employee.

Probably the chances for the labourer of finding work in the Cheese Country remained easier than for those on the Chalk. In the Cheese Country, small farms practiced mixed farming, the fields were often rearranged, drainage ditches dug and hedges created and more animals taken on. The share milker and herder may sometimes have succeeded in accumulating enough money by creating a small surplus each year and, after a time, to

(Opposite page) Work on the farm: the frontispiece to a Manual of Husbandry (1685), including illustrations of bird-scaring, pruning fruit trees, growing cabbages, haymaking and netting duck, as well as several more obscure occupations.

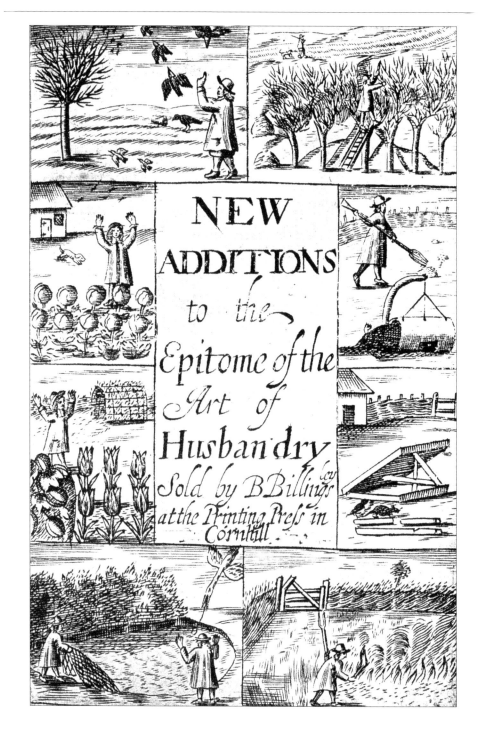

rent enough land to provide him with a living, but to buy land was impossible, as no access to a capital loan existed, even if any owner was willing to sell land. In the Chalk Country, the amalgamation of previous monastic estates, especially their sheep runs, immediately created much larger farms, though the comparative poorness of the chalklands meant more land was needed to make a living than in the Cheese Country. The consolidation also meant less work was available for the labourer, as flocks and sheep runs were also combined and amalgamated. The size of a flock would have to be nearly doubled before another shepherd would be taken on.

The agricultural labourer's daily wages in southern England between 1500 and 1640 rose from 4d to 1s, not including the value of any food, drink or perks in the reckoning. At the same time, the cost of living rose, so purchasing power dropped. No concept existed in the 16th century on the Wiltshire agricultural scene of paying wages beyond subsistence levels, and a labourer could easily dismissed on a slight pretext. Suffering chronic unemployment, sickness, injury or old age, his only resource was the Poor Law, as will be explained more fully later.

The Wiltshire economy

The period covered by this chapter saw the modern capitalistic system of competition, production, monetary payments ending all barter and wages being nudged into operation in Wiltshire. The stagnant economy, from the beginning of the 16th century until the Reformation, then the immediate land sales and later productivity changes in farming, coupled with greater output in the cloth industry, created an economical surge making the county totally dependent on market prices by 1600. As more goods came onto the market, the agricultural labourer would be affected in many ways. Unless he grew some or all of his food, he, too, became dependent on market prices. In 1536, nearly all the food he consumed was grown locally, but a few decades later, the distribution of foods was wider, raising prices as the cost of carriage and middleman had to be added. Though many manors still provided dwellings, a tendency not to replace housing for their workers was beginning, which in time, would add more difficulty to his life, as he had little or no capital to build any kind of shelter for himself and his family, neither would he be able to buy land to build on.

The Enclosure movement

Enclosure of common land in England was a natural development from the open field system of farming, a means of making the land more productive. Compared to other counties, Wiltshire had little totally unused land, such as the heaths of Dorset or the fens in Somerset, unless one considered the forests as unused, but they were not unproductive. Sometimes a community had access to large amounts of common grazing land, and the consequences of enclosure had less impact, than, for instance, on the edges of forest land or the incorporation of a large field system. In the case of an area or field of individually owned strips, their purchase or exchange with the original owners was frequently arranged in order for them to be amalgamated under one owner who then had the exclusive use of the area.

Most poor land around villages was used in some way or another, available to the non-landholders residing in the village as common, rough grazing and for gathering wood for fuel. Before the 16th century, enclosure was carried out mainly on waste land and woodland taken in for cultivation. It did not affect the labourer drastically, as much common land still remained for his use. But common land was not endless and, as after 1536, land sales hastened the taking-in of strips and common land, the livelihood of the smallholder, or the independent peasant trying to exist on one or two acres of land, was to be greatly curtailed. Women especially were affected, as many widows relied on common grazing for their cow, or a goat or two and a few hens. Villagers continued to lose the use of such land when old and new Wiltshire owners in the 16th and 17th centuries made (often forced) agreements with small owners and leaseholders to include such land in enclosure orders. With no other land available, villagers who had relied on common and waste land for a subsistence living, were driven into poverty. Their manors offered them no help, they had to find their own ways to survive. Some did and hung on until the next big round of enclosures, starting in the late 18th century. For others, the choice was clear, find employment with a nearby farmer, seek the very limited Poor Law relief offered, move to an urban area, or take to the roads in the hope of finding work elsewhere. And vagrants received short shrift; parish registers in the 16th and 17th century record many deaths of unknown persons of both sexes and all ages. No statistics exist for Wiltshire, but the rise in vagrancy, poverty and demands on the Poor Laws suggest the fate of some smallholders and labourers.

As the new landowners became more prosperous, they began to put pressure on Parliament to pass laws whereby commons and so-called waste land could be enclosed, hence making it a lawful action. Much has been written about the horrors of enclosure, especially in the Midland counties, where the populations of some villages were totally displaced. In Wiltshire a less brutal picture emerges. This is not to say that the agricultural worker did not suffer; he did, but enclosure was a more gradual process, sometimes taking place by agreement with the original or prospective owner and his small tenants or the smallholders, causing fewer people to move out of their villages. Some evidence exists that on the chalkland, when farms and sheep runs became larger, population in the villages decreased, but this is more likely to have been the result of attrition, rather than a general movement of people having to move all at once from a certain locality. Another factor probably helping the labourer and his family at the time, may have been the number of smallholders still about, whose surplus produce could be obtained more cheaply than at market prices or by barter, but this source would be almost exhausted by the end of the 18th century.

Enclosure was to become inevitable when it was deemed necessary for more efficient production, especially as large sections of land were cheaper to farm than small, scattered plots. Another advantage lay in the closure of fields; besides economy of labour, cattle were kept from straying, grazing could be controlled, grass left undisturbed to grow for hay making, animals segregated to avoid indiscriminate breeding and, in certain instances, isolated from disease. One can truly say that enclosure was an achieving factor in the development of early capitalism in England.

Hundreds of scattered land holdings had existed in Wiltshire. For example, in 1519 Nicholas Goldney held arable and pasture land among five different common fields in Chippenham, Cocklebury, Stanley, Sheldon and Lowden. It would take have taken half a day just to walk round to each holding, and to work all the land took double a labourer's time, than if the plots were all together. The business arrangements must also have been time-consuming; the five plots were rented out by at least four landowners, representing an enormous amount of paperwork, plus the employment of different rent collectors. Bureaucracy at its height!

In 1536, many small tenants rented land at Cocklebury, near Chippenham, from Farleigh Hungerford Priory. As the Dissolution began, King Henry married Jane Seymour and three weeks later granted all the Priory's lands to Sir Edward Seymour, Jane's brother. Richard Apharry, chief tenant at Cocklebury, soon became rent collector for Seymour. Other small tenants, leasing scattered strips and grazing areas, are recorded, but by mid-century enclosure began, larger packages of land were assembled, and a gentleman tenant assumed a lease of most of the area, presumably ousting Apharry. He was to be replaced in 1567 by another gentleman tenant, who leased surrounding land and a nearby house, later to be known as Monkton Manor. He then bought from the Seymour family various land parcels at Cocklebury to resell to local merchants for residential sites and to a few husbandmen with the means to acquire enough land to create a dairy farm. The enclosures meant the ousting of the remaining small tenants, the enclosure of Cocklebury Common and the withdrawal of its grazing rights. Of interest is one of the residential parcels purchased by a leading Chippenham lawyer, whose firm for several decades afterwards handled many land transactions in the Cocklebury area.

Adjoining landowners often cooperated to divide up land for their own convenience. It was done in small pieces, so that any protest by cottagers was easily controlled. Amalgamation of several strips could also be done this way. Enclosure by agreement was also common. Sometimes fictitious disputes were created to ensure action and ratification by a court. Enclosure in Wiltshire usually meant the fencing off of the land, access being made only to the owner or tenant, as is the way of the countryside today, despite the trespass laws. A 1548 survey of Iwerne Courtney manor near Blandford Forum in Dorset, but not too far from Wiltshire, shows how drastic changes happened fast, to both owner, tenant and the land:

> The customary tenants were so smale and so lyittle lande [be]longinge to them that the tenants were not able to paye the lordes rent, but one halfe of them departed the towne, and yielded up ther copies [copyhold leases] into the lordes handes;...then every tenant inclosed his owne lands, so as the more part of the hole mannor was inclosed and every tenant and farmer occupied his grounds several to hymself.

Five years later, only four tenants remained at the manor, with grazing rights for their sheep on the nearby downs.

How enclosure affected the agricultural community

Cocklebury, as can be seen, was another example of a total land rearrangement, though it took some forty years longer than in the case of Iwerne Courtney, and perhaps had less effect on small tenants, as they were probably absorbed into the area as laborers, or could easily reach a job in nearby Chippenham. The social effects of enclosure for the larger landowner are usually catalogued as wealth and status. But for those who went downward on the social scale it was a different matter. Changes in status affected the pattern of economics of a village, and community spirit could be lost. If one neighbour lost his grazing but another still retained his, rapport would be strained. A fence would perhaps legalise the situation, but a human relationship had been lost. Over all, considerable resentment was bound to emerge when a man saw one social group doing well at his expense, while he lost his means of livelihood.

Consolidation of farms and the dispensing of labour also meant a loss of cottages, as many were pulled down. A farmer might build a few small cottages for his workers, but with no land attached to them, they were deprived of growing any vegetables. Enclosure could mean the end of surrendering stubble and the aftermath of harvest to the use as common grazings, though gleaning rights still continued; too much protest would have ensued if they had been taken away.

The relationship between tenant and lord undoubtedly determined the social peace of the countryside. The Acts of enclosure disrupted it; disturbances broke out at Wilton between 1548 and 1549, due to the preparations carried out for creating the extensive parkland required by the Earl of Pembroke around his new residence. Sir Henry Baydon built a new house, Spye, at the top of Bowden Hill, and enclosed a large amount of land, mainly royal forest from Pewsham to Lacock, to surround it. Forest dwellers were displaced and protested, but to no avail. Not far behind was Sir John Thynne, who took woodland surrounding Longleat house for his park, and the Duke of Somerset, whose tenants protested when he enclosed part of Savernake forest for the same reason, thereby denying them rights of pasture. A prosperous farmer, Nicholas Small, emparked common land known as the West Field of Kington St Michael. In Wiltshire very large landowners employed agents to do liaison work, but for the smaller owner, living closer to deprived tenants, it could not always have been easy and no doubt resentment lingered for several generations.

In 1599, Edmund Ludlow enclosed common fields at Hill Deverill 'whereas the ancient tenants kept ploughs,' converted the arable land into pasture and destroyed 'houses of husbandry and building cottages. The new cottagers do live but barely, only by their day labour.' Ludlow made arrangements for some of the displaced labourers to live in a nearby converted farmhouse, to become his 'servants' (farm workers). No mention is made of how other displaced families were able to live, perhaps being reduced to vagrancy or staying and applying for parish relief.

Aubrey's writings confirm that enclosure often occurred by agreement in the Cheese Country. At Whaddon, the manorial court book of 1548 shows an agreement between

Henry Long and his tenants, enclosing 14 acres of farmed land, the tenants making an exchange with other land a little more distant. 'The lord doth grant and agree that at any time hereafter that it shall be lawful to the said farmer and the tenants to permute and exchange any other lands, to inclose and make severed for the wealth of them, or any of them, as need shall require, and the exchange so made be recorded at the next court following.' In another instance, at Dauntsey, tenants of Sir John Longe asked him to enclose Dauntsey waste, or common, of 100-120 acres, 'being voidable, unprofitable and overgrown with brambles and briars and not worth twelve pence an acre.' In 1579, Sir John cleared, hedged and enclosed it, so that it became worth twelve times more per acre. In compensation, the tenants were allowed access to other common lands, plus access to and profits from a section of woodland nearby. Unfortunately one has to report an unhappy end to this enclosure episode. Fifteen years later, upon Sir John's death, the tenants tried to retake the old waste, now presumably profitable land, eventually bringing serious trouble to themselves in doing so.

Forest enclosure

A large amount of land taken by enclosure in the 16th century lay in small areas close to or in the Wiltshire forests. Little protest was recorded, but in the 17th century enclosure of much larger areas began, encountering much opposition. Like enclosure of open agricultural land, the process was inevitable, but the forest lands had for generations nurtured a tenacious hardy peasant, who was willing to fight for his way of life, unconcerned with offending a landlord; so resistance to deforestation in the 17th century was much more organized and prolonged. Forest enclosure often was carried out after parliamentary permission, which then made it that much more official, and hence harder to rebel against.

Large areas of the old medieval royal forest of Braydon were enclosed during the 17th century, causing protest, which linked to other protests due to efforts to enclose the Royal forest of Gillingham, adjoining Wiltshire's Selwood. Charles I and his government had proposed its sale, to be enacted after cutting down of all trees in the area. The Crown employed many foresters and a great number of other persons had common and grazing rights in the area, so from the start the proposal did not sit well. Meanwhile, a few years previously, in 1627, Charles had decided to survey Braydon forest in order to prepare for deforestation and enclosure. Four years later the court of the Exchequer declared that the King had the right to disafforest. The declaration caused widespread dissatisfaction to many, who then lost their rights of common, which they had possessed for centuries. Commissioners sent to investigate the opposition heard opinions that the enclosure of the Forest would be the 'utter undoing of may thousands of poor people that now have right of common within the said forest and do live thereby.' A surveyor wrote 'that all the borderers stocke their Commons by the Forest with sheep, and so by that meanes their Cattell do wholy feede in the Forest.' The leader of the Gillingham protests, Henry Hosklins, proceeded to Braydon Forest, and the commoners rose in revolt. They chopped down fences and hedges, making the forest accessible to all again. Twelve men went to jail, but when released went back and did it all over again. Leading rioters were apprehended and removed from the scene of action. Sporadic protests continued until 1636, when the King gave in, worried about a general popular uprising and the chances of more rebellion increasing the dissatisfaction the Crown had already generated. He granted land to commoners and doled out land to certain freeholders and tenants. It was a long, but well-organized protest, with lengthy communication lines maintained throughout the years of challenge. Those who took part were drawn from every class of rural society, including the Maskelyne family, defenders of local agriculture and the labourer then, again three centuries later. (see *Forgotten Harvest* p186-7).

Revolt and Protest

Protest came out of conflict between two levels of society, those in control and those controlled. As has been shown, the gap began to grow between the poor and those adequately blessed with goods. In England, until 1349, the feudal system had served as a weapon of subjection. After its failure, legal restrictions came into being as another means to retain power over people of lower status. New laws controlled movement, wages, access to land and game, restriction of holidays; all proved major irritants, but difficult to protest against when made in distant London by unknown persons.

An expensive means of protest, demonstration in early modern times proved an ineffective weapon in the long run, as the aftermath of costs, such as job dismissal or changes in people's attitudes, invariably combated any benefits protesters might gain. Demonstration for the Wiltshireman and the fact that he did it, showed how he was pushed to the limit and how little hope he saw in the future for him or his family. Sadly, in most of the recorded demonstrations, he seldom gained more than a short extension of the status quo. Pressure would then be put on him again to relinquish rights or, in the case of enclosures, land. When he rioted because of food shortages or famine, the gain was never more than that of only just the amount of food necessary for survival, to be distributed or put on the market. The increasing wealth of the Wiltshire economy generated, continued to go upwards at the expense of those on the lower rungs of the social ladder. The poor remained poor, and also at their expense, a middle class was to evolve rapidly. Contributing to it were small merchants and shopkeepers, farmers with increasing amounts of land, plus some of the new Anglican clergy, their ranks all almost impossible to break into without capital or education. The close contacts of feudal times between landlords and agriculturists began to disappear rapidly as the monetary economy grew and wages did not keep pace. At the same time, the gap between the newly-forming middle class and the rich landowners and merchants also began to grow, both classes isolating themselves from each other by social mores, as did the middle class and the working poor, the very poor and the vagrant.

Labourers had other problems, besides unpopularity, if they did decide to protest. Two were the difficulty of communicating and gathering, especially on the chalkland where a relatively small rural population lived scattered over a large area, in the main controlled by large and socially powerful landowners and manorial lords. In the Cheese Country, with a denser population and smaller farms, most workers met at least twice a day with their employers; hence the latter found it easy to keep a close watch on what their labourers did. The county's few towns, except in the cloth manufacturing area, were isolated, with wide stretches of countryside between them and always a long distance to reach for most labourers. For the same reasons, communication was slight between the labourers on the chalk and cheese, distance again preventing them from congregating together. Lack of time proved another factor, most worked from dawn to dusk and, in the Cheese Country, on Sundays as well. So protest invariably came from a small number of persons confined to a particular area, sometimes spreading from or into Wiltshire from an adjoining county, making a protest difficult to have effect, as two authorities could be involved.

Few records exist of considerate treatment by a landlord or employer to his employees or small tenants, despite the two examples given above, those of the Long family of Dauntsey and Henry Long of Whaddon. Local surviving documents are sparse on discussion or mediation taking place compared to those of actual protest incidents. After researching protest action in Wiltshire and the character of the Wiltshire agricultural labourer over a period of nearly 800 years, one is drawn to the conclusion that he and his family bore the burdens of their everyday life with little complaint and much phlegmaticism. Not only have the men's actions and their consequences, or Aubrey's opinions of the North Wiltshire 'Aborigine' as he called the agriculturist, contributed to this conclusion, but also my own contacts when working with him in the 1940s at the very end of his life-span.

Besides outward signs of difference, forms of quiet protest began to originate. In 1389 the first of the game law acts was passed by Parliament, restricting the labourers' access to hunting certain wild creatures, a tradition they had always considered an inherited right. Objection to the game laws began with the gesture of poaching, but until the sport of shooting became a gentlemanly pastime, enough animals existed in the countryside for poachers to be leniently dealt with by game wardens and keepers, who in turn kept their own form of gentleman's agreement with the poachers. But as the game laws became more stringent and food and money shorter, poaching increased, and active hostility between poacher and keeper developed, to end up as one of the fiercer countryside clashes between the haves and the have-nots.

Dissent, later to be called nonconformity, was another form of quiet protest. After the Reformation, the seeds of dissent, sown in the previous two centuries, slowly spread in the county. In medieval times one of the chief roles the church played was that of disciplinarian, by attempting to channel its parishioners' lives into paths acceptable to it. In times of great want, doctrines had decreed that the Church act charitably, lessening demands of its tithes and dues, attempting to give comfort. After the 14th century plague years, the church's authority began to wane, as its control over people diminished, parallel to the greater freedoms achieved. By the 15th century, as has been shown, Wiltshire people showed great interest in new religious ideas, especially Lollardy, and set the scene for other dissenting sects to appear and flourish.

After 1536, the more closely-knit manors that retained their entity seem to have kept their labourers' links close to the Church as a means of authority over them, and frequently the lord of the manor had a say in the appointment of his village or manorial churchman.

This happened more often on the chalk than in the Cheese Country, where an employer often showed little interest over his labourers' religious faith. Manors there, often small or fractured, had less say in the choice of local clergy. Eventually a geographical separation began in the county, illustrated by the saying - chalk to church, cheese to chapel. Division of the Church from the labourer began after the Dissolution. New clergy began to replace priests and in 1538 the Church was given instructions to keep registers of baptisms, marriages and burials and to have a Bible written in English present in every Church. These orders probably made little difference to parishioners, but in 1547 came the dissolution of the chantries, the removal of images and crucifixes. Two years later a new English prayer book was adopted. It contained a prayer in which labourers could ask God to provide them with the incentive to work, hardly appreciative of their talents and working skills. 1552 saw the disposal of charitable distributions and church plate. How much this affected the labourers is not recorded, but their enthusiasm for nonconformity did not abate.

There is no belligerence on record against the return of Catholicism during Queen Mary's reign (1553-8). 'Little evidence survives to bear witness to the inner feelings of parishioners,' stated at the time of the Reformation, no doubt continued to be true. The rapid return to a protestant Church of England after Elizabeth ascended the throne must have quite confused people, unless very devout and utterly sure of their faith. Historical evidence does not demonstrate that the Wiltshire agriculture labourer made any effort to stay with the old faith, with notable exception of the southwest corner of the county, where the Catholic Arundell family on the Wardour estate influenced their workers and a few neighbours.

So it is hard to gauge what the Wiltshire agricultural labourer continued to think about the new Anglican Church after 1530s. Whether he found pleasure in worship or derived much comfort from it, except perhaps for the thought of the promised restful after-life for those who were not sinners, is just not known. In a certain sense, the simple church theology he understood must have been very remote from his everyday life and the old myths and folk lore of the countryside, combined with the forces of nature, far more acceptable and believable, along with local society rules governing moral relations and ethical concerns. He probably spent more time thinking of his survival problems, rather than of God, the profane and the sacred. Perhaps the analogies to biblical characters, the work of the tiller and scatterer of seed, formed links between the labourer and formal religion. It is to be remembered that Hudson, in *A Shepherd's Life,* noted that on the chalklands both farmers and shepherds were attracted to the many metaphorical biblical references to sheep - flocks, pastors, good shepherds, for example.

The labourer may have felt the Church establishment to be just another factor to cope with, another aspect of social life with which to deal. His role in the Anglican Church generally emerges as passive; unless he crops up in religious or secular court records, either for moral or legal reasons, he is seldom mentioned at all in social interaction. Any mention of him from the Church is little evident, except for recorded births, marriages and burials. Not until the coming of Wesleyanism after the 17th century and the appearance of 'chapel faiths' appear did religion seem to touch his soul. The Informer Movement sometimes impeded on his life. Originating after the Dissolution, it aimed to search out Catholics and other nonconformists not attending Anglican services, exposing them to heavy punishment. Many rural offenders are recorded in Quarter Sessions Records, as the momentum of these searches built up, not to subside until the 17th century, when, because of their growing numbers, more tolerance was exercised towards dissenters.

By 1562 Bishop Jewell of Salisbury saw the fabric of many countryside churches showing neglect and lack of care. The Church's link with upper and middle classes began to gain strength, undoubtedly influenced by their new wealth, while it ignored the needs of those at lower social levels of society. Contemporary evidence is scant on the start of this alienation, but it is strongly evident by the 17th century and backed by the evidence of the labourers' favourable reaction to the nonconformist movements.

A form of protest with more success arose against grain leaving the county to be sold at more distant markets. Poor harvests are frequently recorded during the 16th century, mainly due to more hard cold winters or excessively wet weather. The price of corn rose and records show that by 1595, Wiltshire men attempted to stop grain from local markets being sent to Bristol, where better prices no doubt could be obtained in those hungry times. During famines in the early 1600s, protests began again when labourers discovered corn still being sent from Wiltshire, while people starved. Riots occurred, mostly in the cloth districts, for instance at Seend, Warminster and Westbury. Disorder and local protests continued sporadically through the first half of the 17th century. Reports of protests occurred less when new market regulations ensured that grain went first to local customers in the markets, while at the same time, farmers on the chalk made sure that their own laborers received locally-produced grain.

Character of the agricultural labourer

The 16th century saw the last remnants of feudalism and the start of capitalism. No turning back was possible. Modern capitalism was here to stay and its establishment began to delete important aspects from the agricultural labourer and his family. The chief cause was the change in status to wage earner, caused by the deprivation of both land and any of the newly-acquired wealth. When the century began, the agricultural labourer and his family still saw their home territory as not only the place where their dwelling and nearest neighbours were located, but also as an agrarian organization of which he was part, manor, village, or a small settlement with common land and a nearby field system. A tavern or inn extended his territory, as would his nearest local market. If he lived in or near woodland, that too was incorporated into his home territory. To this territory and scene, he undoubtedly gave his allegiance, surpassing the loyalties he might have formed to Church, county, country or Crown. A hundred years later, consolidation of farms, enclosure and the ending of common grazing rights deprived many labourers of their familiar territorial structure, giving them far less to relate to in their lives, especially as the social structure continued to widen the gap between the haves and the have-nots. The labourer began to see that his employer and the Church cared little about him, indeed 'Hodge was the one individual whose aspirations were never considered: and scarcely proper he should have any.' These attitudes of the country people towards the agricultural, or indeed any, labourer did not change until the 19th century, when writers such as Cobbett slowly began to break them down.

Fortunately, the social structure of the village did not disappear, its survival undoubtedly helped by the habitual human resistance to change. It was to exist until easier communications with the outside world and lack of affordable housing led finally, in the 20th century, to all but a minute number of labourers leaving the countryside. In the county itself, from village to village, life patterns and customs continued and overlapped, gradually changing in the progress of time and events of history.

For the whole family, the labourer's work is likely to have given them their deepest social roots. All were involved in it, be it working for a local farmer full time, or

Peasant cooking potage.

partly for themselves. Labourers thought of themselves as ploughmen, carters, hedgers, reapers, herdsmen, shepherds or stockmen. Common labourers were probably fewer in numbers than specialists, especially when economics brought it upon the farmer to save wage costs by hiring itinerant labourers to do common work at casual or piece-work prices. The sons and often daughters, if their mothers worked in the fields, followed their fathers' skills as they grew up. For wives who did not work outside the home, besides the domestic work there was likely to be poultry and other fowl or birds to care for, sometimes small animals, their daughters learning their skills to become wives in turn. The work was hard, but they could still take a pride in it, as they still felt they were necessary to the fabric of their society.

From 17th century Probate Inventories, the Wiltshire husbandman or smallholder set great worth by his animals and family care. His possessions and little money were left to benefit family, with thoughtful, often explicit instructions for their future security. In some cases, such as a widower dying, a child or a young girl was officially bequeathed to the head of an outside family to act as a surrogate parent or guardian to assure support and supervision. Perhaps this became customary in a labourer's family also, as manors had ceased to assume responsibility for their labourers, and a widower or a penniless man did not want his children falling into the care of the parish. Such cases, though in different circumstances, resembled the slave or serf in earlier times selling his child for his own welfare.

Despite the changing of the farms and the haste towards greater productivity, the actual work the agricultural labourer did during this period altered little, resembling the work his ancestors had done for nearly two thousand years. This too was a form of social security for him, no surprises in the work place and little confrontational change. His metal tools evolved very little, farming methods changed slightly, but basically he continued to tend sheep, pigs and cattle, plant, cultivate and reap the harvests of grain, legumes and vegetables, make hay, and care for the goodness of the soil wherever he worked.

Housing

Archaeology forms the basis of the knowledge of labourers' housing in Wiltshire until the 19th century, as few changes in its form took place. A late medieval village, Sheldon, near Chippenham, deserted in the 13th century for economic reasons, boasted at least thirteen platform houses, the raised platform creating separation, while providing drainage. One structure shows traces of a central passage, quite typical of a Wiltshire house. The houses had small structures nearby or added to them, confirmed by tofts or mounds around their sites. Linking the houses, a track behind them was well travelled by carts pulled mainly by oxen, though the nearby manor house is likely to have used horses for grain and other goods being transported long distances. A large field behind the village shows traces of ridge and furrow even today, though these are more pronounced in an aerial photograph. Next to this field a small wood of six acres or so remains, probably descended from a larger wood used for coppicing, pannage, timber and even shelter for deer. The remains of the manor's medieval northern boundary can still be seen as a distinctive earthen bank. Sheldon is likely to have been a typical small village, part of the organization of the manor, dependent but adding to the manor's economic and social structure, the land around the village also contributing to the villagers' living. At the village of Gomeldon near Salisbury, excavated 14th century cottages had drains and cess pits, often a yard or an accessory building for animals. Floor plans of a few other dwellings in late medieval times show an area set aside for animals, though the longhouse tradition is at present still considered to be more akin to Devonshire than to Wiltshire.

When Sheldon and Gomeldon were built, labourers' houses usually had foundations of stone rubble or pressed chalk with posts or stone walls rising above them. Cob, wattle and daub between the posts or stones formed walls, exterior and interior. Roofs continued to be some form of thatch over timber beams. Directly above the usually central hearth, a hole in the thatch, perhaps lined with flints or stone tiles, served as the escape route for smoke. This type of building was to gradually replace the traditional construction of post beams inserted into the ground, which generally rotted after a generation, necessitating the whole building to be replaced. However, for the very poor, a stone or chalk foundation might not always be affordable, and the post-in-the-ground construction probably lingered on until the 18th century.

It is possible that by the 15th century the slightly more prosperous peasant or smallholder managed to afford two rooms, one heated and to cook in, the other unheated for sleeping and storage. Examples can be found at Chilton Foliat, Fittleton and Fovant. A farmhouse at Fowlswick dating back at least to the 13th century, is considered the earliest example of a small three-roomed dwelling, but probably inhabited by families more prosperous than a smallholder. A scarcity of housing for people of the lowest social classes began in the 15th or 16th century. It became a common factor of history which is likely to remain for ever, Wiltshire being no exception to this rule. The greater percentage of the rural population in Wiltshire undoubtedly had a roof over their heads until the 1500s, but then the increase in the numbers of landless labourers and vagrants looking for employment turned housing into a steadily growing problem for the poor labourer. Farmers felt no obligation to provide separate housing for an employee, the solution of the tied cottage apparently not coming onto the scene until the 19th century. By the 1600s, mentions of unmarried male farm workers in Wiltshire began. Accommodated by 'living in' i.e. bedded in a farmhouse attic or out buildings, and provided with board by the farmer's wife, the practice did not become as customary as in other counties. It was less frequently heard of in the Cheese Country, where the houses for the newly-consolidated farms contained only enough space to house the family and the cheese. In the Chalk country, farm labourers were sometimes lodged in farmhouses made surplus by the consolidation of farmland.

The 1589 Cottage Act is likely to have discouraged building in Wiltshire by any entrepreneur. Supposedly to counteract the effects of enclosures and loss of land to the small agriculturist, it stated that no cottage was to be built without an attachment of four acres of cultivable land. (The term 'cottage' is misleading; until the late 18th century, very few labourers' homes are likely to have consisted of anything more than a structure not much larger than 12½ feet by 8¼ feet; this applied particularly to casual building on commons and waste land.) At the time four acres of land was considered roughly the amount needed to graze one cow, another mistake made in the good intentions of the Act, as certainly the local landowners did not wish to encourage labourers to further their independence by any means, which possessing four acres would do. The four acre condition is sure to have put off any farmer from even contemplating building, as such acreage was far too valuable to be used by or for a labourer, and far too expensive for any entrepreneur to make a profit on a cottage or house. It is doubtful if the Act deterred any local labourer from building if he had the means or need. Quarter Session records later confirm requests being made to build on small patches of waste or common. Many resorted to illegally putting up a rough dwelling where he could settle or squat, sometimes using the help of local craftsmen and neighbours, sometimes a community effort. As it happened, the Act soon was ignored and eventually repealed, a well-intentioned but worthless piece of legislation.

The absence of labourers' dwellings surviving more than a few decades indicates that most housing stock was made up of poor structures not built to last, customary until late medieval times because of cost, and also lack of understanding of how to create an inexpensive damp-proof foundation. The major deterrent of cost, plus scarcity of land and building materials, were factors all to be aggravated after the 16th century. In Wiltshire, on the Chalklands, both wood and stone were comparatively scarce to build with, while in the

Ploughmen, circa 1525.

Cheese Country, good timber was unavailable to the labourer by the 17th century, and stone, even rubble, beyond his purse. So the cheapest and thinnest of unshaped timber would be used for standposts, driven into hard earth or beaten chalk. Cob, a mixture of mud and straw, plus lime, filled the space between the posts. The blend was built up in layers, each layer allowed to harden first. Wattle and daub, incorporating cow hair and dung, is likely to have replaced cob in the Cheese Country. In limestone areas, walls thinly built with rubble stone were bonded with a soft mud mortar. The roofs consisted of the strongest pieces of timber to be found and an overlay of thatch, perhaps resting on hurdles or strong branches, completed the usually one-roomed dwelling.

Thousands of such dwellings over the centuries were scattered over the Wiltshire countryside, all today unaccounted for and lost. At Cocklebury the farming activity obviously required the presence of several hundred labourers throughout its written history, yet any evidence of their dwellings never emerged, except for traces of a well on the boundary of the old common. The oldest remaining cottage there, built of rough stone and rubble, dates from around the end of the 18th century. Richard Jefferies wrote in 1874 of a fluke of survival of a one-storey house near Swindon. Built by a labourer for himself and his family on quit-rent land, the floor consisted of hardened mud, wattle and daub walls and a thatched roof. Divided into two rooms, one was so small it could be reached across, the other, a little bigger, served as the main living area.

Homelessness had become a chronic problem in the 17th century, squatters another. Quarter Session records in 1631 show that many vagrants and very poor people applied to the courts for permission to build a house, which was usually granted. The Chalk Country, where manors had more influence, controlled squatting forcibly, but in the Cheese Country, near woods and still existing common land, squatters were harder to control. (And as a passive source of casual labour, JPs and local employers turned blind eyes to them.) If the squatters managed to build and so stay in the area, the local labourer suffered severely; competition for locally grown food and casual work increased, a few squatters who successfully established 'a residence' attracted others just as badly off, water supplies were stressed, drainage and sewage problems multiplied, as did the risk of disease. An obvious case concerned the notorious squatters on Warminster Common, beginning in the 17th century. No doubt squatters gave the Poor Law overseers many headaches trying to sort out who was or was not entitled to relief. In Lacock, a village of probably a few hundred people at the most, the overseers in 1610 stated their concern that they might be forced to give aid, or at least deal 'to the number of sixtie persons like to lye in the streets for want of houses.' The vicar requested permission from the manorial lord to erect fifteen cottages on manorial commons in the area. Saddest of all must surely be the case of elderly John Bevin of Brokenborough with his wife, who in 1647, homeless and nowhere to go, took up residence in a hollow tree. With so much materialism today, it is hard to envisage what it was like to live in a Wiltshire community with so little that one could not afford charity to anyone, but such conditions were to continue to overshadow village existence for more than two centuries.

Interior features of small rural dwellings, seldom more than one storey high, are difficult to determine, as so little evidence has survived. However, a few details of cooking and heating arrangements are known, as hearths often survive under flooring put down later and evidence of smoke holes and chimney pots can still be found. Customarily in the middle of the room, a few hearths were placed against an end wall. Though more convenient for cooking and housekeeping, this meant an uneven distribution of heat in the room. Some hearths consisted of stone tiles, flints or cobbles laid on edge, tiles being preferred to a slab of stone, which was more liable to crack from the heat of the fire. Ceramic louvres or chimney pots of various designs are found from the 13th century, but it is more likely that a peasant's house would have used an old barrel, or tiles placed on the thatch surrounding the smoke-hole pierced through the roof from above the inside hearth. A Peruvuian shack dweller living high in the Andes told a visitor in 1999 that because he was always desperately short of fuel, he could not afford to lose any heat up a chimney, so his family put up with a smoky room at cooking time. Perhaps this observation helps us today to understand a little more how people accepted such conditions of living; there was nothing they could do about it.

A similar situation surely applied in Wiltshire in many instances and fireplaces with a chimney, being so expensive to construct in poorer dwellings, were not likely to appear until the end of the 1700s in Wiltshire. As a substitute, a smoke bay might be created by framing the hearth with timber and wattle and daub panels. If money and space were available, provision could be made for smoking meats, occasionally for malting barley. If the house was later divided into kitchen and living room areas, the kitchen fireplace might have an oven, but most managed with a trivet suspending a utensil over the fire, and a metal baking box placed in residual hot ashes.

Shepherds, 1579.

Shepherd, shepherdess and sheep, woodcut published in 1624.

The 16th and 17th centuries were a time when the Wiltshire agricultural labourer became steadily more dependent on his wages for providing his food, particularly bread, even though some were still able to cultivate a little land or run a few sheep on the commons. Hence, he and his family depended heavily on the result of the harvest, which depended in turn on the weather. The many poor harvests in these centuries contributed much hardship to his life. A wet, cold year with too much rain at the wrong time could mean poor grain yields, plus a great deal of disease amongst animals, especially sheep. A very good harvest meant surplus grain carried over to the following year. In turn the amount of harvest, particularly grain, affected the price of bread and other basics such as beans, peas and cheese. As the labourer spent four-fifths of his income on food, and his level of earnings was only just above subsistence, the price of bread was crucial. Each bad year, or even a moderate year, could mean starvation and the need for parish relief. Market prices reflected competition of extra food production and a growing population, so inflation occurred easily, especially if a poor harvest or a harsh winter ensued. In 1545-57, the currency was seriously debased, prices rose 200%, and wages in the west of England barely increased. The wage earner immediately began to face another factor putting him at a disadvantage, compared to some other workers in the countryside, such as craftsmen who could ask more for their work, and farmers who raised prices.

Poor Law

After the Black Death of 1349, legislation against idleness and vagabondage was passed by Parliament, the first official recognition that such conditions of life existed in England. But no effort was made or funds allotted to relieve any person who suffered either state. Then people began to move away from the family or community seeking work or land, and the problem of poverty became more visible. By 1388 legislation was passed, stating firmly that the liability for helping the impoverished or destitute lay in local organization; it was not to be a national responsibility. This liability, again stated in 1495, prevailed until the 19th century. The parliamentary statutes of 1391 and 1403 nudged the bishops to see their churches set aside money from parochial revenues for alms, but the sums were always very meagre. Some churchgoers organized customs such as holy loaf and the giving of bread and ale to the poor at certain times of the year. In the mid-15th century, churchwardens are supposed to have kept a parish box for donations, to be distributed at their discretion, but records of how many did are non-existent.

About 40 monastic houses and hospitals run by the Church provided the only in-house health care for the Wiltshire agriculturist in the late medieval period, and that care of rudimentary form, due to lack of medical knowledge and finance. Both houses and hospitals were scattered around the county and due to absence of transport, could only have served a local nearby population or walking cases. Nearly 20 hospitals are listed in 1536 before the Dissolution, mainly clustered in towns. Bradford on Avon, Calne, Cricklade and Wootton Bassett each boasted one. Other towns, Salisbury, Devizes Marlborough, Malmesbury and Wilton had more than one each and were comparatively well served. Only the hospitals at Great Bedwyn and Easton would have served a strictly rural population. Presumably at the Reformation these hospitals ceased operation, the new Church of England unable to fill the gaps left by the disappearance of the monasteries and most of the hospitals.

The major source of charity is likely to have remained within the network of family and neighbours who tried to look after their elderly and sick; presumably everyone else worked until he or she could no longer do so. The only form of in-village charity to emerge later was individuals' bequests held and managed by the local church. In the case of widows, custom allowed a poor widow to sublet or lease her land if she was unable to farm it. The practice of dower gave widows the right to keep one-third of their husband's land, sometimes a rental agreement allowed her the whole tenancy. But if land was involved, manorial provisos often existed, stating that the widow remain continent and that only family live in her house, male friends or lodgers definitely not permitted! Some widows took to making and selling ale from their doorstep, and laws encouraged them to do so as an alternative to penury. Orphaned children were likely to be taken in by their family relatives, while servants often had their children or child with them in their employ.

In 1535 Parliament passed what may be considered the first Poor Law of England, which gave authority to churchwardens and constables of the parish to administer relief from church alms, but it did not give any specific means as to how the alms were to be obtained. Permission came in 1572, when parishes were allowed to levy Poor Rates and appoint 'Collectors for the Poor,' (later called Overseers) to gather and distribute the monies raised. In one Wiltshire parish, Lacock, the first account books show money raised, amount in hand, monies laid out, and yearly remainders. In 1590 for instance, £13 was raised, nearly £19 was in hand and, after pay-outs, 18s remained. Between 1590 and 1600 Lacock doled out to its poor an average of £10 a year. As the years went by, more detail on how the monies were spent and particulars on the life and travails of the agricultural labourers in Lacock parish begin to emerge from the account books; these will be recounted later.

In some ways, a growing handicap for the agricultural labourer came about from the new Protestant belief in the work ethic. Labour was the alternative to poverty, whether work was available or not (an ethic which welfare authorities today still try to put in effect at times). Therefore if he or she could not find work, a lazy person was implied. Gradually through the 16th century, hostility against the poor began, mainly because of their visibility and the fear of losing one's job to them. The local labourer resented the job competition and he probably begrudged parish monies spent on vagrants or those locals who, for various reasons, could not work, because of sickness, disability or just lack of employment. Towards the end of the 1500s, due to rising population, penniless war veterans and increasing lack of work on the land, vagrancy increased, as both men and women went 'on the road' to seek work. Wiltshire is likely to have seen many such people, having a larger percentage of rural population than most southern counties, a large cultivated area therefore attracting job seekers, and being crisscrossed by the major routes coming and going in all directions. All meant competition for local labourers of both sexes.

Those who had no means, if injured, permanently sick or disabled, had few alternatives but to send their children out to work early, obtain a maintenance order from their manorial lord if common custom allowed this, ask help from their working offspring, or failing all or any of these means, continue to work for as long as possible. The old so-called right of building a small dwelling between sunset and sunrise on a piece of waste land and therefore being allowed to occupy it free of harassment or rent, by the 16th century apparently was to be well exercised, despite opposition from land owners and sometimes local residents.

The 1590s were a particularly harrowing for the rural poor of Wiltshire the majority of them farm workers. Wages were roughly 7d a day in summer and 6d in winter, (bread a penny a loaf), conditions stressful due to fewer jobs, little protection from destitution, and several bad harvests. Wheat prices increased tenfold, wages increased hardly at all. People were dying in the streets from lack of nourishment. Conditions were so bad that in response to a government order in 1595, the Vicar of Lacock and '4 substantial householders' (a JP and three yeomen farmers) each lent 40s for poor relief. It was not to be fully repaid out of the church funds for eight years, doubtless due to the longevity of the bad times.

A system of charitable distribution, carried out by local ecclesiastical authorities, settled into place by the beginning of the 17th century and would be the only source of official charity available to the underemployed or destitute labourer until the 1830s. The need for Poor Law relief continued in Wiltshire into the 20th century, though parishes ceased administering it to all intents and purposes after 1834. Many flaws existed in the system from the very beginning. Local administration of the Poor Laws meant each parish had to raise its own money for the poor, which varied from parish to parish, hence the amount distributed was uneven, as the wealth of each parish varied. Church officials, wardens and overseers had become Poor Law administrators, whether they liked it or not, and were bequeathed great power as they controlled who received the pay-outs. And some, according to records, seemed devoid of the ability to incorporate any humanity into the system; but that is a 21st century judgement, from a perspective of radically changed values, and not a fair one when so little relief money existed. Almost certainly overseers were constantly having to work with a situation amounting to triage, having to make crucial decisions on when and how to pay out the monies available and to whom. The most critical flaw from the agricultural labourers' point of view, however, was the means available to a parish to obtain the monies for the relief of the poor. The source, rateable property owners, in the overwhelmingly rural parishes of Wiltshire, signified local farmers, therefore their employers. The fox had access to the hen house at will. The system ensured that in time it would become financially more feasible for a farmer to keep wages to a minimum, discharge a man when no work existed for him and have him paid minimum relief rates, rather than employ him full-time.

How well the Poor Laws were administered in Wiltshire deserves a careful study of rural parish records. It certainly varied from parish to parish, depending on the skill and humanity of the administrators, local wealth and local politics. Unfortunately neither JPs nor church officials could administer the laws objectively; they always had some kind of land, legal or monetary interest of their own involved with any relief action or ruling. In 1563 a statute put the power of assessing wage rates into the hands of the employer class and those assessments were later to be confirmed by JPs. In Wiltshire the latter realized that they were legally unenforceable, and so nothing more was heard of them.

Other difficulties of administration constantly appeared. JPs, while commanded to monitor the laws, could be appealed to by the recipients of relief pay-outs who felt that they had suffered unfair treatment, but as leading citizens, often landlords, JPs were almost always on the side of the farmers. Dealing with local administrators, a complaining recipient and his family could easily be marked as a persistent trouble-maker. To discourage the lingering of passing vagrants and to absolve responsibility for them, whether male or female, the parish wherein they begged had legal rights to immediately force them back to their home or birth parish, besides having them whipped, as a punishment for trying to remain. If their home parish was outside Wiltshire, they would be moved to the county border, to be passed on by other county parishes to their destination. Lacock administration seemed comparatively kind, giving care to the vagrant if very pregnant, sick, or otherwise unable to travel, but this meant relief monies taken from local mouths, and would be sure to stir up resentment among parish residents.

Beginning in 1597 and probably induced by the difficulties caused by poor harvests, codifying Acts had gone into effect and laid out a basis for poor relief: supporting almshouses, to be created for those who could not work - the old, sick and disabled; work to be

Woodcut of beggars, published in 1621 on the title page of John Taylor's, The Praise of Beggery.

provided for the destitute but able-bodied man, woman and child parishioners who were unemployed; an apprenticeship scheme to be run for children; punishment for those who could, but did not work. With the slender funds available, none of these requirements of the acts could be fulfilled at first, humanely or inhumanely. To quote one writer, the Poor Laws became 'a long slide into unimaginative impotence.' After all, what could be more unimaginative and expensive than to order a person back to his own parish to be relieved?

In time, however, parishes levied poor rates, appointed overseers, set the poor to fabricated tasks and placed children out to work or into an apprenticeship. Lacock tried to fulfill the work orders by establishing a bakery, which never produced a profit. The parish did not issue raw materials for the poor to work on in their homes, such as hemp, flax, wool, thread, iron or other goods as suggested, mainly, no doubt, because few of the materials were available in the parish, except wool, and to supply that would have caused much resentment from the many Lacock wool weavers. Here is yet another illustration of conflicting administration difficulties always facing hard-put overseers.

As the 17th century progressed, an increasing proportion of the population became dependent upon wages or poor relief for the major part of its livelihood. By 1641 a contemporary report estimated that one quarter of the inhabitants of most parishes in England were miserable and poor, except at hay and harvest time, without any sustenance.

In 1696 labourers, cottagers and paupers supposedly made up nearly half the population of England, 47%. The farmer, increasingly having to work with larger external markets, continued to economize on wages. Prices steadily rose through most of the period, so more men and their families who had been self-sufficient, were thrown on the labour market. Never enough jobs existed, particularly on the Chalk, so the Poor Law administration became an ever-increasing factor in labourers' lives.

Just the mention of the Poor Law frightened people. And that fear still remained in the 20th century. As a child in the 1930s, a housemaid told me of her parents' dread of ending up in Chippenham Workhouse when her father became too old to be employed. Fortunately, the old age pension had come to their rescue, plus contributions from their working offspring. Working at Cocklebury a decade later, farm labourers related stories told by their grandparents of Overseers' begrudging charity to local families suffering hunger in the first half of the 1820s. Hopefully, people of the Western world will never know such fears again, but once experienced, they are remembered for generations.

Wattle and daub – frequently found in Wiltshire dwellings from medieval times until the late 19th century.

Besides workless and hungry people, the parishes also had to provide medical care for the chronically sick, the disabled and the mentally impaired. Early Lacock parish records give some expenditures, showing the sick and infirm nursed in their own homes by others paid to do it from church funds for the poor, or they were boarded out to neighbours' houses. Villagers obviously had to depend for medical care mainly on the local midwife, a barber-surgeon if close by, folklore, the local herbalist or a walk to the nearest town, if able to do so. Home visits by doctors to poor rural people would not occur until after Poor Law reform in 1834.

The Poor Law as administered, tends to make gloomy reading, and in 1592, in Shakespeare's *Henry VI, part II*, one of his characters observed 'it was never merry world in England since gentlemen came up.' But in the next chapter it will be seen that despite the hard work and setbacks villagers endured over trying times, their lives were not all drudgery. Holy days provided festivities, ale celebrations and other money raisers held in the local church certainly provided camaraderie, while contributing to the self-esteem and unification of the community. Sports and other recreational activities, even poaching, played an enjoyable part of in laborers' lives, and within the ale-houses, despite puritanical opposition, many relaxed after their toils.

Chapter 5 Bibliography

Volume IV of the *Victoria County History of Wiltshire* gave much guidance for agricultural matters in this and my other chapters . Volumes four onwards of *Agricultural History of England and Wales,* gave me helpful direction, particularly in the relationship between agriculture and economy after the 16th century through to the 20th century.

The following books provided an insight into aspects of Wiltshire agriculture in the 16th and early 17th centuries:
BETTEY, J., 2005, *Wiltshire Farming in the Seventeenth Century,* Wiltshire Record Society 57
*KERRIDGE, E., 1970, *Agrarian Problems in the Sixteenth Century and After.* Allen and Unwin
THWAITES, J., *circa* 1992, *The History of the Wiltshire Horn Breed of Sheep.* Privately published.

Some of the earliest reports and concepts of social behaviour in rural Wiltshire can be found in:
INGRAM, H., 1987, *Church Courts, Sex and Marriage in England 1570-1640.* Cambridge University Press.
The agricultural labourer began to be more socially active (or he was documented more fully?) in the 16th and 17th centuries. The writings of A. M. Everitt gave me background to the Wiltshire scene, while the books and papers cited below provided more specific detail for this chapter and Chapter 6:
ALLAN, D., 1952, The Rising in the West 1628-31. *EcHR* 5, 1, 76-85
CHARLESWORTH, A., 1983, *An Atlas of Rural Protest in Britain 1548-1900.* University of Pennsylvania Press
KERRIDGE, E., 1958, The Revolts in Wiltshire Against Charles I. *WANHM* 57, 64-75

STAPLETON, B (ed). 1992, *Conflict and Community in Southern England*. NY: St Martin's Press

SPUFFORD, M., (ed). 1994, *World of Rural Dissenters 1520-1725*. Cambridge University Press

YOUNG, G M., 1944, Some Wiltshire cases in Star Chamber. *WANHM* 50, 446-51

I am indebted to the series of books published by the Wiltshire Building Record, documenting aspects of the county's housing, and particularly to the ever-present help of their author, Pamela Slocombe. Two further studies contributed knowledge of very early dwelling-places for rural laborers:

GIBBS, E., 1986, *A Walk Around the Deserted Medieval Village of Sheldon*. Privately Published

MUSTY, J., and ALGAR, D., 1986, Excavations at the deserted medieval village of Gomeldon, near Salisbury. *WANHM* 80, 127-69

For information of Poor Law Relief supplied by Wiltshire parishes from the 16th century to 1834, the chief study is:

HINTON, F. H., 1940. Notes on the administration of the relief of the poor in Lacock, 1583-1834. *WANHM* 49, 166-218

A world of contradictions, ushered in by the Civil War: woodcut from John Taylor's 1642 pamphlet, Mad Fashions, Od Fashions.

6
Downhill all the way

'No-one has written his signature more plainly across the countryside; but no one has left more scanty records of his achievement. A few lawsuits , a handful of wills and inventories, a few manorial surveys, subsidy assessments, royal commissions and parish registers, a few contemporary observations.'

The Civil War 1642-46

Since 1629 Charles I had constantly quarrelled with parliament over taxes, religion and his own powers of monarchy. Gradually these disputes spread to the countryside and in a few places had even led to violence, but the west of England remained quiescent. By the eve of the Civil War, the aristocracy and clothiers of Wiltshire had aligned themselves, supporting either the King or the parliament, roughly a division of Anglicanism and Catholicism or Puritanism. The county also expressed itself geographically, generally the chalk supporting the royalist cause, the cheese more comfortable with parliamentarian concepts.

Unfortunately, except for the Clubmen's activities (see below) which led protests at the very end of the Civil War against the fighting of both royalists and parliamentarians, very little consideration has been given to the effect of the war on the common man in Wiltshire, particularly those in rural areas. Neither is there a great deal of information on the war's long-term social and economic effects on him. But the Civil War years, 1642-46, caused great uncertainty in the everyday lives of Wiltshire people as royalist and parliamentarian troops crossed and re-crossed the county. Writing two centuries later, Canon Daniels, vicar of Langley Fitzurse, described how civil war activities around Chippenham frequently disrupted normal existence. The troops are recorded as commandeering food, animals, ale, clothing and boots, thereby revealing the material shortages both sides had to endure. The better-off smallholders, rural workers and their families most likely suffered all through the war from petty pilferage; particularly vulnerable to robbery were foods a labouring family might have had in storage – bacon, root vegetables, cheese and preserved goods, while garden crops, poultry or even the family pig could be filched. Isolated cottages were extremely susceptible to looting. Farmers losing more than

a sheep or two were able to claim
compensation. And though both armies often
paid town corporations with promissory
notes, it is doubtful if these were handed out
to the common people. Led by Charles'
commander, General Goring, royalist soldiers
generated much hatred in Wiltshire, as he
gave them free rein to plunder and destroy;
in some incidents, even rape occurred. On
the opposite side, General Fairfax kept a tight
rein on his troops, hence they were better
received by the populace.

Wiltshire, besides hosting several major
battles between the royalists and the
parliamentarians, was also a focus of east-
west and north-south routes spanning the
whole county, so the armies, under varying
commanders, had a great deal of contact with

Shepherd, 1642.

the populace. Apparently those contacts did not change commitments to either side, for
the Wiltshireman's immediate loyalties appeared to be to county, village or community,
King or Parliament came second. 'They care not what government they live under so as
they may plough and go to market.' So said Aubrey, who also maintained that the Cheese
Country people mostly supported the parliamentarians, while those on the chalk, due to
their different character, were royalists, but he may have claimed this to justify his previous
judgement of what he considered two disparate groups, due to terrain and occupation.
This differentiation he also applied in general to the yeoman farmers in both areas. Higher
up in the social scale, the leading families of the county soundly declared their allegiances,
the very wealthiest, the Herberts, the Arundells and the Thynnes, for the King; the less
wealthy, such as the Baytons, for Parliament and Cromwell. The Hungerford family split
their loyalties. But all classes (and town administrators) frequently dealt with both sides
during the course of the war, not only once but often several times, as battles in different
localities resulted in troops having to scatter to the nearest towns or across the countryside
for what shelter and sustenance they could find.

Pockets of local loyalty existed, particularly in towns, which could be defined more
positively than in rural areas where people kept their views and opinions more quietly to
themselves. Salisbury strongly supported the royalists, as did Devizes. Chippenham and
Marlborough inclined more to the parliamentarians. Aubrey blamed much of the area's
puritanism on the vegetation. North Wiltshire, he observed, abounded in 'sour and austere
plants, as sorrel, etc., which makes their humours sour.' But he also had an economic
explanation. In the arable regions, people had to work too hard following the plough to
bother about religion or politics. In the cheese country they had time for such diversions:
'the Bible and ease, for it is now all upon the dairy-grassing and clothing, set their wits a-

running and reforming.' The cloth villages especially, Aubrey felt strongly, were 'nurseries of sedition and rebellion.' However, Highworth, Wootton Bassett and other small market towns of the cheese country showed a tendency to support the King. In the final analysis however, the war years, despite so much contact with both royalist and parliamentary troops, did not, to any extent, change the geography of peoples' original sympathies and leanings.

Besides theft and pilferage, inflation added more deprivation to people's lives, particularly to the labourers who depended on bread as a major source of sustenance. The demand for food and all goods increased as the conflict continued, and due to war conditions, farmers had problems with growing and harvesting their crops and getting their animals to market. Prices rose, but wages did not. Justice of the Peace Sessions records show how difficult it was to move food and other goods to market, making it hard for ordinary people to obtain everyday supplies. At one Wiltshire Quarter Sessions the Justices considered the roads 'very dangerous to travel by reason of interruption of the soldiers' and so decided not to fault anyone for non-appearance at the courts. In 1645 Sessions were not held, 'for the whole of Wiltshire was up in arms and large bodies of soldiers of both sides were stationed and fighting throughout the country.' (For further information on local civil war incidents in the county see *Cocklebury* pages 54-6.)

In May of 1645 the common people, 'the lower orders' as contemporary writers described them, began to stage protests against the war throughout southern and western counties. In Dorset and Wiltshire the actions of Goring's army proved a major provocation. Protesters called for meetings in Wiltshire at Harnham Hill, Stonehenge, Upavon, Whiteparish and in villages between Salisbury and Shaftesbury, all rural areas on the edge of the chalk. The Clubmen, as they called themselves, did not support either the royalists or the parliamentarians, they declared themselves neutral, while protesting against the destruction of property and requisition of goods by both armies. The fear that their old community customs and religious lives would be undermined is thought to have played a large part in their protests. The movement spread and Wiltshire Clubmen met and resisted royalists in Pewsey Vale. More Clubmen allied with their Somerset counterparts and marched to the top of Lansdown, to meet Prince Rupert, the King's cousin, accompanied by one of his generals. There they rejected the Prince's overtures. Later, Clubmen attacked men of both armies in several places, only to suffer defeat, but not subjugation. In the following year, Clubmen kept active, undoubtedly creating some excitement in normally torpid villages.

A few months before the war ended, in the summer of 1646, troops had come to Market Lavington, seeking monetary contributions towards the royalist cause. They ran into much objection from the locals who rang the church bells to alert nearby villagers. According to contemporary reports, one thousand Clubmen supporters walked to Devizes to gather and protest in the Market Place. In addition, other skirmishes between royalists and Wiltshire Clubmen took place at nearby Calstone Wellington and Wootton Rivers. The rural flavour of the Clubmen makes it certain that agricultural labourers involved themselves in these activities, particularly in North Wiltshire, where their employers were more likely to sympathise with the parliamentarians than the royalists. But these protests seemingly made little difference to the last few months of the Civil War in the county, or indeed to the years of parliamentary rule that followed. The puritans abhorred rural amusements and managed to suppress some of them. The Church of England, particularly in the Cheese Country, lost more of its influence to nonconformity. A growing trend before the conflict years, the dissent was to gain even more strength after the Restoration in 1660. By then the deeds of the Clubmen were no doubt forgotten; other problems had arisen that called for protest.

Aftermath of Civil war

The cessation of battles, plunderings and lives in danger no doubt left Wiltshire people thankful and hoping to resume the peaceful life they had enjoyed before 1642. Unfortunately, post-war conditions brought new tribulations, especially to rural life. Vagrants wandering the roads were not an unusual sight in Wiltshire; to these were now added ex-soldiers without means. Some of these, if able-bodied, competed for employment on the Wiltshire farms. The processes of enclosure and consolidation of farms began again, particularly to be pursued in the Cheese Country. And wages still did not keep pace with prices. These factors the labourer could see before him, but there were others, mainly economic and far more complex, which were to cause him much continual hardship and to eventually set in place a gradual fall in his living standards over the next two centuries.

The Civil War had greatly stimulated the Wiltshire economy despite the difficulties of increasing production due to war conditions. Afterwards, the woollen trade resumed its previous vigour, later to expand into silk making, to become the largest employer of labour in the county, except for agriculture. Market towns grew through the 17th and 18th centuries, as the country's whole population doubled from an estimated 5½ million in 1600 to 11 million in 1801, the first year of the census. Better methods of cultivation increased yields on Wiltshire farms, especially of cheese, corn and meat. The new laws passed to regulate the services supplied by inns and ale-houses showed an increase in their numbers, another indication of prosperity. This economic growth bypassed labourers to benefit mainly the larger landowners, farmers, tenants, merchants, and, presumably, local craftsmen. Some smallholders continued, though many probably lived not far above subsistence level. Most are likely to have worked part-time on a larger nearby farm at haymaking and harvest time. Share milking and sheep herding provided a living for some families. For the cloth and agricultural workers, financial difficulties in their lives continued; both groups were ill-paid, and the concept of paying an adequate or living wage had yet to be thought of by either an employer or employee. A wage was considered the lowest possible sum a master could pay to a workman without protest. The workman, in turn, was not in a position to bargain except occasionally at haymaking or harvest time, and had to accept what he was offered. So both men and women and certainly children (the employment of children on Wiltshire farms is still an obscure subject until the middle of the 19th century, but can be taken for granted) were hired cheaply and discarded at will, unless they were employed by contract, usually for a year. If a farmer and worker got on well, both fulfilling their obligations to each other, and the worker remained quiescent, it is likely they remained together for long periods of employment, perhaps even for their lifetimes, but at the time, how common was such a relationship cannot be ascertained.

Briefly summarized known wage statistics for the Wiltshire agricultural labourer in general show him earning 4d a day in the period 1450-1550. By 1650 he was able to earn 1s (12d) a day, but due to market forces the cost of living rose so high that his purchasing power dropped by 50%. Between 1650 and 1750 wages rose and prices dropped, but by then other factors had to be reckoned. He was steadily losing access to land which grew him extra food; the unprecedented population growth and more intensive farming, especially on the chalk, lessened the work available to him. So his standard of living again declined. The Napoleonic Wars, beginning in 1793, caused further price rises, especially of bread, then starting to be the crucial index for the labourer. By 1800, his wages could be as high as 1s 6d a day, but prices rose nearly twofold, so he was worse off than ever before.

The 18th century began to see the start of a tradition of paying a lower wage to farm labourers than to any other type of workers in Wiltshire. As a consequence, a widening of the already social and economic gap between master and servant increased, not to begin reversal until the 20th century; as farmers became more prosperous, the lot of their labourers proportionally diminished. A good master and regular work is far more likely to have happened in the cheese than the chalk areas, due to the nature of stock farming. It needed daily labour and contact, in contrast to grain cultivation, where work was spasmodic and men could easily be laid off several times during the farming year; so unemployment, whether partial or total, was a constant factor. The farmer was not always to blame; it was said in the 19th century that an efficient farmer on the chalk, if he had planned correctly, was always able to find enough work to keep his labourers employed all year round. But as

early as the 17th century Wiltshire farmers began to face a competitive market; to farm became more expensive as new innovations and ways of cropping evolved; cutting wages was just a part of business, humanism did not come into it. Any surplus profits were invested as capital into the farm, not to be expended as costs which gave no apparent return, except a more contented labourer, another concept seemingly not considered of much worth. Old-fashioned paternalism, the little there was of it, first of the monastery and manor, then of the early farmers before they entered a market economy, began to fade out in Wiltshire. Aubrey never mentioned it, except to say ploughmen lost their occupations by enclosure and were hence impoverished. From the 17th century, the landless labourer was well into becoming a separate social class of the countryside, poor, to be only tolerated for his work by people of classes above him. Low wages became acceptable and protesting in Wiltshire was seldom about pay rates, it was mainly about politics, enclosure and food shortages.

Labourer chopping down tree, 17th century.

Countrywoman with pattens, 1640.

The Civil War had prised open further the split between the two parties that had brought it about. The tendency to puritanism by the ruling parliamentarians after the war, enlarged the split and in 1655 supporters of the exiled Charles II organized a revolt against Cromwell's regime. Amongst several small uprisings in the south, one originated in Wiltshire, organized by a John Penruddock, who lived near Salisbury, and who considered himself a member of the local gentry; amongst his few hundred supporters were small farmers, agricultural and other workers. Badly-led and coordinated, most of the participants soon encountered arrest just outside Salisbury, but Penruddock managed to flee and Cromwell's troops chased him into Devon. Once captured, without attempting to bring him back to Wiltshire, the parliamentarians immediately had him sentenced and executed.

As a result of these protests, Cromwell divided England into twelve military districts, each ruled by a major-general. Greatly resented by all, this militant approach to law and order, particularly its attempt to impose rules against immorality and irreligion, sent up a warning signal to beware of extreme governmental measures and religious fanaticism. It may have contributed to the apparent acquiescence shown in Wiltshire when Charles II returned to the throne five years later. Certainly no objections are on record, not even in areas considered puritan strongholds.

Those persons in Wiltshire who had supported the parliamentarians during the Civil War may have continued to support Cromwell for several years, but resentment against the throne died down as the Commonwealth's rule became increasingly severe. Charles II made the Restoration more acceptable when the monarchy encouraged the revival of the old sports and pastimes, relaxed restrictions on ale-houses and did not deal harshly with dissent and nonconformity. When Charles' illegitimate son, the Duke of Monmouth, landed at Lyme Regis in 1685 in his attempt to claim the throne from James II, he gained no support from Wiltshire people, not even in the strongly Catholic area of the Wardour estates. Only the Thynne family at Longleat declared for Monmouth, perhaps influenced by support from nearby counties south and west of Wiltshire.

If the agriculture labourer took part in any protest in Wiltshire during the next 80 years, none seems to have been recorded, though cloth workers demonstrated at times. In the 1740s, several bad harvests, an epidemic of rinderpest among cattle and terrible winters caused protestations in other parts of England, but the county remained quiet. Not in 1766, however, when heavy rains in the Spring and Summer led to a poor harvest, with especially low yields of wheat. An economic depression already reigned in the cloth areas and a threat that wheat would be sold outside the county led to protests.

Disorder spread from the Gloucestershire cloth-making areas into Wiltshire in early September. People began to march to combat the threat of grain leaving the area. Troops from Salisbury created order at Bradford, but farther north near the county border protesters marched in an area curving from Malmesbury to East Tytherton and Wootton Bassett. The march encompassed villages where people had previously protested at the time of the Bradford uprising. Their targets seemed to be mainly the large local dealers in corn and provisions. The disturbances ceased when the government adopted a previous embargo on grain being moved from local areas and had grain returned from the London markets. Though there is some contention as to whether farm workers actually participated in these disturbances in Wiltshire, as in all villages, most inhabitants were linked to work on the land, so the agricultural labourer can hardly have avoided demonstrating. To curb subsequent disorder and to set an example, seven men were executed and 57 convicted as felons in the county's courts.

The agricultural labourer himself – Aubrey

No book on the Wiltshire agricultural labourer is complete without John Aubrey's observations on him and the countryside he lived in. Aubrey, born in 1626, had grown up on the limestone in the northwest corner of the county between Malmesbury and Chippenham. He felt certain that agriculturists took on particular characteristics depending on geography and the work they did. He divided them into two groups, those residing in the north of the country and those living on the chalk.

He described the Cheese Country dwellers as living in a dirty clayey area, having pale skins, often deep(gallipot) black eyes, general plumpness and the characteristic of being 'feggy,' (handsome enough), with 'drawling' speech. He did not have a high opinion of their character. Their heaviness of spirit, phlegmaticism, slowness and dullness, he blamed on their high consumption of dairy foods, which cooled their brains too much and hurt their 'inventions.' 'These circumstances make them melancholy, contemplative and malicious; by consequence whereof come more law suites out of North Wilts, at least double to the southern parts.' They also tended to be fanatical and inhospitable. Attributes of laughter and cheer receive no mention whatsoever, but Aubrey explained it as all due to the area being ' a woodsere country, abounding with much sowre and austere plants, as sorrel, &c. Which makes their humours sowre, and fixes their spirits. In Malmesbury Hundred, &c. (ye wett clayy parts) there have ever been reputed witches.'

To the men of the downlands he gave a different aspect of character, though still much linked to sobriety. They were industrious, but weary from hard labour, so weary they had no contemplation for religion. A curious comment, considering the Wiltshire Downs had bred many secret heretics and in Aubrey's time had begun to show strong leanings towards nonconformity. But no doubt they still often had to be secretive, especially in closed villages. On the chalklands, he sums up the native character succinctly: 'The south part, where 'tis all upon tillage, and where the shepherds labour hard, their flesh is hard, their bodies strong: being weary after hard labour, they have not the leisure to read and contemplate of religion, but goe to bed to their rest, to rise betime the next morning to their labour.'

Forest dwellers, according to Aubrey, avoided many of the problems employed labourers faced. 'Given to little or no kind of labour, living very hardly with oaten bread, sour whey, and goat's milk, dwelling far from any church or chapel, [they] are as ignorant of God or of any civil course in life as the very savages amongst the infidels...'and 'For the people born amongst the woods, are naturally more stubborn and uncivil than in the champion countries.' These remarks certainly signify that the Wiltshire forests in his time still bred a very different labourer from those on chalk or pasture countryside.

Security and Social issues for the Agricultural Labourer

Property and land rights have meant security to man throughout history. When one considers how many Wiltshire smallholders and holders of common-rights had their land taken from them by sale or enclosure from the 16th century onwards, to be reduced to labouring, their lives and those of their families take on a particular poignancy. Court cases illustrate the attachment the labourer had to his land (and often too, his stock and tools); an attachment still held by landholders today, as shown by the value we place in land ownership and the infighting we engage in, when necessary, over boundary and property rights.

At this period of his history, the labourer still took a pride in his work. According to contemporary sources such as agricultural writers, his skills gave him self-esteem: sheep shearing and successful lambing, hedge laying, thatching, even threshing corn, one of the most unpleasant jobs on the farm, being dusty, tiring, monotonous. Valued by all while the community depended on them, these skills were passed on down the generations by father to son to grandson.

But the 18th century also produced another kind of writer of the labouring scene, termed at the time labouring or peasant muses, a few (of both sexes) who produced poetry describing their lives of toil, trying to show how hard a worker's life could be. To be published they had to soft-pedal their message to reassure their audience they did not aspire to the pursuits of the upper class and agreed with the contemporary concept that the poor were born to labour, views that no doubt gave them great conflict of mind. They were cautious to uphold social values of honesty, industry and piety and made plain a practical imagery of country life, avoiding the poetic, rural, idyllic existence. They might be considered pre-cursors or informers to the reform movement, which began in England after the French Revolution of 1789. One of the earliest poets was a Wiltshireman, Stephen Duck, perhaps a yeoman, perhaps a labourer, (his origins are hard to sort out) who achieved prominence in 1730 with a poem, 'The Thresher's Labour,' literally describing the work of those who laboured on the farms. His poem paid short shrift to women field workers and nine years later, in a specific answer to Duck's poem, appeared 'The Woman's Labour' by Mary Collier, who described herself as a washerwoman from Hampshire. Both poems are worth reading for their descriptions of manual labour and the workers' feelings and aspirations, but Collier's poem strikes a modern chord, still applicable to a working woman's life today, as she graphically described their long hours given to family care, before and after a day's work in the fields.

At the same time that peasant muses struggled to pen and convey their message, the labourers' work had begun to be undervalued or taken for granted, and both male and

Shepherd, circa 1650-1700.

female toilers were looked upon as a menial class doing menial tasks, an attitude to continue into the 20th century.

Even after the 1930s this viewpoint still occasionally surfaced, and it certainly did when I began my training in agriculture as a labourer at Cocklebury farm in 1943. Some people treated me as a social contaminate, whose parents had made a dreadful mistake in allowing me to work alongside farm labourers. But the skills I learnt, milking, carting, scything, caring for horses, poultry and pigs, tractor driving and towing various implements, I was really proud to accomplish and do. And my regard for anyone who did farm work increased correspondingly. Thankfully, such attitudes have changed. To work on the land is a respected calling with status, though sadly the future is still economically uncertain.

The amount of work required by the agricultural labourer and his work environment always has presented problems to him. Weather in Wiltshire is frequently uncomfortable for outside work; it is too often wet, cold, windy, and occasionally, too hot. Farm work, when powered by human or animal energy, is always exhausting after a few hours. I may have taken a pride in my skills, but when doing tiring work, one had little time to really think or observe one's surroundings. Our well-being depended so much on the weather; when cold or wet, nothing was really pleasurable on the farm, except going home when the work was done, or, on a dairy farm, getting to the milking shed. There, despite the draughts and rain sometimes beating in, depending on the direction of the wind, one was next to a warm animal and in the companionship of other milkers. Comfort doing farm work also depended on one's muscles, however fit; if a job took all one's strength, it was onerous after the first hour to have to continue with it until done. And on the farm, especially a dairy farm, jobs nearly always had to be completed; no matter what the hour, one had to stay and finish. Certainly this applied always at haymaking and harvesting, sometimes done by moonlight during the double summertime days of WWII! No labourer could guarantee what time he would arrive home and get his evening meal. Notoriously, farmers always took advantage of their labourers' time and energies, despite their own always long working hours, often twelve hours a day, more at haymaking and harvest, right up to the 1950s.

The earliest agricultural manuals, dating from the 16th century, frequently mentioned the sluggishness of farm workers. But farm labourers in reality were not slow and slothful, they just knew how to pace themselves to get through the whole working day, week and year. Every man, woman and child realized that they would never last out the day if they did not pace themselves, the work was so arduous. In a rural community, with few people and little input from the outside world, life was naturally slow; one lived by the light, not the clock, the daily and seasonal demands of family, crops and animals being the chief concern of everyone. Beginning in the middle 1700s, the wages of the Wiltshire farm labourers were often not high enough to provide nourishing food, clothes and warm shelter for himself and his family. His work habits became slower and this phenomenon is constantly mentioned in literature of the day. The criticism was doubly cruel, as dim-wittedness, procrastination, laziness and other shortcomings blamed were rarely true. Farmers at Avebury in 1794 concerned with their labourers' lack of output tried to discipline them by threatening to extend working hours. Whether they were successful cannot be determined, perhaps retreat was the better part of valour on the farmers' part.

At the same time Avebury farmers voiced their objections, Thomas Davis, an acute observer of agricultural England, wrote of Wiltshire labourers as 'slow, strong and robust.' He added, however, 'farmers are great sufferers of the habitual indolence of their workmen.' Here was a typical class statement, but to give Davis his due, he did mention their low wages, subsistence living and shortage of fuel. A Dorset farmer, James Warne, kept a diary in 1758. He documented how he hired his labourers, often quite casually, then dismissed them for what he considered disobedience and sloth, which, from his descriptions of the circumstances, they may well have exhibited. These men Warne wrote of were far more defiant than the seemingly passive Wiltshire labourers one reads of repeatedly. Dorset men continued to have a reputation more active than their neighbours, especially in the 1830s during the Captain Swing movement and later efforts to establish unions, resulting in the sagas of the Tolpuddle martyrs.

During the 17th and 18th centuries the Wiltshire agricultural labourer's loyalty seems to have been first to his family and community, sometimes to his employer, depending on his treatment, certainly to the animals he cared for. It then extended outwards to county, king, maybe country, (but that is a guess, no evidence exists of the extent of his patriotism) and religion. Custom, tradition, inheritance, rules of cultivation and animal husbandry, the use of his skills; such rights as fuel collecting, use of footpaths, some mild poaching, the local ale-house, sports and pastimes, all these gave security to his life. In these centuries the Wiltshire agricultural labourer likely can be divided into three types, the husbandman, the skilled, (sometimes) contract worker, and the unskilled day worker. Commenting in the late 19th century the writer Richard Jefferies wrote:

> work for the cottager must be work to please him; and to please him it must be the regular sort to which he is accustomed, which he did besides his father as a boy, which his father did, and his father before him; the same old plough or grub-axe, the same milking, the same identical mowing, if possible in the same field. He does not care for any new-fangled jobs. He does not recognize them, they have no locus standi- they are not established.

Though this observation was somewhat out of date when written and Jefferies had biases while being prone to recognizing only certain facets of the labourers' lives, it no doubt had applied to many generations of Wiltshire workers. Despite increased output on the Wiltshire farms between the Civil War and the end of the 18th century, and the new crops grown, on the whole the work changed very little for our labourer, especially for the small or share-holder, who was unlikely to have any access to capital for changes or improvements on the little land he worked.

In Wiltshire the chief grain crops were wheat, barley (a bigger crop in the south than in the north) and oats, a little rye. Peas and beans were also cultivated and the end of the 17th century saw the introduction of turnips, swedes and rape. Potatoes came a century later, a very unpopular vegetable until starvation drove people to accept them because of their cheapness to grow and their high crop yields. The work involved in ploughing, harrowing, rolling, seeding, weeding and harvesting had remained basically the same for several thousand years, except for the introduction of metal tools, oxen for ploughing and certain forms of cultivation, and later when horse power came on the scene, more metal implements and wooden carts. Grass for hay was cut with a scythe, ripened grain stalks cut with a sickle, often by women until the 18th century, when the scythe began to replace the sickle, and hence the work became too heavy for women to do, except in very short spells. But women still assisted with the threshing, using the traditional and very laborious method of flailing with a swing stick attached by a leather loop to the end of another stick.

Animal manure remained the main source of fertilizer until the very end of the 18th century. The labourer's work with animals encompassed sheep, cows, beef cattle, oxen and horses. Harness for cart horses and oxen held the same set patterns, right through to the 20th century, as did most of the equipment to take care of the animals. The implements on a North Wiltshire dairy farm in the 17th century differed very little from those on Cocklebury Farm used by myself, nine men and the working farmer. Most of our work was done by hand, little was mechanized. Admittedly the threshing machine (the crew made up of two mechanics and several land girls) visited us after the harvest, a puffing Lister pump drove our hay elevator and the two tractors pulled various cultivating equipment – a plough, sometimes a harrow and a roller, sometimes the hay cutter and reaper. With seven horses, five wagons, two dung 'potts' and a little outside labour at harvesting and haymaking, we hand-milked 200 cows, raised pigs, poultry, (and sheep for a short period), brought in grain and vegetable (kale, potato, sugar beet etc.) crops and took good care of the farm. Our work certainly compared equally to that done by the labourers of centuries before us.

At Cocklebury the farmer supplied us with tools, though by preference, one or two men used their own when rick thatching, hedge cutting and laying. The tradition of the

Woman milking, 1640-1700.

agricultural labourer in Wiltshire supplying his own tools for the skilled work of hedging, ditching, hoeing and tree cutting, probably began in the 1600s when the hiring of agricultural labourers began to be competitive, due to excess labour and the farmers' desire to cut costs. Probably every labourer had his tools made by a local blacksmith, individualized to his hand and his particular skills. No doubt this is the reason why so many slight variations of numerous tools had evolved by the early 19th century.

The first simple mechanical tools used on Wiltshire farms are likely to have developed in blacksmiths' workshops. The earliest and most prominent is Robert Reeves, who set up his forge at Bratton about 1774 and whose descendents, by the early 1800s, led the way to greater production by starting a small foundry and making, among other implements, plough shares and corn-drills. By 1848 Reeves had won a silver medal at the Royal Agricultural Show at York; the firm had obviously acquired national prominence. The diversity of Wiltshire agriculture, both arable and dairy, allowed the firm to stay in business for 150 years, despite competition from far larger worldwide enterprises. But in time it was engineers who mainly initiated the making of most equipment in the county, the output of their factories following closely the development of agricultural machinery of the 19th century.

Agrarian Practices and the Agricultural Labourer

In a period of 150 years, some changes in the agriculturist's work were bound to take place. He still continued to exercise his age-old skills in hedging and ditching, haymaking and harvesting, carting, taking care of stock and horses, all the work of the farm that the changing seasons presented. But for some their work narrowed as the production of main crops – corn, sheep and milk   intensified As dairy herds enlarged to 40 cows or more, the cowman concentrated on his cows, and jobs such as carting and ploughing were done by others. On the chalk, carters and ploughmen also became specialists, but a harvester remained a harvester and, out of season, a general worker. Shepherds, certainly skilled labourers, like dairymen, had to work every day, even if they managed a few hours off on Sundays, except in lambing time.

Dairy farms with herds of up to fifteen cows were likely to be run by family labour, or with the help of a live-in dairymaid. On the Chalk, as the farms became bigger and the farmers wealthier, family labour was not used; indeed, on the largest farms, 'the boss' was often not the farmer at all and hired bailiffs managed the farms. On the chalk manors they are likely to have replaced manorial stewards, as the manors gradually lost their authority over their tenants in the 18th century. This tended to increase even more the class and social gap between lord and tenant, labourer and employer, not to mention the income gap. Farm buildings produced other work differences. On dairy farms during the 18th century, cow byres began to be built to accommodate cows at milking time and during the winter months the cows did not always go out into the pastures. This meant no more field milking, making the labourers' and dairymaids' work of milking and feeding the animals in the winter easier and a little warmer. For the cow, she appreciated the warmth of the cowshed, and if she was lucky, being fed at milking time, far more comfortable than being in a cold field or messy yard. When working at Cocklebury Farm it did not take me long to discover that a happy cow is easier to milk. It is sad that farming methods still seldom consider an animal's comfort unless it is profitable to do so.

On the chalk arable farms, the shepherds always had their own routines, quite separate and different from other labourers; they stayed with their flocks on the sheep runs, sometimes so far from the farm house that they seldom saw the other employees. At lambing times they lived and slept in their moveable huts (somewhat like small gypsy caravans), abandoning family life for several weeks. The carters and plough teams on a large farm, 100 acres or more, also had their specific work. General labourers who worked at haymaking and harvest did routine chores around the farm at other times, but the moves towards more intensive agriculture began to create the problem of finding enough work for a farm's labourers during the slow and winter months. By the 18th century, market pressures for cheaper food production caused many farmers, especially in the corn country, to dispense with as much labour as they could, raising unemployment levels to the point where the men had to rely on the Poor Law to keep them and their families during the winter. This custom spread to the Cheese Country, creating serious economic problems for the labourer and much hardship. In addition, hiring for piece-work became more common, adding further wage reductions.

Few figures are available for Wiltshire, but it is definite that some labourers and smallholders supplemented their income in the cloth-making areas by spinning or weaving in their homes, being paid piece-work rates. The spinning was usually women's work, the weaving men's work, because of the heavy frames and skills needed. By 1793, the spinning jenny came into general use in Wiltshire and was used at first in the putting-out system. Within a few years, however, economic savings ensued if machines and workers were accommodated into factory buildings. This meant an income loss to the labourer and to the women on the small family farms. Other local industries in Wiltshire were also likely to have made a contribution to a labourer's household income, included lace-making, straw plaiting, knitting and glove-making. Wives and daughters would have worked at these in the home, the latter as soon as they were old enough to hold the necessary work tools. None of these occupations was practical in isolated areas, as the raw materials had to be distributed and the finished items collected, so it did not pay to put the work out further than a few miles from a central collecting point, usually in a town. Hence Wiltshire, with its small scattered rural population, spawned few home industries, compared to other counties. Aubrey, when discussing the shepherdesses of Salisbury Plain, recalls that many made straw hats before the Civil War, but by 1680 'doe begin to worke point [pillow lace-making], whereas before they did only knit coarse stockings.' (This mention of shepherdesses in Wiltshire, the author finds unique and would welcome information of any other references.)

New Agrarian Practices

The growing of 'industrial' crops, seemingly mainly tried out in the south of the county – tobacco, woad, hemp – for various reasons did not survive more than several decades in Wiltshire, though the introduction of new crops must also have increased the labourer's skills, if only for a short time. For a few years, woad had been grown around the Salisbury area on the rich soils by the rivers, but it proved too labour-intensive to be profitable, and water meadows are likely to have replaced those cropping areas. Some flax growing, turnips, rape and the planting of leys with mixes of rye grasses and clovers persisted, as did cabbages, said by Aubrey to have been introduced at Wimborne St Giles (Dorset) from Holland during the 17th century.

During the 17th century, rabbit warrens with artificial burrows were created as a market proposition, especially on the chalk lands, where well-drained, steep land provided a congenial habitat for the animals. (Referring to rabbits in warrens, coneys described the adults, rabbits referred to those up to six months old.) A warren created by a Bristol businessman at Hazelbury, Box, supplied the household with at least 200 rabbits a year, and other commercial warrens are mentioned, producing from 100-300 rabbits yearly. The animals sold at 6d each, making a warren was a profitable enterprise for a landowner or leaser. The man who looked after it, the warrener, was considered a skilled worker under contract, not part of a farm workforce. Undoubtedly the farm labourer used warren animals as a source of food, poaching for them with ferrets or wires. However, due to escaping animals and the damage they did to crops and hedgerows, over the years warrens became a liability, to be gradually replaced by arable crops.

Large scale development of water meadows as a means to increase early grazing became feasible at the beginning of the 17th century. Constructed by the Wylye, the Salisbury Avon and other chalk streams, water meadows needed a great deal of capital to initiate and so on a large scale was prohibitory for a small farmer. Their yearly care did not come cheap either. The skilled work of primary installation, the grading and ditching of riverside meadows, the creation of hatches to control water flooding and discharge, all were hired out to a contractor, the work supervised by a 'floater' also brought in on contract. The yearly floodings or drownings were mostly carried out by estate or farm laborers, who knew intimately the layout of the individual meadows and who earned as much as 1s 6d a day. The concept spread into the Cheese Country wherever suitable sites occurred; recently evidence of water meadows at Seend has emerged, undoubtedly other sites exist. Seend's Semington Brook ran fast enough to maintain a water meadow system and its affluence at the time is obvious. Large farms, the cloth industry nearby,

A likely site for water meadows at Seend, photographed from Row Lane.

corn mills on the brook, charitable donations to Seend church; all provide clues to prosperous resources.

To induce early grass growth, the meadows were flooded at the beginning of winter and the ever-moving water kept at a depth of about an inch. If a scum formed, the meadows had to be drained and re-flooded, a job requiring some skill, as the flow of the supply river had to be gauged. Draining the meadows in early March allowed the sheep to be put in to graze, no doubt a pleasant change for the shepherd as well as the sheep, both enjoying a change of scenery from the bare sheep runs on the Plain to the warmer river valleys. After a month or so of grazing, the meadows were again floated and drained and allowed to rest to promote the growth of grass for hay. Water meadows, if their silt deposit was rich and adequate, could produce as many as three hay crops in the early summer. Because of the extra food available, more sheep could be carried on the farm, beef and dairy cows grazed until October. Each year the hatches, sluices and drains had to be checked and repaired if necessary, hedges and ditches taken care of, in preparation for the water meadows' yearly cycle. More work was created for labourers, but unfortunately, being seasonal, it was adaptable to piecework and mostly given to casual workers, except perhaps in the case of second and third hay crops, when the regular farm employee was likely to be given the work and paid less, as the hay was harvested out of season.

The Wiltshire villages

By today's standards, Wiltshire villages were small at the beginning of the 17th century, perhaps 100 persons or so at the most, and many smaller rural communities existed, especially in the Cheese Country, where often, over a long period of time, they acquired the title of hamlet. Records tend to confirm a constant population rollover in villages, the major reason being shifts to new employers. Scarcity of employment often forced men away to seek work or take their chance at a hiring fair, or compelled smallholders to sell up and relocate. Girls married and moved too, but marriage patterns changed little until the 19th century in rural Wiltshire; a spouse usually came from within 10 miles, the farthest a working suitor had time to walk, unless much enamoured. Emigration to other continents began in the 17th century, but probably at a very slow rate for Wiltshire. These migration factors, the low life-expectancy, especially among children, suggests a 60% turnabout of village populations within a span of twelve years, but cannot as yet be confirmed for Wiltshire.

Many Wiltshire villages and communities lay away from the beaten track, so visitors were few and tidings of the outside world slow to arrive. Newspapers did not appear until the middle of the 18th century in most rural areas; few read or wrote, so letter carriers had little reason to call. The village is likely to have seen pedlars often, except in mid-winter; they carried packs containing haberdashery, thread, needles, combs, belts and other small personal items for sale. They were certainly greatly welcomed, not only for their goods, but also for news of distant happenings, or just the pleasure of talking to a new face. Other fresh faces came from adherents of small religious groups who travelled to various villages, to speak or lead a cottage service.

Custom and habit endeared people to their community, whether it provided them with an adequate living and shelter or not. Several elements bound villagers together, the efforts to make a living no doubt the chief one, and as long as no outsiders came into the community to dilute the employment pool, a village was likely to have continued for many generations on a fairly even keel. If in want, people looked out for one another. Once strangers came in and robbed locals of work, or numbers of people became too many for the area to support, the balance of the village could be upset and difficulties would have arisen. A major historical event, such as the Civil War, provided another type of upset and distress. These aspects of Wiltshire village life have yet to be studied in detail, Gandy's study of Aldbourne is the nearest we have so far.

Housing

As mentioned previously, it is unlikely that few, if any, 17th or 18th century dwellings housing the agricultural labourer and his family in Wiltshire exist today. They were all small and poorly built, for the simple reason, that the labourer could afford nothing better, and the idea of estates or farmers building cottages for labourers did not develop until the very end of the 18th century. Up to the mid-19th century, any surviving cottages are hard to find; far more noticeable in Wiltshire villages are the those built between c.1860 and 1914.

A day labourer may have built a hut on waste land with the help of neighbours. If employed full time, he is likely to have lived in a village or near his place of employment. On the limestone, his house, if he could afford it, had thin stone rubble walls bonded with a mud-based mortar. If of wood, some kind of a sub-base was not an option, because of cost and lack of materials, so posts were still put straight into the ground. By the 18th century, houses were possibly larger and clay or mortared walls, strengthened with timber made them a little more durable. Sometimes flagstones appeared on the floors and a fireplace replaced a hearth. 'Outsets' – extra lean-to rooms – could be added onto the main walls to serve as extra sleeping space, a larder, or a shelter for a pig, relieving the cramped living quarters of the nearly always large family. Even so, these houses, because of the lack of foundation and invariably poor drainage, still seldom survived longer than a generation or two. (See *Cocklebury* page 47)

The smallholder's cottage may have had an upper floor by the 18th century, or part of one, it seldom had a staircase. I recall in the 1930s an early 19th century cottage at Allington, near Chippenham, with a narrow ladder to a minimal sleeping space, divided into two by a flimsy partition. In rural housing, ladders prevailed for a long time, no doubt due to the expense needed to replace them in such limited space as a cottage offered. The 16th century farmhouse at Cocklebury had a Victorian addition which provided a main staircase, but in the original section, a ladder remained until alterations made in 1928 provided an extra staircase to the original first-storey sleeping area. An early staircase in a farmhouse can certainly be used as an indication of the farm's prosperity and an owner's appreciation of the better things in life!

Records of cottage furnishings and household goods of poor people on relief at Clyffe Pypard in 1767, taken by the overseers and churchwardens of the parish, give a picture of

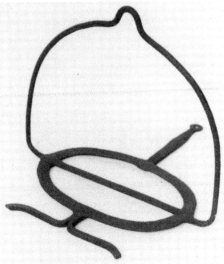

Downhearth with faggot supported on brandirons with matching andirons on each side. Fire backs such as these were expensive, hence not often available to poor households. The faggot was bound together for easy handling and giving a fierce heat. The utensil under the hearth is the essential grisset, 17th century, of cast iron, used for melting fat for rush lights.

A hanging brandis, suspended above the fire, could hold a pot or frying pan

Reflector or Dutch ovens, the shields can be tipped forward. Placed on a trivet and stood in front of a bar grate fire, they served as a simple oven.

A cast iron baking pot known as a spider. Covered with ashes and hot coals, it served as another form of oven for baked goods.

*Five frying pans 18th and
19th centuries*

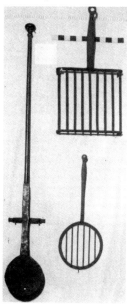

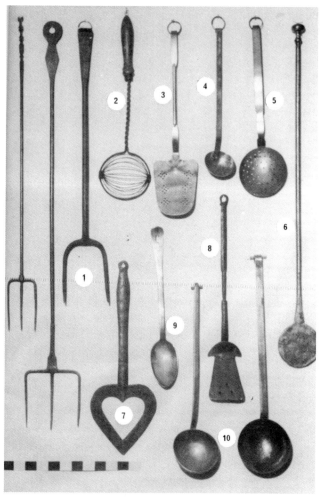

*Common metal instruments, most appearing in the Clyffe Pypard cottage
inventories, including brass skimmer, brass ladle, beef fork, 'culliner'.*

(above) Salamander and grid irons.

*(right) Tinder box, which served as a candle
holder as well. The tinder was usually a piece
of charred linen, and a flint when struck with
the iron steel supplied the spark which was
applied to the linen or a wooden spill dipped in
a sulphur compound to produce a flame.*

the meagre living endured by nearly 50% of the population at the time. Of 21 persons documented, one John Watts owned neither bed nor candlestick, while Ann Swansborough had only a bedstead, bedding, box and chair. Perhaps John slept at a son's or daughter's house, while Ann used a neighbour's household goods. Only one of the poor law recipients had a coal fire grate, unlikely to have burnt coal however, as the cost of that fuel would have been prohibitive in Clyffe Pypard at that time; wood was the fuel used, presumably in a hearth of stones laid on hard earth in a smoke bay, or below a chimney. Others had andirons for wood, with tongs and sometimes a fire shovel. None possessed pokers, a few had bellows.

Almost all owned a dough trough in which they kneaded their bread, probably baked in a shallow pan in the ashes of the wood fires, unless they were lucky enough to have an oven in the hearth recess. For cooking they managed with an iron pot on a hanger and crook over the fire; all had a frying pan. Tin cooking pans and a bacon rack are mentioned. They ate off wooden, pewter or earthenware plates and bowls. A few cooking utensils, forks, ladles and skimmers are listed, but no eating utensils, perhaps too humble to record. So too were tinder boxes, as reference is made to steels which provided the spark for tinder. A knife box and even a grindstone are listed, a sharp knife being an absolute necessity. Teacups and dishes are not surprising, for tea drinking was already a habit of all classes, the leaves sold in a screw of paper for a few pennies. Several had warming pans to take the chill off their bed covers. Four had mirrors. Many had ironing boxes. One man had an oil lamp. All had wooden tubs, probably for washing clothes, perhaps sometimes themselves, if they had enough fuel to heat the required amount of water. Buckets, pails, kettles, barrels, all show the necessity of containers for carrying and keeping water on hand, and wooden bottles may have held other liquids such as beer, which to some was still considered as essential to life as water in our time.

Cupboards are seldom recorded, coffers more common, boxes even more common. Most had bedsteads and bedding. No clocks are listed, but people still lived by sunrise, high noon and sunset times. One close stool (commode) is listed, but no mention of chamber pots appear, perhaps the church wardens valued modesty and were reticent on such matters! Usually only one table appears, with one or two chairs and/or stools. Totally out of place is the listing of a glass cupboard and a writing desk, perhaps cherished gifts from an erstwhile employer. All in all, sparse living indeed, but little evidence exists that the working labourer had more in the way of material possessions.

Food

Even if regularly employed and with a dry roof over his head, the agricultural labourer, by modern standards, led a very frugal life indeed, with very little to spare. Compared to his father, grandfather and great-grandfather, he bought more staples such as bread, dried beans and peas. Fats, cheese, tea and meat by the 18th century, because of cost, were purchased in very small quantities. Ale would not be extravagantly consumed unless he was extremely partial to it. To obtain much of it, in many cases, he is likely to have had to deprive his family of food. Most households brewed their own beer, a milder drink than ale, and farmers supplied beer to the labourer at hay and harvesting time; but cider and perry seem to have been a more common work beverage in the Cheese Country. And neither would appear in a cottage home, as both needed land to grow the apple and pear trees, expensive barrels, machinery and room to operate a press and mature the juice extract. William Marshall, the agricultural observer, commented bitterly in 1790 on the custom of small beer being drunk by the labourer at work during the winter, some farmers allowing as much as a gallon a day. Whether his comment applied to Wiltshire is not clear; by this time the labourer was often on a sustenance food level and known to take beer back to his family, a welcome food supplement, besides being an alcoholic beverage. A whiff of moral disapproval from Marshall is sensed here, a reaction frequently surfacing in the 19th century; for by then, a strong temperance movement had materialized in rural Wiltshire.

It should be born in mind that the amount of cooking done depended on the amount of fuel available to a household. Manors had early on instituted rules pertaining to fuel gathering. Purton manor tenants, according to a circa 1597 custumal, were permitted to gather only ' all Toppes starved trees and wyndfalls and shrowdes all underwood as thorne maple hazell and withy.' Workers of the manor are not mentioned and later records all confirm the decrease in the meagre supply of fuel available to labourers and the poor throughout Wiltshire. Coal was unaffordable to nearly all in Wiltshire until the building of the canals began in the late 18th century, except perhaps on the western edge of the county near to the Somerset coal fields, where carts brought it to better-off households; and to village blacksmiths it was an essential. Utilization and the later enclosure of waste and common land continued to rob the wood gatherers of fuel, by definition, leases began to specify that all rights to timber, both large and small, were owned by the landholder or his tenant. By the 18th century, stealing wood had become a frequent crime, but the courts, though meting out extremely heavy punishments to offenders, had little success in combating it.

From the 16th century onwards, the process of enclosure accelerated, gathering wood became more difficult, particularly on the Chalklands away from the wooded valleys. Cottagers had to burn dung mixed with straw and village by-laws indicate that in some Wiltshire villages, a communal fire was used to cook meals. Doubtless this was a source of much argument and in-fighting as to who should achieve cooking on the hottest part of the fire. It does not bear thinking about. Later village bakers hired out oven space for roasting the Sunday dinner and baking bread. By the 18th century chances were slim or remote of staying warm and cosy on a cold winter's evening in a labourer's dwelling after the evening meal had been cooked, such was the shortage of fuel.

From the 1500s, fire dogs raised wood logs from the hearth floor and for the next 200 years, even longer in rural areas, downhearth cooking as it was called, utilized this open fireplace, much of the operation being done very close to the fire itself, despite difficulties. Cranes, hooks, spits, hangers, trivets, cradles, drip trays, tin reflector ovens, pot standers, all were used around or in the fire, to aid the cooking processes. Spatulas, salamanders, iron spoons, toasting forks and other utensils further helped food preparation by the fire. Many fascinating details on Wiltshire cooking utensils and other hearth equipment can be gleaned from H. D. Roberts, *Downhearth to Bar Grate*.

Bread was the main food staple in Wiltshire. Evidence from food riots indicates that wheat was the main staple of bread flour, perhaps sometimes mixed with oats, barley or peas if wheat was short or the labourer poor. If diet in later centuries is any guide, pease pudding, a pottage of dried peas and perhaps dried beans, made up another food staple in the county; certainly this agrees with what labourers told me in the 1940s about their parents' and grandparents' food. The local market supplied the flour for a household, purchased in small quantities, probably weekly, so the labourer was very dependent on the price of grain and often severely deprived if the harvest was bad and corn prices rose. 17th century market regulations and Quarter Sessions records show how close a watch was kept on grain sellers to avoid engrossing and cheating, especially after food riots.

According to contemporary records, labouring families ate very little butcher's meat until after the mid-19th century. The cheapest cut or scraps brought home from the market would be added to vegetables and cooked into a pie or stew. Occasionally poaching supplied a meat meal, a rabbit or hare, a pigeon, partridge or pheasant, depending on local resources and the ever-disappearing forest. Bacon was more easily obtainable, from the cottager's own pig and in the Cheese Country, where pigs by the 17th century formed a tradition on the dairy farms, their meat was perhaps a little cheaper to buy in the local market than in the Chalk Country markets. Evidence of bacon smoking is occasionally revealed in the chimneys of small Wiltshire houses, as was the practice of malting barley for beer and ale, the grain probably laid on a hurdle covered with horse hair and heated just enough to prevent germination.

Probate Inventories until the end of the 17th century show that some smallholders salted meat in an outset, mostly ham and bacon no doubt, but perhaps beef if a neighbour had killed an animal. When affordable, a cottager may have preserved a piece of beef by soaking it in a brine solution with added peppercorns and spices. So much must have depended on the labourer's wife. A man in steady employment, married to a thrifty hard-working woman, was far more likely to be able to preserve food by buying when the opportunity for a bargain occurred (or an animal died), than one who was unemployed or thriftless and hampered with a wife of poor management skills. This goes for other aspects of household goods, such as candles, rush lights and soap. The end of the Civil War, a watershed in marketing enterprises, made such items available in markets, though rush lights continued to be used for another hundred years. They are mentioned in the 1767 Clyffe Pypard cottage inventories.

Little is known of the Wiltshire agricultural labourer's consumption of fish during the period of this chapter. Perhaps very little, being a long way from the sea, and unless in a town, few markets would have offered it for sale and fishponds had become a rarity. The privilege of river fishing, as with gathering fuel, was restricted to landowners or tenants, which left poaching, the possibility of sneaking access to a stream, or catching eels as they moved across the land in the Spring.

Poultry are likely to have been kept by many labourers' wives. Besides eggs, the young cockerels provided a chicken for the pot or oven, no chicken sexing in those days! When a hen came to the end of her few years' laying life, she too contributed to the soup pot. To feed the poultry, besides scavenging, gleanings and table scraps, the 'tailings', or broken corn, could be obtained cheaply from the farmer, particularly if the labourer had participated in the flailing of the grain during the less labour-intensive winter months on the farm. A pond included in rights to a common meant ducks and geese could also be kept, to contribute both eggs and flesh for the household. Poultry feathers ended up in pillows and bedding. By the late 18th century, for some unknown reason, poultry and eggs are seldom alluded to, perhaps the labourer no longer had enough land to keep fowl, the costs were too high, or they were too common to be mentioned.

Turkeys were introduced into England from Mexico at the beginning of the 16th century, so it is probable that some householders may have raised a few in Wiltshire after this time. They were tricky to raise, being delicate and fussy in their choice of food, so a patient housewife was needed to cope with them. During WWII a few turkeys were raised at Cocklebury. In their first weeks the delicate poults ate better than we did on the farm. The farmer's wife found all sorts of treats for them, such as chopped hard-boiled eggs daily when the egg ration for people was one per week. But how good the Christmas turkey tasted!

Presumably more cheese was eaten in the cheese country than on the chalk, but whether the cheaper, but much hated, skimmed milk cheese, was marketed before the 19th century, when the cream separator appeared on farms, is unlikely. If a labourer still had grazing rights, his wife may have made cheese from either cow or goat milk. Whitehouses (small dairies) often occur in smallholders' Probate Inventories. Bread and cheese was probably the basic carried lunch of the Wiltshire labourer for many centuries. Butter, unless he had his own milch animal, would have been a rarity, as a proportionately expensive food item. The much cheaper lard replaced it in a labourer's household, or dripping, the fat left over from cooking a roast, when available. As a child, I recall eating beef dripping spread with a little salt on toast or bread as a treat, but not bread and lard, which was considered the fare of the poorest of the poor. With the pig being common, lard was a staple, making good pastry, especially for savoury pies, always a way of stretching a little meat and many vegetables, as long as one had enough fuel to cook the pastry.

Frying – quick, easy and using less fuel – is likely to have been the cooking method of choice, frying pans used in dwellings at Gomeldon in the 13th century indicate its importance in cooking. Lard or dripping was no doubt used for frying eggs and that Wiltshire standby of 'bubble and squeak.' In my time it consisted of left-over potato and cabbage, mixed into a large patty and fried on both sides, but it was probably invented utilizing other vegetables long before potatoes came into the labourer's diet in the late 1700s.

In Wiltshire's cool temperate climate, everyone's diet, except for that of the well-off, would have been fairly monotonous, especially in the winter and early Spring. What rang the changes can only be guessed, as little is known of Wiltshire food traditions before the 19th century. Nuts from the countryside may have brightened some dishes, or herbs, dried easily in the summer sun, a little spicing if affordable and no doubt raisins at Christmas time. The first wild Spring greens, such as dandelions, were certainly gathered, and later watercress. Sorrel is sometimes mentioned as another green used. Of the various methods of preservation used by poorer households, drying, smoking, salting, boiling and pickling were no doubt the most common; if fuel was short, salting and pickling seem the most practical. Preserving mushrooms is likely, easily obtained from the fields in the late summer. They could be salted or pickled, vinegar in the form of sour wine likely to be obtainable and cheap. Pickling walnuts was also feasible. Drying depended on weather and a dry atmosphere in a cottage, hard to obtain in the damp English climate with only sparse fires. Other vegetables and fruits may have been pickled, barberries in particular. They are now eradicated, as the plant often bore Black Rust fungus which can attack growing or stored cereals. Cabbage, cauliflower and green beans, none of these needed much salt or vinegar to preserve and only a crock for storage.

A kilo of sugar cost a day's wage in 1797, but if affordable, jam could be made from fruits, whether domestic or wild. An extra cost is likely to have been a container for the preserve. Honey, no doubt, provided a substitute, some households kept bees, and an occasional find of comb from wild bees did not come amiss. Homemade wine, using honey or sugar for sweetener, mead, beer, ale and other fermented beverages were certainly made, even by the poorest, contributing to a long Wiltshire tradition; dandelion, cowslip, parsnip, rhubarb, elderberry and elderflower to name a few of the favourites. With the advent of cheap spirits during the 1700s, fruits – cherries, sloes, damsons, raspberries – added with some sweetener to rum or brandy produced homemade liquors always enjoyed, if only on special occasions.

Clues to what poor people ate can be gleaned from the Lacock parish poor relief records. The overseers gave out hundreds of food portions to the needy, mainly bread, cheese and beer, but some commodities are named. Meat is usually mutton, a shoulder, a sheep's head and henge (a head with the lungs and liver attached), or offal. Oat and barley meal were issued, the least popular of grains, (therefore its cheapness no doubt appealed to the ever-short-of-funds overseers); the Wiltshireman had always shown a preference bread made with wheat flour. Soap handed out showed it to be considered an essential item.

A garden, however small, supplied carrots, parsnips and turnips; by the beginning of the 1800s the potato had assumed a far greater importance in the diet of the labourer. Late Spring saw the gathering of the first plantings of salad greens and herbs and perhaps rhubarb. Larger cottage gardens had a few fruit trees, particularly apple and pear, but sometimes cherry, medlar, plum, greengage and damson. The concept of allotments and potato grounds came into being at the beginning of the 19th century and will be discussed in the next chapter.

Clothing

The labourer's clothing was doubtless made at home, except for leather items. Men wore an under-smock of light wool or linen, a loose shirt or smock, a leather jacket, breeches and hose, leather boots, or shoes and some kind of leggings. As the 18th century proceeded, leather clothing items began to be unaffordable. The exceptions were those absolute necessities – a pair of serviceable boots and leather gloves if the labourer was a hedger. Probate Inventories often mentioned a husbandman or smallholder's leather jacket, waistcoat or breeches, demonstrating their high value, to be willed to a son or son-in-law. Evidently these leather clothes lasted through many years of wear.

Labourers probably wore wool garments under leather in the winter and linen when warm enough. Poverty no doubt popularized the traditional Wiltshire smock as a cheaper, long-wearing substitute for leather garments. To protect his work clothes and himself from the rain, he wore sack-cloth. His wife would have knitted all the family stockings or hose, perhaps gloves and, no doubt, woollen caps, or the labourer had a leather cap made. I never remember labourers or myself wearing gloves while working at Cocklebury, but colder winters prevailed in the past and gloves perhaps became a necessity at times. Chilblains were a common ailment in my childhood days among those who did not wear gloves and lived in unheated dwellings, so they must have been very common in previous centuries. From medieval times leather gloves were sometimes provided by farmers at harvest time, when stooking corn could tear one's hands to pieces, thus hindering working efficiency.

Aubrey, and later Defoe, mention a substantial white woollen garment worn by shepherds on Salisbury Plain: 'a long white cloake with a very deep cape, which comes halfway down their backs, made of locks of the sheep.' That traditional garment lasted until the 19th century.

Sports and Pastimes

Certain basics united people in every village. Gathering together to go to market was one activity, church-going another. The ale-house or inn was of great importance, where the men got together as often as they could. Sports and other forms of entertainment generated concord. It is human nature to celebrate and enjoy, but little is really known of rural pastimes in Wiltshire until the 17th century. Supposedly pagan seasonal revelries slid into Christian celebrations in Saxon times, as the Church adopted them to its calendar. The Reformation and counter-Reformation in the 16th century began to bring in secular supervision of some sports and pastimes (which is when our knowledge of them really begins) and the growing nonconformity, as a combatant to the Anglicans, set off a decline. Researchers have disagreed regarding the strength of the decline between the Chalk and the Cheese. At the end of the century Puritanism had definitely begun to put a crimp in people's desire and ability to celebrate and, if people's religious preferences were followed, more restrictions may have been made in the Cheese Country than on the chalk. Later, the Commonwealth is known for its restrictions and the Restoration of the Monarchy for bringing back the Anglican ritual year and traditional popular festivities.

So it is difficult to determine how much entertainment a villager enjoyed and no doubt different customs prevailed in different villages. Presumably, the remoter the village, the less it enjoyed visits from groups of travelling players such as puppeteers. Potterne and All Cannings had a tradition of a mummer's play and continued to enact them until the end of the 19th century. Though presumed to be of long tradition, it is now thought that these plays in the traditional form we accept today originated no earlier than 1738. Fairs played a large role, local seasonal fairs meant a day from work to enjoy the lighter side of life. Food and drink, fortune telling and illegal gambling, cock fights, bull-baiting and occasionally bear-baiting, some if not all were offered at fairs. Ingram, in his book, *Church Courts, Sex and Marriage in England 1570-1640,* offers a huge amount of information he gathered from Wiltshire church court records and shows how the puritan attitude to enjoyment in these years certainly dampened celebratory customs. Further interpretation of these records indicates a tendency to disapprove of any unsupervised large gatherings, especially those which might lead to sexual activities. Such behaviour, aside from the moral point of view, was to be condemned, as it could increase the chances nine months later of bastard or pauper children who might have to be maintained by parish church revenues.

Christmas and Boxing day, Easter and Whitsun were the traditional religious holidays, but others dated back to long before Christianity – Spring Festival Day, May Day, Midsummer Day. Two more celebrations were added in the 17th century, Oak Apple and Guy Fawkes days. Entertainments on these days matched the season, some form of religious play at Christmas, Morris dancing on May Day and in the summer. Shrove Tuesday, traditionally noisy, a reaction perhaps to shriving the previous Sunday, often provided an excuse for cock-throwing.

Churchyards conveniently supplied a site for recreation and some villages, on Sundays and holy days played games and sports in them at the time of church services, – tennis at Colerne, cudgels at Lacock, stopball at Slaughterford, bowls at Damerham, stoolball at Sherston Magna. In addition, people indulged themselves in dancing, card-playing and drinking. At Newton Tony cock-fighting is recorded as taking place within the church building. But objections to churchyards being used for such activities began to be recorded on sacrilegious grounds, and by the end of the 16th century the puritanical conscience promoted the notion of enjoyment as being unrighteous, particularly by the lower classes, as it distracted their concentration and energies from their work. Later came a condemnatory attitude to time spent on Sundays watching animal sports, cock-fighting, bear- and bull-baiting. However, the people's propensities for these sports continued unabated, though in places they moved away from the church or churchyard.

In 1645 Mercurius Britannicus referred to people's means of enjoyment as ' the wondrous old heathen customs, of Sunday-pipings and dancings, with the meritorious maypoles, garlands, galliards, and jolly Whitsun-Ales.' Many other means appear in various documents referring to Wiltshire, bell ringing, dancing in churches; Aubrey's writings mention wassailing, midsummer bonfires, harvest home and sheep shearings as causes for merriment. Were things as jolly as the writers wished to make them appear? It is unlikely that it will ever be known, but there is a trace of mawkishness in the writings; did the labourer really long for the 'wondrous old heathen customs?'

Animals played a large part in entertainment until the 19th century. Bear- and bull-baiting, certainly badger-baiting too, though curiously it is very seldom mentioned. At Warminster, bull-baiting is recorded in 1677, and cock-throwing on Shrove Tuesdays, a

A medieval ale-house.

custom not abandoned at Chippenham until 1756. (see *Cocklebury* page 52) Cock fights were apparently frequent occasions; they may have been organized locally or the birds taken round the countryside to sites, as were bulls and bears for baiting. If local, breeding the cockerels may have been a common hobby. A commercial enterprise would have allowed opportunity for the local 'champions' to combat the outsider. Kilvert wrote in 1874 of a very old man who remembered well a cockpit and a bullring at Langley Burrell. The bullring was enclosed by a ditch and near to common land. The old man did not recall the ring being used within his lifetime.

The local ale-house (or tippling-house, a lower class version) was an integral part of labouring life from time immemorial. Ale-houses in the towns are better recorded, since they were supervised more easily and activities within them sometimes ended up before the local magistrates. The country ale-houses may have received less notice, but they were there in great numbers, as many as the village or hamlet was able to support. Some were undoubtedly run by smallholders who used the profits from running a house to supplement a meagre income obtained from their holding. The rural laborer's drinking places are never likely to have been very comfortable until the age of the motor car, and some may have been very poor establishments indeed. The image of the cozy English village pub with a roaring fire cannot be confirmed until well into the 18th century, and those were probably mainly on the coaching routes.

Another unknown is the complex question of whether Wiltshire village women patronized the ale-house on any occasion. Clark in *The English Alehouse* suggests perhaps only during courtship or with her husband at a celebratory event, but there is very little to confirm this in records or literature. Puritan ethics certainly would have discouraged females from alehouses, and until WWI, a rural labouring-class woman who drank at a pub was not considered wholly respectable by the locals, unless she was quite elderly. Not to say that women did not drink, they did, if only on certain occasions at home, for it was the women who made beer and later wines and cordials.

Ingram considers the ale-house a rival of religion. Various rules and regulations applied to all, to ensure an orderly house. The rise of Puritanism had encouraged official informers, who besides disclosing unlawful sports, had field days in taverns, citing disorderly conduct and drinking on Sundays before church. Their unpopularity grew, finally causing the central courts in 1624 to be closed to 'Informations,' except for those concerned with customs, usury and maintenance. But the same problems continued when in 1627, at Clack, then a market centre, the authorities suppressed all four alehouses for disorderly conduct and 'the poor inhabitants in their misery did beg the justices to grant a new licence.' The Saracen's Head re-opened a year later, but card-playing in the tavern soon was to be reported to the court. Complaints did not cease. Marden churchwardens protested in 1652 of alehouses open for business on Sundays, keeping people from church services, and the courts continued having to deal with card-playing and gambling, while disorderly behaviour sometimes contributed to closure of a tavern

Tobacco and ale-houses are synonymous, and evidence of early smoking is still easily found in Wiltshire. 'There is not so base a groom that coming into an ale-house to call for his pot, but he must have his pipe of tobacco,' a contemporary writer remarked in 1614. Tobacco, introduced to England in 1565, soon found its way to Wiltshire. According to tradition, Sir Walter Raleigh smoked at Great Wraxall Manor while on a visit to the Long family. Aubrey claims Sir Walter Long then acquired the habit and introduced it to his friends, who soon spread it over the county. Poorer people rapidly picked it up, using a half walnut shell with a straw piercing it as a pipe. Innumerable clay pipes have been picked up all over the county and can still be unearthed from agricultural land and gardens. The pipe illustrated was discovered at Cocklebury around 1950, three hundred years after being made by a Richard Greenland, perhaps of Marlborough, the vicinity where most of his pipes are found.

So many discoveries of pipes scattered about the countryside and the tradition of tobacco in ale-houses indicates that the Wiltshire agricultural labourer thoroughly enjoyed his tobacco. Smuggling was rife, due to the high rates of duty tobacco always commanded. For a while, it was grown in southern counties, including Wiltshire. To protect the duties, several Acts of Parliament banned the cultivation of tobacco in the 1660s. This did not deter farmers and an enquiry committee in 1675 found it still

A Country Ale house.

growing in Wiltshire, but a few years later the crop had
finally disappeared.

Nothing discouraged smoking; tobacco was easily
available, particularly in inns and ale-houses, while
tobacconists opened up in all the Wiltshire towns.
Tobacco leaf, shipped into Bristol from Virginia, was cut
and made into ropes and rolls, to be bought at so much
an inch and stuffed into a pipe bowl. (The author's family
possessed a brass tobacco rope dispensing machine once
in use in the late 19th century at The Bear in Chippenham;
a customer put in a penny, and could cut off an inch of
rope tobacco all ready for his pipe.) Richard Anstie retailed
snuff in Devizes in 1696, and began to manufacture it
from ground tobacco soon after. The tradition of the farm
labourer and his pipe continued well into the 20th
century. With his dreary life, 'a bi'uff baccy' provided
much comfort to him (and occasionally her!), with no-
one associating smoking with any bad side-effects. When

*Clay pipe found on Cocklebury
Farm.*

I worked at Cocklebury we used to think a cigarette warmed us up. Not necessarily an
illusion, as the nicotine may have dulled the cold we felt throughout the winter.

Besides entertainment in the ale-house, some labourers also spent time outside
cultivating vegetables, if they had access to a little land or a garden around their dwelling.
They were a vital supplement to the family diet, as would be a pig and poultry if they had
room and means to keep them.

Skimmingtons provided recreation to a whole village or district. They had deep roots
in the Wiltshire countryside and apparently originated as a demonstration against nagging
wives and scolds. A form of derision, a skimmington stemmed from the old belief that the
community had a right to take the law into its own hands and supplement it if they judged
that a case within their midst deserved punishment. Domination of a husband by the wife,
manifested by beating him physically or verbally, a husband beating his wife or child, and
cuckoldry were the main excuses for holding a skimmington. But a straying husband
seemed never to be included in the community's judgements. The event followed a
traditional pattern and afforded an excuse for revelry and noise in a community. It needed
planning beforehand and several hours to execute, then sometimes continued into the
next day. One at Potterne in 1857 took up three evenings, and blocked the main street to
carriage traffic. Sometimes skimmingtons were used to deride a neighbouring village and
had no connection with marriage misdoing. Burbage demonstrated in skimmington form
against Wilton in 1625. Sometimes processions might 'unintentionally' move over a
boundary, as when a Quemerford revel invaded Calne in 1618.

Demonstrations, whether large or small, involved several basics: a procession, noise,
the chance to make mischief without retribution,(unless the event got out of hand, and so
appeared in court records) and the possibility of showing disapproval (or envy?) of other

people's transgressions. In Wiltshire rural areas, the skimmington continued well into the 19th century, perhaps to the 20th. When originating in a village, the agricultural labourer was inevitably involved, though possibly farmers contributed by supplying the horse for the customary ride and the sets of cow horns participants often wore. Ringing bells, beating drums, raucous playing of musical instruments, the beating of household pots and pans, all made rough music, sometimes to be accompanied by the discharge of guns or fireworks. Sometimes 'armed' men marched, adding to the procession. Staves, rakes or pitch forks imitated weapons, attempting to convey force and power. Mocking the husband, the marchers sang rhymes, likely with derisive sexual innuendos in the case of a cuckold.

A horse available, a husband was placed on it, usually facing the tail (another insult), and sent along in procession. Sometimes his wife was forced to ride back to back with him. A substitute for a horse was a stave carried by several men, the husband astride it, a painful ride to endure, both physically and mentally. Or stuffed images were made of an errant couple and similarly carried. Much laughter and jeering accompanied the procession, by both men and women, and sometimes the crowd indulged in further demonstration by

A Skimmington revel.

beating a husband, or tying the wife to a stool and ducking her in the local pond. In a controlled form, symbolism played a large part in these revels. The horse might have its hair trimmed from its mane, ears and tail and a pair of horns attached to its head, or the husband might be hooded. Further insult was provided by men in women's clothes, today possibly to be interpreted as an example of transvestism.

These demonstrations happened infrequently as far as records show. But they only are noticed if they reach a court of complaint, so many more may have taken place than is realized. They were an outlet for high jinks and a way for lower classes to assert themselves in a time of growing restriction on their social actions in the countryside.

But revels, sports, pastimes and religion were outside factors to his life, how happy or unhappy was the agricultural labourer and his family were during the 17th and 18th centuries, or at any time in his history? What constitutes happiness and unhappiness changes from society to society, decade to decade, individual to individual. Until the 14th century, the Wiltshire agriculturist perhaps saw happiness as the security of estate or manor life, adequate food, clothing and shelter, no more work than he had the strength to do. Events up to the 16th century expanded his horizons; if he was enterprising and had the opportunity and the money he gained a little land to work, and also the concept that his path to happiness lay in the factor of possession, seemingly the road to security. As society stripped him of more and more, he began to see himself as a deprived person. Some may have turned to the ale-house, but family life no doubt gave much comfort; he had yet to see his children starve as the 19th century labourer did. Looking at the question from a 21st century viewpoint, what represented happiness for the agriculturist can be little more than conjecture. And for the woman, too, though until the 20th century, her wants were probably more modest than her father or husband. The basics of sufficient food, clothing and shelter, not to be overworked, to be able to live cheerfully and create a happy home; but ultimately, security may have topped her list. For children, one can only surmise that their fundamental happiness depended on kindly parents and a fair employer.

At the end of the 18th century, reformers began to take an interest in the life of the agricultural labourer, and in time came to their conclusions. Give him better housing, more food, fewer working hours, security in his old age and he would be happy. Until he had all of these, he would remain unhappy. But man has a capacity for looking at the brighter side of life despite the odds against him. The Wiltshire agricultural labourer was evidently not unhappy all the time, or he would have rebelled more strongly, protested more loudly. He and his family endured far too much hardship by the standards of today, but for him to find an alternative life was extremely difficult; he just had to carry on. From our viewpoint, in the 21st century, we cannot imagine any contentment at all in 18th century rural Wiltshire, but it is apparent that not all hours were gloomy for the labourer and his family.

Crime and Punishment

Life could be grim for those considered lawbreakers and sentenced. Punishments for vagrants were incredibly harsh, whipping, transportation, prison being some. So harsh that most JPs in Wiltshire forbore to administer them and if possible, just moved the vagrant on. But Salisbury poor records show beatings ordered for vagrants, to discourage them from lingering in the City. So many crimes called for the death sentence, prison conditions were appalling, and a transportation sentence from the 1780s meant being shipped to Australia, with little hope of ever being able to return; unlike a sentence to America, where a little more hope existed of family reunion, due to more shipping being available. Extreme punishments cited in Quarter Session Records horrify: a man to be whipped until his back bled, then slowly pressed to death; 1623, at Devizes, 'four men were ordered to be conveyed from hence to the place of Execution and there to be hanged by the necks until they are dead' for sheep stealing. Elizabeth Bennet, who had apparently hidden two of them. was sentenced to be burnt on the hand with the letter F (for felon) and after to be whipped about the Market Place and then released. But it is not always confirmed that a punishment was invariably carried out as specified.

Not all punishments were unreasonable by modern standards. John Shengellton, an apprentice of John Scott, ran away frequently from his master's service, begging bread and other victuals in his master's name. He lodged in hayricks and barns, robbed cheese presses, (i.e. took fresh cheese curd out of presses in the dairy, as it was more accessible than maturing cheese, usually stored in farmhouse attics) and, by presumption, hen roosts. He was ordered to remain in the house of correction until his former master, or some other person, take him into service.

How the common law and its administration affected the life of the Wiltshire agricultural labourer is beyond the scope of this book. Existing court records show that by his numbers and poverty alone, he could not help but be involved at times. If convicted, unless given unusual circumstances, his crime almost always resulted in a jail sentence, transportation or death. Harsh punishment was the chief method to be used at all times to maintain the law, however trivial the crime might be. Seldom did it seem to serve as a deterrent. The respective roles of justices and judges in executing the law in the 17th and 18th centuries are explained by Cunnington in his notes to Quarter Sessions records, and illustrated by the comments of William Hunt, a JP active during the years 1744-9.

Society – Escape – Emigration

Due to lack of money and connection, desire to get away from Wiltshire to create a new life was rarely an option for the agricultural labourer. A job, perhaps, could be found on the edges of adjoining counties, but pay and living conditions seldom differed, offering little inducement to leave the familiar. To find an employer farther away, a rural would-be migrant always faced a serious problem due to the vagrancy laws, for unless he had a definitive job to go to, he was likely, if caught, to face a vagrancy charge and to be punished by transportation back to his home parish. And how would he set about finding a distant employer, when he could not read or write, lacked communications, and found the transport of the times prohibitively expensive?

Of the overseas emigration of Wiltshire labourers during the 17th and 18th centuries, little is understood. In the Caribbean and America, a servant or prisoner sometimes had an offer of land at the end of his indenture, but this had ended by the 18th century, though in America a servant could find land by trekking further west from the Eastern seaboard. The background of emigration to New England from Wiltshire between 1630-60 has had some study. The numbers in this category are likely to be only in the hundreds at the most, mainly from towns or socio-economic groups usually not including rural labourers. A few artisans are mentioned, however, and some correlation exists between religious radicalism and emigrants from pastoral areas, although the ecclesiastical authorities, the clergy or the courts apparently had not harried those who left for religious reasons.

Religion

Puritanism in Wiltshire slowly died out by the end of the 17th century, but though not always parallel, nonconformity increased steadily, particularly in the Cheese Country. In 1646 a John Browne of Semley hoped that the puritan Parliament's religious decrees would change the rhythm of rural life. In one way his hope came true, for in time, in numerous villages and towns, nonconformist denominations would arise, giving meaning to people's lives and these denominations, for many agricultural labourers and their families, were to become a far greater influence and give much more comfort to their lives than did the Church of England. Aubrey passed judgment on this spiritual conversion by saying about those living in north Wiltshire: 'In all changes of religious they are more zealous than other; where in time of the Rome-Catholique religion there were more and better churches and religious houses founded than any other part of England could show, they are now the greatest fanaticks, even to spiritual madness.' Forest areas also produced many nonconformists; a strong link can be shown between them and radical religious behaviour demonstrated in Wiltshire between 1640 and 1670. Even some chalk villages noted for their royalist leanings such as the Donheads, Newton Tony, Aldbourne, Barford, boasted strong Puritan ministers. This may have been a local phenomenon, since most literature conveys the impression of Anglican ministers on the chalk supporting the restored monarchy and the values for which it stood.

A new prayer book officially appeared after the Civil War, finalizing the change in direction which the new Anglican church had begun to take after 1536. Its thrust was now to nurture only the soul and not the body as well, as previous creeds of the Catholic church had done. The Church began to change its direction regarding its clergy, seeking a more educated candidate, mainly drawn from the middle classes or upwards. The new clergy quickly and more easily related to their own social level and the church began to move away from their underprivileged parishioners towards the more affluent. A class separatist movement began and during the Commonwealth, with its emphasis on simpler religious practices which workers related to more comfortably, the gap widened further between middle and lower class churchgoers. In towns, particularly Bradford on Avon, Trowbridge and Warminster, religious nonconformity paralleled similar beliefs in the surrounding countryside. They were strong enough for the government to fear uprisings in 1655.

The Anglican church played a strong role in the movement to restore Charles II to the throne and in the 1660 declaration of Breda he gave assurance of respect for those of religious 'tender consciences.' Two years later in 1662, Parliament passed a new Act of

Uniformity, endeavouring to restore harsh treatment against dissenters and nonconformists. It is well documented that Puritan clergy in Wiltshire had to leave their churches because of the Act, which undoubtedly raised more feelings of dislike and opposition to the Anglican church and more support for nonconformist sects. Nonconformity began to be accepted by more people and eventually dissension was officially acknowledged in 1689. Meanwhile, John Earle, Bishop of Salisbury, a fair and enlightened man, insisted gentleness of action against dissenters and the ecclesiastical courts handled them reasonably.

Ingram, studying church court records between 1570-1640 points out that they indicated the period to be one of lax religious observance and indifference and that church attendance should not be correlated with religious beliefs. Little is known about the degree of religious knowledge possessed by uneducated people and 'rustic characters with at least a jumbled and misty half knowledge may be closer to the truth.' It was obvious from the court records of the period that the church had great difficulty in trying to maintain conformity. When the Toleration Act of 1689 spurred the growth of nonconformity in Wiltshire, it undoubtedly enlarged 'the rustic characters'' understanding of Christian doctrine.

After the Restoration, the church buildings desecrated by the parliamentary troops during the Civil War, were put in order – their statues, stone ornamentation, decorated walls and furniture. Pews were installed, in later years to be rented out for fees far beyond a worker's pocket, even if he could obtain an allocation. Pew rents were to spawn a further form of alienation from the Church, as the agricultural labourer and his family, forced to stand at the back during services, were made conspicuous.

Much money would continue to be spent on Wiltshire churches, but on the furniture and fittings, not the fabric, especially monuments dedicated to the glory of benefactors rather than the glory of God. These added and enhanced the material side of the Anglican faith rather than the spiritual, which was already being put in place by the new prayer book approved after the Civil War. That theme continued through to the end of the 19th century, despite the efforts of some clergy to try to relate to their poorer parishioners. George Herbert (1593-1633), famous for his religious poetry, during his four year stint as vicar of Bemerton, also made a name for himself as a clergyman who tried to get close to all his parishioners, well or sick, whatever their station in life. He was an exception, and the 17th century became a time when many parsons began to identify with the sporting squire and the prosperous farmer, ceasing to relate with the rural labourer and other lower classes. Some parsons were magistrates, which did not add to their popularity, as cases of petty crime came before them, particularly poaching. Clergyman JPs are likely to have judged poaching offences harshly, as the concept of game not being meant for the poor grew ever stronger. Later, many clergy in Wiltshire were absentees, the parish being run by a curate, poor and invariably overworked, hence not in a position to provide much help, spiritual or material, to the scattered rural workers.

Official recognition of dissenters and the increasing unwelcoming attitudes of the Anglican church encouraged the interests of the labourer and his family in the less rigid forms of Presbyterianism that allowed a direct approach to their God. This was particularly evident in the open Cheese Country villages, where a lord of the manor was not often in control. The Ranters, the Quakers and the Congregationalists never made much headway in Wiltshire, except in a few small areas. Few were able to deal with the sects' demands of personal participation and in the case of the Ranters, aspects of unconventional morality. Baptists and Anabaptists set up small congregations in the cloth-making areas (conveniently located by rivers!) and no doubt attracted rural attendees from the Anglican churches to their uncomplicated, less structured beliefs.

Besides the growth of Baptists and Anabaptists in the first half of the 18th century, the tremendous success of Wesleyism (leading to Methodism) headed the beginning of a long period of chapel building. Erected mostly by local labour with local funds, many of these chapels, some empty or converted into housing, still exist today in the towns and the villages, extremely visible on any Wiltshire rural drive, especially in the Cheese Country. But it was not only workers whom Wesleyism attracted; many dairy farmers had a tradition of sympathy to nonconformity. In time they made a strong alliance to Methodism, which in turn led to clashes with the Anglican church. It still retained the right to the tithes of all produce of the land, and the farmers' objections continued until partially relieved by the Tithe Commutation Act of 1836. Smallholders and even cottage gardeners also had to pay these tithes, so they too had joined the farmers to fight the Church's authority in this matter.

The second half of the 18th century is known as an era of great preachers, of which John Wesley is best remembered. In Wiltshire he preached mainly in urban areas and is unlikely to have reached the agricultural labourer unless he lived close to a town. It was the circuit preachers who went about the countryside, tramping from village to village, covering many miles on a Sunday, nurturing the early seedbeds of nonconformity. David Saunders is well remembered in Wiltshire lore. Walking seven miles from Seend, he preached to many shepherds and labourers at meetings in a cottage in the tiny village of Inmarsh. Many licences were granted to dwelling houses in rural areas, making small gatherings accessible to travelling preachers. John Cennick instituted Methodism in NW Wiltshire and drew supporters from many small villages. Congregationalism followed by the end of the century, and, with Unitarianism, made gains in Wiltshire at first, but their popularity was overtaken by Baptists by the mid-19th century. A tremendous expansion of Methodism occurred in the 18th century and chapels reached into many villages. Methodists constructed their chapels plainly, sometimes with a gallery. These drew many labourers and their families, not only for the religion, but also for the music, singing and sociability the chapel supplied. Revival meetings also spread Methodism in north Wilts; in the Brinkworth area Primitive Methodism particularly appealed. It is hard to trace any evidence in Wiltshire of swings back to Anglicanism from any of these faiths at any time.

Numbers of chapels continued to rise, with nearly as many chapels of various denominations in Wiltshire by 1851 as Anglican churches (352), though their seating capacity was nearly one third less. As will be seen in the next chapter, chapels played an important role in bringing early education to labourers' children in the form of Sunday schools.

Meanwhile, 18th century nonconformity proved a liberating influence for the labourer, not only in the chapel activities, but the numerous cottage meetings which created a basis for better social relationships in a small community. In the chapel, services also allowed farmer and labourer to hear each other's points of view, often through the medium of lay preachers from both sides. Methodism was less class-conscious and more outgoing, a contrast to the Church of England, which continued strictly to maintain the *status quo*. The concept of cottage meetings later brought about village reading rooms and some early adult education, which reached the agricultural labourer and older male members of his family.

There is no doubt that nonconformist sects touched the soul of the agriculturist and his family between the 17th and 19th centuries. The time was ripe for an upsurge of new religious beliefs, and they were given to hope that by directly reaching a god who cared in particular for them, a happier future would be assured. This was especially relevant to them, as it was growing quite apparent that many of their 'betters' had no interest in them as human beings, only as producers of wealth for their society. Unfortunately, by the middle of the 19th century, gradual disillusionment for the Wiltshire agricultural worker had set in. Life was still very difficult and he was beginning to realize that any hope for a better future lay not in religion, but in emigration, education and the unions.

Poor Law

As has been shown, to present a balanced picture of the Wiltshire agricultural labourer, many factors have had to be considered and evaluated. The main factors were his work, living conditions, recreation, his place in the local community, how he felt and thought, how society regarded him and how the economic world treated him. But dominating all these issues and crucially affecting him in the 18th and 19th centuries was the Poor Law. It was to impinge on every facet of his life, every day, directly or indirectly.

Before discussing the distribution of Poor Law relief in Wiltshire (mainly based on Lacock parish distributions), charity should be considered. Very little can be gleaned from church records or contemporary sources, though the spirit of charity is touched on in literary sources by the end of the 18th century, the novels of Jane Austen being an example. Social writers of the 19th and 20th centuries have always emphasized that charity seldom came from the heart, but was dispensed with some underlying motive and beneficial interest of the donor. Private charity can be faulted for its frequent discrimination of recipients in terms of the 'deserved' and the 'undeserved' (still sometimes true today), at the same time emphasizing the social differences between the donor and the recipient. The provision of food, shelter or clothing by the cleric, the gentry and the well-off farmer increased the recipient's obligations, making him or her vulnerable to pressure from givers to accept their control, philosophies and concepts. It also encouraged the giver's expectation of deference from the recipient. Early 19th century education was to come into the same category as charity for these very reasons. And charity was thought of as a supplement to wages, thereby creating another reason to keep wages low.

Wiltshire is of particular interest in matters of poor relief. By the end of the 18th century the county invariably held bottom place on English wage scales and the county's relief measures were sometimes particularly cruel. The reasons for this are several. Wiltshire had little industry and hence was always short of capital. This meant a county poor in infrastructure. Almost all the agricultural land was tied up in the hands of owners and speculation had ceased. Tenant rents were low enough to permit hard-working farmers to supply their own capital, enabling them to keep up-to-date with advances in agricultural production, but not able to pay more than minimum wages to their labourers. When the industrial revolution occurred, it bypassed Wiltshire, because of the lack of mineral sources and ports. Then the cloth industry lost out quickly and heavily to the north country mills, so it was mainly landowners and their tenants who were producing the wealth of the county by agricultural products. The low wage levels did not allow the labourer to produce any wealth by spending, as he had only enough to provide himself and family with subsistence living. By the mid-18th century, few labourers had grazing rights or any addition to their income except, perhaps, a garden, so constant deprivation, poor housing and food began to be their lot.

Poor Law expenses increased steadily during the 18th century, because of a lack of alternative employment in rural areas, continual population growth and more prospective labourers coming on the market as the birthrate climbed. The inequalities of relief from parish to parish exacerbated the inequalities within the parishes, e.g. a parish lacking housing put pressure on the population and housing stock of the parishes around it, especially on the chalk, where parishes were large and population scattered. Remaining common rights were also under constant pressure for the same reasons.

As has been seen from the previous chapter, a system of administration and distribution of relief for the poor had been put in place in England by the 17th century. The Lacock parish records of overseers' disbursements give a clear indication of how a rural Wiltshire parish in the Cheese Country administered its Poor Law relief. (Records from a rural chalk parish have yet to be studied in similar detail as F H Hinton did on Lacock,) A parish committee, usually known as the vestry, through its appointed overseers, executed the relief scheme. It authorized the levying of poor and other rates and arranged for revaluation of property when more taxes were needed. In addition, it assessed the overseers' work and added or subtracted doles to individual cases of poverty. In turn, the JPs examined the overseers' accounts annually, usually approving them. Each year, the vestry also nominated potential overseers, of whom two were then chosen by the JPs. This system of choice could be good or bad; if one started with a parish who wanted to avoid spending more on the poor than was absolutely legal, whose Vestry consisted of miserly members, who nominated inhuman overseers, who were in turn accepted by uncaring JPs, the system of relief in a community could be quite brutal. On the opposite face, it could indeed be compassionate, and the records give the impression at Lacock that overseers were perceptive and empathizing. However, it cannot be verified how many persons applied for relief and were turned down, as the records fail to mention such incidents. By Poor Law regulations any applicant for relief, if dissatisfied, might appeal to a JP, but no requests are entered in the Lacock records. A built-in discouragement to this procedure existed, as any complaint is likely to have affected future relief applications to overseers.

A clue to the Lacock overseers' lenient perceptions of the poor lies in their administration of some of the Poor Law rulings. The 1724 legislation insisted on all members of a poor family wearing a patch on the right sleeve with a large P (for pauper) 'cut thereon in red or blue cloth.' This law was not amended until 1810, but to their credit, the overseers seemingly did not enforce it, for after the first entry of 6d, no more sums for the badges appear in the records. Appeals for medical treatment are invariably answered quite generously by the standards of the times, and despite the harsh regulations dealing with vagrants, the parish records show that Lacock just moved them on, not involving any more severe punishment by JPs, which laws permitted as a discouragement to seeking help. The records give the impression that none of Lacock's parishioners ever lacked subsistence or shelter.

The supervision of the Lacock overseers' expenditures on Poor Law relief over the course of three centuries fell, by law, to local JPs. Mainly three families, all small landowners, typical of Cheese Country parishes were involved – the Talbots of Lacock Abbey, the Montagues of Lackham and from the 18th century, the Awdrys at Notton. If the recipient of poor relief had been born in the parish, one of the current JPs is likely to have known him from childhood. What was kept a secret (illegally) were the values of the property ratings in the parish and the amounts paid out regularly for the vestry members' dining enjoyment at local inns or a prepared meal after they had met on Poor Law business. The moneys were recorded in a sealed book and known only to the vicar.

Relief paid to a labourer, either disabled, employed or unemployed, residing in the parish, was generally known as 'outdoor relief.' If a person was disabled, unemployed and homeless and not of Lacock parish in general, they were given money and had to walk back to their birthplace, or to the last parish where he had had more than one year's employment. If unable to walk, means had to be provided to escort them back. Sometimes a child or an indigent person was boarded out; at Lacock and in other parishes 'poor houses' were set up where these people were put out to exist the rest of their lives. This was a relief in kind, or 'indoor' relief.

Poverty and Punishment

By 1700 various local Acts allowed for public moneys to be used to set up shelter for the poor and indigent, wherein they could live and be set to work, hence the dreaded term 'workhouse.' Differing from finding employment or a regular job, this indoor relief, as it would in time be called, was slow to be implemented and at first the poor and indigent were housed together, kept in conditions of near imprisonment, with no system for provision of work. After 1723, individual parishes were allowed to establish their own workhouses, with the major aim of providing a deterrent to the poor; hence, conditions of living within were stark and harsh, the one at Lacock no exception. Many of the inmates over the years appear to be children, whose parents could not support them. A few shelters, including Lacock, managed work schemes, but little if any profit emerged. Lacock, and most parishes in Wiltshire and other counties, failed to successfully put to work the 'diligent poor' – a term for an unemployed employable person. Throughout history, forcing people to work has always proved too expensive a proposition, especially when tried as a means towards paying the costs of welfare received by recipients. The Lacock overseers found the situation in their parish no exception to this rule. As the indigent poor in any parish usually outnumbered spaces in workhouses, it made outdoor relief essential, a state of affairs to continue into the 19th century.

The growing poverty meant that more people applied for relief and the Poor Laws stipulated that people receiving outdoor relief should be listed. By 1724 Lacock had 22 persons on their 'monthly list,' some described as old, infirm, blind, lame, 'a Natural' and three children – one parentless, two with their fathers 'lame.' Each was allowed an average of 3s 9d *per month*, when a labourer's pay was roughly 7s a week. A widow and four small children received 7s a week. By the end of the 18th century, 125 people were on Lacock's monthly list.

Cases of this type put a very heavy burden on the Lacock Poor Law rates and partly account for the ever-increasing outdoor relief payments the overseers made through the 18th century. The steep climb of the figures for Lacock are hard to believe, despite continuing inflation over centuries. From 1590, for ten years, the average amount given to relief of the poor was £10 a year. At the time, the labourer made about 6d a day. Between 1666 and 1674, the average annual expenditure by the vestry was just over £113. 120 years later, the average number of poor people 'on the list' for receiving relief had jumped from 22 persons in 1724, to 63. By 1817, an average of 160 individuals received monthly 'pays' at an annual cost of £1,000, and even more persons needed 'extraordinary' reliefs.

'Extraordinary' described various forms of relief. Rent subsidies were one of the most common in Lacock parish, particularly after 1750, as the purchasing power of the agricultural workers' wages decreased. Great consideration was given to each case. The overseers in such cases invariably found themselves in a catch 22 situation; if the tenant could not pay his rent, he was liable to have a distraint put on his goods, then needing more help than before. Lacock dealt with one case as follows: 1752, 'Bought the Goods that Farmer Perce Seized for Rent belonging to William Heath and lent ye Goods to Heath again, £3; the Rent due to the farmer £7 15s 0d.'

As poverty deepened, extraordinary payments grew. Often the payment was by order of the JPs who intervened on the paupers' behalf. Commodities frequently were given in lieu of money, and items show on how little poor people had to exist. Bread, meat (a shoulder of mutton 9d), oatmeal and soap (6d), 2 sheep's heads with lungs and livers attached (8d), cheese, beer, shoes and clothing, tools, shrouds, (presumably to comply with a 1660s law, passed to aid the cloth industry, stipulating that a person had to be buried in a wool shroud), medicine, medical treatment, rent payments. Each year Lacock distributed hundreds of charitable items and payments. In times of want, some items were bought in bulk: 1741 saw £1 being spent on 'Barley for the poor,' and offal meat £1 7s 1d; the following year bread and meat purchases cost £3 3s 2d. Another expenditure is recorded thus: 26 ells of linen cloth at 11d per ell. (an ell measured a little over one metre).

Other aspects of the labourer's life can be found in Hinton's records. The fact that the overseers bore the cost of a full funeral is surely indicative that it was an important

ceremony to people. A coffin and shroud, money for laying out, bread, cheese and beer,
All were supplied to the mourners and presumably to the coffin bearers. Bearers of a
smallpox victim's coffin received, in addition a payment, compensation for the risk of
infection involved.

Conditions in Wiltshire jails, as in the rest of England, were abominable, and until
1774, a prisoner could be held beyond his sentence if he had no money to pay the fees he
'owed' to the prison keeper for his keep (food and straw to sleep on). At Bridewell jail,
Devizes, if the prisoner was penniless, his parish sometimes helped and paid the prisoner's
debt to his keeper. In 1751 the Lacock overseers paid out Mary B's debt from her time in jail
as 10s 6d. Later in the year the widow Spundley's son served a sentence for a minor offence.
Apprenticed to Master Isaac B. and almost starved to death in the jail, a payment of 2s
obtained his release. But what happened if a working labourer was convicted and sent to
jail? How did he get out if he was in debt to the keeper? Did the neighbours or family pay
or appeal to the Parish? Whatever the case, it all no doubt proved a harrowing experience
to everyone, prisoner, family or friends; but perhaps very little to the rest of a community
used to such circumstances and treatment.

By 1642 Lacock had assessed its poor rate at 4d in the £, which yielded nearly £20
yearly. As more moneys were required for poor relief, properties were reassessed, and the
value of stock needed in trade also rated, though farmers were not liable to the latter. Fines
imposed by JPs for certain offences and paternity money from putative fathers provided
another funding source. But just the pay-outs to illegitimate mothers often exceeded
paternity money by more than 50%. It was the local JPs' responsibility to check that the
rates were correctly dispersed, but in practice the overseers performed this function, so
few checks and balances existed.

Apprenticeship

The 1597 Act gave parish officers the right to apprentice children, who could not otherwise
be maintained, to farm, domestic work, or other occupations meeting the JPs' approval.
The source of the child is not revealed. At Lacock the records begin a year later with children
being sent to households, with some clothing provided, for varying lengths of time, with
the stipulation only that food, lodging and clothes be provided. Thankfully numbers were
not great, only 15 children were apprenticed between 1669 and 1673; until 1832 a total of
194 indentures were recorded, a method the parish used to avoid the responsibility of
maintaining a child.

With the aim of saving rate moneys, the overseers could place a child in apprenticeship
outside the parish. They often gave a master a premium of £1-£3 to accept a child and paid
for some clothing at the start. Boys remained in apprenticeship until the age of 24, girls
until age 21, a deterrent to early marriage unless pregnancy occurred. The apprenticeship
could be of many years, as children went to a master sometimes at the age of seven. As
many apprenticeships were to trades or occupations that required little skill, it was a form
of slave labour and very harsh. No education or religious training was specified and the
records give no indication that the overseers cared at all as to the child's fate, no follow-up

being made. A brutal master or mistress, or sexual assaults – there was no limit. Perhaps living in a small community, gave some protection from abuse. (But in the 1930s, I recall people looking the other way at mistreatment of servants or employees, unless extraordinarily outrageous.) Only five Lacock apprenticeships stipulated a payment of wages, a shilling or two a week. Most of the apprenticeships were to the clothing trade, or domestics (49 girls and 125 boys out of the 194). Children were unlikely to be apprenticed to farmers, as they could obtain plenty of labour from the offspring of the labourers they employed, though girls may have been apprenticed to farming households as servants. But some apprenticed children may well have been the children (or bastard grandchildren) of agricultural labourers who could not afford to keep them, yet were not in receipt of poor relief, and so turned the children into the care of the parish.

Medical Attention

By the 18th century, the labourer could receive some medical help from parish relief funds, but only when in dire straits, either through a disablement leading to unemployment, or not having enough means to cope with a chronic medical situation in his family.

The labourer and his family, until the 19th century, remained silent as to their expectations of medical help. For England in general, early medical practice in medieval times is known to have reached different social levels, but mainly in urban areas. Sometimes serfs referred to as *medicus* appear in medieval records. Rural areas mainly had to depend for medical attentions on barbers, barber-surgeons, 'leech men,' midwives, wise women (sometimes to their detriment considered witches), apothecaries or even astrologists if they could be found. Examples are known of blacksmiths giving medical help, particularly in the case of broken bones and other serious injuries. For the services of a trained physician or medic taught by the church or later at a university, it is unlikely that the Wiltshire agricultural labourer and his family ever had access in his village to one until the 18th century. As had always been the case in village life, rural people depended on women to help them with childbirth and sicknesses, and relied on herbal and plant medicines, the cost of sending for a doctor being quite beyond the means of any inhabitant.

Relief administrators had to provide medical treatment for those in poverty and unemployment, though the hiring of physicians did not commence until the 1700s. The working poor fell between two stools in this period, not poverty-stricken enough to get medical relief through the Poor Law overseers, and not able to pay for a doctor. But rural life was supposed to be healthier. The 17th century recorded a body of medical opinions such as that of Tobias Venner, a Bath physician, who firmly believed that high open land was healthier to live in than low and marshy places, and rural life much healthier than city life, his viewpoint based on the better the air, the better the breathing. Echoes of Aubrey can be heard in this belief too, and 19th century census and death statistics tend to indicate that rural peoples' life expectancy was higher than that of town dwellers. Life in rural Wiltshire may have been healthier on the chalk and higher land; certainly privies and standing water drained off better, but despite a long life span, poor food, clothing and

The plant birthwort, used for many centuries by midwives to ease childbirth.

shelter undoubtedly increased his need for doctoring and medical attention.

Lacock vestry records show that a considerable percentage of the poor rates was spent on the care of the sick poor, and perhaps half the time and energy of the overseers was engaged on their behalf. No detailed expenditures are given until the 1700s, the sick and disabled apparently being nursed in their own homes by family, or by neighbours paid for their services by the overseers. For instance, in 1702, the overseers agreed to pay a woman to nurse a neighbour for one shilling and were willing to exceed the allowance if there was cause. 1749 an entry reads 'To Drugg Hiscock and his wife setting up 3 nights with Edmund Duck and his wife Laying light Headed and Restless..........1s.' A pauper was nursed by her sister in 1724, costing the parish 8s. After her death, the sister received 1s for laying her out. Sixteen years later the same sister fell sick and her daughter tending her was given 6d for expenses.

Until the middle of the century, payments were made to apothecaries and doctors for treatment and medicines, but in 1751 a Dr Savage began to receive £10 a year for medical attendance on the poor. In 1827 Mr Edward Spencer of Chippenham accepted £30 yearly for his duties as parish surgeon. As he had to travel at least three miles each time he was called out for accidents, the pay does not seem particularly high.

1772 saw entries in the parish accounts for with taking children 'to the Water' (£1 1s) and 'going to the Salt water.'16s 6d). To the water perhaps referred to visits to nearby Broughton Gifford, Melksham or Holt waters, thought to be beneficial, or to Bath. The salt water may have been a visit to the Bristol channel, for the belief that a mad dog bite could be cured by sea water still prevailed at this time. Chippenham overseers in 1739 had paid 10s to a father to take his child, bitten by a mad dog, to the 'Salt water.' Nearly as far away as the salt water was the shrine at Glastonbury, where a Lacock man sought a cure for his leg, 'having several holes in it.' The overseers allowed him 5s for the journey, perhaps enough for him to travel by carrier cart. Lacock poor were sent to Bath hospital to obtain treatment for various ills. The parish gave the hospital 'caution money,' which, if not used up, the treasurer refunded at the end of the year. By 1789 the hospital received an annual subscription of two guineas and 'caution money' is no longer found in the accounts, saving considerable bookkeeping by both the hospital and the overseers.

With wages at 1s 6d a day, these expenditures seem very generous, but it cannot be determined how far the help extended. Were all sick persons treated equally, or was it a case of the squeaky door getting the most oil? And with Lacock being a large parish, were those who lived within the village, on the doorstep so to speak, given more attention and care than a family living a mile or more away?

According to Hinton, by 1766 the parish had created an institution at Lacock 'where the sick and infirm might receive nursing,' but no details are given of the care being offered. In 1723 parishes were given the power to build workhouses for 'profitable employment of the poor,' based on the theory that a reduction in poor rates would automatically follow. Lacock at the time had what was termed a Poor House, where a few favoured poor families lived, and in 1758 the tenement was converted into a workhouse for unwanted children, or for those whose parents were not able to afford their keep. In 1766, this house was to be enlarged to several houses, to provide for 20 poor paupers and presumably it was here that the sick were accommodated.

Wiltshire's history of plague outbreaks parallels that in the rest of England, constant outbreaks occurring until 1665, with high death rates, mainly in towns. Then it disappeared. Death rates were often aggravated if the outbreak took place in the years of bad harvests and subsequent food shortages. Today typhus is suspected as being a cause of epidemics in Wiltshire in the 1650s, as so many late autumn and winter deaths occurred in certain areas, such as Chippenham and Warminster; perhaps due to their situation on the well-used east- and west-bound routes frequented by vagrants and other walking travellers. Perhaps other areas suffered too; mortality rates determined by parish records need careful examination to prove this.

Smallpox was another matter. Endemic in England for centuries, occasionally flaring up into an epidemic, it was greatly feared, due to its high infection and death rate and the permanent scarring of the face. Five epidemics are recorded in Lacock between 1736 and 1756. Isolation was the only weapon known to combat the spread of the disease and small pox houses are frequently recorded, one existed in Chippenham (see *Cocklebury* pages 77-8). According to vestry records, Lacock parish rented two in order to confine patients, at a cost of £1 10s and £2 10s. The patients fed very well indeed by 18th century standards, plenty of beer, wine, meat, bread and biscuits. Finally, inoculation reached the village. After another epidemic in 1776, a Dr Banks was paid £1 3s to inoculate poor persons. In 1803, the parish surgeon charged ten guineas for 100 inoculations, about 2s an inoculation. By 1840, the government had forbidden inoculation and ordered the Poor Law authorities to use vaccination instead, a much safer practice. One wonders how many people in the Cheese Country were immune to smallpox due to their contact with cows, and therefore had in effect already received their vaccination. And whether compulsory inoculation and vaccination reached all the working poor in the villages.

Mental illness

What treatment, if any, mentally afflicted persons in the Wiltshire countryside received until the 1700s, is just not known; presumably a violent or dangerous person was confined or otherwise restrained. And families looked after their own. When poorhouses were instituted, the mentally ill paupers mingled with the others, not a practical solution to such a serious problem if the person could be violent.. In Lacock, after 1750, records of care begin to crop up. A year later, an overseer, Jeremiah Beswick, had to ride to Reading to bring back a woman 'out of her mind.' The total cost, £31 6s 7d, paid for three horse changes for the cart carrying the woman and reimbursement to the Reading overseer. Beswick received one guinea a month for his care of the woman and the parish bought him a lock and chain for her. Another woman pauper, taken all the way to Bethlem in London, cost one guinea in expenses for the journey and £2 4s for admission to the asylum. Because of ignorance and lack of cures, treatment of the mentally afflicted was frequently cruel, especially for the poor, a situation to continue well into the 20th century. I can recall the threat some parents used to discipline their children in the 1930s, 'ull be sent to 'vizes sylum' if you b'aint careful,' illustrating the fright which just the mention of Devizes mental asylum still created. Not until the advent of National Health Service did Wiltshire provide what is considered today kinder care for the psychologically disturbed.

The relief pay-outs made by Lacock parish records are some of the earliest historical insights available to a few aspects of the life of the Wiltshire labourer and his family. Studies made of relieving records from other Wiltshire parishes, along with analyses of the same parishes' population categories and numbers, certainly would lead to some understanding of just how much of the wealth of a parish was expended on the poor, as parish overseers administered an ever-running, very complex operation.

But Poor Law records cannot convey any of the feelings and thoughts of the Wiltshire agricultural labourer until the 19th century. He remains faceless and his emotions can only be imagined; no-one was interested in recording them. But change was in the air, due to the new reform movement sweeping across Europe into England. The existence of the labourer was about to be acknowledged and his importance to society and the economy started to be understood. It would, however, take longer for society to recognize his human characteristics and his individualism.

Chapter 6 Bibliography

Much of the Civil war action and its aftermath I have described is based on general readings. The paper: DANIELL, J., 1870, Chippenham and the Neighbourhood, during the Great rebellion. WANHM 12, 293-317, though written long ago, is still relevant.

The writings of David Underdown (including UNDERDOWN, D., 1980, The Chalk and the Cheese: Contrasts among English Clubmen. P&P 85, 25-48) convey well the feelings of the rural population and the continuing protests during this period. The Avebury farmers' protest is recorded in Avebury Parish Register (WSRO 1569/31), and the Dorset farmer's protest is taken from MINGAY, G., 1990, The Diary of James Warne, 1758. AHR 38.1, 72-78

Discussion points on villages, their inhabitants and occupations benefited from:
KENNEDY, D. and L.(eds), 1999, *Marriage and Rural Economy in Western Europe since 1400*. Turnhout: Brepols
CUNNINGTON, P., 1967, *Occupational Costumes in England from the eleventh century to 1914*. New York: Barnes & Noble

For background to Wiltshire sports and pastimes I drew heavily on:
HUTTON, R., 1994, *Rise and Fall of Merry England: the ritual year 1400-1700*. NY: Oxford University Press

For greater depth on Skimmington activities see:
INGRAM, M. 1984, Ridings, Rough Music and the 'Reform of Popular Culture' in Early Modern England. *P&P* 105, 79-113
ROBINSON, P., 1990, Royal Justice and Folk Justice: Conflict arising over a Skimmington in Potterne in 1857. *WANHS* 83, 147-54

In the introduction to volume XV of the WRS: *Tradesmen in early-Stuart Wiltshire: a miscellany* (1960), the editor, N. J. Williams, set the scene for trading in the county, including information on alehouses and inns. But early drinking habits of the Wiltshire agricultural labourer still need to be gleaned,. Peter Haydon's *The English Pub* (1994, Robert Hale) showed the contrast between drinking establishments in rural areas, compared to those in cities and towns.

Anthony Salerno's unpublished thesis, *The Character of Emigration from Wiltshire to the American colonies 1630-1660* (University of Virginia 1977) demonstrated how immigration at this time was seemingly limited to the better-off labourer, husbandman or townsman.

For the history of, and sources of information on, nonconformity at this period the best introduction is the chapter written by Marjorie Reeves in volume III of the *Victoria County History of Wiltshire* (1956)

7
1795–1900
A Little Light towards the End of the Tunnel

'A rich land breeds poor labourers.' Cobbett

Introduction

The revolutionary events of 1789 in France deeply affected liberal thinkers in England; they began to hope that the democratic ideas and the rights of man they had championed might become more firmly established. Their expectations were soon dashed to the ground, the political face of Europe changed rapidly and by 1793 Britain and France were at war. Conflicts, always a drain on a country's economy, made the Napoleonic Wars no exception. England, already financially strained by colonial responsibilities, suffered bad harvests and rising wheat prices, both continuing into the new century. The poor suffered accordingly, in particular by the introduction in 1795 of the Speenhamland system of paying out poor rates, calculated on the price of bread. The price of grain had always ruled the well-being of the labourer since a market economy had begun in the 17th century; if grain was cheap, he fed well, if expensive, his food intake dropped to subsistence level. The hard line is illustrated by the statistic of wage portions spent on bread; in the 1760s it equalled 44% of total family expenditure, by the 1790s, 60%. This disparity between wages and the grain prices widened in the 19th century to create 50 years of subsistence living and often actual hunger for the Wiltshire agricultural labourer.

Despite the reformist movement and a whig-liberal Parliament for the next fifty years, few reforms aided the agricultural labourer. He had no representation and limited franchise for most of the century, while landowners and the aristocracy outnumbered other parliamentary members. Franchise bills are an example, the first being in 1832, which helped the 'ten-pound voter,' certainly not the agricultural labourer unless he owned his own cottage; he had to wait until the 1880s to get a vote. But gradually more reforms came.

Capital punishment for horse-stealing and house-breaking was abolished in 1832. In 1836 an Act commuted the much-disliked payment of church tithe in kind into a fixed charge, which mainly affected farmers, though a few smallholders as well. At the same time, the Church of England had to forego the privilege of allowing a clergyman to hold two benefices if more than two miles apart, while increasing the salaries of notoriously poor clerical postings. This was a move to attempt closer contact with the rural population of Wiltshire and their churches, which alas, did not help as much as had been hoped, because of the clergy's prevailing class attitude to the lower levels of society. However, by 1836, perhaps earlier in some places, sometimes with the help of their families, curates and vicars struggled to create and maintain village schools. By the same Act dissenters were permitted to be married in their own chapels, or before a registrar. These were all small concessions perhaps, but they showed a slightly softer approach to working-class welfare and benefit, both rarely taken into consideration in the past.

The Wiltshire farmer did well through most of the Napoleonic War years, general economics and government policies taking care of him. Most farmer-owners budgeted for capital improvements and kept their land in good heart, a custom handed down from the 16th century, particularly in the Cheese Country. A farmer-tenant expected and received capital improvements to his buildings from his landlord. His lease stated explicitly, that the goodness taken out of the land must be returned by restrictions on the sale of hay, straw and manure, and crop cycles. But both owner and tenant, dependent on a market economy, still had to sell their farm products as cheaply as possible, which meant counting every cost. The farmer cut wages to the bone and dropped them to subsistence levels. He felt quite justified in trimming wages, as it was he who paid out the rates for Poor Law relief. By 1820 land and grazing rights had almost run out for the labourer, and with prices doubled in the previous 60 years, he was in very sorry shape. The farmer and the land came through the Napoleonic Wars in good heart and, except for a few years immediately after the Wars, both remained so until the 1880s, but the labourer's plight steadily worsened until the 1860s and was not to show much improvement until the 20th century.

The dire straits endured by many agricultural labourers in southern England in the 1820s began to attract public attention, especially after William Cobbett, the pamphleteer, began to hold a parliamentary seat, according him a political pulpit. His rural rides in Wiltshire and other counties produced some of the earliest writings on the economic plight of the agricultural worker to reach the general public. An influential, though controversial, political reformer, his impact on Parliament lingered long after his death in 1835. Cobbett, and those reformers who came after him, did not solve the labourers' problems, time and economics did more, but they made people aware of the rural labourer's plight.

Cobbett, born in Surrey of a labouring family, had as a child toiled in the fields. So he understood countrymen and their lives. He told society constantly of the rural labourer's contribution to the country's economy and society and the lack of reward he received in proportion to the amount of work he did. But he misjudged the labourers when he thought that enough remuneration in wages and perks to take them back to their old ways of life would keep them on the land and give them happiness, for Cobbett was blind to any desire for social progress. He felt strongly that the agricultural labourer should still keep his place, rather than try to better himself as other social classes in 19th century England were trying to do. Though Cobbett had jumped class barriers himself, he did not seem to understand that to change social status at the beginning of 19th century England was a feat beyond the means of most. He maintained that the government economic system kept the agricultural labourers poor, totally discounting local social customs of other class members who rigidly maintained social ranks, blocked access to land, whether by renting or purchase, and most of all, refused to raise their wages as their purchasing power steadily diminished.

Obviously a man of contradictions, Cobbett also wanted the countryman to keep his rural values, yet he encouraged the rising labour movement. He believed strongly that the poor should not have access to wealth or better themselves; if they did, they would take from other social classes above them. He also did not seem to understand that when a person, through his labours, contributes wealth to his society, he gets restless if he is not allowed to share that wealth; which is what the agricultural labourer in Wiltshire perceived more and more as the 19th century moved on and he continued to receive less and less.

Cobbett contributed to anti-clericalism, an influence which continued to grow long after he had left the political scene. He strongly resented the Church ignoring the needs of the poor and putting the social mores and needs of the other classes first. But he was happy to leave alone the limited education provided for the rural poor, agreeing with many clergy that more schooling would make them discontented with their lot, destroy their morals, give them ideas above their station. And if the Government meddled with education, the Church would gain too much power, so he opposed the first £20,000 national education grant in 1833. On the other hand, he asserted frequently that education should be in the charge of working class people, not of the clergy. But for all his drawbacks, Cobbett's comments drew a vivid picture of the Wiltshire countryside in the 1820s. And as with those two Wiltshire natives, Richard Jefferies and Francis Kilvert, who also wrote of the rural labourer's life, Cobbett's words are still frequently quoted today.

At the beginning of the 19th century, Wiltshire continued to be a county of large estates, particularly in the Chalk Country. The tight control landowners exerted over their estates greatly affected those employed on them or by their tenant farmers, as the estates controlled farm rents; which in turn dictated market prices to some extent; which in turn dictated wages. In the Cheese Country smaller estates meant fewer owners letting to fewer tenants, and many small farms both self-owned or tenanted. This meant a greater number of farmers who regulated themselves, with varying policies. The final land Enclosures added thousands of acres to existing farms. In 1851 21% of Wiltshire farms were over 100 acres, 20 years later, lands in the county controlled by the Longleat, Wilton, Bowood and Savernake estates totalled over 30% of the county's agricultural land. Domination indeed, but less control over tenants and labourers began towards the end of the century, when due to the agricultural depression and the huge debts of Savernake estate, land began to appear on the market.

It is difficult to get a picture of the average Wiltshire farmer in the 19th century. He seldom wrote anything and is mainly disparaged by reforming writers of yesterday and sometimes even today. Farmers were human beings living in a particular social climate that dictated their attitudes and economic actions. The class division between labourer and farmer was wide, and it existed all through the historic period. His need to make a living and the customs of his time, looked at by our values today, sometimes seem appalling, but not all Wiltshire farmers made harsh masters, and perhaps a clue to this is the numbers of long-term service awards to labourers and farm servants made during the century by agricultural and other associations. Many indisputably held the loyalty of their servants for a lifetime, no mean feat. But much of what was written about them was seldom flattering and benevolent farmers rarely achieve a mention.

Caird, author of a well-known description of Wiltshire farming in 1851 and a perceptive man, criticized the Wiltshire farmer for too easily laying-off his labour in the winter. Conversely, a decade or so later, farmers in South Wiltshire were recalled as being on the whole 'kindly in their disposition', wanting to employ their labour year round if they could find the money to do so. The 'hoarding' of labour during slack times, to be used at peak times, comes in for particular criticism. Various ways existed of making sure labour was on hand when needed, but not employing men full time. Avoidance of an annual contract was one way of doing this, as was piece-work. Later reported from Charlton near Salisbury was a farmer who 'did with his labour as he did with his potatoes. He did not keep all the potatoes out for use every day, and he did not like some farmers try to find work for men all year round. When he did not need them he put them in the workhouse until they were needed.' Perhaps this example was an extreme case.

Little information is to be had on the character of the farmer's wife. A key figure in the Cheese Country, she ran the dairy, making the cheese herself or employing a dairymaid. To hold a skilled employee, (for such was the dairymaid), she could not be harsher than current social values permitted, or the dairymaid would leave at the end of her annual contract, presenting an economic loss if a newcomer had to be trained. On larger farms, particularly if arable, she is unlikely to have participated in any matters concerning the employment of her husband's labourers. She seldom, if ever, gave evidence at the various government agricultural inquiries in Wiltshire, though her husband frequently participated. From his remarks and information one gets the impression he was usually carefully chosen to testify and often expressed what the enquiry wanted to hear. So gleanings from these inquiries are informative, but have to be interpreted with care.

Some farm wives had to run their households to accommodate the boarding of farm servants, a term often used early in the century to describe unmarried male labourers living on their employer's farms. They ate communally in the farmhouse, but often slept in out-buildings, such as over the stable loft. More likely on the dairy farms, family labour was more widespread, the houses smaller and the tradition seemingly not established, except for the live-in dairymaid and female house servant. Cobbett in 1826 pointed out that farmers preferred paying wages to giving bed and board as it was cheaper; it also gave the farmer and his family more privacy. The 1851 census revealed 85% of Wiltshire labourers did not live within the farmhouse. The remaining 15% would have included the dairymaids left in northwest Wilts, and probably farmers' sons, as reports of farm servants are few at

Sheep shearing gang - Chitterne c. 1895

this date. A government enquiry indicates by 1867 farmhouse boarding had disappeared. At about the same time, a farmer from the chalk at a government enquiry decried putting unmarried labourers in cottages (especially those remotely situated), as it encouraged excessive drinking or possible immorality linked to 'forward' young village girls. The farmer may have resented the lack of social control over such individuals, or perhaps his assertions were a case of what the commission wished to hear. However, from economic necessity, the Wiltshire unmarried labourer invariably shared a domestic life with his parents.

The Male Workforce and Wages

The size of the workforce on farms started to fall in the 1850s, though the number of farmers remained roughly the same. Male laborers available declined through emigration overseas and filling jobs that were becoming available in the county, such as those created by the police, army, railways, post office, gas manufacturing and better roads. Wiltshire had begun to creep into the 19th century. The introduction of mechanization meant fewer farm workers were needed. Some arable land in south Wiltshire began to be converted to grass. Female workers declined as Victorian morality decreed farm work to be less acceptable for females, and the women themselves tried to avoid it. Dairy work had become more intensive and hence very demanding and field work hard and rough, not to be contemplated unless a woman had no other means. Victorian morality meant that few unmarried girls worked on farms, but widows were another matter and often did so by necessity, there being no pension, only Poor Law relief or the workhouse. Labourers' wives, who had time or the need to work, did domestic service if not living too far from a job, or took in washing.

The traditional work on the Wiltshire farms began to change in the early 1820s with the arrival of small machinery, such as chaff-cutters and bean mills, rollers and harrows. Then came the threshing machine on big farms, seeding machines and drills, iron and steam ploughs. In the Cheese Country mechanization was extremely slow to arrive, except for the small machinery and some dairying equipment; practically nothing in the 19th century, unless a farm also grew grain. Until the arrival of the reaping machine, all grain except wheat was cut mostly by scythe, occasionally by sickle. The advantage of threshing machines on small farms was marginal at the time of the Swing Riots, most threshing still being done by flail which produced straight, non-bruised straw. Until the 1850s more grain in Wiltshire is likely to have been hand-threshed by flail rather than machine-threshed.

On the larger farms on the chalk, the 1851 census records a few labourers as engine drivers or steam ploughmen. But farmers did not attempt to train their men to use machinery, or pay them more if they did learn to use, drive and repair them. They always seemed to exhibit hostility to any form of education and this animosity continued until 1944, when secondary education finally reached rural areas. Instead they preferred a quality of labour that did traditional jobs and skills in the conventional way. Machines did not always contribute to farm productivity, but they were labour-saving and hence made the worker more dispensable or expendable. On the other side of the coin, several reports exist of farmers continuing to pursue a policy of non-mechanization from habit, dislike of change, sometimes to provide more work for employees. By the 1890s in Wiltshire farm machines were usually purchased due to lack of labour, rather than to replace men. And because of machinery, harvest earnings had dropped to as low as £3, from £8 to £6 in the past, so labourers found little reward in the work.

Average wages over the course of the 19th century began at 6s weekly and ended at 16s, not including extras such as relief, allotments, perks such as those at haymaking and harvesting, charity and friendly society benefits, sometimes housing. At various times threats of reductions occurred, but few materialized. According to Caird, in some parts of south Wiltshire the lowest wage rate of 6s still existed in 1851. Fifteen years later wages edged up to 10s and by 1880, as Wiltshire entered into an agricultural depression, the average weekly wage ranged from 10s to 14s. It fluctuated similarly to the end of the century, but falling food prices increased the labourer's purchasing power.

Farmers used several means to keep wages low over the 19th century, not only by laying off men, which forced them to apply for relief, but also by piece-work payments instead of a weekly wage, and various other manipulations. After the Napoleonic Wars, actual wage reductions occurred between 1815 and 1822. On the farms the number of workers was reduced whenever possible. A calculation for 1839 estimated that dairy farms employed one man per 50 acres, a seemingly low figure, and for arable farms, one man for every 30 acres. Often men from the Cheese Country, if not involved in milking, went south during the grain harvest to work and if unable to find work on his return in the autumn, had to seek relief. After the 1860s, surplus labour in Wiltshire declined, Irish imported labour replaced it at haymaking and harvest time, particularly on the chalklands, a custom continuing into the 20th century.

Sail Reaper near Avebury c. 1880

Role of Fairs in Agricultural Employment Practices

Many farm workers, male and female, moved yearly at the beginning of the 19th century. Especially if single, they changed employment from one farm to another, usually at Michaelmas. A good worker with skills could always find employment, but lack of housing often created difficulties after 1820, especially as the custom of live-in farm servants decreased. For young women in Wiltshire a fair was the certain road to a position of dairymaid, so great the demand, so few willing to do such hard work. (See *Forgotten Harvest,* page 158-162)

Part of the Wiltshire agricultural scene for several centuries, hiring fairs were usually located in a busy market town. Other fairs, especially the big sheep Michaelmas Fair at Tan Hill, served as additions to the hiring scene. When the business of the day was done, celebrating a new job, eating, drinking and general merriment began, and the fair livened up. People found old friends and made new ones, and young people of both sexes had a rare chance to mingle with no social restraints. The need for hiring fairs lessened as farmers cut down on employment by annual contract, and their doubtful reputation had begun to create some moral disapproval by the 1850s. Non-agriculturalists, and even a few farmers, began to look on them as humiliating to the job-seeker from the aspect of a person trying to sell himself, which had been the primary reason for hiring fairs in the first place. Cirencester Mop Fair, to which some Wiltshire people walked many miles to obtain a job, had a particularly notorious character, supposedly fostering promiscuity. However, there is no doubt that these fairs, whatever their reputation, gave much pleasure in different ways to many people.

Chippenham Hiring Fair, held in March and September, was one of the last to survive in Wiltshire. Those requiring jobs paraded in the Market Place with smocks, whips, crooks or a pail to indicate their talents. By 1853 it had turned into a very sober affair, being supervised by clergy, gentry and the good ladies of the town. The secretary of the local Agricultural Association cited it as being totally unlike a certain raucous Scottish hiring fair where, 'a general scene of dissipation wound up the business of the day.' Like Wootton Bassett Hiring Fair, Chippenham Fair died out by the end of the 1850s, perhaps due to its dullness, but more probably because the railway had made communications easier between prospective employees and employers. A register of the Chippenham Fair shows both job seekers and employers drawn from not only local areas, but also Gloucestershire and Somerset, quite logically as the town lies close to sections of both counties.

Besides the fairs, hiring naturally took place locally as well, essential for a family man who could not move far away, due to cost and accommodation being hard to find. A boy or a girl was hired to a farmer by arrangement with a parent, or sometimes by the parish if the child's family was on relief. Sometimes this was accomplished by a harsh apprenticeship, but this changed after the 1834 Poor Law reforms and surplus children went to the workhouses, doubtless a little better fate for many.

Women's work

Women do not seem to have gone to hiring fairs if they sought work on a farm, unless looking for a dairymaid position. Apparently they hired themselves out locally, or made an arrangement with their husband's employer. Sometimes a wife had to work on a farm as a requirement for tenancy of a cottage. Little is known of how gang work for women was organized in Wiltshire.

Women agricultural labourers in Wiltshire during the 19th century can be divided into two groups, the inside dairy workers and the outside field workers, and their situation was to change drastically through the century. By the end of the 1860s hardly any dairymaids remained and cheese was being made by farmers' wives or daughters. Field labour for women, not inherently in gangs, continued until the 1880s, when it became financially less necessary for labourers' wives to seek employment outside the home. The impression is obtained from contemporary documents that it was not customary for women to perform field work in the Cheese Country, and so few women did outside farm work; but until the mid-century they apparently threshed grain with a flail and did other barn work, such as milling roots or chaff-cutting. They often hired themselves out as milkers on larger farms.

On smaller farms with fewer cows, the dairymaid sometimes milked, but according to tradition, the farmer's wife never, so Mrs Self of Cocklebury Farm always maintained.

Female apprenticeship on Wiltshire farms is a topic needing investigation. Parish poor records indicate it existed into the 19th century, but how many girls worked outside and how many inside the farm house is not known. In North Bradley it had been very common, but in Lacock, ten miles away, little indication occurs of females being sent to work on farms.

The shortage of labour due to men going to fight during the Napoleonic Wars put more women than ever into the fields; Berkshire called them 'petticoat harvesters.' After the Napoleonic Wars, returning soldiers apparently did not change the previous employment situation for women. Plenty of evidence exists for women labourers, especially on the large corn-growing farms. Henry Methuen, the Vicar of All Cannings (1810-69) commented how he had to restrict his parish visiting, since both men and women worked in the fields throughout most of the year. A Victorian lady, Mrs Haughton, writing of life in her village in the Vale of Pewsey in the mid-19th century, commented that the local women worked in the fields as regularly as men. 'It is a hard life, especially for the young girls, and at a very early age the women looked prematurely worn and haggard.' Yet despite this, some lived to reach eighty or ninety.

Female gang-labour in Wiltshire began to attract a great deal of attention after 1843, when the moralistic point of view began to be put in front of government commissioners. Members of a gang working in a remote area were suddenly considered to be at risk from a male gang leader, unless elderly, and the younger or unmarried women a target of corruption from older 'unvirtuous' married women of the gang. The presumption existed that, given these circumstances, immorality was bound to occur, and it was insinuated how easily this could happen because of the lack of a certain undergarment few poor women could afford to buy, and had never been in the habit of wearing.

The commission of 1867-8 investigating the 'Employment of Children, Young Persons, and Women in Agriculture' is a mine of information pertaining to Wiltshire on the subject conveyed by the title. For instance, a Mr William Long of Amesbury, representing himself as a most righteous person, farmed 1,800 acres. He paid out £1,800 in wages annually and despite the great need for cottages in the area, he had eight on his farm, one family per cottage. He employed 30 men, 16-18 women, and 17 boys age nine and upwards. He favoured education, as he considered an informed labourer was a better worker. His cottages on the downs were isolated, hence very bad in which to put single man. Among the girls, aged twelve to fourteen years, he saw much immorality. He felt that the law should prevent women working in the fields with men, or with girls under the age of fourteen, for fear of their bad moral influence on either group.

A clergyman followed on, pointing out how inconsiderate people were to the poor and the need for the labourer to work his children for the money they earned, often 50% of the total money coming into the home. He also felt that many squires showed little interest in the poor unless they could see them, otherwise, 'out of sight, out of mind.' Various other view points were later presented to the Commission on the pros and cons of education and the employment of women, mainly thought to be physically good, but morally harmful.

Another farmer, Mr George Brown, farmed 467 acres at Avebury. (Interestingly he admitted to being an ardent supporter of Free Trade.) His women employees who lived only a half a mile away in the village, worked at weeding, haymaking, and spreading manure, the latter job seldom in the winter. Perhaps this work was considered too tiring for women at that time of year, I certainly found it so. They earned 8d a day and 1s a day at harvest time. Brown paid his men a basic wage of 10s a week, but claimed with overtime, they took home an average of 12-13s weekly. He was ambivalent about the value of education and it is to be noted that the idea of education for women was never mentioned before any commissions, indicating that it was not worth consideration.

Later on in the same hearings, an agent from Savernake informed the commissioners that the estate, for moral reasons, had ceased to employ female gang labour, but did allow women to go into the woods and gather acorns.

It was not so at Castle Coombe on a 250 acre farm. The women (the farmer did not employ girls) worked on a part-time basis, in spring and summer 6 am to 6 pm, and in the winter from dawn to dusk, especially 'when the [threshing] machine comes.' Hours at harvest time were also longer. They earned 10d a day.

Edward Little at nearby Lanhill, a well known local agriculture figure, employed women on his farm in clod-breaking and clearing the pastures in the spring, though he claimed that chain harrows were taking over this work more and more. No employment, he felt, was injurious to women, though he conceded cleaning turnips in the winter to be exposed, cold and wet work, as was feeding field sheep sheltering under thatched hurdles. The women worked from 8 am to 5 pm, earning 9d a day.

Child labour

For the first two decades of the 19th century, all sons of agricultural labourers inevitably went to work for a local farmer at a very early age, often as young as five years if no school existed in his village. A Norfolk widow, Elizabeth Dickson, stated the case for child labour succinctly before a government commission: 'My children were obliged to work very young, some before they were seven years old. If you have nothing but what comes out of your fingers end, as they say, its no use, you must let them [work], they want more victuals.' After 1830 schools in Wiltshire became more numerous, and conditions by 1867 were perhaps a little kinder, as boys seemed to be allowed to stay in school until they could read and write at nine years old. Girls stayed on until the age of eleven or twelve, then might be employed in light farm work if parents permitted and not 'go out to service.' An Agricultural Children's Act of 1875 would then make it unlawful to employ a child under eight years of age in any kind of agricultural work; to hire a child between eight and ten, proof of 200 school attendances in the previous twelve months had to be supplied; but if the family needed the earnings and took the child out of school to work, to enforce the clause a school teacher probably found it caused hardship and unpopularity. At any rate, the clause was suspended at harvest time.

In Wiltshire, boys in 1867 still started work on the farms younger than in other southern counties generally paying higher wages. In those counties the boys started at nine to ten years old, the girls at fourteen to fifteen. The practice of hiring and boarding a boy for a year still existed on large farms, which needed the boys' work. They were paid 30s yearly plus food, and perhaps clothing. A Salisbury doctor testified, to another commission, of boys suffering from rheumatism, heart disease, (rheumatic fever?), and lack of sleep. However, a farmer did not think the health of the boys was seriously injured by farm work.

Some landowners after the 1850s cast a benevolent eye on children on their estates, setting up schools, or providing them with instruction. The Vicar of Calne reported in 1868 that boys on the Bowood estate cultivated small patches of land and received instruction in carpentry. Girls on the other hand learnt needlework only and Lady Lansdowne supervised them herself. However, at Savernake active domestic science schools existed for the girls. The girls preferred service in large houses rather than small; reasonably so, as working conditions and supervision were doubtless better than in a small household, where a young girl endured almost slave conditions, and if working on her own, could be very lonely. Mr Spencer, the agent at Bowood, informed the same commission that 'crow boys' working from dawn to dusk earned 3-5d a day, as did boys assisting carters.

The very young boys worked at bird-scaring, or other 'light' work, as for instance preventing animals put out to graze in stubble from straying. Small boys were not much good at ploughing, understandably as it needs considerable strength. Farmers made constant references to boys not making good milkers until over twelve years of age. Probably not, children of that age lack concentration and application, the cow, if not handled correctly, would refuse to let down her milk at first and, when she did, failure to milk her sufficiently 'dry' was an easy fault for a young boy to make.

Many boys ran small errands for the farmer. Fewer children worked on dairy and mixed farms, more on arable farms, and most seem to have endured appalling work conditions and worked days as long as their fathers. They were paid 4d-6d a week up to the 1850s, up to a 1s a week by the 1860s. On Mr Brown's Avebury farm, the boys worked 5.30 am–6 pm, and by 1868 averaged 2s 6d to 4s week with £1 at Michaelmas, apparently much higher than other local current rates. But Avebury was a village with a history of protest, leading to trade union activities in the following decade, and working conditions therefore marginally better.

Boys and women at Broughton Gifford, on the clays, engaged very little in field work, according to the Vicar, Reverend Wilkinson. The girls stayed at school until aged eleven or twelve years, the boys until eight or nine years. One third of his parish engaged in hand-loom weaving, the young children assisting in 'quillying and changing shuttles.'

Edward Little also had much to say on the employment of young boys. He had four boys working on his farm. He liked to start them at six years old and one of that age, working for him in 1869, could already read and write, due to the 'excellent school system at nearby Chippenham.' He always needed boys aged nine or over for full time work on his farm and after the age of eight he paid them 4d a day.

Giving evidence before a government commission the Reverend Payne of Downton complained in no uncertain terms that owing to shepherd boys often being employed on Sundays, they were unable to attend religious school, and he suggested it be made illegal that boys be employed on two successive Sundays, particularly as the *only* work done was stock-feeding and milking. Boys should not have to work on farms until the age of twelve, often not fit enough because of lack of sleep and good nourishment. Supporting the temperance cause, he suggested that the boys' fathers should give up beer to provide them with better food!

Child labour lessened after the 1870s but the suspension of the 1875 Education Act at harvest time and the conditions of proof of school attendance were undoubtedly stretched when necessary for boys, especially if the parents needed the child's wages. Young boys and girls gleaned with their mothers, (gleaning often began as early as 2 am) and girls often went out in the fields with them, hoeing and doing other 'light' work by the age of twelve. Two other alternatives existed for the girls as they reached their teens – going into service, or eventually marrying a village boy. By 1870, the service route seemed to be the most frequently chosen, little future for a girl existing in a local marriage.

Reports often occur until the 1860s of girls straw-plaiting and pillow lace-making in the home. Glove-making is likely to have been practiced in the Corsham area, dependent on the delivery and return of leather cuts making the money worth while. In the cloth districts children are sure to have helped their parents with weaving at home, like those at Broughton Gifford.

Village Life

Enough contemporary documents exist through the 19th century to enable a picture of village life to be drawn. Wiltshire had more than 300 villages, all in their way individual, yet all sharing certain generalities. Distance and lack of communications kept many villages isolated, some until the end of WWI, so residents depended on their own input to form a communal society. To survive, villagers still looked to agriculture; for some living within a

few miles of the cloth valleys, weaving and piecework provided irregular additional income. Home industries produced a little money. Various craftsmen and people of other métiers also lived in villages. Everyday needs and supplies came from the nearest market and their own resources. Not until canals and the railways appeared in the county did goods and newspapers come regularly into a village. Regular deliveries meant the emergence of the small village shop, mainly dealing in food and other simple items. Some were run by widows from a front room in a house, preferably on the village street, and later a section of such an establishment might serve as the village post office.

Cohesion of village society had stemmed from traditional sources, from the top, the lord of the manor, local large landowners and JPs, then smaller local owner or tenant farmers. Differences in many villages came from whether they were open or closed. Generally a closed village meant a local landowner, whose land encompassed the village and its buildings. He or she had great power over the villagers, especially when combined with the Church and local tenant farmers. Housing, roads and sanitation were usually of a better standard than those in an open village, but charity could be rationed according to the deserving and undeserving, employment controlled, and church attendance monitored. In addition, from the 1840s onwards until the end of the century, many landlords, like other middle- and upper-class Victorians, developed an interest in moral standards, particularly those of women, but these extended to the men of the village if they showed any interest in unions or other benefit societies. In addition, land owners scrutinized the goings-on at the village pub and kept an eye on its attendees. Residents of open villages on the other hand were less observed, as more than one landowner held lands in and around the area and did not influence the clerical appointments. Hence villagers had more freedom and were able to attend nonconformist activities if they so chose. Today a chapel or nonconformist building in a village frequently signifies an open village.

Open or closed, the Anglican Church and the parish vestry played a large part in village life until 1834, as it had to organize the poor rates and handing out of relief. If schooling existed in the village, it came mainly from church or chapel Sunday schools, Dame schools and private enterprise ventures until the 1840s , when day schools began to appear in some villages. Church or chapel activities and the villagers themselves created community gatherings and functions. But the gap existing after 1800 between the haves and the have-nots widened more rapidly and community life followed the separate divisions made. Custom kept progress at bay as Thomas Davis observed in 1813, but the inescapable changes in social patterns eventually made their mark on even the remotest village, mainly due to news of the outside world reaching the villages and improvement of communications, especially after the coming of the railways to the county.

By the mid-century, from contemporary writings and censuses we get an idea of the work of the village inhabitants. Craftsmen still predominated. Trades represented in the 1851 census show many large villages had a thatcher, hurdle-maker, blacksmith, shoemaker, baker, grocer, mason, carpenter, and mole-catcher. Some had a resident herbalist, a miller, tailor or dressmaker. Women worked as laundresses, nurses, midwives and small shopkeepers. Agricultural labourers were still the most numerous of all the villagers, either permanent or part-time employees and those who moved around at harvest or hay-making time.

In All Cannings in 1848, there were 7 farmers, 3 bakers, a blacksmith, carpenter, tailor, shoemaker, the parish clerk, the landlord of the King's Arms who also ran the post office, the mistress of the Free School and a relieving officer. In 1851 the census also lists 2 dressmakers, 1 lacemaker, 2 cordwainers, 3 Chelsea pensioners, 3 canal labourers, a police

A Wiltshire pub in the 19th century: The Waggon & Horses, Beckhampton c. 1890s

constable, a shepherd and a higgler or carrier. The largest farmer, Simon Hitchcock of Green House. farmed 1380 acres and employed 67 labourers. Other farmers were Henry Neate, a solicitor and farmer at nearby Allington, farming 1000 acres and employing 42 persons, Joseph Parry farming 870 acres and having 36 employees, down to a farmer with 4 acres and no employees. These statistics hide the endemic poverty present in the village at the time.

Twenty years later Earl Nelson of Trafalgar House, Downton, testified at a government hearing:

> In 25 years labourers have advanced – great improvement in soberness, general intelligence and independence; the young carrying themselves better, are brighter and their appearance altogether in advance of their forefathers. I cannot agree with the political economist who would place the agricultural labourer below the same class in towns, either in intelligence, position or morality, and although their conduct of morality is not so high as that among the upper classes of society, it is much more generally and strictly observed than the higher code attempted among ourselves.

Obviously a decade of better food and a little education had improved the labourer's life in the Downton area.

One room cottage near the Wiltshire–Somerset border at Radstock 1846. The artist recorded an earth floor and an inside height to the eaves of four feet. Most Wiltshire agricultural labourers and their families lived for centuries in little or no better accommodation until after the mid 19th century when housing slowly began to improve for them.

Housing

By any standards through most of the 19th century the agricultural labourer and other villagers were still housed abominably. The few, who after the 1860s obtained a newly-built cottage were the only lucky ones, thanks to large estate owners or landlords who could afford and were willing to make a large capital investment giving little capital return, due to the traditionally low house rents in Wiltshire.

By the end of the 18th century, the supply of houses in Wiltshire villages had diminished due to several factors. Population grew, jobs became scarcer, wages lower. The system of the labourer himself replacing or repairing his own cottage when needed broke down; he just could not afford the repair materials. Enclosure allowed a landlord to terminate a lease, raise a rent, or, if a freehold cottage, the land could be bought up, some compensation given, the cottage torn down and the inhabitant moved on, as he was no longer needed in that particular place or job. Or a cottage was deliberately neglected by a landlord and combined with unemployment, created circumstances forcing a family out of a parish, a saving on the poor rate. Even Poor Law overseers were known to reduce the number of dwellings available by allowing them to fall into decay. Caird, the agricultural observer writing on the farming scene in Wiltshire in 1851, reiterated the same scene and accused 'large proprietors' of diminishing the number of cottages on their estates, so that families were driven to accepting open-village housing. Another factor always reducing the stock of houses was fire. A cottage fire made good local news and from the late 1830s the newly-established north Wiltshire paper, the *Devizes and Wiltshire Gazette* (DWG), frequently reported on them, invariably citing total destruction because of thatched roofs and lack of fire-engines. The fire hooks at the side of a house in West Lavington, seen from the main road when passing through the village are a relic of those days.

Though ever ready to praise the 'pretty' ones, Cobbett was one of the first reformers to document the disgraceful state of housing in Wiltshire villages. He described at Erlestoke a group of white houses spaced a few yards apart, covered with flowering creepers. But in contrast he saw many bad villages, where misery among the workers showed in their gaunt hungry faces and scarecrows of paupers wandered in the roads around.

Twenty years later, the true state of cottages began to be documented at government hearings. A typical description invariably included the following: a floor of stone, often lower than outside levels, no drains, streams of refuse, privy and pig liquid all around. The 1843 report of the Poor Law Commissioners on Women and Children in Agriculture has the now-famous portrayal of a cottage in Studley, Calne, where 29 persons resided, the interviewee deploring the lack of decency in such living conditions. The new age of morality had begun, and women and children's morals especially were to be frequently used as an excuse to expose bad housing and employment conditions. After 1860, when new cottages began to replace the old, economic reasons, mainly the retention of labourers in the countryside, motivated their building, rather than the labourers' lack of 'decent' morals.

Progress was slow however. An 1868-9 commission showed very little betterment of rural dwelling conditions. According to one authority, Wiltshire cottages fell into three groups; those on larger estates usually the best maintained, 'fair' cottages built by speculators, and the worst, those still being built or repaired by employers or labourers with wattle and cob (gravel, straw and mud) with straw thatched roofs. Rents ranged from £1 to £4 a year. One witness suggested that money spent on cottages should be used sparingly, as the labourer did not appreciate model cottages. Probably not – he knew their rents were unaffordable to him. Before the same commission, Earl Nelson claimed that he still gave facilities to squatters on common lands and supplied sites for the freeholder and speculator. But despite new cottages in time replacing the old wattle-and-daub dwellings, (and these ostensibly had disappeared by the 1880s, according to Jefferies) the chronic shortage of rural cottages in Wiltshire continued into the first half of the 20th century.

Large families were still the norm in the 1860s. Signs of labour shortages had begun however and plans of building more cottages in the countryside were aired. Designs for model cottages abounded ever since Prince Albert had, at the time of the Great Expedition of 1851, specified that the minimum cottage should consist of a living room, scullery, a privy and three bedrooms. Such a cottage cost at least £100 to build and, to make the investment worth while had to return a rent of £6 annually, or 10s a month. The average annual wage of the labourer in Wiltshire at this time was 10s a week, so he could not pay that high a rent; furthermore he was not used to high rents. To build cottages was a losing proposition to all but the largest landholders. A few estates were willing to take that loss and began to build. Records of the Neeld estate at Grittleton make frequent reference to cottage maintenance and building after the 1860s and Joseph Neeld's architect, James Thompson, rebuilt worker's cottages at Alderton and Grittleton, out of sight of Neeld's great house. They happily fulfilled Prince Albert's requirements and left room for small additional 'outsets.' The Wilton Estate had always taken pride in its laborers' cottages, and was able to pay for maintenance and rebuilding by charging its farm tenants higher rents. On the other hand, the Savernake Estate, at mid-century, proposed rebuilding unsanitary and overcrowded cottages on the estate at an annual investment rent of £1,000 a year, but due to family financial problems did not live up to the decision.

The large landholders and estates invested in many more cottages than ever before. They can still be identified by their recognizable style in many Wiltshire villages today; Bremhill and Grittleton are two clear examples. Sadly this trend slowed down, especially on the chalk, as Wiltshire entered an agricultural depression not to be lifted until the start of WWI. But much more remained to be done, and labourers frequently had no chance of decent housing until after WWII, despite the drift from the land meaning a lessening of demand for rural housing, and the provision of council houses after WWI. Through this time, due to the demand for urban housing, the County Council had faced particular administrative problems financing and executing rural housing. And health authorities, though they had good reason, did not condemn houses when people had no alternative accommodation. So the bad housing remained.

Contrasts in open and closed villages still prevailed in 1880. According to Heath, barns and stables were better-constructed than rural housing and the concept of offering housing as a form of social control prevailed in the closed villages. He described the closed village of Wilcot as a mixture of brick and stone, thatch and slate, fifty or so 'pretty' cottages making up the village. All had good-sized lattice windows, two or three bedrooms, a sitting room and a kitchen. Most had attractive gardens, with fruit, vegetables and flowers, so that 'over all, there is a brightness and freshness, and there is especially an absence of the sort of soiled appearance which too frequently is noticeable in workman's dwellings.' Rents were no higher than one shilling a week, plus eight-pence a year for a contract chimney sweep, who came twice annually. The landlord allowed no lodgers, so to make best use of accommodation, the families moved from house to house as more children came along, grew up and left home. Drunkenness or a daughter 'getting into trouble' meant eviction. The only pub closed on Sundays as there was no demand. (Surely wishful thinking on the part of the writer!) In contrast, at nearby Oare, an open village, pubs were plentiful, as were Saturday night fights, but the village lacked the paternal care of a landlord-owner. At Wroughton, the standard of cottages was generally higher, influenced by Swindon's better housing supplied by the Great Western Railway (GWR). There the company paid their employees enough for them to afford higher rents, threefold or more than the agricultural labourer was able to afford, which indicated the difference in rural and urban wages. But Jefferies is exceedingly critical about the standard of housing in Swindon under GWR regime, conditions being, in his opinion, being more unsanitary than country cottages because of overcrowding.

A cottage at Avebury perhaps photgraphed circa 1920s. The comparative abundance of building material in this more prosperous agricultural area made for a substantial building.

It is difficult to determine when the system of tied cottagers came into being in Wiltshire. One of the triggers may have come from farm servants and other labourers who had previously lived in the farmhouse and commenced to live out at the end of the 18th century. Another trigger was possibly the chronic storage of housing, leading to the farmer who could afford it to invest in a few cottages for his labourers, especially if the farm lay far from a village. But few records of tied cottage can be found until the 1860s, and by then it was a phenomenon taken for granted. Probably large landlords also let cottages to their tenant farmers, who then sublet on a tied-cottage basis. By 1868, at a government commission, a large farmer in the south of the county stated that tied cottages abounded, but often the wife had to work in the fields as a condition of tenancy. The tied cottage system was quickly adopted, to remain commonplace until the 1950s when total mechanization reduced labour needs and at the same time gave the farm worker affordable wheels, so that he could live some distance from his job.

General renting of cottages in villages was always a norm. The longer the tenancy the better, as it lessened the chance of being turned out at short notice. A [Stoke] Bishopstone widower with three sons is recorded as always attempting to obtain a year's lease on his dwelling and in 1868 had a cottage with three bedrooms.

Houses and their Contents

Not much information is obtainable regarding the interior of a labourer's cottage in the 19th century. In the first place, much must have depended on the quality of the building. A wattle-and-daub house with an earthen floor cannot generate or offer much comfort. By mid-Victorian times, artists were beginning to produce large numbers of cottage interior scenes, but most were depicted as respectable. clean-living households, looking fairly well-fed and dressed, whereas the Wiltshire setting was generally far worse, with one room down and one up, the up-space under the roof approached by a ladder or a very steep staircase, divided by a partition or two. Some cottages managed to have outsets, maybe in the form of a scullery, a wash- or a bread-house. A one-up and one-down cottage had its front door opening into the living room. In a slightly larger cottage, the door opened into a narrow passageway the depth of the house, with a connecting doorway to the kitchen-cum-living-room where the chimney hearth was located, and the space up above consisted of two rooms of the same size as those on the ground floor.

The brick or stone hearth or fireplace did not change much until after the 1850s, when due to the railways, coal could be purchased and a hob grate sometimes installed. Additions to the fireplace depended on the household, the ingenious labourer and a thrifty wife might manage to create a bread oven, add a rod above the fire to hang pots or even a frying pan in a triangular frame or a crane that swung a pot over the fire. By the beginning of the century, thanks to the industrial revolution, cheap tin utensils were being manufactured, such as skimmers and ladles and little tin reflector ovens. I recall as a child seeing the latter used in farmhouses and cottages; they were just a three-sided tin, pierced through with a rod on which were hung hooks. The meat or bacon was placed on the hook and the oven put in front of the fire on a stand or a lip extending from the hob grate. This method of cooking needed very little fuel and the fire, in addition, heated a pot hanging from the chimney. Local blacksmiths made fireplace implements and fittings of cast iron if a labourer could afford it.

When the new cottages began to be built after the 1860s, a hob grate was standard, sometimes with a cistern for hot water. These continued as the main means of cooking until the 1920s, then paraffin cooking and heating-stoves appeared on the scene. Hob grates were still being inserted into both urban and rural council houses in the 1930s, but gas and electric stoves were often beyond a labourer's pocket until after WWII.

Privies were often shared, and probably always a bone of contention as to who was to empty them and where their contents were to be disposed. One Wiltshire labourer, whose family ate more meat than most of his neighbours, thought so highly of the contents of his privy that he offered them to the local farmer at a higher rate than was usual. Away from a farm, the garden or an allotment absorbed the 'night soil, ' and unless care was taken could be a source of disease. At a double cottage near

A tied cottage at Manor Farm, Stert , 1928

Chippenham in the 1930s, occupants had permission from their farmer- employer to dump their privy buckets weekly on a manure heap in a field adjoining the cottage. It was a fairly safe procedure, as their well was 50 yards away. At Easton Royal, in a house on the main street, though it had running water in 1951 the only sanitary arrangement was still a bucket privy in the back garden, a two-seater with a crescent in the door!

One farmer in front of a government hearing in 1868 swore the solution to the privy problem was what he called Maule's system for privies, in reality a dry earth closet. Not very practical for cottagers when earth had be obtained from a distance and then taken back again, time-consuming

Council houses at Rowde. Not as attractive to look at, but at the time of building (1926) far more comfortable and labour-saving.

and needing large containers for the moving. But earth-closets had a long life in Wiltshire, the largest house in Chippenham, The Ivy, relied on them until after WWII, moving the earth in buckets via a special dumb waiter system located at the far end of the house.

The water supply, or lack of it, dominated the labourer's household and its cooking, cleaning, washing of bodies and clothes. If a wife took in washing, it became even more critical and often more back-breaking to fetch and carry if the cottage did not have a nearby well. Supplies to many cottages were primitive or non-existent. Nearby streams often had to serve; if there were none in the vicinity, wells were dug, many of them probably dating back a century or more. The rainwater butt was another supply, complete with little 'wigglies' in it. Village standpipes needed valves, pipes and other equipment, plus a steady water supply. To the best of my knowledge, standpipes did not come into villages until after the 1870s and many, e.g. Urchfont, relied on them into the 1930s. At Eastwell, near Potterne, villagers carried water from the only well. Piped water had arrived, but was not laid on to privately-owned cottages, landlords being too tight-fisted to supply a standpipe. Jefferies in the 1870s confirmed that most water-carrying was done by the girls in the family. To supply so many remote Wiltshire villages with running water was a problem in logistics and money, a challenge from the middle of the 19th century until the 1950s to both landlords and the County Council.

Cottage furniture and furnishings are likely to have been of the minimum, the many budgets published of a labourer's household expenditures never allowed for items of either, there was just no money for them. Some would be inherited pieces, others made by the labourers themselves or perhaps by the local carpenter, paid for by barter of labour, pig-money, or perhaps vegetables. Bedding was often supplied by overseers or charity. General household possessions were probably not much more than those the pauper cottagers had at Clyffe Pypard in 1767. (See previous chapter.) What a household possessed must have depended on several factors: whether the head of the household held a year-round job, whether both he and his wife were good managers, how healthy they were, how many children they had and what they might have inherited or were given by other family members.

Fuel

If the agricultural labourer's standard of living is gauged by the amount of energy coming into his home, he was very badly off indeed in Wiltshire after the 16th century. Eden, in 1797, draws attention to the labourer in the north, being able to enjoy more hot food, bread and soups because of the availability of cheap coal. In the south the scarcity and high prices of coal and wood made the introduction of any dish needing much cooking an impossibility. Frying and short-boiling were the most economical methods of cooking over a fire of collected wood or faggots. Adding together poverty, endless food shortages and the fact that many women had to work in the fields or dairies, are some of the probable reasons why Wiltshire has no tradition of peasant cooking.

Getting enough fuel for the hearth 'by hook or by crook' began to be problematical for the Wiltshire labourer after Enclosures began and the rights to gather wood were gradually taken away from him. In the 18th century wood theft had become a very common

Gathering wood circa 1930. Mrs Smart of Urchfont, 'ooding.' An age-old task that did not die out until the 1950s, and done by many more in the in the terrible winter of 1946-7.

rural crime. Ruth Pierce of Devizes market fame appeared in court accused of it. Throughout Wiltshire it seems that only the villagers in the Great Wishford and Barford area retained the old traditional rights to gather wood in nearby Grovelly forest, despite the opposition of the owner, Lord Pembroke. He attempted to take away the rights several times during the 19th century. They still remain today and are celebrated annually.

Coal came into the county by barge from Somerset and the Forest of Dean at the beginning of 19th century, but like the very few cartloads brought in before the canals and later railway transportation, still beyond the labourer's purse. The further the distance from a station, the costlier the coal, so remote villages seldom saw it. A blacksmith's family was fortunate, his trade demanded it, so they are likely to have had it for their household use as well.

Cobbett in 1826 commented on the lack of fuel in villages around Salisbury, which added to the 'hopelessness that rotted village life in southern counties' and the woes of the 'poor creatures living there.' In the same year he drew attention to the fuel shortage, when he observed girls at Great Bedwyn carrying home bean and wheat stubble, not exactly a long-lasting fuel. In the Cheese Country, with almost all the land in private hands, the situation was no better, with fallen timber, green or dead, inaccessible except from any remaining common land or roadsides. A little peat came into the south of the county from the New Forest, but in such small quantities that it probably made little difference to the average cottager. Furze, if obtainable, could also be used as fuel.

The Vicar of Hinton Charterhouse, a Somerset village just over the Wiltshire border, wrote in 1836 with little understanding of the need of the poor for fuel:

> However poor the rate-payers of a parish may be, the parish itself is regarded by the paupers, as an inexhaustible fund, from which they can never get too much. We see this tendency in all who have lived in idleness on the property of others. On the rail-road leading from the coal pits [to the Somerset Coal Canal], may be seen a dozen women, following the waggons of coal, under the pretext of picking up all that falls from them; but, this casual supply not satisfying them, when the driver goes forward to open a gate, some of the gang knock off lumps of coal, which are immediately divided amongst the whole company; and by this traffic they have for many years chosen to live, rather than by the usual methods, which are attended by less excitement and liberty.

The reverend gentleman had all the makings of a Victorian moralist; in contrast, the waggon drivers and the colliery authorities evidently turned blind eyes to regular filching by people too poor to buy coal at the pithead. Of interest too is the accepted practice amongst the women of fairly dividing their spoil, illustrating long-term organization on their part.

The critical fuel situation continued until the end of the 19th century, when cheaper coal, slightly higher wages and coal clubs all began to relieve the situation. Also linked with the fuel shortage was the dearth of lighting in a cottage. Candles were expensive, and so was oil or fat for rush lights. Often the fire was also used as a source of light, candles and rush lights being very sparingly used.

Food

By the end of the 1790s, the static wages and sky-rocketing prices of bread meant that the Wiltshire labourer became heavily dependent for his entire diet on bread, a little bacon and cheese, occasionally a cheap piece of meat or scraps and his home-grown vegetables. His only luxury was tea and sugar, both bought by the ounce. At a village near Swindon, presumably though given away in the past, poor people had to buy skim milk or whey for 1d a gallon, but on the other hand, the farmer had to consider profits carefully after the Napoleonic Wars. After a bad winter causing a shortage of even cheap bits of meat, the poor in Calne could not afford even old cow beef. At the time, wages were approximately 7s week for a male agricultural labourer, to go down to 6s or less between 1820-1840, and not to move upwards until the 1860s when 10s a week was reached.

When Cobbett travelled in Wiltshire in 1826, one of his major impressions was of 'half-starved labourers.' Near Tetbury he prevented an old man from being chased after stealing cabbages from a garden. He calculated 22s week was needed for a family of five children and their parents for base victuals and drink. But at the most a man earned 9s a week, with a parish allowance of 7s 6d for that size family, making a deficit of 5s 6d. Cobbett contrasted it with a soldier who received 7s 7d a week, plus clothing, firing, candle and lodging.

A credible description published in 1874 of how the agricultural labourer had to manage his poverty is told in 'Skeleton at the Plough.' George Mitchell, son of a farm worker was born in 1827 near Yeovil, a few miles from the Wiltshire-Somerset border. Put to work at the age of five for 6d a week scaring birds on a local farm, he cites himself as one of the worst cases of poverty. He worked almost full hours (dawn to dusk), often Sundays, though not on days of snow. Unlike Wiltshire families, his family ate a great deal of barley as their starch, being cheaper than wheat; a 'hot' dinner was an onion with a few pieces of bread soaked in hot water, or perhaps bread and hard skim-milk cheese served the same way. Sometimes he had no food before he went to work in the morning or at night on his return. He supplemented his diet by pulling a turnip, stealing peas or beans or picking up acorns. He hunted and roasted hedge-snails. His employer rewarded him with a cup of vinegary cider when he ran an errand. He claimed to have been much abused and finally found a more reasonable employer where he had better treatment and food, but more work. Mistreatment of children by violence is well-documented in the 19th century and, one suspects, molestation and sexual exploitation may not have been uncommon, but those subjects in the Wiltshire countryside were never to be mentioned; therefore nothing is known of them and their knowledge would have remained just between instigator and victim. On the other hand, incest and immorality in the lower classes received a great deal of open attention, but in the countryside were seldom alluded to as taking place in other social levels.

The poverty Mitchell endured increased as wages stayed the same and grain prices continued to rise. Wiltshire had a tradition of mainly wheat bread; barley, rye and oats had seldom been added. The custom of gleaning seems to have continued and remained important until the 1850s, but it is uncertain how the labourer and his family used the recovered grain. Home grinding had certainly been abandoned, perhaps it was ground by a local miller, then sold, or used in some households for poultry or pig feed? By the early 1800s, due to the change in grinding procedures, two-thirds of bread consumed was white, by 1850, nine out of ten loaves. The nutrients lost in the discarded bran and wheat germ from the flour were never replaced and white bread can be thought of as the first junk- or fast-food, creating a taste for bland, smooth foods that 'went down easy.' Dried beans and peas, with the exception of pease pudding ceased to be referred to in the labourers' diets or their purchases, hence another cheap source of nutrition was lost. Potatoes, introduced in the 18th century, were most unpopular as a cheap bread substitute in Wiltshire, but they were easily grown, seldom prone to crop failure (except in the late 1840s when the potato blight reached Wiltshire), readily cooked and digestible. Deprivation forced Wiltshire folk into finally accepting them as a basic item of diet. Meanwhile more nourishing foods disappeared from the labourer's table as cottagers generally ceased to brew beer or salt meat, except perhaps bacon if they had a pig or a share in one. Eggs are never referred too, it was not customary to drink milk and cheese had begun to cost 4d a pound by 1800, more than the occasional bit of meat at 3d a pound.

During the 18th century where a village baker remained, custom still decreed that villagers bake their bread or their Sunday dinner in the baker's oven for the cost of a penny or two. But village bakers decreased steadily in the 19th century, town bakers substituting with bread deliveries by horse and cart. Cobbett says the practice of home baking was dying out when he travelled about Wiltshire in 1826. Perhaps one in twenty baked at home by 1857.

Lack of money and resources ate into a woman's time, especially if she had to work. With water to be carried, wood to be collected or chopped before starting a fire for cooking or heating water, the washing and other chores to do, plus being able to afford only bread and a few basics, it is no wonder that meals became the minimum to prepare in time, money and ingredients. Bread, hot water poured over burnt (to add flavour) crusts, even hot water poured over a little butter and some flour, is mentioned frequently as served for

Wishford bread plaques: The periodic placing of these plaques illustrates the importance of the price of bread to the 19th century rural Wiltshire worker and his family.

breakfast. Bread and sometimes a little cheese made up the mid-day meal for all family members; home-grown vegetables boiled up, with a little bacon or bacon fat for flavouring, the addition of suet dumplings or dripping on accompanying bread with the stew provided supper, or a fry-up of vegetables with a few meat bits added. A little tea, maybe with sugar at night, and that seems the basic daily diet at the extreme edge of poverty. Porridge or gruel is not recorded.

Additions to diet depended on the family and where it lived. A rabbit or other animal for the pot could be available all the year round if the head of household or his son were willing to take the risk of poaching. If the bank of a river or stream was public land, a labourer could fish from it. Rooks, larks, blackbirds, sparrows and other wild birds substituted meat in pies, but the time and opportunity to catch them must have been limited for the agricultural labourer with his long hours of work, and the law of trespass hindered his opportunities. At pig-killing time, usually November, if a family had not sold the family pig, lard would be rendered down, perhaps some bacon salted and smoked, offal and cheaper cuts of meat used for the table. The best meat seems to have been sold to a butcher or neighbours.

After March, nettles could be cooked, and wild greens eaten raw; dandelion leaves, lung wort, liverwort and purslane and a few weeks later turnip tops appeared. A garden or allotment allowed lettuce and other salad vegetables to be grown, besides later vegetables for cooking: peas, green beans, carrots and other root vegetables. Raw greens as an item of diet are never mentioned however, so one has no idea if they were used, or unmentioned because they were taken for granted. The same applies to cabbage and kale crops which could be available almost throughout the year, but nothing is heard of their consumption by labourers in Wiltshire until the later decades of the 19th century.

Others ate them however. Gandy tells of the Crown Inn at Aldbourne serving up a meal for the local Commissioners celebrating the enactment of the 1805 Enclosure Awards. They ate shin of salt beef, ox tongue, half a loin of boiled veal, a neck of pork, plenty of bacon and a pair of boiled ducks. Accompanying vegetables included cauliflower, blockles (broccoli?), spinach, turnip tops, sprouts, tates, watercress, parsnips and turnips. And plenty more of all sorts, which no doubt included puddings, cold sweets and drink. The cheaper meat cuts and the lack of 'the roast beef of Old England' is a sign of the comparative expense of a joint of beef and, perhaps, lamb.

No allusion is ever made through the 19th century to collecting wild fruit. Again the price of sugar inhibited gathering more than could be eaten in a day or two and, except by jamming, no other means of preservation was used as far as can be ascertained. Bilberries, wild medlars, dew berries and of course the ubiquitous blackberry grew well in the Wiltshire countryside, the right of picking them lasting to the present time; surely used as a food source, but again no allusions occur.

Home-made wine and liqueur-making are old Wiltshire traditions, but how far down the social scale they went in the 19th century cannot be determined. At the end of the 18th century sugar cost 6d or more a pound; at that cost a serious limitation to making either wine or liqueur. Although beer-making generally seems to have been abandoned, one or two references are made at government hearings, when it was brought up to illustrate thrift in a household. In 1868, the agricultural labourer, Thomas Halliday of Stoke Bishopstone, the thrifty widower with a growing family, made his own beer from 2 bushels of malt, yielding 72 gallons.

Celebratory meals after the hay and grain harvests, paid for by the farmer, gave the labourer and his family the chance to eat a square meal and to imbibe freely during the festivities. As Victorian morality increased, the 'indulgence in liquor' would be much condemned, to lead, by the end of the 19th century, to curtailment of this aspect of the meal. Pork, beef, a medley of vegetables, plum pudding, porridge, plenty of bread and cheese and other items were among the food served, washed down with beer and cider.

Cider has a long tradition in Wiltshire, crab apple trees grew at Windmill Hill in the Bronze Age, so it does not take much to imagine a fermented beverage being made from apples and honey. Anglo-Saxons drank *seider*, and later manorial documents refer to apple-pressings for cider. Perry also was consumed more than people realized; in 1653 Gervase Markham wrote of perry and cider as equals and certainly old pear trees dotted about West Country orchards back up a healthy consumption of it. Judging by my own memories of many old sour pear trees and orchards in the Chippenham area, some farms made perry up to the end of the 19th century.

Cider was the common harvest beverage in northwest Wiltshire and other parts of the county, where it was cheap or cheaper than beer for a labourer's beverage. The best cider, made from select apples, went to the gentlemen's table; farm labourers drank rough cider pressed out from windfalls or any apples available. North Wiltshire farms provided it all the year round, South Wiltshire farms furnished it at haymaking and harvest. Was it because it was cheaper than beer, or just more thirst-quenching? By 1794 Thomas Davis claimed that cider in North Wilts was made only for farm consumption and, in 1813, his son, in a new edition of his father's book, stated that orchards are more frequent as appendages to farmhouses than gardens; but cider, and he believed, perry-making, lingered on. In 1879 Mr Long of Kellaways Farm near Chippenham employed three labourers at 14s a week and allowed them three pints of cider per day. At haymaking and harvest allowances went up to as much as a gallon a day; it was thirsty work and even women drank it! By the 1870s, a better diet, more beer, and the temperance movement inhibiting the giving of alcoholic drinks in lieu of wages on farms, decreased the amounts of cider made in northwest Wiltshire. Like the cheese, it was easier to purchase it off the farm. The taste for it remained. Frank Collet, a brewer at Langley Burrell offered Prime Devon, Hereford, and Holbrook's American ciders in 1889. Ralph Whitlock in *Lost Village* mentions at least four portable cider presses operating into the 1900s at Pitton in the south of the county. They were let out on contract and pushed around the orchards as apples ripened, ready for crushing. Thomas Hardy even wrote a poem about portable cider presses

As early as 1848 Harris of Calne began to import American bacon and cheese, probably the first imported foods eaten by the Wiltshire labourer. Thirty years later these imports had became an influential factor in the slow demise of both the bacon and cheese industries in the county and had reduced prices on the local product. The Australian and New Zealand trade began by the 1850s, bringing in more cheese, butter and then meat. A 'trickle down' effect started and meat slowly began to replace cheese as a protein source, though it happened first in urban areas and took until the 1880s to reach the country labourer. Cheap sugar from the Caribbean and the Americas appeared on the market. Wheat imports made flour cheap and bread, pastries, cakes, biscuits and other sweets quickly became more affordable items to the labourer and his family. Lower prices also had put coal within reach of most people, if only by clubs or charity. It is at this time that Wiltshire dishes come into our ken, the lardy and dough cake, polonies, porkies, faggots and other meat delights. Traditional jams and preserves could be bought cheaply, while the practice of home wine-making increased. A few more food choices were to be had, but never in abundance, as wages were still low and went only so far. The pauper could go hungry in Wiltshire in the 1890s and many lacked a balanced and nutritional diet. The plenty we know today, both of choice and nutrition, would not be seen by every Wiltshire labouring family until the 1960s.

Clothing

Poverty depleted wardrobes. From the end of the 18th century until the 1850s, mention is made occasionally of some labourers not having boots to wear to work, boys with their feet wrapped in felt going bird 'scoring' and children arriving at school barefoot. As has been noted, the money from the yearly pig kill was often reserved for the footwear of the labourer and his family. Frequent mention is made of the ever-present problem of damp boots and the impossibility of drying them overnight due to lack of fuel. Getting wet and staying wet was always a problem for the farm workers at Cocklebury, though we had rubber boots (a special allowance during WWII) and a few extra clothing coupons. But the oilskin waterproof garb was clumsy, an incumbrance to work in and uncomfortable to wear. A rainy day and my overalls between the bottom of my raincoat and the top of my 'wellies' stayed permanently wet. Thankfully I could dry them off at home, but it wasn't so easy in the workers' farm cottages, particularly in the summertime when there was little or no heat in them. In the 19th century, when he could afford them, the labourer wore leather gaiters, sometimes stuffed with straw for warmth; they helped to keep his feet dry as they covered the top of his boot. We hear little of the ordinary farm labourer's real working attire in the 19th century, and though by 1839 the DWG ran advertisements for waterproof clothing, could he afford to buy it? He tried to keep dry by wearing a hemp sack around his shoulders. Still plentiful on farms in the1940s, always at hand, we at Cocklebury used them too, to keep water off ourselves in a downpour.

Materials used for farm work had to be hard-wearing, fustian in the 17th century, moleskin later, both being types of twill. Brown corduroy then became the favourite for work trousers from the middle of the 19th century until after WWII 1950. No jeans, though I recall denim garments in the 1940s. The traditional county linen smock, gone by the end of the 19th century, but probably worn for several centuries before, came in various lengths, some opened up, others went on over the head. The milker and general farm worker could unbutton his smock, the carter kept his closed (though it may have been easier to have it

Carter: in smock and hard crowned and brimmed felt hat, circa. 1890s?

open when he clambered up onto the cart, or took the occasional ride after taking a horse from field to stable). Shepherds' smocks were closed and could be worn at a longer length; as on the chalk, there was less mud to deal with, and the smocks provided a certain amount of warmth to the legs. If a man milked, he is likely to have worn a different smock, or apron, as did the dairymaid, for the smock skirt would be stiff with milk after a day or so, making it unpleasant to wear, and extraordinarily difficult to wash, as my mother found out when I brought back my dirty white milking coat and cap after my first week of milking. Before caps, milkers often wore old cloche-shaped hats, positively stiff with hairs and grease, the heavy felt having acquired that shape from pressing into the side of the cow as the worker milked. For hygienic reasons, the Government insisted on washable cloth caps after 1940.

In Aubrey's day, shepherds were traditionally represented as wearing white cloaks with a very deep cape 'which comes halfway down their backs, made of locks of sheep.' By the 1860s, some were clad 'in a cast-off infantry great coat.' Ida Gandy, writing of her childhood at the end of the 19th century explained this phenomenon thus: 'All the shepherds in our part wore these blue cloth cloaks lined with red and my father told us that they were relics of the Crimean War, brought home by the soldiers and handed on in the family.' A durability unheard of today.

Smocks had several advantages, they were very sturdy and the linen was tightly woven, therefore making them washable, and if necessary, spongeable. They were practical to wear except in extreme temperatures, for linen does not feel too cold in the winter, or too warm in the summer. At hay and harvest time linen gave protection from the scratchy stalks of grass and corn. The looseness of the smock meant comfort and the accommodation of as many layers of clothing underneath as the wearer needed or could afford. The reverse applied in the summer. But a disadvantage of smocks lay in their propensity to slow drying after being rain-soaked, like woollen garments. Another drawback was a smock's light colour, which caused all the dirt to show, but people were used to that. (Even today, some country people still hate dry-cleaning their raincoats and other wet-weather gear!) What

Shepherd on Salisbury Plain wearing cloak.

specifically the Wiltshire labourer wore underneath his smock and cords is like asking a Scotsman what he wore under his kilt. A vest, shirt, long underwear in the winter, possibly of linsey, a cotton or linen shirt in the summer. Whether smocks were the universal working garment of choice in Wiltshire is hard to determine; few paintings, drawings or photographs exist of labourers actually working in one and those actually photographed look so pristine, they had obviously not made contact with the dirt of farm work.

Gloves were clumsy to wear and hard to work in, though ones of heavy leather were essential for hedging and clearing ditches. Presumably some form of socks were worn, probably woollen handknits. Most important was the hat. Inevitably felt, 'a billycock' for Sundays and best towards the end of the century. An 1890s photograph of a group of shearers at Chitterne exhibits a great amount of individuality in the range of their headgear, from a Derby to old caps. The traditional woollen, hard-peaked cap was seldom worn until after WWI and then usually by the farmer rather than by the labourer. Until after WWII, most garments, especially hats, reflected the wearer's class (see picture on page 193).

Women farm workers are often depicted in 19th century rural paintings, usually idealistically attired in very clean, neat garments, all quite impractical for the work they are depicted doing. Particularly romanticized are depictions of dairymaids and harvesters, dressed in light-coloured clothing and shoes giving no protection to chaff, dirt or rain. Some East Anglican paintings towards the end of the century are more authentic, as they often show the woman field worker in worn dark clothes, bundled up against the cold and wet, wearing heavy sensible footwear.

What did Wiltshire women farm workers wear? It is hard to say, since so few records remain. (For what the dairymaid wore see *Forgotten Harvest,* page 152) Obviously garments had to be loose and easy to move in, skirts long and full for protection, but able to be hitched up if the work called for it or to avoid soaking the hem. Aprons were commonly worn in an attempt to keep outer garments clean. Mrs Anne Hoves of Latton, a mother of thirteen (the eldest not at work minded the younger children), told a government enquiry in 1869 she had worked all her life at various farm jobs, which included spreading manure, hoeing, haymaking, harvesting and general field work. 'I have been in the turnip field pulling up turnips with ice covering my dress half way up.' For such work and conditions, it would be impossible to wear anything but practical clothes made of hardwearing materials. Felt hats are depicted in the winter, sun bonnets in the summer, head scarves at anytime of the year. Long-sleeved, buttoned blouse-type bodices were worn above the skirt, covered by an apron. Presumably beneath the bodice was some sort of undergarment, a bust bodice (no bras until the 20th century) or vest, and petticoats under the skirt. A cloak or shawl tied at the waist and woollen or cotton stockings and sturdy boots completed the woman fieldworker's outfit. Mid-century moralists assumed the lack of 'bloomers' contributed to promiscuity, particularly in women's work gangs, which was why one Wiltshire farmer assured an 1867 government hearing that he employed an old man to supervise his gang! He also insisted he did not force his women employees to do gang work or to stay in the fields for more hours than they wished.

Sports and Pastimes

Despite remoteness and a small community, villagers, when they had a Sunday or holiday, entertained themselves with zest, seemingly the major problem being getting time off from work to enjoy various sports and other mostly traditional pastimes.

May Day meant dancing and the maypole. One stood on the village green at All Cannings, donated by the Hitchcock family. It lasted until 1829 when it was blown down and not replaced. Sylvia Young who provided this information (see *Wiltshire Folklife*, Autumn 1996, page 35) also added that the nearby pound and stocks lasted until the 1850s, which, except for the occupants, supplied a bawdy amusement to some village inhabitants.

Whit Monday in many villages provided an annual feast and a procession. Often if the village had a Friendly Society, it organized the procession which wended its way to their club meeting place, invariably the local public house, accompanied by a band and waving banners. The villagers themselves indulged in a large meal and later a traditional local walk or dancing, ideal for promoting prospective romances. St Valentine's encouraged the chanting of traditional rhymes by the children and visiting in the village asking for pennies and sweetmeats.

Until their gradual demise due to the coming of the railway, fairs gave villagers a day out. The most famous in Wiltshire was held at Tan Hill in the Pewsey Vale. People travelled all night to them and Victorian morality throughly disapproved of them due to: 'the swearing, drinking and general immorality' as Henry Methuen, Vicar of All Cannings, phrased it. Thomas Moore, the poet who lived at Bromham for many years, visited the Whitsuntide Fair at Bromham in 1825 with his family and their maids. They made a great sensation 'among the clods.' Moore's opinion of the rural population was obviously not very high, but he appreciated one of the dancers there, 'a rather pretty girl.'

Village cricket, quoits, bowls and football matches abounded. And rougher sports. Alfred Williams recorded the comments of an old man he knew who regretted the demise of the old traditional pastimes and games. 'Us could hae a bit o' fun then, an' 'twasn't allus rough; 'twas oni now and 'agyen as us 'ad a bit of a row, an' then 'twas nothing. We bwoys ood run fer miles to see a bit of back-zoordin and wrustlin.' Williams continued: 'His old head was covered with scars – several of five inches in length. His legs too were covered with scars from wrestlers' boots. The wrestlers were forbidden to have iron tips on their boots, so a great many used to soak them for a month in horse urine; this made the leather very hard, and they were enabled to kick their opponents black and blue.' Fighting with cudgels used to draw admiring crowds to the village green at All Cannings and Henry Methuen, the Vicar, reported that he knew some doughty exponents still alive.

Harsher by today's standards were the still-apparently much relished animal sports: bear-, bull- and badger-baiting and cock-fighting. In 1771 Parson Woodford noted a two-day cock-fight between Somerset and Wiltshire at Ansford, which Somerset won. All these went on until the mid -1800s, after which they cease to be mentioned. Probably the coming of the railways, starting in the 1840s, destroyed their tradition, while cock- fighting became illegal in 1849.

Harvest Home celebrations at Lacock circa 1880s.

Mumming, as a symbol of the earth's eternal fertility rather than as a mereYuletide celebration, obviously continued in many villages. Potterne kept its traditional play going until 1890, a very late date. Skimmington revels could happen at any time of the year.

Henry Methuen described a game called 'Maddle', played by shepherds on the downs, using a board of turf and beans or marbles. Possibly this was Shepherd's Puzzle, to which Hudson drew attention to in his travels on Salisbury Plain.

Poaching

Though considered as a sport, pastime and a source of food in the countryside, by the 19th century the Game Laws had made poaching a very dangerous endeavour. But the Wiltshire agricultural labourer still felt it was his inalienable right to hunt wild game. Besides fulfilling an innate love of the hunt or the 'sporting instinct,' he viewed the hunted animals as no-one's personal possession, their killing a part of country living, particularly if his family were hungry. The Game Laws stretched back to 1389, originally created to protect the King's deer and to limit the right of hunting to certain social orders. In 1671, manorial lords were permitted to appoint gamekeepers authorized to carry guns and seize guns and goods from others. By the 19th century, the Game Laws conflicted, not only with the agricultural labourer, but with the many emerging small tenant farmers, as they legally could not hunt the land they rented and farmed and were bound by their leases to preserve the game on it.

Aubrey claimed of Wiltshire: ' no county in England had greater variety of game' and most of the countryside was accessible to the labourer to hunt it. To the middle of the 18th century, when hunger began to strike some labourers, 'a bit o' poaching' was not heavily prosecuted or so frequently reported. But shooting amongst the landowning classes had steadily gained popularity and, as hunger and poverty grew, poaching increased. Gamekeepers, with their rights of seizure, clashed with the more numerous poachers and conflict began. Keepers who lived in nearby villages or came from local families could create much antagonism. They often used an informer to apprehend a poacher or his cohorts, splitting family loyalties and causing resentment throughout a community. A meal from the poached hare or bird had to be kept a secret and the remains of the animal before cooking and the subsequent carcass hidden or buried carefully. Thomas Bright, a Ramsbury labourer on an Ailesbury estate, informed against a higgler who was in possession of and intended to sell four hares. Bright had been snaring hares in 1767 on the estate, and was in dire need, as his application for relief had been refused and there was no bread in his house. His informing had made him most unpopular with other villagers and they were 'ready to knock hime on the head.' A year later he was before the local JP for laying 29 snares, and he again saved himself by informing, this time on another higgler to whom he had sold a brace of hares for 4s.

Sometimes when accused, a man fled his village. William Bray of St Martins, near Marlborough, left for London and sent back money to support his wife and children. Perhaps he obtained a job as a middleman to a game supplier of the city. Middlemen were frequent; not all labourers poached because of hunger or poverty. Convictions and complaints during the first half of the 19th century illustrate how much game was poached for sale in the nearest town, or sent away as far as London. According to Jefferies, who knew first hand the ways of poachers and gamekeepers, a few men made a good living at poaching. Well able and always careful to avoid the local keeper, they created their own systems to dispose of the game to town markets. They were known and sometimes went to jail, but they still craftily carried on their chosen profession. For the occasional poacher, publicans were in a convenient position to act as a middle man; what could be easier to convey in a capacious pocket to the pub than a bird or a rabbit he'd 'just happened to come across', have a drink and at the same time, receive a shilling or two for his trouble and risk.

Lacock Gamekeeper circa 1840s: Probably the first photograph of an English gamekeeper, taken by Fox Talbot.

Few labourers risked having possession of a gun; aside from discovery if a house was searched by police at the request of a keeper, a gun needed ammunition and was noisy to use. The snare of choice was the wire, looped in the best way to catch the creature of choice, mainly rabbit, hare or pheasant. Jefferies explained how labourers set their trap wires hidden among the hedgerows or sometimes in their allotments. Rabbits, as all gardeners know, are attracted to many green plants, while planting a patch of corn encouraged a pheasant, easily dispatched while feeding with a quickly thrown stout stick conveniently at hand. Shepherds were in a good position to poach, usually worked in isolated areas away from the footstep of the keeper and always had a legitimate need for a working dog who was dually trained to hunt as well as to round up sheep. Like other countrymen, while pointing out gypsies as chronic poachers, Jefferies also complained of men coming out from the towns on Sundays to poach. Their nefarious activity would be covered by the excuse of gathering bunches of primroses, fern sprouts, watercress or mushrooms, depending on the season, the bottom of a basket or small sack providing the hiding place for a rabbit or a hare.

Jefferies, writing mainly of poaching habits in his home area of Coate, mentions briefly that the occasional fawn might be come upon, killed and brought home without detection, being small enough to hide. But an adult deer was not, and invariably left alone by the locals. This apparently did not apply in Cranborne Chase on the Wiltshire borders, where poaching deer was a very ancient custom, despite being a risky practice.

Estates in Wiltshire dealt with poaching in various ways. Lord Ailesbury at Savernake ruled that if a man was accused of poaching he was to be cut off from poor relief. His steward complained, 'he commences [as a] poacher and [turns into] a thief with all his might,' a logical act as immediate starvation stared a culprit in the face. But harsh punishments were the rule on large estates, it being very costly to prosecute a violator of the Game Laws through the courts. For instance, in 1797 it had cost Longleat £37 5s to secure convictions for several poachers. But at least the Marquis of Bath never used man-traps. They were forbidden by law in 1827 and had provoked enormous resentment among country people, not only for the horrible injuries they could cause, but also the psychological resentment that humans were no better than the animals also trapped. That labourers thought as little of the animals they trapped was an irony of the situation seemingly unnoticed.

Wiltshire has many records of sheep stealing during the hungry years and, if caught, punishment by hard labour and transportation invariably followed. Harsher sentences materialized for those detected poaching, but the war between landowner and gamekeeper on one side, the poacher on the other, continued unabated. In 1770, taking game by night became punishable by up to twelve months' imprisonment. By 1800 a single Justice had the power to sentence poachers to imprisonment with hard labour; three years later armed resistance to arrest became punishable by death. In 1817, armed poachers caught at night could be transported for seven years. Hunger continued in the countryside, harsh sentences failed to curb poaching and convictions rose. A Marlborough JP convicted 170 poachers between 1780 and 1800. Over 60% of these convictions were of labourers, earning only a few shillings a week. But 75% of those paid hefty fines, perhaps indicating that they were not only poaching for food.

Poaching laws began to be mitigated in 1828, when the penalty of transportation for first offence was removed and night poaching was replaced by a measure reserving transportation for the third offence. But due to hunger poaching convictions multiplied. In Wiltshire from 1839 to 1843, offences committed increased from 597 to 847, as did the percentage of Game Law offences from 21% to 26.4%. By 1862 a little more food was available to labourers and poaching lessened, especially those cases involving assault and stealing; obviously the countryman was not quite so desperate. The Sykes trial, a famous poaching case in 1865, made it quite clear that the verdict and newspaper reports showed public opinion did not agree with the stringency of the poaching laws and during the remainder of the century their severity was gradually reduced, parallel with the desperate need to poach for supplementary food. Poaching continued well into the 20th century in Wiltshire, sometimes exhibiting much hatred between poachers and keepers, occasionally producing violence and tragic incidents. By the 1940s, however, encounters between the two adversaries had dwindled to practically nil, but a few village enthusiasts still continued to poach, more to exhibit their skills than for need of sustenance.

Crime and Policing

One of the purposes of the Law is to protect people, but as has been shown it responded harshly to crimes against property in the late 18th and 19th centuries and regarded property as 'the measure of all things and far more valuable to society than any member of the labouring classes.' Between 1727 and 1830, many related convictions for attacks on property were punishable in England by death. Four out of five sentences were carried out. These offences included sheep-stealing, cattle- and horse-stealing and highway robbery, of which many incidents took place in Wiltshire after 1780 because of poverty and hunger. A highway robbery, commemorated by a stone still at the site of the incident, took place 1839 at St Joan a Gore's Cross two miles from West Lavington. Carried out by four men, one was a farm labourer from Bishopstrow. The mitigation of death sentences changed conviction rates and by 1838 almost two thirds of convictions were for simple larceny. But the extreme attitude to criminal punishment was not to relax until the organization of professional police forces. By the 1860s, only two crimes, treason and murder, called for the death penalty.

The criminal system bore hard on the Wilshire agricultural labourer, as he had no property and was surrounded with situations wherein he encroached on other people's. He saw daily how his labours produced assets and a decent living for others and not for himself or his family. He resented many of the law's actions which he encountered, and most attempts at keeping him in order. He remained a convenient scapegoat, in sight and powerless. The behaviour and judgement of the local magistrates and JPs were almost an incentive to crime at times. A culprit considered an undesirable character could get the maximum punishment with ease. If a criminal seemed penitent, or was normally one of good character, the punishment could be mitigated or even pardoned if requested by a local gentleman. At times the fear of antagonizing the local populace existed if the maximum sentence was to be given, so a lesser sentence would be handed out. Over generations, aversion among the general public grew against heavy sentencing, particularly that of transportation, to culminate, as will be shown, by the Swing Riots and Tolpuddle Martyrs sentences handed out in the 1830s.

Few private police existed, but in some villages at the beginning of the 19th century, constables, derived from the manor court appointee of tithing man, served to enforce the law in extreme circumstances. They also collected tithes from cottagers, which did not add to their popularity. James Tucker apparently acted as a constable at Seend when he apprehended a Daniel Bingham. Bingham, accused of stealing the belfry door key from the parish church, received a sentence of seven years transportation. Constables, untrained and, except on singular occasions, unpaid, seldom excelled at keeping order. When the Swing Riots took place at Aldbourne in 1830, despite the local constable, the difficulty of keeping the peace so frightened the local gentry that a private association for the prosecution of felons was appointed, creating yet a further insult to the poorer members of the village. A considerable number of villages had such associations, according to records in the WSRO. The office of parish, or petty constable, was declared unnecessary in 1872, making village pounds and lock-ups redundant, two very demeaning forms of punishment seldom, if ever used, after the mid-19th century.

Villages varied as to their degree of compliance with the law, 'some villages notorious, others extraordinarily stable in a sea of discontent.' An investigation into these villages

Broadside printed for the Castle Combe Association for the prevention of Robberies and Thefts, listing rewards paid for information against offenders

and whether they were open or closed and other reasons that might account for their difference would make an interesting study. The authorities' harsh suppression and later convictions during and after the Swing movement left much bitterness among the Wiltshire rural population and the founding in 1839 of the Wiltshire police force (which claims to be the earliest rural county force established in England) increased many working people's alienation to the law; they looked on it as another move of a hostile government and an interference. Around Devizes in particular anger developed, especially as the police now had to enforce the payment of rates by cottagers. The Potterne 'lambs' (sobriquet probably because the village policeman was called Wolfe!), a group of small farmers' sons and agricultural laborers, actively showed hostility to the force and were often reported in the local press. However, in time, early directories show an elaborate chain of command embracing most villages with village police stations, and the rural population seemingly began to accept the Wiltshire policeman. As the 19th century went by and crime decreased, persecution against the labourer lessened. With a little more regard for him as a human being, the police began to command respect, and resentment against them appears to have died away or been left unsaid. Towards the end of the century, when police were called to incidents involving assemblies to organize trade unions, rancor is seldom inferred in subsequent newspaper reports.

The effect of prison sentences on the agricultural labourers and the consequences for their families are easily imagined. 19th century conditions in Wiltshire prisons are beyond the scope of this book, but awful as they were, they did not deter crime, especially in the sixty years or so of hunger in the county. 'To countrymen reared in open spaces and used to fresh air, the rigid discipline, close confinement and isolation of the ` separate system' were objects of deep fear and hatred.' But far more pervading after the 1830s would be the fear of the workhouse system.

Constable Coles, village policeman at Bishopstone, north Wiltshire, c 1910.

Though police were seldom mentioned in connection with the everyday village scene in the 19th century, other personnel, official or unofficial, came into villagers' lives for various reasons. The Church, and now the Chapel, often played major roles in village life, not only through religion, but also by starting a patchy rural education system which when taken over by government decree, would be compulsory for most villages by the end of the century. People offering charity came into villages, especially in the first half of the century. Well-meant no doubt, the assistance was often clumsily bestowed and hence at times resented. Medical treatments and services continued to be meagre, even after local government Acts beginning in 1835 implemented help to villages. The powers authorized were narrow and Wiltshire had little funding and less enthusiasm to do much for rural communities, so the Acts made little change and few medical personnel visited the villages until after the turn of the century.

Religion in the village

Religion and its influence on the village labourer and his family can be divided into two parts, physical and spiritual. The division of life by a religion's sacred and profane was likely to have been somewhat remote to the agricultural labourer trying to survive and deal with his material problems. To think through and achieve a faith that sustains one through all travail takes time and a certain amount of leisure time at that, which he or she did not have.

What religious feelings the agricultural labourer may have had in the 19th century is a difficult question and answers are hard to find. From religion, did he acquire a belief in the Christian God, derive comfort and the hope of an afterlife to mitigate the endless poverty that was his lot? In my childhood the working people I knew gave me the impression that they thought nothing at all of the Church as a factor in their lives and certainly not as a social element, which still was important in the 1930s to many rural people of the middle and upper classes.

Clergy did not seem to understand the problems of the labourer. At all Cannings, between 1810 and 1869, the Reverend Henry Methuen, though concerned for the villagers' souls, apparently could not reach them at all. His successor had no sympathy; he thought labourers generally apathetic, with no appreciation or understanding of the blessings of education. At nearby Bishop Cannings the Vicar complained in 1870 of no spiritual life, fervour or devotion on the part of the labourers, their sole thought being to scrape together enough daily sustenance. Justly so, one cannot live on religious promises.

A writer from Lincolnshire at the end of the 19th century commented that many of the old ways and beliefs persisted, despite organized Christianity in the villages. But many probably practised both to be 'on the safe side!' Mob anger against witches had disappeared, but belief in them still persisted. The familiar myths and folk laws of village life were time-honoured and easily reached, 19th century Christian theology, especially the Anglican, remote, All societies need rules governing moral relations and ethical concerns, and in not reaching the labouring classes, the Church of England in the 19th century let down the agricultural labourer very badly indeed. The tremendous growth of nonconformity in Wiltshire through most of the century illustrates how ably chapels catered to their needs. To survive and thrive, not only are devout people needed who really believe in the god, religion, or way of life being offered them, but they also need people who are loyal, willing to work for the religious organisation and willing to indoctrinate the next generation. This happened in the chapels in Wiltshire, but input from the agricultural labourer was non-acceptable by the Anglican Church. Perhaps in the long run, the forces of nature he met in his work had far more reaching effects on him than religious ethics.

In a Wiltshire village at the beginning of the 19th century, people, whether Anglican or nonconformist, accepted and did not query religion, at least on the surface. The gradations of secular society were faithfully represented in the Anglican pew system, pews being allocated according to status of parishioners. Box pews, benches in side aisle pews or in galleries were not to disappear until the end of the 19th century. In the nonconformist chapels the seating arrangements appealed more to villagers, especially to the labourer and his family, as they symbolized equality of persons.

Cobbett on one of his famous rides counted 31 churches in the Salisbury Avon valley in 1826. In his opinion, though each had a vicar and curate, none helped the starving poor, having lost touch with the labouring classes. And the poor themselves just did not go to church. Cobbett's statement is confirmed by the Vicar of Aldbourne, John Elderton, who in 1783 explained that numbers of poor were habitual non-attendees and others refrained from attending church for want of proper clothing. Nearly a hundred years later Joseph Arch, the trade union leader and ex-farmworker, described communion in his parish church at the age of 14: 'squire, farmer, tradesman, shopkeepers, the wheelwright, the blacksmith and then, very last of all, went the poor agricultural labourers in their smock frocks. They walked up by themselves; nobody else knelt with them; it was as if they were unclean...I said to myself 'if that's what goes on – never for me.'

Many of the Wiltshire clergy are likely to have been unpopular with poorer parishioners because of absenteeism. By the 1830s half the parishes in the county lacked an incumbent, as parsons were allowed to hold two or more parishes. The empty parish was run by an overworked curate, paid hardly more than the labourer. Many other incumbents earned the reputation of sporting parsons, often absent from their duties to enjoy hunting and shooting, fishing and horse racing. Their curates remained to run everyday church matters. By the 1850s these anomalies were rectified by law and the Diocese of Salisbury sought more education and training for their prospective clergy.

Another reason for unpopularity of church and clergy concerned the one-tenth tithe payments, always a bone of contention. These extended to those cottagers who held large allotments or gardens, the payments biting deeply into their slender food resources, though by 1836 tithes could be paid by money instead of in kind. Enclosure groupings sometimes resulted in Church lands doubling in value, certainly enclosure commissions made sure that the Church never lost value on its property, unlike so many of the smallholders and labourers. Often the increased land values meant a rise in social stature as clergy became landed gentry and mixed with the higher social orders of the neighbourhood. Some enclosures made clergy eligible for an appointment as a magistrate and in that role they were far more likely to administer the rich man's justice based on property values, rather than one that considered the labourer's poverty. But admittedly, social mores of the times did not expect the Church to cash in the profits made on land and spend them on the poor.

Cobbett also observed, perhaps somewhat excessively, that wherever he went, clergy were known better as JPs than as religious ministers, but he wanted to make the point of their unpopularity. Magistrates having to administer the law in Swing Riots cases caused local resentment, not to mention sentences they imposed for poaching. It required a great deal of tact to stay popular if one was on the bench and at the same time fulfilling the clerical duties of dispensing charity and helping the sick and needy. Often secular concerns overrode pastoral duties. But to the mid-century, the church was to provide in Wiltshire 'a very low quality social cement and it did little to prevent the appearance of large cracks.'

On the other side of the picture, the clergy often had to play a difficult role. In remote and poorer villages, over bleak downs, many curates lived an isolated life, with erratic newspaper deliveries and perhaps just a few village children for company during the day, as they struggled to teach them the three Rs. Any enterprising clergyman usually tried to be posted to a more fruitful area than a Wiltshire village 'far from the madding crowd.'

Sometimes the clergy themselves had to play a submissive role to advance themselves, the curate at the whim of his rector, the vicar at the whim of his bishop. Many clergymen may have strongly supported or at least were sympathetic to the efforts of the labourer to obtain better conditions of living. But that being so hard to obtain may have caused one rector's wife in a country parish to open her weekly Mother's Meeting with the prayer: 'Oh God, make these poor women contented with their lot.'

Few clergy in Wiltshire actually championed the poor, perhaps afraid to incur the displeasure of their congregations and social equals. However, an ex- vicar of Cholderton did. As Bishop of Manchester he reported to a Royal Commission in 1870 on the condition of the Wiltshire poor in the hungry forties:

Bread was dear, and wages were down to starvation point; the labourers were uneducated, underfed, underpaid, their cottages were often unfit for human habitation, the sleeping and sanitary arrangements were appalling. Naturally they took colour from their environment... It was impossible to exaggerate the terrible state of things then existing; they were so bad physically, socially, economically, morally and intellectually that it would be difficult to make them worse.

Politics, too, made things difficult for the clergy. When male labourers obtained the vote in 1885, congregations looked to the clergy to influence them, or at least to promote the return of candidates supportive of the Church. Farmers on the chalk tried to influence their employers to vote conservative, but in the Cheese Country, home of smaller land-owners and tenants, the liberal vote was encouraged. A conflicting situation emerged, causing Charles Buller, a genial radical of the time to remark: 'For heaven's sake do not destroy the Established Church, it is the only thing that stands between us and Christianity.'

Nonconformism

During the 19th century, nonconformism continued to play a bigger role in the life of the Wiltshire villages. Always involved in its growth from lay preaching to cottage meetings and to the building of chapels, the labourer obviously found much solace in the faith offered him. To him and his family, to be considered social equals of their ministers, gave them an added advantage to become Methodist, Wesleyan, or Baptist, the main nonconformist sects. And these all combated the role the Church of England presented to the labourer: – formalised worship, dispenser of charity and the reminders of his lowly place on the social ladder. In contrast, nonconformity offered the possibility of speech- and thought-sharing, charity dispensed with dignity, a freer form of worship and less rigid social barriers. One small but well-confirmed factor was the opportunity which chapels gave to village musicians to play at nonconformist services, as the Church gradually restricted its musicians to those of higher classes.

Naturally nonconformity was considered a rival by the Church. John Furze, a Methodist preacher, stated that in the 1790s, the vicar in his home parish of Wilton had described the new religion as a plague that affected whole families. Landlords would exclude dissenters from among their tenants, supposedly some would exclude them from their labouring employees. But nonconformity continued its growth in Wiltshire, in town and in country. Bratton, a good example of growth, had nearly twenty Baptists in 1777, 117 by 1822 and 160 or more in the 1860s. Labouring men and women in their chapels were given the opportunity to run their own affairs and thereby acquire self-confidence and administrative expertise. And at their chapels they heard one another's view-points at meetings after the lay preachers had spoken. Local preachers and class leaders among the Primitive Methodists, for example, were labourers, but they were less prominent among Wesleyans, as that sect was more dominated by the middle-class.

Many small farmers continued in their nonconformist beliefs, especially in the Cheese Country. They had clashed with the Church regarding tithes until 1836, and probably felt in sympathy with their workers regarding Church of England attitudes to them Nonconformity in 19th century Wiltshire however, although usually paralleling the Cheese region, illustrated that geographically many small communities did not conform. Village ownership supplied the key, a village with a squire or lord was far more likely to lean towards Anglicanism, with nonconformity in areas consisting of smallholdings and surrounded by small single-owner farms.

The 1851 Census showed Wiltshire had a total of 158,694 church and chapel seatings provided by 352 churches, and 369 nonconformist places of worship. Anglicans numbered 87,843, 55% of the population, nonconformists numbered 70,851, 45% of the population. Wiltshire was fairly representative of all counties in England.

Nonconformity opened up a range of thought and feeling far beyond the conception of the agricultural labourers' Protestant forbears and undoubtedly exposed their lives to greater emotional and mental experiences. The emphasis on the importance of family life and the intensification of human fellowship and brotherhood by nonconformist faiths in turn is likely to have revealed differences of social attitudes in villagers as chapel attendance increased. Intolerance and narrow-mindedness doubtless decreased and contributed to breaking the hold of the Anglican Church over village and parish, especially in an open village, and probably altered village politics. Above all, it made the labourer more aware of himself. And very importantly for his wife, it gave her a status as chapels accepted her as an important part of their establishment.

Changes in the role of the Church and Chapel in the villages came slowly after the 1850s. Moral concerns began to emerge and both groups became more involved with trying to alleviate village poverty, poor housing, low pay rates and drunkenness. The latter led to much action in trying to curb public house opening hours. Then the 1880s agricultural depression caused a drop in both Church and Chapel incomes, due to the poorer economy in the first instance, and lower attendance in the second. The Disestablishment campaign was at its height through 1868-1886. In the seventies, incumbents complained of Joseph Arch's campaign for the National Agricultural Labourers' Union, whose speakers, often nonconformist lay preachers, urged the disestablishment and disendowment of the Church.

Both church and chapel-going for the working classes peaked in the 1870s. Twenty years later participation in Church activities continued to decrease, except in the more remote Wiltshire villages. The few charms and distractions of the towns, a little more education and falling village populations led to the demise of religious influence over the life of the agricultural labourer.

Charity

Charity is usually defined as benevolent actions to the needy without expectation of reward. The distribution of charity in Wiltshire in the 19th century fulfills the first half of this definition, but the donors often ignored the second half and much charity was dispensed with beneficial interest to the dispenser.

Gerard makes the point in her book *Country House Living*: 'Charity also legitimized social subordination, not just in demonstrating the giver's superiority and the recipient's dependence, but in rewarding the deferential.' In some instances in Wiltshire a form of charity was showing a personal interest in long-term tenants, elderly servants and employees, particularly if they were obsequious. But Roman Catholic charities did nothing for the labourer unless he worked for a Catholic family or estate. Towards the dawning of the 20th century some forward-looking English women began to perceive that they could help other women change their position in life by showing them how to attain skills to help them enter the employment market at a higher work level, but evidence of such help reaching rural Wiltshire has yet to emerge.

Real want existed in the Chippenham area when I was a child in the 1930s. I can remember food being given to our dressmaker and other domestic employees when they left at the end of their day's work and they were grateful for it. But my mother disbursed charity with discretion, and never tried to enhance her status with it. Not everyone was as tactful, some making very clear their distance between them and the recipient, and expecting deference and humility as their reward from the donor. Charity in the Wiltshire countryside a hundred years previously apparently had to be received with great appreciation and submissiveness, the deserving being plainly singled out from the undeserving. It was often used as a weapon to make people toe the social line, those who did not confirm would not be included in a Christmas distribution of meat or coals, holiday meals, clothes or red flannel – of which one recipient in a Wiltshire village was reported as saying, when given flannel to make warm clothes, 'I du wash it afore I du make it up to get the smell o' charity ut of it.'

Visits to the poor and sick added to the genteel image so favoured by the middle-class 19th century ladies and sometimes by the clergy. Reading about it nearly two centuries later the gentility is infected with patronage, as evidenced by the wife of Parson Bowles of Bremhill who only ventured forth in the summer. Henry Methuen, Vicar at All Cannings from1810 to 1869, tried harder, and visited his villagers regularly in winter and summer. As he was always short of ready money, despite a good income, he probably dispensed cash on his visits or brought goods to the poor. He often reached them at home in the winter, but in the summer, he called himself the village policeman, as when he appeared in the village, groups of villagers dispersed rapidly. He likely lacked the personality to have the ability to show his real concern for his parishioners, as he sadly lacked influence in the village. To his chagrin, several of the Swing activists came from All Cannings. Religious comfort was not a successful form of charity in rural Wiltshire, if one was an unsuccessful practitioner. However, when he died, still Vicar of All Cannings, a large number of older villagers from around attended his funeral, as did clergymen of other denominations. Obviously he was well-thought-of, which, if he had known, would no doubt have pleased him greatly.

Many churches and meeting houses ran benefit or clothing clubs or asked for donations, particularly cloaks and coats. Seend Church had an endowed charity, started in 1651 with £50 left by a William Tipper to be used for the poor of the village. The money was invested in a field and the rent provided a yearly distribution of warm coats for men in the village. 'Bugge Coats,' made from a thick white wool cloth and fastened with brass buttons continued to be handed out until 1906, when they were changed to a practical colour in an updated style. Thomas Hughes in 1830 'bequeathed £330 6s 8d in consols upon trust that the dividends should be distributed at Christmas for ever in blankets and other articles of useful woollen clothing among the most deserving and necessitious (sic) poor parishioners at the discretion of the vicar and chapel workers.' As late as 1901, Henry Hungerford Ludlow-Bridges gave £1000 to be invested and the annual proceeds distributed to the poor for fuel. Seend was a reasonably well-off parish, other churches were not always so generously endowed with moneys for charity, but most had some bequests. Other churches and authorities, it must be admitted, were not always scrupulously honest in distributing funds meant for charity as has been shown at Cocklebury in the 19th century. (See *Cocklebury*, pages 61-2)

At North Wraxall charitable distributions were systematically distributed by the end of the 1870s. The Charity Commissioners held £3,172 at 2 ½% consols. They belonged to the village school, contributed by local worthies, including Lord Methuen of Corsham who held land in the area. The consols contributed an income of £79 quarterly. Other moneys held by the commissioners belonging to the village totalled £1908 and yielded £47 quarterly. Clothing club members paid 1½d to 3d weekly, with extra contributions from local worthies and other funds. The charity moneys yielded enough income in 1905 to distribute £31 each plus a 7s bonus to the club's 49 members. Carefully spent, this paid for a complete set of clothes for each family member. The Coal Club handed out 55 tons in the same year. It cost 15s a ton, but a donation from a carrier meant ten tons were hauled free of expense. Obviously North Wraxall, at least six miles from a railway station, had to count haulage costs. In addition to the yearly distribution of clothes and coal to the clubs' members, other local charities donated specific items of clothing. bedding and fuel to other village members. A share club for children aged one to four years consisted of a matching weekly pay-in of 1d for each child if the parents contributed the same amount. Both the coal and clothing club were limited to persons earning less than £1 a week. Such clubs for the poor were enthusiastically endorsed by authorities, being considered a means of teaching thrift and money management. And doubtless it did.

Poor Laws

The Poor Laws in England by the 17th century can be seen as another form of charity to persons in need whether working, non-working, sick, disabled, too young or too old to work. The system of pay-out had gradually become more expensive to parishes as hardship increased after the 1750s due to growth of population and further afflictions caused by the Napoleonic Wars. William Marshall, the famous observer and writer on agriculture, commented on the situation at the time: 'The poor rate of a village falls principally on the farmer, and if he does not employ the poor he must support them in idleness,' acknowledging that enough work for every labourer just did not exist.

At Speenhamland (Berks) in 1795 justices decided to give outdoor relief to families, on a sliding scale based on the cost of bread. If an 8lbs 11ozs loaf cost 1s, a man had 3s weekly for his own support, his wife and other family members 1s 6d. When bread prices increased, the support increased at the same rate as the rise in cost. Supposedly the only assistance a poor family could receive, the Speenhamland System as it became known, was adopted in principle by other counties. Wiltshire overseers continued in various other ways to support the unemployed, the sick and the disabled, but the employed person suffered from the new system. Labourers' wages from 1794 advanced from 6s to 12s by 1814; but in 1785 a weekly wage bought fourteen loaves, in 1812 only nine. The plaques outside Great Wishford parish church, recording bread prices during this period of Wiltshire's history show how significant to people was the cost of bread. And to the Wiltshire labourer potatoes, which had reached Wiltshire by 1790, were no substitute for bread. Considered fit for pigs only, the 'new-fangled' food provoked much opposition. Poor harvests and high prices finally broke down the prejudices against them, eventually making them a staple food in the labourer's diet until the 1950s. But despite cheap potatoes, (if the labourer had a small plot of land where he could grow his own), he was still in the same situation of being paid a wage on which he and his family could not live on, with no existing alleviation.

With wages below subsistence level, did many labourers enjoy the combination of a fair employer, a little cultivable land, good family management and were hence able to avoid extreme poverty? Certainly none from Wiltshire ever appeared in print, yet some villagers surely had one or all of these advantages. How many practiced extreme thrift and, with inward pride, went to great lengths to avoid applying for relief? And if circumstances forced them to apply, how many did it for the sake of his children? None of these points can be determined from existing records. But it is known that some families had to give up their children to the parish to be housed and fed, or apprenticed.

The Speenhamland System caused great distress and so did another form of relief practiced in Wiltshire – the ticket employment method or roundsman system. The principle was to distribute the unemployed, to be hired on a daily basis, amongst the rate payers. If a man was not wanted for work, he tried other farms, and if no work materialized, he returned to the overseers for a handout. Begun in the 1780s, by 1830 it had become a common practice. The process soon became demeaning to the labourer. He might be employed for a few hours on piece-work, then given a ticket which he took to his parish overseers for relief. He had no recourse if a farmer claimed him a bad worker and dismissed him. Regular employees would resent him for taking 'their' work. At all times the system was open to abuse by farmers who could become even more reluctant to keep on a regular employee, especially in the months of the farming year when work was scarcer. It was then far cheaper to dismiss a full-time labourer and use piece-workers. Some parish overseers made efforts to prevent farmers from misusing the roundsman system, which seems to have happened at Lacock.

An alternative of the same system was 'found' or created work, of which a description of paupers picking stones in a field outside Westbury in the early 1830s makes heart-breaking reading. Stone-breaking by roadsides was also assigned to paupers, in the 1920s a few still could be seen in the Wiltshire countryside. As can be imagined, having to take this type of relief, demeaning and demoralizing, was far worse to one who had once enjoyed regular employment in his own parish.

In 1830 the Lacock Vestry took tenancy of 25 acres of Lacock Abbey land in agreement with Mr W.H. Fox-Talbot of photography fame, paying £2 5s an acre. Here poor labourers of the parish were put to work on the 'farm,' to raise barley, beans and potatoes, perhaps for themselves. Supposedly this 'farm' continued until 1859 when the Lacock poorhouse closed. Undoubtedly a philanthropic gesture on behalf of the landowner, yet the yearly rental received made the arrangement with the Vestry extremely remunerative for him.

Due to the chronic lack of employment and low wages, the numbers of rural poor in Wiltshire increased steadily in the first three decades of the 19th century. Between 1802 and 1815, some 7,000 adults were on permanent outdoor relief in 374 rural parishes, the total population of the county being 184,000 in 1801, increasing to 192,000 in 1811. Government reports of the 1830s and contemporary writings portray the labourer as deprived, semi-starved, often churlish, but who could blame them if they were? But he was still slow to protest, and not until the Captain Swing movement came to Wiltshire, did he do so, to no avail as will be seen. At the same time, the labourer faced with the ever-rising price of bread began to understand the consequences of the Corn Laws and how they affected his life-style.

In 1813 Parliament had passed a protectionist bill, later to be known as the Corn Laws. The bill had the effect of permanently increasing the price of bread for several reasons. It set out regulations prohibiting foreign corn from being sold on the home market until grain grown in the country had reached a certain price level. No allowance was made for home sales of surplus grain to be sold more cheaply. The bill had tremendous repercussions on the Wiltshire agricultural scene and by 1815, further tinkering with the Corn Laws had brought the price of English corn to famine levels by making the cost of bread exorbitant. But the farmers made a guaranteed income and Parliament, dominated by rural landowners, maintained this class legislation until the Laws were repealed in 1846.

However, protection was not always to guarantee the farmer high prices. If a good harvest year occurred and prices went down, more 'adjustments' to grain prices took place, not always to the benefit of the farmer; but however modified, wheat prices stayed high for the consumer. Farmers in the 1820s, especially in the Chalk Country, began to see bad times, despite reduced rents and labourers on minimum wages. The issue of the Corn Laws became more and more of a political 'hot potato' which neither the Whigs nor the Tories wished to handle. Meanwhile population started to outstrip food supplies, pushing up prices again. Protectionist associations sprang up to little avail and the necessity for relief continued.

Wiltshire labourers made little complaint until the Swing agitations, and even then the protest actions related more to employment than to the price of bread. The appalling sentences meted out to the agitators and, a few years later, to the Tolpuddle Martyrs, ostensibly deterred the Wiltshire agricultural labourer from continuing formal protest and little is heard from him, despite two more decades of near starvation. In June 1845, a meeting was held at Upavon, attended by over 1000 people. Labourers spoke on the laws at the gathering, but nothing came of it. Farmers agitated all through the rest of the 1840s for the extension of protectionist policies on corn prices. But influenced by the working class protests all over England, Parliament finally repealed the Corn Laws in 1849. Bread prices soon began to drop, which helped the agricultural labourer to buy a little more food.

Because of high bread prices at the end of the 1820s, as pay-outs continued to increase, the Poor Law administration reached a severe crisis. Several Government select committees reported on the state of the Poor Laws and demonstrated that most people wanted to work; few were innately lazy, but the labourer worked slowly because but he had endured three generations of undernourishment and poor housing and clothing. A Wiltshire witness on the 1833 Select Committee for Agriculture, Robert Hughes, related that in almost every parish surplus labour abounded, the men being very badly off, with full-time work only during the summer. November to March were the harshest months for them. He cited an extreme case (committee reports generally dealt in extremes, hence they have to be interpreted carefully) at Urchfont, where fifty men remained unemployed for all but five weeks of the year. 'The parish pays 3s a week during that time and enquires no further about their time of labours.'

Government commissions continued to report the need to alleviate harsh conditions of living in the countryside and it became obvious that the provision of more work, higher pay and lower bread prices was the key to reducing relief rates and poverty. Except for the reformers, (including Cobbett), Parliament paid little attention to the commissions' findings. Then came the Captain Swing incidents in 1830. They frightened not only governing authorities but many ordinary people who saw law and order disappearing in the countryside. Parliament hardened its heart and in 1834 passed the Poor Law Amendment Act, containing rigorous and incredibly inhumane reforms.

The new Poor Laws, concerned with relief costs tripling in the previous thirty years, worked on the principle that if made disagreeable enough, people would avoid applying for relief. In addition, the bill aimed to level out the differences between relief offered by poor parishes and that by versus better-off parishes. The unsatisfactory Speenhamland System of administering outdoor relief ceased, to be replaced by one far more costly. More indoor relief was to be provided, despite being proved time and time again more expensive than outdoor relief due to shelter and food costs, and the unsustainable expense of forcing people to work. The new laws did not entirely prohibit outdoor relief, but Lord Lansdowne's Cabinet had had a loophole built into the 1834 Act that meant application could be forbidden. Curiously enough the first order prohibiting outdoor relief was issued to the Calne Union on May 1 1837, the town immediately adjacent to Lord Lansdowne's Bowood estate. The Act did not 'nationalize' the management of the new Poor Laws, but it diminished local participation by removing the powers of relief of the local JPs and overseers and the relief administration from the individual parishes. This meant that the poor no longer could apply for relief to a local person who already had knowledge of their circumstances, but had to seek out a stranger, often several miles away from their home.

The new Act divided Wiltshire into seventeen Union districts each with a Board of Guardians and with relief to be focused on a central workhouse. Some Union districts overlapped with nearby counties; for instance, persons in the Tidworth area went to the infamous Andover workhouse if awarded indoor relief. Designated workhouse rules

Pewsey Union Workhouse: Before the greenery grew on the building and railings topped the surrounding wall, this workhouse looked very grim indeed.

deliberately made life disagreeable for its inmates in order to discourage relief appeals. The separation of husbands, wives and families, minimum provision of food, bedding and heating, no allowance of tobacco or beer, and compulsory monotonous work, all guaranteed to generate almost unendurable conditions for inmates. Particularly devastating to pauper children, the system herded them together with no personal life or affection and exploited them for labour, despite the fact that they were supposed to receive education to equip them for their adult labouring working life.

The newly-appointed Boards of Guardians built workhouses to accommodate the new laws and, seemingly deliberately, constructed dreary, forbidding buildings, many of which are still in existence today, a reminder of how fortunate one is not to be threatened by them. Two built in Wiltshire that immediately come to mind are Semington and Pewsey. For those unable to find work, too poor, sick, or disabled, or who had no family to look after them in their old age, or with no means and carrying an illegitimate child, indoor relief at the workhouse was often the only choice, turning into a form of punishment and workhouse confinement, just because of their unlucky circumstances. And all suffered loss of human dignity.

The original ideals for a workhouse – instruction of youth, encouragement of industry, relief of want, support of old age and comfort for the infirm and suffering – made pretty reading, but bore no relation to the treatment a workhouse inmate received. The elected Boards of Guardians in rural areas included JPs, local farmers, ratepayers and other property owners, of whom all had reason to cut down on relief to lower rates. Statistics show that between 30,000 and 36,000 paupers received either indoor or outdoor relief each quarter in Wiltshire in the years 1840-46, of which between 26 and 29% were able-bodied. (Between 1841 and 1851 the annual population of Wiltshire averaged 255,000). But, as with the idea of forcing people to work, indoor relief for all was found impossible to administer and eventually more than three-quarters of relief applicants were given outdoor relief, despite the workhouse rules. Authorities kept levels of outdoor relief to the old and the sick as low as possible. Older progeny were supposed to contribute to parental welfare, yet another strain on families' purses and village resources, and neighbours also probably did their best to help. Overwhelmed by so much existing poverty, the new Poor Laws failed completely to live up to any ideals; and the different relief standards of parishes were only replaced by the variations in the administrations and services of the seventeen Wiltshire Unions.

Widespread discontent with the new 1834 Poor Laws and the establishment of the detested Unions and their workhouses erupted all over England between 1835 and 1837, though apparently not in Wiltshire. Especially hated was the rule separating families within the workhouses. Complaints of poor care given to inmates, particularly children and the sick, were constant over the rest of the 19th century and little really changed. By the 1880s, less pauperism existed in the county and fewer persons entered workhouses. Poor Law relief limped on piecemeal through the rest of the 19th century. In the first half of the 20th century, the dread of workhouses began to lessen, partly due to families being more able to extend home-care to their elderly, sick or disabled members, and partly to the start of a social services safety net beginning in 1908.

The threat of the workhouse would linger on for decades, sometimes the local workhouse being used as a disciplinary form on children in the 1930s, similar to the threat of being sent to Devizes Asylum. I recall our household maidservant who used to take me to have tea with her parents. She and her sisters and brother had long decided to do all they could to support their parents in their old age, to assure them of remaining in their home for the rest of their lives. Sometimes she and I walked past the Chippenham Workhouse and waved to the inmates. Still separated by age and sex, they exercised behind high railings on non-rainy days. I always looked for one lady, erect and slender in shabby black clothes who usually wore a tall battered hat. In 1930, Boards of Guardians were dissolved and the County Council assumed responsibilities for workhouses. They continued however, essentially functioning along the same lines until after WWII when, new social legislation abolished the system. I detected fear of the workhouse in my fellow labourers at Cocklebury, who always expressed strong condemnation of the system. In 1944, those men understood thoroughly the significance of the Beveridge Report.

Today it is still difficult to be objective about Wiltshire workhouses for lack of comparative evidence. Specific records sometimes show kindness and compassion, but in general it seems that life behind the workhouse walls was devoid of any comfort or peace of mind for those forced to live within them. What good existed in the system is hardly ever mentioned. Purton and Andover had notorious reputations, but little is heard of the others in the county and a relative study needs to be done of all seventeen. By present standards, it seems that the treatment meted out to inmates is shocking, but the attitudes of the times, limited funding, the lack of understanding of nutrition, hygiene and medicine, the day-to-day psychological effect of living in a workhouse, and finally the dearth of trained carers – all have to be considered in order to make fair judgment.

A new approach to relief of the poor began in 1908, when minimum old age pensions were initiated and limited medical services and unemployment benefits legislation passed three years later. The affliction of poverty and the stigma of being a pauper slowly lifted in rural areas, but the real end of Poor Law concepts did not come until the National Assistance Act of 1949. Today the terrifying aspects of the 19th century Poor Laws that created 'more embittered unhappiness than any other statute of modern British history' are, thankfully, completely forgotten.

Medical Services

The 1834 Poor Laws, though trying to eliminate out-relief, continued to allow medical attention to be given to eligible able-bodied persons, the sick and disabled. The Guardians of each Union hired doctors, often by tender, meaning that the cheapest, not necessarily the most competent medic won the contract. They mended bones, performed midwifery, gave free smallpox vaccinations, prescribed and supplied medicines, their costing strictly reckoned. In cases of general illness a house-call was permitted. As can be imagined, serious bone fractures and toothache caused immediate problems, the former needing skilled setting, then careful nursing, the latter, often a long walk to the nearest barber-surgeon. For the average Wiltshire villager, obtaining medical help at short notice obviously created a problem if the nearest doctor was more than a few miles away and the patient not ambulant. As far as can be ascertained the Salisbury Infirmary is the only hospital at the time in Wiltshire that provided out-patient services to a wide area and local parishes subscribed to these services. Hudson in *A Shepherd's Life* points out that the Infirmary was one of the most important buildings in Salisbury as far as the labourer was concerned. Country doctors often lacked training, and not until 1858 did government regulations insist that district medical officers had to be qualified in both surgery and medicine. Most Wiltshire records show a great deal of compassion by doctors towards the poor. Those hired by the Lacock parish overseers in the 19th century rode many weary miles in bad weather to treat their poor patients. In the case of one Marlborough practice, the Drs Maurice, the tradition of assisting the poor went from father to son, to become the longest-serving family practice in the county.

Workhouse records reveal the difficulties doctors faced when giving medical attention within the workhouses, such as when one of the Maurice doctors who had trouble in entering the Marlborough workhouse as porters kept him waiting at the locked entrance door. After complaint, the Guardians finally agreed to let him have a latch-key. This illustrates one of the living conditions inmates had to endure – being locked up like prisoners at all times. Nurses (their qualifications somewhat hazy) began to be hired by the Guardians in 1863, but as with others in subsidiary jobs, few stayed very long, conditions of employment and pay being low.

𝕭𝕽𝕰𝕸𝕳𝕵𝕷   𝖂𝕵𝕷𝕿𝕾.

O R D E R S,

TO BE OBSERVED BY THE

Friendly SOCIETY,

Inftituted at the DUMB-POST, in the Parifh of Bremhill,

The Firft of January, 1770.

By {Jofeph Thrufh,}{STEWARDS.}{Wm. Gregory, John Gingel, Wm. Harding, Abel Ferris, Mathew Wheeler, Jacob Killing, Wm. Broadhurft,}{Edward Manfel,}{Thomas Flewefter, Thomas Brown, Robert Gauf, Jacob Gauf, Thomas Clerk, AND Wm. Haderel, MEMBERS.}

A R T I C L E I.

THIS Society fhall confift of Seventy-Five Members, and no more in being at once, forever. There fhall be a Meeting once in Six-Weeks on Monday Night, at Seven o'Clock, and continue 'till Nine, except on Two Meetings, which fhall begin at Midfummer Yearly, and then to begin at Eight and continue 'till Ten, at the DUMB-POST; each Member to fpend Two-Pence and put One Shilling in the Box, which fhall have Three Locks and Three Keys, Two of the Keys to be kept by the Two Stewards, and the other by the Clerk. If any Member for Two fucceffive Meetings neglects to come, or fend, his fpending and Contribution Money, he fhall forthwith be Excluded.

II. Four Members fhall ferve as Stewards for the fpace of Two of thefe Meetings, Two being chofen every Six Weeks, and Two Difcharged at the fame time, that the new Stewards may the better be inftructed thereby ; and the Two Stewards Difcharged fhall ferve the Office of Mafters, to affift the Clerk in receiving the aforefaid Monies, and then to give a full and fair account of fuch Monies received, for the fatisfaction of all, that there may be no caufe of jeloufy, or the leaft fufpicion of Fraud or Deceit. Any Member refufing to ferve the Offices when it is his regular turn, fhall Forfeit Two Shillings and Six-Pence, or be Excluded.

III. No Member fhall be admitted into this Society but thofe that are known to be found healthy Men, and not under Fifteen, nor more than Forty Years of Age, except thofe Entered at the Firft Meeting ; if after Entry it be made appear that any Member was under or above the age here mentioned, he fhall be Excluded without return of Money.

IV. No Member fhall have relief from this Society un-till he has been entered a full Year, and then to have relief according to the tenor of thefe Articles.

V. If any Member of this Society is taken fick or lame by Gon's Vifitation, fo as to render him incapable of working, he fhall have Six Shillings per Week, but with this Reftriction, if he does not Recover in Three Months, his pay fhall be reduced to Three Shillings per Week, during the Time of his Affliction.

VI. No Perfon after this our Firft Meeting fhall be admitted a Member, without coming or fending a Letter the Meeting before he is Admitted, and then not to be Admitted without the Confent of the Society then prefent ; he fhall receive no benefit from the Box 'till he has been fick a Week, which the Stewards are to give proper notice of.

VII. If any Member, by Debauchery or Fighting, or any other Diforderly means, brings Sicknefs or Lamenefs upon himfelf, fhall have no benefit from this Society.

VIII. WHEN it fhall pleafe GOD that any Member departs this Life, he fhall have full Power to bequeath to whomfoever he Pleafes One Shilling, to be paid by each Member belonging to this Society, at or before the fecond Meeting after his Burial ; if he fhould Die without making a Will, either by word or deed, it fhall be paid to his neareft of kin. Any Member refufing to pay his Money for the faid ufe, fhall be immediately Excluded.

IX. No Member to have Relief from this Society until he have been Sick a Week, and then to have the above-mentioned Allowance, and if he finds himfelf able to work before the end of the next week he may work, and fhall be allowed One Shilling a Day ; but if pleafe GOD he fhould Die, there fhall be Two Pounds Ten Shillings taken out of the Box to Bury him, and Ten Shillings to be fpent at the Dumb-Poft the Day of his Funeral, timely Notice being given by the Stewards to as many of the Members as they poffibly can, and the Stewards fhall likewife give Notice to as many of the Members as poffible of the Time of his Burial, and he that does not attend fhall Forfeit Six-Pence to the Houfe, or be Excluded.

X. If any Member of this Society is fufpected to feign himfelf Sick or Lame, and is by an able Phyfician found guilty of Difimulation, he fhall be forever Excluded.

XI. Two of the Stewards fhall be obliged to Vifit every Sick Member belonging to this Society, that Lives within Four Miles diftance, and carefully infpect and diligently enquire into the Cafe of the Sick Member, that there may be Relief as before-mentioned, if lawful, according to the true meaning of thefe Articles, otherwife to have no relief that there may be no Deficiency or Impofition on either fide.

XII. If any Member of this Society refiding at a greater diftance than Four miles, is, by Sicknefs or Lamenefs, rendered incapable of working, he muft give Notice in writing, figned by a Doctor, and Two Parifh Officers, of the nature of his Cafe, that he may have Relief, according to the tenor of thefe Articles.

XIII. THE Clerk of this Society fhall not belong to this Club, but fhall receive One Shilling and Six-Pence every Club Meeting for his Attendance, which fhall be taken out of the Box, and if he fhall not attend within a Quarter of an Hour after Seven, and a Quarter of an Hour after Eight, at the Society Houfe, he fhall Forfeit Six-Pence, unlefs Sick or Lame.

XIV. Every Member ferving in the Militia, if drawn, fhall pay, according to the tenor of thefe Articles, during his Servitude, as before ; but if he enlifts, fhall be immediately Excluded.

XV. Every Member, at his Enterance, fhall pay Five Shillings to the Stock : and as thefe Articles are Printed by the Confent of the Society, every Member fhall Buy one of them, that they may be the better acquainted with the Rules of the Society, the Price being Six-pence, which will be laid up for the benefit of the Stock.

XVI. The Stewards, Clerk, and Mafters, fhall attend at the appointed time of Meetings, and fhall not exceed a Quarter of an hour after Seven, and a Quarter of an hour after Eight o'Clock, on Society Nights, on pain of Forfeiting fix pence for every fuch neglect, unlefs fick or lame.

XVII. If any Member Foments a Qnarrel, or Challenges to Fight any one on Society Nights, or Feaftival-Days orNights fhall Forfeit Two fhillings and fix-pence to the ftock if any Member fhall Curfe, Sware, promote Gaming, or offer wagers fhall for every fuch Offence Forfeit Two-pence to the ftock, or be Excluded.

XVIII. If any Member upbraids another for having received Benefit from the Stock, he fhall, for every fuch Offence, Forfeit fix-pence to the ftock.

XIX. If any Member of this Society is found guilty of Theft, he fhall forthwith be Excluded ; or if he is guilty of any other mifdemeanour, he fhall be kept in, or be excluded, as the majority of the next Meeting fhall think fit to Determine.

XX. No Member fhall propofe to remove the Box with out a very juft Caufe, but if the Landlord neglects the Society, and the Stewards, Mafters, and Clerk thinks proper to remove it, the Stewards are to give Notice thereof at the Meeting, and that they are to Vote at the next meeting in the Society Hours, and then, if fairly Voted, the majority to Remove it, but to have good fecurity for the ftock before fuch removal. If any Member propofes to break the Box, he fhall be Excluded without delay : the Box or Club fhall never be broke whilft there are Five Members in it.

XXI. ANY Member may talk about his particular Bufinefs in the Club-Room, but where Ordered by the Stewards for filence, the fame is to be Obferved, or Forfeit Three-Pence to the Box after being ordered Twice.

XXII. IT is farther agreed, that on Whit-Wednefday fhall be held our Feftival, which fhalt be at Ten o'Clock, or half an Hour after, in the Forenoon, each Member to be at the Dumb-Poft, to attend Divine Service at Brimhill Church, and he that does not attend fhall Forfeit One fhilling, and to pay One fhilling and fix pence for his Ordinary and Extraordinary.

XXIII. There fhall be fixty peices of Paper, marked. No. 1, to 13, the reft Blanks, made up in fuch a manner that no Perfon fhall fee the Numbers, which fhall be drawn by the Members then prefent, and they Thirteen fhall vote 'it out amongft themfelves ; they fhall go into a private Room, and no Member, nor any other Perfon, fhall be allowed to go near them ; it fhall be voted in Fifteen minutes, and the moft Votes to Carry the day.

XXIV. IT is agreed by this Society, that after the ftock amounts to 116£. that they fhall Reduce it to 43£. the Members that was at the laft Reduction to go fhare alike, and they that Entered fince to have it according to every man's Enterance, and if ever the ftock is reduced to 40£ every Member to Subfcribe fhare alike to make 43£ with-in Two Meetings after fuch reducement ; any Member that refufe to fubfcribe fhall be immediately Excluded.

XXV. IT is further agreed, that after Dinner, on our Feaftival Day, being Whit-Wednefday, every Member, being at Dinner, fhall walk in an Orderly manner Two and Two, according to their Entering, from the Dumb-Poft to David Rumming's, the Bell-and-Organ at Brimhill, and walk round the Crofs Twice, and to have a fhort Pot of Beer each Time, which each Member is to pay for ; any member refufing, or breaking his Rank, fhall Forfeit Three-Pence to the Box, after being ordered by the Stewards once.

XXVI. IT is farther agreed, at our Feaftival to give the Ringers Six fhillings, and for Mufick Ten fhillings, and their Dinners paid from the ftock.

Bremhill Friendly Society certificate issued to author, a facsimile of original 1770 certificate used for current membership.

Doctoring in the early 1800s had many drawbacks in rural Wiltshire, where overcrowded dwellings, bad water-supplies and lack of food were so prevalent. The 1830-40s saw many epidemic outbreaks, but little detail is known before 1837 when compulsory registration for births and deaths began, and many deaths from typhus and scarlatina, smallpox and consumption were revealed. Devon in 1838 had as many as 615 deaths from typhus and scarlatina, 460 from smallpox, 1,649 from consumption and a mortality of 18/1000. (A comparison of similar statistics for Wiltshire would be of great interest.) The concepts of preventative medicine were not to be fully understood for another twenty years or so; the link between diet, housing, working conditions and health came even later. And when understood, little was done in Wiltshire. Lack of drive and funds and the isolation of rural communities all conspired through the whole of the century and beyond to make the development of social service policies particularly slow.

Countryside living had several drawbacks to good health. Sanitation was the worst. Water for household use and drinking came from wells or streams, easily contaminated by seepage from middens or manure heaps. Cottage floor levels were often well below the surrounding ground or road, pig styes in the garden sometimes meant drainage into the houses, the wells or surface water sources, while shallow, stagnant pools lay around. Dampness, crowding, poor heating and ventilation of the home, limited clothing and food, all contributed to the spread of disease and poor health. It would not be until the 1870s before housing improved and child mortality rates dropped, particularly those of infants. But the newly-created statistics recorded many rural Wiltshire people surviving to a ripe old age, despite their adverse living conditions.

In the middle of the 19th century in Wiltshire, only workhouses supplied basic hospital services to the poor in the countryside and rural towns and villages; in 1861, one hospital bed existed per 1,800 population in England, statistically about 140 hospital beds in Wiltshire, with half the population more than three miles away from a hospital. By this time the county population was approximately 250,000, with five people urban to four rural. In 1868 a new Poor Law Act guaranteed an infirmary in every workhouse, but materialization proved slow; even by 1900 probably more than half the sick poor of the county were still being cared for in the workhouses' general accommodation rather than in a separate infirmary. Cottage hospitals had begun in 1869, but because of lack of transport few in Wiltshire received the rural patient, though doctors had the authority to send them.

Some charity existed locally, ladies of middle- and upper-class families giving care or soup to sick people in their villages, and local clerics offering limited help. For instance, the Rector of Chilmark maintained a trained nurse for the poor of the parish at his own expense, an extremely practical charitable gesture. 19th century medical charity to villagers in Wiltshire is certainly a topic worthy of research. And the patchy care offered created an ironic situation for the 19th century working agricultural labourer as, except for Friendly Society members, paupers had better access to skilled medics. Hospital care in the workhouse was avoided whenever possible; some would die rather than allow themselves to be admitted.

For any medical services, probably the most fortunate of all the poorer labourers were those who belonged to Friendly Societies. In payment for a small regular contribution of a few pence, the societies provided sickness and funeral benefits to their members, all working men. Apparently their families did not share any benefits. Keevil Friendly Society, formed in 1765, is the earliest recorded in Wiltshire. The societies increased slowly, numbering 30 in 1801 and 250 by 1866. About 6% of the Wiltshire population held Friendly Society membership in 1801. Statistics are misleading, as they do not reflect financial failures which often occurred through having too few members paying enough dues to fund necessary benefits. Corsley, not a large village, supported seven Friendly Societies at one period. But encouraged and regulated by the Government, some continued into the 20th century when, under the National Insurance Act of 1911, they were given a new role as state health insurance agents.

The Bath and West of England Society, soon after its foundation in 1777, had recommended that farmers support the Friendly Societies, expecting them to help lower the poor rates, but the farmers and some officious members of the public retained uneasy feelings about them. The organizations were independent, run by labourers for labourers, with ceremonies and rituals no outsider could join, hence supposedly possible rivals to Church and Chapel. Their monthly meetings held at a nearby inn were convivial and lively, their outdoor processions and annual feast created local legends, so they raised suspicions that they contributed to the ever-present temptations of excessive drink and debauchery. The latter, among other insinuations, was an euphemism for catching VD! Most threatening of all, Friendly Society gatherings supposedly encouraged that 19th century bogey, the labourer getting above his station in life.

After Poor Law eligibles and Friendly Society members, those left among the agricultural labourers and their families had to pay for medical attention. To have a doctor make a house-call in a remote area was costly. No doubt exists that, whenever they could, villagers relied on traditional folk and herbal knowledge and their families to nurse them through illness. Barbers still set bones until well after 1858, when the law began to require that surgeons be licenced before practising. For childbirth, if a village or hamlet had no local midwife or nurse (usually self-trained or working from knowledge inherited from her mother or others), neighbouring women rallied round the prospective mother. Because of the scattered population and lack of industrial income in the county, the Public Health Acts, Sanitary Reforms and Local Government Acts between 1848 and 1888 just did not reach out much beyond urban areas until the 20th century. The Wiltshire County Council (WCC) then authorized and organized visiting health officers, concentrating on midwifery and infant welfare. In 1911, the arrival of national sickness insurance, which applied to 15 million wage earners making less than £160 a year, did somewhat remedy the shortage and difficulty of paying for medical attention in Wiltshire and some of the controversy always arising over charitable hospital care. But a panel doctor could only deal with minor complaints and some chronic diseases; the more seriously ill, if lucky, went to the voluntary or cottage hospital, the unlucky to the workhouse.

Slowly, other county services came into being, school doctors and dentists, optician services and visiting services to older children and later to house-bound adults. But until the 1946 National Health scheme, by our present high standards, adequate medical coverage and services in rural Wiltshire were often difficult to obtain and retain.

The agricultural labourer and other workers slowly realized self-help as one of the roads to self-reliance and struggled to help himself first with Friendly Societies, then by general protest calling attention to his plight. And by the 1860s, Church and Chapel and some landowners began to give more practical help besides charity.

Education

In the mid-19th century, both the upper- and middle-classes feared the revolutionary events taking place on the Continent, and shuddered at the thought of their spreading to England and so upsetting the social strata. Limiting charity brought forth arguments that the Poor Laws and the workhouse took care of the indigent and the labourer when in desperate need. Charity was handed out in small enough amounts to make sure that the poor would not be able to 'ape their betters' by making any money or accumulating goods from it. For the same reasons, society made sure that education, a form of charity, particularly in church or non-denominational schools until the 1870s, was limited to reading, writing, a small amount of arithmetic (boys and men), and religious instruction; seldom anything included could be practically applied to increase job skills.

The only education open to 18th century Wiltshire agricultural labourers' children undoubtedly was linked to church or chapel schools. No totally state-funded education existed until the 1870s, private schools were far too expensive and, of course, above the agricultural labourers' station in life. At first mainly Sunday schools, the religious-linked schools, taught children moral guidance and catechism in Anglican classes and reading enough to understand the Bible. Day schools began to appear at the beginning of the 19th century, some of these early schools known as 'Dame' schools, but most were Anglican, a few nonconformist. How many reached village children early in the century is difficult to estimate before school inspectors began to be appointed in 1839. The schools charged about a 1d a week for a child's instruction, so with several children of school age in a family, until the 1860s, this small fee was usually beyond the poor labourer's purse. In them, learning meant the three Rs, religious instruction, and needlework for the girls. Primarily the emphasis was put on the pupils' lowly station in life which they were required to accept unequivocally. The Poor Laws allowed expenditure for school fees on poorer children and apprentices, but after 1834, this was often refused to parents.

By the 1840s, the Government awarded grants to the religiously-linked schools and instituted a system of school inspectors to raise standards of education, though the religious schools always emphasized indoctrination rather than scholarship. Grants for teaching trainees followed soon after. The grants were small and schools apparently had minimum standards of accommodation, equipment and supplies, with few qualified teachers, seldom decently paid. Canes were in abundance, corporal punishment being thought of as an essential of discipline. According to Rex Sawyer his book: *Collett's Farthing Newspaper,* the 'Principal' at Bowerchalke dame school obtained her cane sticks from the apple orchard of a nearby vicarage! But there was little or no tendency to encourage or spend money on any education directed towards the working class, especially in rural areas.

Not all parishes in Wiltshire boasted a school and in those which had, attendance was not compulsory. Parents took their children out of the classrooms at will to work in the fields, apparently more often in the Chalk Country than in the Cheese Country, where the farms offered less juvenile work by the 1860s. Haymaking, harvesting, gleaning, potato-lifting, sometimes even hoeing, caused schooldays to be skipped. Compulsory elementary school attendance for all children did not come into force until 1880, but even then children continued to work in the fields when their parents desperately needed their earnings to help support the family. As early as 1858 a report on education in Wiltshire contained the observation on parents: 'unhappily it cannot be said that they appear very sensible of the value of education for their children.' But education did not put food on the table and the long-term value of schooling was especially hard to perceive, when so little opportunity for the future existed in the county for either the labourers or their children.

In 1841 a government inspector wrote: 'the inner life of the classes below us in society is never penetrated by us. We are profoundly ignorant of the springs of public opinion, the elements of thought and the principles of action among them – those things which we recognize at once as constituting our own social life, in all the moral features which give to it form and substance.' These remarks parallel the author's own difficulty in understanding the intrinsic nuances of the Wiltshire agricultural labourers' lives. 19th century Education Committee reports, village school records, inspectors' reports and bishops' visitation records contain an enormous amount of information on village schooling in Wiltshire and await a diligent researcher, particularly one with a love for statistics. From them can also be determined how many agricultural labourers' children actually attended school and for how many years. For example, the 1858-9 report of 364 Wiltshire parishes and chapelries, 72 parishes had no schoolhouse (though nineteen of these parishes required no school having no children of school age), 208 had one or more school buildings in good condition, 55 had defective buildings. Schools were grouped into various categories, including Dames' schools, Dissenters' schools, endowed schools, parochial Union schools and two Roman Catholic schools. Not all categories required inspection. 720 schools were reported with a total of 33,217 scholars, an average of 46 attending each school. Of the masters, 42 had qualifications or registration, 134 remained uncertified or unregistered, 40 mistresses had certification. Pupil teachers numbered 167, of whom many were young girls, which may have provoked the wry observation from a farmer before a government commission who felt that schoolmistresses had no disciplinary skills and boys do not learn from a woman!

The 1858-9 report lists schools by parishes, with the date of inspection given, the population of the parish, its rateable value, followed by remarks. The comments are especially revealing. A random sampling on page 30 of the 1858-59 report mentions no schools at Steeple Langford (population 634) – 'the farmers violently opposing the building of them.' 15 to 20 village children are kept out of mischief in two cottages, perhaps 50 to 70 scholars would appear if a school was set up. Then an additional remark is made: 'I learn that a good school, under a master and mistress, is to be established here next year, to be open to children from Stapleford, Wylye, Fisherton Delamere and Little Langford where no school age children are known.' In the Cheese Country at Langley Burrell (a closed village) with a similar population, Mr Ashe, the local squire, had built a substantial school (still standing, now a private residence) and supported it. One mistress and a girl teacher taught 30 or 40 children 'Bible and Catechism, and reading, and writing and needlework. The manager disapproves of any more advanced instruction.' A good report came from Lacock, where in the two-roomed school, a certificated master and three pupil teachers endeavoured to instruct nearly 120 children out of a village population of 1,653. 'Mr Hughes reports very favourably of the discipline and instruction, and especially of the writing and arithmetic.'

Sunday schools were very prevalent in the county. In 1835 there were 142 with supposedly over 13,000 students; with an average of 95 pupils per school, one assumes not all attended every Sunday. By the end of the century every Methodist chapel had its Sunday school. Night schools existed in Wiltshire to reach older children and adults, usually attended by males. 9,078 students attended in 1858-9. Due in great part to the influence of several Bishops of Salisbury, night schools existed for boys *and* girls in the Wylye area . An average attendance of 453 boys out of 586 is recorded in 1860 and they were taught by clergy, paid teachers (both male and female) and volunteers. Winterslow had a night school and by 1867 a reading room, hopefully established to keep men out of the pubs. At the time an estimation had been made that the villagers spent £500 annually on beer, and so a recommendation to initiate licensing laws was added, presumably to discourage spending on alcohol.

The Church clergy figure frequently in efforts to establish and maintain Church schools and by the time of the 1870 Education bill half the children in England receiving an education obtained it in a church school. Ten years later State schools formed the main thrust towards educating children. Meanwhile conscientious clergyman monitored their village and Sunday schools. Francis Kilvert can be mentioned as outstandingly assiduous in his duties as a parish priest. Besides the two sessions of Sunday school at Langley Burrell, according to his diary, he visited the village school daily between 1872 and 1876.

Overall, the quality of schooling available to the Wiltshire agricultural labourer appears variable, but probably not much better than that offered in other poor rural counties of England. An 1854 statistic stated that 7% of Wiltshire's population was enrolled in day schools, a high percentage compared to most other counties in England. However it cannot be judged today what should have constituted an adequate education and it is a subject too complex to discuss in the confines of this book. But even if literacy was a chief requirement, schooling was deficient, the estimated figures for literate Wiltshire labourers in the 1860s being 40% to 60% for males, 25% for females. By the 1870s 80% of brides and grooms could sign the register at their wedding ceremony, and due to the Education Act most likely 100% by 1890, but the scope and range of education for the labouring classes in Wiltshire grew only slowly. Very few of the brighter rural pupils obtained a secondary education by the 20th century, partly due to lack of selection and partly to absence of transportation to the schools, all located in urban areas.

So much of the education received in villages depended on the schoolmaster's skills and attitudes and the attendance of the children. Much information on this topic still needs to be uncovered, the figures are there for the asking in the school attendance books. The bright student, especially if male, was often singled out and given more attention. What happened to them would make another intriguing, but difficult research project. Girls, however clever, had little chance of making their way in the outside world; it was domestic service and/or marriage for them until well into the 20th century, except for a lucky or persevering few who became pupil teachers and sometimes made it as school teachers. Not a prosperous way of life, but better than staying in one's home village in most cases.

Adult education came slowly to the agricultural labourer and then it was mainly through the almost secretive attempts of nonconformist village groups to supply talks and later reading rooms, first in cottages, later in village halls. After the 1870s the influence of the Trade Union movements and the Workers Education Association helped towards the acceptance of adult education, but how extensive it was still has to be tracked down. The Swindon branch of the WEA made great endeavours to extend its reading rooms and educational ventures into nearby villages, but seemingly few other Wiltshire towns made much effort to do so.

Emigration

Although education had yet to make any attempt to provide an escape route from his harsh life, emigration was one way for the agricultural labourer to leave drudgery and poverty behind. By the 1830s, and for the next thirty years, the option to emigrate became increasingly available. If a man and his family were willing to take the risk and fulfilled the necessary requirements pertaining to health, age and character, the chance for a new life was to be had. But it seems for many that the option was too fearful to take, so very little was known of those distant countries which would accept him as an immigrant. For others the cost or family ties did not allow them to contemplate such a move, while for some, the enormity of the step was not to be considered.

One of the earliest references in 19th century writings on emigration comes from Cobbett, who was concerned that overseers might transport paupers and orphans to avoid them being a charge on the Poor Laws. In fact, this apparently happened in 1830 at Corsley, where the overseers arranged for 66 of their 'least desirable residents, poachers and 'men suspected of bad habits'' to sail from Bristol to Quebec. Perhaps they were told to go or else...! By 1836, 200 people from Downton received assistance to move to Canada. The DWG of 21 March 1833 discussed emigration to USA and Canada after advertisements offering passages had begun to appear in the newspaper. The new Poor Laws permitted the rates to be used for assistance in emigrating. About 340 people from Wiltshire used this route to migrate by 1837 and in 1842, over 500 had emigrated from villages in the county. Among them was a group of thirteen males and seven females from Purton, mainly from three families. Eight migrants were children between the ages of five and thirteen, all described as labourers, as were the rest of the party. The far-ranging preparations made for the group are described in a fascinating document drawn up between the parish and the shipping agent (WSRO 212B/5644).

Emigration served as a limited method of coping with surplus labour and surplus people. In Wiltshire a gradual process, it did not apparently decimate village population, which continued to grow in the villages until the mid-19th century, then slowly decline, mainly for various other reasons, mostly movement to towns and a lowering in the birth rate. By the 1840s, Australian and government agents came into the county to choose migrants. In one instance, Pitton rate payers borrowed £65 to allow the Waters family, Obadiah and his wife and children, and Henry Wadhams, a shepherd, to sail to Australia in 1843.

Not all labourers favoured emigration overseas, some moved into urban areas where more jobs were opening up. After the coming of the railway to Wiltshire, jobs opened up in the north of the county, on and along the railways themselves. And with a personal contact, a man could bring his family to a town or city, or a young man or girl took their chances and left their homes for unfamiliar work in an strange place. But always there existed families so closely linked to their village, relatives, or even their employer, that they stayed put despite their poverty, their large families, poor accommodation, hunger and shortage of work. Mark Baker cited a carter who firmly refused an offer of retirement; he felt he belonged to the farm where he had worked all his life and could not bear to leave it. And he didn't, for his employer made sure that he was never allowed to want. How many other such cases existed is impossible to calculate, but a few are remembered for posterity by the long-service awards made by various local agricultural associations.

A larger emigration scheme appeared in 1849. Founded with the help of the Marquess of Ailesbury, his son and Lord Shelburne from Bowood, all concerned with over-population and under-employment on and around their estates in the north of the county, the Wiltshire Emigration Association helped 258 people to Australia by 1851. Money was solicited by subscription and the families who went were all chosen for their suitability. Because of the high mortality rate of small children on the Australian passage, those with several youngsters were excluded, as were children unaccompanied by their parents. All came from rural backgrounds, the family heads claiming to be agricultural labourers or 'country mechanics' (craftsmen). Some emigrated without their family members. Sponsored single women were expected to become farm servants. (The actual experience of single women on arrival in Australia was to enter a highly competitive market of prospective husbands because of the shortage of females in the colony; so few ended up as servants for very long.) It is on record that some of these emigrants found a good life in their new country; Mark Baker's paper in the WANHS library (box 249) recounting the story of the WEA and the results of the emigration makes fascinating reading. Baker recollects that large numbers of inhabitants from Burbage emigrated to Australia in 1851, perhaps due to over-population, but maybe from bad living conditions, as Kelly's 1848 Directory describes Burbage as a picturesque but not particularly clean village. Baker suggested Wroughton had seen considerable emigration, perhaps for the same reason, or perhaps because living near Swindon and the new railway gave labourers a wider outlook on life, making it less difficult to contemplate the implications and complexities of migration.

Lord Herbert of Wilton also helped families to emigrate in 1850, but other large Wiltshire landowners showed little interest in such schemes; though Baker cites the

Marchioness of Bath who (when trustee for her son, the 4th Marquess) helped young men to emigrate from Longleat. Emigration continued to Australia, then New Zealand, later opening up to the USA and Canada. Gandy mentions several Aldbourne men who went to Patagonia in 1874; other families from Wiltshire ended up in Brazil. In some counties after the 1860s the newly-founded Trade Union movement gave financial help to its members to leave England. Little evidence is found so far of such assistance to Wiltshire men, but the TU movement was always poorly supported and financially weak in the county. The flow of emigrants continued until the 1880s when numbers dropped as opportunities overseas grew less, passages became more expensive and surplus labour in Wiltshire almost non-existent, thus eliminating the greatest incentive to move. A population of Moonrakers came into existence in many parts of the world, their success rate unknown; but their harsh background must have equipped them to deal with the worst adversities emigrants had to face.

Allotments

Opportunities to obtain land for growing or raising food, or for grazing, steadily dropped well into the early decades of the 19th century as the Enclosure movement continued to appropriate most cultivable and waste land previously available to the agricultural labourer. The need for even a garden plot became more desperate as wages lost their purchasing power and hunger increased. The idea of providing a small allocation of land to a labourer to work for himself began nationally at the end of the 18th century and Wiltshire had several far-seeing landowners who became pioneers of the movement in the county, setting an example for other counties to follow.

The constant lack of food, before and during the Napoleonic Wars, had prompted the passing of several parliamentary acts to promote the concept of more land for allotments, but opposition was always present, especially from farmers. They wished to keep total control over their labourers and the local land supply and felt strongly that an allotment would distract the labourer from his work, take away his energy and might lead to theft of pig food, seed potatoes or manure from a farm. Even the idea of potato grounds did not really find favour in Wiltshire; they get little mention after 1840, though in the early part of the century farmers made good money by renting to a labourer as much as an acre on which to grow potatoes. Needless to say, the perennial objections of making labourers more independent, the blurring of social distinctions, an increase in life ambitions or other changes to his social station were all brought forward against supplying allotments to labourers. Some farmers retained these arguments for much of the 19th century, undoubtedly linked to their fear of losing their cheap workforce.

In time, allotment schemes won public approval, as it was thought that they kept labourers closer to their home in his leisure hours and out of the local inn. Communal allotments supplied 'safe' companionship with fellow neighbours, all of them far too busy digging to conspire to sedition or revolt. A few labourers voiced suspicions of any scheme to provide allotment land, fearing more authoritative control over them and ever-increasing rents, but their fears apparently proved unwarranted as regards the rents. For many, especially those who rented church glebe land, the charges were minimal and sometimes nothing at all.

The Captain Swing movement and subsequent action of the Tolpuddle Martyrs in the first half of the 1830s made headlines in people's minds, but provided more support for the allotment movement in Wiltshire. Reformers, more large landowners, some sympathetic farmers and clergy donated more land and Wiltshire, by 1837, had allotments 'to a greater extent than any other county' and remained in this position for many more years.

A landowner on the Wiltshire/Gloucestershire border, Thomas Estcourt seems the first to have established a scheme in 1801 to award allotments to local cottagers, including residents of Ashley and Long Newton; no rents are mentioned, so they were perhaps a form of charity. The family also sponsored many allotments in the Little Cheverell to Devizes area. The schemes were successful, reducing relief costs by 1805. The local workers then proved 'more able, willing, civil and sober, and property never so free from depredation as at present.' A few years later the Reverend Stephen Demainbray, Vicar of Great Somerford, pioneered an allotment system 'giving part of his glebe land to the poor cottagers of the parish', according to a plaque still to be seen in the nave of the village church. In the following decade allotment schemes appeared in many villages in the county including Colerne, Fittleton and Rodbourne. At least eighteen allotment sites are recorded well before 1830, and many more probably existed unmentioned.

Travelling between Warminster and Highworth in September 1826 Cobbett noticed numerous labourers digging in small plots of land for their potatoes for Sunday's dinner. He thought their rents, the equivalent of £8 an acre, most profitable for the farmer, but he refrained from mentioning that farmers often supplied manure to a potato ground site and sometimes allowed the labourers to work on them in the farmers' time. Cobbett being Cobbett, he eloquently characterized the diggers as honest and laborious men compelled to starve quietly, whether all at once or by inches, 'with old wheat ricks and fat cattle under their eye.'

Due to the prevalent hunger, by 1827 the Marquis of Lansdowne set up a procedure for renting out pieces of land, beginning in the village of Bremhill. The concept quickly expanded, not only in the form of allotments, but by adding cultivable pieces of land to estate cottages. Some allotments were given to older men 'to keep them off the parish.' Unfortunately, a few of these recipients then lost their right to relief. Another pioneer was Joseph Neeld who let out more than 200 plots on his Grittleton estate. The Earl of Radnor followed suit, as did parishes with rentable land.

A survey made in 1833 of cottages with gardens in southern England stated that in 57% of the parishes surveyed most cottages had gardens, in 32% some had gardens and in 11% only a few or none at all had gardens. In Wiltshire 82% of parishes had allotment schemes. At Alton Barnes, the vicar charged no rent for allotments in 1832. A survey of 26 parishes, carried out by the Devizes Branch of the Labourers' Friend Society in 1833-4, indicated that in a population of 20,000 in 1831, of which agricultural labourers numbered approximately 2,200, some 1,450 cottagers held allotments varying in size from 1/40 of an acre to 4 acres, with an average size of 1/4 acre. The LFS, founded by persons of reforming minds in 1816 besides advocating allotments, published a journal *The Labourers' Friend*, with no other purpose than to influence landed interests on the plight of the labourer. Rents for allotment land varied from 5s to £7 acre, usually 20s to 60s, and were paid punctually. Poor relief payments had dropped in the area. A rough rule of thumb was the deeper the poverty, the higher the number of allotments in a parish, so it is no wonder Wiltshire had such a long tradition of allotment cultivation and, with this steady supplement to living expenses, a continuing history of low wages.

Often a wife and children helped cultivate a piece of ground. Working twelve hours a day, six days a week and on Sundays, if a cowman, shepherd or carter, a man no doubt was glad of any assistance. But the holder of a large enough allotment could not keep a cow on it even if he wanted to, it would then have turned him into a smallholder; which was not one of the rationales in supplying allotments; landowners did not want to add to the labourers' independence. A good gardener could produce 20 cwt of potatoes on as little as a quarter of an acre, enough to feed a family and fatten a pig or even two. And a pig yielded the equivalent of 6d a week to a family income, whether sold or eaten. Traditionally the 'pig' money still provided boots for the men of the family, if not the wife and children. At this time many reports crop up of children going around bare-footed in all but the coldest weather, when those still without footwear bound their feet in rags. The pig, the allotment or garden unquestionably kept many labouring families from starving and poor relief during the harsh years of the 1800s.

The allotment movement kept its strength in Wiltshire all through the 19th century. The West of England Labourers' Association in 1872 strongly supported extending allotment schemes for labourers and two of its organizers in the Calne area claimed to have acquired enough land to become self-sufficient. They seem to have been rare cases, however. The Association, like many other hopeful attempts to establish Union support in Wiltshire, fizzled out by 1876. By 1887 the Government reported that the number of allotments had grown by over 40%, in Wiltshire, no doubt any labourer who wanted a piece of land to cultivate could find one easily. By then the moral benefits of allotments were hardly mentioned, just the material advantages. Much government legislation continued to be passed to maintain the supply of allotments, now being demanded by urban as well as rural labourers. However, towards the end of the century, agricultural labourers lessened their calls for an allotment, food was more plentiful and they chose other activities in their spare time, rather than gardening. Suppliers of allotment land changed from private landowners to public authorities and in the next chapter it will be seen how the demand for smallholdings rather than allotments began to increase in Wiltshire as the 20th century opened.

Enclosures

One of the factors that increased the need for allotments in the first thirty years of the 19th century in Wiltshire was the authorization by Parliament of the residual enclosures of farming land. Little hope then remained for any agricultural labourer that he would ever gain access to any cultivable land in his own right and the potato lands and later allotments were made available as a substitute. In time the final round of enclosures were to change the fabric of many villages, particularly on the Chalk. There, consolidation of the land meant larger farms, encouraging machinery and more technology, in turn offering less employment. Local protests against the last enclosures had some success for a few years, but in the end, the labourer lost any access to unowned land or grazings; even if a cottage owner and therefore franchised, there was little he could do in a county mainly represented in Parliament by landowners. Another class of person who lost everything through enclosure was the squatter living on common or unused land, who was promptly driven out as the new owner took possession.

Langley Burrell Common suffered enclosure in 1820 by the Ashe family, the new owner of the tithe. It took away grazing rights from cottagers in the village. They had no means of protest and the land was rented out to estate tenants and farmers and divided into fields for stock and dairy cattle. This situation is summed up by the protest verse:

> The law locks up the man or woman,
> Who steals the goose from off the Common.
> But leaves the greater villain loose,
> Who steals the Common from the goose.

Gandy drew attention to the enclosures in Aldbourne resulting from the 1805 Act. Four big common fields were lost, but users received allotments in exchange. Some had already lost grazing rights on the downs and keeping forage animals had to end. Cottagers had also lost their supply of dung, unless they kept a pig. The bitterness generated was remembered for several generations. To rub salt into the wound, the Commissioners held a celebratory dinner at a local inn, consisting of 'a plenty of all sorts' and accompanying drink.

As happened at Aldbourne, a common practice of land-exchanges existed, implemented by the enclosure's commissioners. They persuaded men who possessed limited common rights to grazing land to part with these rights, in exchange for cash or exclusive rights to a smaller and different parcel of land. As the commissioners always set the terms (according to existing records, though maybe sometimes bargaining took place), the deal, to all intents and purposes, was forced. And seemingly very often, those who elected a land-exchange found a few years later that they could not make ends meet, even with part-time employment (if they could find it) and had to sell their land. If farm size statistics for Wiltshire are carefully examined, it will probably be seen that very few self-employed smallholders existed by the 1850s. At present, statistics are blurred by the ownership of small separate parcels of land that belonged to larger farmers and run in conjunction with their farm, but were listed separately.

Enclosures at Fovant and district began in 1785. The minutes book recording the whole procedure is held by the WSRO #2057. The licence, in actuality a permit from Parliament to enclose, was taken out by the Earl of Pembroke, but the factual plans and execution were done by an appointed Board of Commissioners and their clerks who met regularly at an inn in Salisbury (perhaps the Red Lion?) and had dinner afterwards, presumably at the ratepayers' expense. All meetings were published in the Salisbury Journal and in the parishes involved, a notice being posted on the church door.

The enclosure was to be paid by rates from landowners involved, the 'paying and defraying the charges and expenses incident to and attending the obtaining and passing of the act.' For most parishes the amount totalled approximately £600, for several it was more. The biggest share of the expenses fell to Lord Pembroke at £250 per parish. At the other end of the scale, three freeholders out of a total of 65 paid less than £1, most others paid a few pounds each. There is no doubt who benefitted the most from this enclosure. Some favouritism seems to have crept in; 13 lifetime leaseholders at Bowerchalke paid very low rates, and at Broadchalke Jane Emms, holding several small pieces of land, paid only a token amount, unlike 35 other holders in the parish.

Plans and maps of the area to be enclosed were drawn up. The courses of public highways were slightly changed where necessary, private roads, bridle-ways and footways sorted out. Some bridle-ways and footpaths were closed, despite protests received. Others were rerouted, causing more protest, particularly ones well used. Various objections were heard, acknowledged and settled with only one disagreement, but no specific objections or names or details are recorded in the minute book. 'Tidying up' boundary lines frequently occurred, but care was taken to allocate Church lands without taking away any value from the Church.

The Board then began to hear claims and objections to the 'beneficial enclosure' proposals. Some claims were justified, others quickly dismissed. Most came from poor people. From the tone of the minutes written up by clerks, the proceedings frequently show evidence of previous agreements made by the commissioners before the meeting. One gets the impression of a steamroller steadily moving to its objective at each meeting. By the Spring of 1787, grass seed was ordered for the laying down of allotted arable land. Common grazing rights were to be extinguished by October, the end of the farming year, but privileges to some woodlands were retained. All ancient rents had been cancelled. The day after commons rights were withdrawn the commissioners threatened to impound all cattle and horses not removed in 24 hours from the enclosed land and any rescuers of the animals would be indicted. No objections were recorded at the time, but in 1788, a Samuel Parnot refused to pay his rate of £11 8s 3d, and his goods and chattels were ordered to be seized and sold. A sad ending to such an upheaval for smallholders and labourers with common grazing rights.

The commissioners ceased regular meetings during 1788, but various decisions, such as water rights, were arbitrarily defined during that year. Their last order came on April 3 1793 – payment of the clerks and the announcement of the Act executed fully and completely. Enclosures authorized by Parliament before and after the Napoleonic Wars had continued to create great hardships for the agricultural labourer, particularly in the Chalk Country, but always benefitted the larger landowners by increasing the value of their land by better usage or consolidation.

Protests and Riots

The enclosure movement turned out to be only yet another problem of many existing in the life of the agricultural labourer at the end of the 1820s. By the 1830s, criminal acts had increased, especially theft of food, sheep, clothes and fuel, and poaching and the extreme punishments meted out by the courts were no deterrent to a starving man with a hungry family. The Wiltshire labourer was in such a bad way that he finally dared to challenge the society he lived in. His first protests did not involve any damage to property. Men from Corsley, Ramsbury, Wroughton, Christian Malford and other villages held peaceful demonstrations. At Ramsbury, men threatened to make a march round the villages to protest against wage reductions; in Wroughton men walked out of Church during a service and smoked pipes in ceremony. A hundred labourers at

'Captain Swing' letter.

Christian Malford took possession of the church to prevent the overseers attending a vestry meeting, thereby drawing attention to their plight. which they felt to a great extent was determined by their overseers. In hindsight, these incidents show how severely the laborers were stressed, and had to force their circumstances into the sight of the authorities, the middle- and upper-classes who controlled their lives. But it was to no avail; being so scattered about the countryside made it hard to assemble enough persons to make an effect, without careful and prolonged organization beforehand.

So people took little notice of these first Wiltshire protests and the labourer began to feel that the only way to increase his wages was to act more strongly. But the events of the French Revolution, and Peterloo in 1819, still frightened people and they were wary of any protests; current thought had evolved into law and order being more important than the welfare of the poor. Then came the Captain Swing movement. The threshing-machine loomed large as a threat to employment in corn-growing country and protest incidents began in Kent. By November 1830 they had spread to Surrey, then continued along the London road to Newbury and into the Kennet valley. The public was rightly disturbed; even allowing for exaggerated newspaper reports, the burning of ricks and destruction of threshing-machines were not isolated incidents. Some local leaders readied themselves to strike back with violence at any protesters, despite sympathy for the labourers' cause in some areas.

In reality, in Wiltshire the threshing-machine, except on the largest farms, did not take away employment from most labourers and until the 1850s, more grain in Wiltshire is likely to have been hand-threshed by flail rather than by machine. It was still cheaper to thresh oats and barley by hand; furthermore flailing had the added advantage of producing better straw. Many farmers, especially those on smaller farms, were quite content to ignore the threshing-machine, making use of hand labour to extract the grain and at the same time providing more winter work for both men and women.

But the time was ripe for protest and outside organizers met Wiltshire labourers in their villages, persuading some to strike. Though statistically very few Wiltshire men actively participated in the 208 Swing incidents recorded in the county and no threshing-machines were burnt in the Cheese Country, the movement had far-reaching effects for the labourer. Larger villages apparently produced more 'disturbers of the peace,' than in small villages; some incidents seemed the fruit of impulsive local action, with no outside motivation. Other incentives may have fired labourers to protest: a strong local leader, or a local perennial irritant such as an overbearing squire, an unpopular parson, an absentee landlord, a tight-fisted farmer or a harsh overseer.

All Cannings, Aldbourne, Great Cheverell and Urchfont all staged strong protests. On the reverse side, several local leaders kept the peace ably, showing leniency, sympathy or even paternalism towards the protesters. In the South-West of the county John Benett, M.P. and Lord Arundell; at Calne, the Marquis of Lansdowne; at Devizes, Lord Churchill; all are cited as individuals who used their power and influence towards benefitting the worker. Many local JPs handed out lenient sentences to men who came before them, some farmers gave protesters money to leave their threshing-machines alone, or took the attitude 'get it over and done with' and proceeded to lead the labourers to the site of the machine. But the protests continued and incidents became rougher.

The first-threshing machine destroyed in Wiltshire was at All Cannings on 21 November 1830, where the mythical Captain Swing supposedly appeared beforehand on a prancing thoroughbred horse. At Alton Barnes, Robert Pile fired a shot into a rebellious crowd and they then assaulted him. He was carried into his farmhouse and the mob attacked it. After threatening to break another machine at nearby Hippenscombe, the crowd left, to return the next day to do so, despite the farmer, William Fulbrook, having previously given them a sovereign (20s), the equivalent of 2 ½ weeks' agricultural wages for one man. Men smashed nine other machines in the same locality, plus cloth-making machinery belonging to Thomas Gaby at Figheldean.

Meanwhile, labourers gathered around Ramsbury and broke threshing-machines. At Enford, church overseers called a meeting to discuss farm wages. The labourers demanded and settled for a doubled wage of 2s a day and a gallon loaf, but these terms were never fulfilled. Machine-breaking continued in the area until the following day. when authorities called out the Yeomanry from Marlborough and they confronted the militant labourers on the edge of the Downs. Seven men were arrested and the rest dispersed quietly.

But disturbances lingered on for several more days, despite arrests being made after capture by Yeomanry troops riding out from Devizes, Chippenham and Melksham.

Labourers attempted to rescue fellow rioters, but were caught and committed to the Old Bridewell in Devizes. The riots spread north to Highworth and further south in the county, men marched to Quidhampton Mill, subsequently wrecking cloth-making machinery, throwing parts into the nearby millpond. At Wilton Mill around 500 people broke up the machinery so thoroughly that it was not worth repairing and replacement costs were estimated to be around £500 (note the neatly rounded off figures).

The climax of the rioting came to be called 'The Battle of Pythouse' which took place near Tisbury, where the previously-mentioned M.P. John Benett, resided. He confronted as many as 500 men and told them of the King's Proclamation of a reward of £50 for information leading to an arrest of a rioter and £500 for information leading to the arrest of any incendiaries. The men insisted they had had nothing to do with any incendiaries and proceeded to Fonthill Gifford where they smashed more farm machinery. The Yeomanry caught up with the men, who began to pelt the troops with stones. About half an hour later came the first shot, followed by hand-to-hand fighting. Armed with axes, sledgehammers, picks and bits of broken machinery the rioters fought the troops for about 20 minutes, then broke and fled. A John Harding was shot dead and 25 others suffered arrest. John Brickle, an employee of Benett, told of the journey he made with the prisoners from Tisbury to Salisbury: 'We had to get our farm horses and wagons and take them to Salisbury – and the blood did trickle out of the waggons – the whole way to Salisbury – I was carter – and drove the first waggon. When we did get to the Black Horse at Chilmark they did cry out for summat to drink poor fellows but the Cavalry wouldn't let em have nothing – they wouldn't. It were an aweful cold night and they were most shramm'd with the frost – and some of 'em couldn't wag a bit. When we got to Salisbury we took one load to the Fimary and t'others to jail.'

In December, burnings continued on the edge of the Chalk, near Cricklade and Poulton. A few hayricks were later destroyed at Broughton Gifford, Coate near Devizes, and Christian Malford, all on the clay. Everyone in the county was on the alert; John Hatherell told Kilvert how he recalled 'pad rolling' (patrolling) with Squire Ashe when the disturbance occurred at nearby Christian Malford. But the momentum had gone and disturbances ceased by Christmas.

The aftermath of the Swing Riots in Wiltshire illustrated how a great fear of repetition existed. Hasty trials resulted in severe sentences, even by 1831 standards. At Salisbury Assizes 336 men and 3 women appeared in dock, 239 accused of machine-breaking, robbery or riot. Other counties had meted out much less harsh sentences. In the end 150 were transported to Australia (they included several residents from All Cannings where the first incident occurred), 46 went to prison and 133 were acquitted or bound over. Though 50 men received capital punishment, only two were sentenced to execution and they, James Lushe of Broad Chalk and Peter Withers of Rockley, were spared after a campaign for mercy.

All those transported went to New South Wales (NSW) or Tasmania and, in the custom of the time, were assigned to a job, mainly in rural areas to various employers, mostly farmers. Isaac Cole of Wilton ended up in Government employment. Charley Davis, the leader of the riot at Alton Barnes, died soon after arrival in the colony, age 33. William Lewis, another labourer from Wiltshire, died in a fire, as did Albert Cook in 1834. William Rogers succumbed to tuberculosis soon after his arrival in Tasmania. One official who had dealings with the transported men observed that these men died from disease induced, apparently, by despair. And he added, 'from also a deep sense of shame and degradation.'

James Toomer, a ploughman of Hannington, accepted the Governor of NSW's offer to have his family shipped out, his wife, five boys and three girls. Peter Withers married in Tasmania; George Durman, William Francis, Henry Toombs and Thomas Whately married in NSW. John Forbes, a ploughman from Wiltshire had to obtain a legal guardian's consent before he could marry a minor from NSW. And David Bartlett, also from Wiltshire, committed bigamy, not to be discovered until seventeen years later, when his conviction called for a sentence of one year's hard labour at Port Arthur!

Due to protest in England, many of the prisoners shipped to Australia were pardoned or their transportation sentence shortened. Records of any returning to Wiltshire are few. W. H. Hudson at the end of the 19th century claims from local hearsay 'not more than one in five or six.' William Francis was one; he returned in 1837. John Shergold, a Wiltshire labourer, moved from Tasmania to Port Dalrymple in 1832 and, like most of the tranportees, stayed on in the colony.

A few are recorded as prospering in their new country. By 1842 Robert Blake and William North from Great Bedwyn together leased a farm in the Bothwell district of Tasmania. William North, a 23 year old ploughman, and his brothers Daniel and Samuel had endured transportation on the same ship. The latter married and prospered, in 1851 becoming licensee of the Cape of Good Hope Inn near Oatlands. He bought land at Bothwell, and died aged 64 in 1871. Despite so many sentenced, no record shows that they carried a tradition of rebellion to Australia. They made their lives in Australia without causing any ripple of political activity or dissent.

Any paternalism shown in the days of the Swing Riots died as soon as the emergency was over, it had been just an expediency to quell further protest. A few had their wages raised, only to be lowered again to a base of six or seven shillings a week. Unprotesting, with no zeal remaining and no support, the labourers docilely accepted the treatment which farmers meted out to them; they understood the message of the punishments dealt out to the Swing rioters.

Coming so soon after the Captain Swing incidents, the case of the Tolpuddle Martyrs no doubt left another lasting influence on labourers in Wiltshire when it came to protesting. Not far from the Wiltshire border, six men in Tolpuddle (Dorset) had formed an independent association, asking labourers who joined to stand together for solidarity and withdrawal of labour if they faced a wage reduction. Though not illegal to form a trade union, it was unlawful to administer secret oaths, which their meetings had included. The Captain Swing incidents had made authorities anxious and they overreacted. Spied on, the men were caught and tried, and in 1834 sentenced to seven years' transportation. Much public anger and protestation followed, but the men went to Australia. Protests continued and in 1836 they were pardoned and returned, the last to reach England having endured an absence of three years. One of the martyrs, George Loveless, on his return, wrote in his book *Narratives of Sufferings*: 'nothing will ever be done to relieve the distress of the working classes, unless they take it into their own hands;...nothing but Union will or can even accomplish the salvation of the world.'

Some controversy exists as to how much influence the Chartist movement had on the Wiltshire agricultural labourer. In actual fact, it seemed very little, but like the Captain Swing movement, it must have impressed the labourer, influencing his thoughts, in time affecting his behaviour towards changing his life, if only by emigration or leaving his work on the land to find other occupations, such as openings in the new police force, or opportunities created by Brunel's railway being built through north Wiltshire.

Chartism, a workingmen's political reform movement derived from the 1838 People's Charter, drafted by the London Working Man's Association (WMA), spread into Wiltshire from Bath. It reached Trowbridge first, and a large and enthusiastic meeting held in November 1839 is likely to have attracted rural workers. The first rural meeting in Wiltshire was held on Crockerton Green, near Longbridge Deverill, where labourers joined forces with cloth-workers. Walter Long M.P. told the government in March 1840 of many members enrolled in the Trowbridge area, including, he suspected, his own gardeners and farm hands.

On Easter Monday a meeting at Devizes, having been previously brought to the notice of the magistrates, caused the Yeomanry to be called out and special constables sworn in. Supporters from nearby towns who marched to the town included navvies working on the London-Bristol railway track at Box. Violence erupted, resulting in many arrests. Never again did the Chartists hold a meeting in Devizes! Other meetings during April took place in the cloth country. At Steeple Ashton a farmer sacked three of his workmen who attended a meeting there. One man went back to work the next day, perhaps by invitation of the farmer, causing fellow-attendees to pull down his cottage.

In the early years of the Chartism movement, some Meeting House Certificates issued in the Trowbridge and Bradford-on-Avon area are thought to have been due to an active Chartist involvement with nonconformist evangelism and perhaps by 1841 provided added strength to the movement. It became more organized and less radical in Wiltshire, ceasing to advocate violence, holding regular indoor meetings in the towns and villages. Officers of branches were appointed and delegates sent to organized conferences. By 1842 all associations and village classes were asked to contribute weekly to the central Executive committee of the Chartists, located in Manchester. But by 1843, directed mainly from Bath, the thrust of much Chartist organization in Wiltshire concentrated on the middle-classes and the Anti-Corn Law movement.

WMA's members supported the Chartists and. though they did nothing directly for the farm workers, they surely strengthened their resolve to continue to protest their low wages and poor living conditions. And, as with the Captain Swing incident, probably influenced decisions to emigrate from the countryside to urban areas or overseas. As the GWR engineering works at Swindon developed, a branch of the National Charter Association founded there gained strength. But Chartism slowly died of inaction, though there were many talkative meetings and classes in Wiltshire. By 1848 it had failed. The rural population of Wiltshire distrusted Chartism, it appealed more to town people and at the time distrust between the two groups was very deep. Perhaps the situation of Chartism in Wiltshire was an example, as one member is attributed to saying: 'Political progress cannot outdistance public opinion.'

Anti-Corn Law League activities created opportunities for labourers to protest between 1843-46. The centre of the movement was really one man, George Reade of Goatacre, near Lyneham. Reade, a lay preacher at the tiny hamlet's Independent Chapel, founded the Goatacre Reform Society, holding its monthly meetings at his house. Besides fighting for repeal of the Corn Laws, the Society put a good deal of effort into publicizing 'working-class distress,' while instructing people who wished to speak at public meetings. It also had idealistic hopes of creating 'a union of all classes for the betterment of the country as a whole.'

A meeting organized by the Goatacre Reform Society at Lyneham in June 1844 attracted 1000 labourers, 'mechanics' (craftsmen) and a few farmers. A month later, 500 gathered round the cross in the centre of Bremhill village. A few miles away, Spirithill Wesleyan Chapel hosted a smaller gathering in September. The following year, a few labourers dared to speak at an Upavon meeting, attended by (another!) 1000. Seven months later, on a cold winter's night, labourers with their wives and children met again at Bremhill, where wives spoke for their husbands, therefore lessening the risk of job loss. This last meeting for some reason hit the national press, to create much publicity, being reported in both *The Times* and *The Illustrated London News*. Even the DWG felt bound to mention it two weeks later, drawing their readers' attention to the vicious reputations of many of the attendees! (*Very* Protectionist, the DWG had naturally oriented its reporting to farmers, their main readers.) Speaker after speaker recounted their sufferings and nearly a thousand attendees listened. A reporter described it as ' a heart-rending sight, when the moon shone out from time to time behind the clouds, and revealed the upturned faces worn with anxiety, want and hunger.' Consequences of the meeting included five Spirithill laborers, who had attended but apparently had not spoken, being fired by their employer, Mr S. Jefferies of Bremhill. As *The Times* reported, '*fear* predominated, dread of being marked men, of losing even the small pittance they now receive, kept back their desire [to speak].'

All Reade's meetings followed a pattern; first handbills were distributed a few weeks beforehand. A large open-air space was chosen, the time of the meeting set for out of working hours and families encouraged to attend to give voice to their concerns and troubles. Inadequate wages, uncertain employment, the Poor Laws, the desire for representation in Parliament were some of the issues aired. Two wives, Mary Ferris and Lucy Simkins, spoke at several meetings. One of Simkins' speeches at a Bremhill meeting inspired Charles Dickens to write a poem: 'The Hymn of the Wiltshire Labourers,' later published by the *Daily News*. On the other side of the coin was the Reverend Drury, Vicar of Bremhill who tried to stop the famous meeting. Failing to do so, he requested police to attend, should 'the slightest confusion' take place. If they did attend, they were not needed. The previous vicar's wife, nearly ten years before had deplored 'ranters' in the parish (ranters usually being a derogatory term for Primitive Methodists) whom she and 'Parson' Bowles had met while making charitable visits to the poor during the summer. Sometimes 'a gentleman' holding the pro-Corn Law position appeared, but no disturbances were ever reported at Reade's meetings.

An independent local protest began at Stert, later in 1846, against paying labourers by piece-work. One farmer suffered £1400 damage by arson, to warn him to cease piece-work and in turn, other neighbouring farmers heard the lesson. But the meeting had no effect outside the area, piece-work pay continuing in the rest of the county. A year later, at Erlestoke, situated in the same 'protest-prone area,' women stopped bread carts and insisted that bakers sell their loaves to them at the same price as elsewhere.

Nearly twenty years later, Elihu Burritt, in his walk from Land's End, relates the result of a conversation he had with a hedger in Wiltshire. After detailing his own hardships, the man told him:

> that his son-in-law had six children, all too young to earn anything in the field, and he had to feed, clothe and house the whole family out of eight shillings a week. They were obliged to live entirely on bread, for they could not afford a little cheese with it. Take one-and-sixpence for rent, and, as much for fuel, clothes and candles, and a little tea, sugar, or treacle, and there was only five shillings left for food for eight mouths. They must eat three times a day, which made twenty four meals to be got out of eight-pence, only a third of a penny for each.

Food shortages in the countryside continued. The DWG reported a February 1849 meeting of the Swindon Protection Society, where Jacob Baker, a married labourer aged 40 with nine children, owner of his cottage and therefore safe from a landlord's eviction powers, protested lack of employment, low wages and the separation of families in workhouses. Evidently an enterprising man, Jacob, who lived near Swindon in the hamlet of Hodson, emigrated in 1851 to Australia with all the family. He wrote back: 'Poor pipel in Hodson do not know what good living is...this is the contrey, my boys.' He died at the age of 80, owning four acres of land and £25 worth of personal property.

A week after Jacob had protested at Swindon, the DWG reported a wage reduction threat from 7s to 6s a week by farmers in the West Lavington area. Apparently 150 'malcontents ' met in front of the farm of Mr Spencer, one of the leading farmers of the district, hindered his labourers from getting to their work in his fields, opening sheep folds and setting horses loose from the ploughs. There was no breach of the peace, no personal hostility and no beer around. Captain Meredith and 'a strong body of men' (no doubt police as a Samuel Meredith had been appointed the first Chief Constable of the county in 1839) arrived in the parish at midnight, to leave the following morning as everyone quietly returned to work. Labourers objected to one person being taken into custody and tried unsuccessfully to rescue him. He was brought before the Devizes magistrates and remanded. Nothing further was heard of the incident. Two years later in July the DWG reported a disturbance of 'country people' at Warminster, but no serious consequences followed. During the same week a death by starvation occurred at Malmesbury. Soon after, the DWG reported a strike for a weekly wage of 9s in the Wylye valley.

The labourers' protests led nowhere and though the Corn Laws were repealed in 1846, as can be deduced, bread remained the key item in their diet. But prices did not come down for several years, while butter and meat prices continued just as high. Finally food market prices changed, beginning in the early 1850s. At the same time imports of cheese and butter began. Both imported foods were on sale in Wiltshire markets almost immediately, but while wages remained low, even with a little cheaper food, only with Poor Law supplements, low rents, charity and perhaps a garden or allotment could the labourer keep his family living at the barest subsistence level.

On July 16th 1865, the Reverend A Headley presented a sermon at St Paul's Chippenham, berating country people who, the week before, had come into the town and created a 'demonstration of the lower orders' to support the Radical candidate for Parliament, Mr Lysley. No doubt the congregation approved the sermon, as the candidate did not get elected in this first election for only one M.P. to represent Chippenham and district instead of the traditional two members.

For some labourers, especially in the Cheese Country, one gets the impression from parliamentary reports that they knew just how far they could go in their protest. Sadly, for the real sum of their request was so little, just a few shillings, the difference between subsistence and starvation, not even the cost of a pair of leather gloves for a middle-class family member. But the few shillings materialized eventually, ten years later, not by any action on the part of the government, reformers local or national, or by farmers, but by local labour shortages forcing farmers to increase pay levels and the change in overseas food production and economics making food cheaper. Better living conditions and wages had to wait for another hundred years, but still the Wiltshire agricultural labourer was destined never to reach a parity with the urban worker in any way, except perhaps he enjoyed more fresh air. Protest won him little, trickle-down economics beyond his control eventually gave him more.

Trade Unions in 19th century Wiltshire

In nearby counties, support for trade unionism began to appear after 1870, to reach Wiltshire in 1872. 700 labourers and their wives gathered at Lyneham Green to support and cheer union speakers; perhaps among them were descendants of those at nearby Bremhill who in 1846 had stood under the moon, their faces reflecting their 'anxiety, want and hunger.' But the DWG, addressing their middle-class readers in 1873, berated Joseph Arch, leader of the new National Agricultural Labourers' Union (NALU) for journeying to North America to see for himself if better conditions there were available for the agricultural labourer. The paper connected his journey with reports being received from Canada regarding immigrant labourers being cheated either by promises of land or terms of employment bad enough to be considered slave labour. In addition, the paper felt Arch's action belittled the good conditions in the UK. 'He may perhaps come to see when too late, that a man who has a decent master here and is making a reasonably fair wage...is more comfortable and practically quite as independent as if he goes to the Prairie for a living.' But how many Wiltshire labourers had a decent master and what was the criterion for a reasonably fair wage?

Unfortunately the Union movement in Wiltshire, until after WWI, had a history of sizzle and fizzle. The expectation of unions that a man is entitled to a job while wanting to work full time and earn enough to buy essentials of life plus a few extras and security in old age, is still challenged today in many countries. In the early years of unionism in rural Wiltshire the concept was totally unfamiliar. Large NALU regional meetings, such as one at Crewkerne (Somerset) trying to draw attention to local low wage levels, continued to be ignored and were treated by newspapers and other media as just another Oliver Twist appeal, a failure to encourage Union support.

In 1873 a Union organizer, George Grove, reported that the North Wilts Union, a district section of the West of England Labourers' Union with a membership of 15,000, had met in London with other leading agricultural labourers' unions to form a federation with a membership of 50,000. Each union was left in full charge of its funds and business, reporting to a head executive committee. A fatal arrangement, as by 1875, the federation failed because of local drainage of HQ funds to separate branches.

The year 1874 was a time of lock-outs and evictions across the south of England. Small unofficial strikes by local union branches in the countryside usually meant eviction for the men who led the labourers. Though the Union tried to help ousted families by moving them to other counties or even another country, due to circumstances leading up to the eviction, it was almost always a devastating period for the families. One Wiltshire eviction took place at Cherhill and received, by standards of the times, a great amount of publicity.

A squire-dominated village, virtually owned by the Henage family, Cherhill as has been shown in this book, has one of the longest recorded histories of any community in Wiltshire. Mrs Henage had a deplorable reputation of severely punishing female members of the village for any transgressions in behaviour, dress, or attempting to marry without Henage approval. The Durham family had lived in the same cottage in Cherhill for 28 years and William had the reputation of being a good citizen and an excellent worker. But he and his two sons made the mistake of joining the NALU and, to compound their troubles, the family were ardent Wesleyans, hence even at this late date in the century, considered dissenters. On February 10th 1876, the Henages ousted the Durhams from their rented house, along with their household possessions.

C. W. Henage, Esq. V.C., J.P. had previously applied for an eviction order and had Durham's daughter, aged twelve, turned out of the village school at the same time. The Union had promptly called a meeting in a nearby field, lent by a Mr John Clark. Attendance numbered (the usual)1000, many speeches were made and songs sung, but as the Henages held local power of dismissal from work on their tenants' farms and/or expulsion from their houses, protesters went no further and the Durham eviction proceeded. However, the secretary of the Salisbury district of the NALU had anticipated the event and hired a photographer to go to Cherhill by pony and trap on the day. The resulting carefully arranged but authentic portrait of the family posed before their house, with cat, furniture, a picture of Joseph Arch and the collection box for the Wesleyan Missionary Society, sold well and provided enough money for the family to be settled elsewhere.

The new Union journal, *Labour Union Chronicle* (LUC), did not report on any further eviction cases, perhaps this example was a case of once is enough, and any other ousting in Wiltshire cannot be traced, with the exception of very notorious cases at Foxham and Chitterne in 1912, concerning allotment holders and the Wiltshire County Council, which will be explained in the next chapter.

Reading through the LUC monthly publications, one feels the fervency of the Union movement, but also its difficulties in organizing and getting members. The June 1876 issue describes a conflict at Shalbourne between 'a drunken farmer and an equally drunken milker.' The worker complained of his 17s weekly wage, his poor cottage with broken windows and deteriorating thatch. He was not dismissed, but how long he remained on the farm after the report cannot be determined. Undoubtedly both employer and employee parted company as soon as possible. In the same issue, the journal gave a report on Ramsbury, where a carter with four children and a seven-day work week earned 13s, the family living mostly on bread. The women of the village toiled in the fields, often walking several miles a day to do so. One event, a sit-down tea in an orchard 'kindly lent by a Mr Talmage,' illustrates an attempt to keep up local support of the Union, and Ramsbury responded nobly, having 149 members in the area.

Various villages, usually small, (which probably meant less hostility to be faced from local farmers) hosted meetings all over Wiltshire during the next five years. Attendees donated a few coins at meetings and obviously the local branches kept themselves going on pennies, which did not give them much heft. Due to the start of labour shortage, wages had gone up in the late 1870s and had reached 17s a week. More men and their families moved to the towns, or emigrated, sometimes with the help of assisted passages (as advertised in the LUC) to New Zealand or Queensland. To go to North America, the necessary ticket had to be paid for in full.

At some meetings the local band turned out, as at Mere in July 1873. Unfortunately the event also attracted anti-unionists. Meanwhile farmers complained of high wages, and tried to cut down on labour costs. Those who tried to dispense with labour and 'grow thistles instead of corn' were called dog-in-manger farmers. The journal lamented that a decent wage for a decent day's work remained unheard and reasonable living conditions were still quite out of reach for the agricultural labourer.

Fear of the squire or landowner often crops up in reports; for example, a meeting planned at in the schoolroom at Heytesbury suddenly moved after threatened retribution. The support of the clergy and their sympathetic attitude to the Union is mentioned in the LUC, but, oddly enough, never any interaction with nonconformists, though from other sources they were extremely supportive of all unions and working men's associations. Joseph Arch came to a big meeting held at Swindon in 1876, but by then support for unions had lessened, they achieved so little for the working man and had no power or money; so their life span in 19th century Wiltshire began to run out.

Joseph Arch contested in a race for MP against Lord Herbert at Wilton in 1877, a brave action, but it was almost inevitable he would lose, as agricultural labourers still were not franchised, unless house owners. The decline of the agricultural union movement in

Wiltshire continued through the 1880s, despite the 1884 Act giving agricultural labourers the vote and increasing the radical element in the electorate. But a long period of agricultural depression had begun by 1879, creating another difficult economic period for the workers and farmers. However, some union support broke out anew in the 1890s. The Wiltshire National Agricultural Union, financed by Devizes resident Louis Anstie of snuff fame, existed for only a few years, to sputter out before the end of the century, heralding another period of quiescence on the labour-protest front. During the first five decades of the 1900s, Union activity and support in Wiltshire was to vary greatly according to the ups and downs of the economy in the country, but by never developing the successful organizational and indoctrinational skills that industrial trade unions managed to attain, were only able to achieve minor successes on the agricultural labour front.

Agricultural Labourers' Union delegates signing petition at Memorial Hall, Farringdon Street, London, 1876

Chapter 7 Bibliography

The 19th century demonstrates the rule that the nearer to present times, the more information one can obtain on a subject. A complete biography of material consulted during the preparation and compiling of this chapter makes tedious reading, hence I have concentrated on the most important and less familiar sources.

Cobbett's character and activities are ably covered by:
SCHWEIZER,K.. & OSBORNE, J., 1990, *Cobbett in his Times*. Leicester University Press

Marjorie Reeves in her book, *Sheep Bell and Ploughshare* (Paladin Press: 1980), besides describing the growth of her Bratton family's agricultural engineering business, also discusses the work of the 19th-century agricultural labourer. The Parliamentary Agricultural Commissions, sitting all through the century, contain a vast amount of information on the housing and working conditions of men, women and children in the countryside, not to mention the attitudes of Wiltshire farmers towards their employees.

References to Henry Methuen, vicar of All Cannings, and the village inhabitants of his time, are taken from the article: 'A Victorian Country Parson', by Sylvia Young, published in *Wiltshire Folklife* 33, Autumn, 1996

Details of cottage building on the Neeld and Savernake Estates are taken from WSRO 1305.

The remark of the poet, Thomas More, on 'the pretty girl' at Tan Hill fair is taken from Dennis Powney's article in *Wiltshire Local History Forum Newsletter* 56, September 2003

For sources on poaching, besides the writings of Richard Jefferies (particularly *Field and Hedgerow, The Amateur Poacher,* and *The Gamekeeper at home)*, the government report of the Select Committee on the Game Laws proved helpful, as did :
MUNSCHE, P., 1981, *Gentlemen and Poachers*. NY: Cambridge University Press.
Paul Sample's 2003 reprint - *The First and the Best,* is a definitive history of the Wiltshire constabulary, and their early attempts to keep poaching and other crimes under control, helped by popular movements to mitigate the laws of punishment during the 19th century. *The Hatcher review,* 48, dedicated to crime and punishment in Wessex, fills out further social aspects of the impact of policing and changing attitudes to crime in Wiltshire.

A. Tindal Hart's writings on the relationship of the English clergy to their 18th- and 19th-century congregations in the field of religion and education can frequently be applied to the agricultural worker in Wiltshire.

The most comprehensive insight into Wiltshire Friendly Societies is:
FULLER, M., 1964, *The West Country Friendly Societies*. Lingfield (Surrey): Oakwood Press

BURCHARDT, J., 2002, *The Allotment Movement in England 1798-1873*. Rochester, NY: Boydell & Brewer, is a fine objective study of the allotment movement. It pays particular attention to the movement in Wiltshire and surrounding counties.

In her writings on the Captain Swing Riots, Jill Chambers has shown sympathy and understanding for the motivations behind the participants' actions. *The Wiltshire Machine Breakers,* Volumes 1 & 2 (1993, privately printed), cover not only the spread of violence in the county, but events leading up to the riots, and their aftermath.

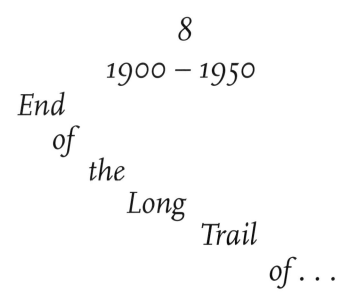

8
1900 − 1950
End of the Long Trail of . . .

. . . 'keeping the poor in that station of life which I, for one, am sure it did not please God to call them.' (F. E. Greene)

Preliminary remarks

The 20th century in Wiltshire saw the end of a triangular tie between large estate owners, the individual farmer and the agricultural labourer, an interdependency of two thousand years or more. By 1800, enclosures and enforced poverty due to the social and economic system had begun to disturb this balance and with it the labourer's last claims on the Wiltshire land. Strong mores, mainly in the guise of various social activities and legal actions came into the picture, to prevent his benefitting at all from the general agricultural prosperity in Wiltshire, until the beginning of the depression in the 1870s. That depression lowered prices and allowed his wages to buy more. Finally, total destitution became rare, though the dread of it seldom was to be absent. So many moved from the land between 1882 and 1902 that half of the advance of the national average of wages was due to the transference of labour from low paid agricultural work to more highly paid employment.

The disparity between industrial and manufacturing wages on the one hand and agricultural wages on the other continued through the 20th century, making it difficult, often impossible, for the agricultural labourer to make, by modern standards, much financial progress towards a better life. His wages allowed him just enough food, clothes and shelter to make existence bearable. Any village offering good housing and fair living conditions was a rarity in the Wiltshire countryside until after 1950. Ten years later the movement of town people coming to live in the country for the weekend had begun, and the price of any residential building for rent or for sale began to climb out of reach of the workers' pocket. Even the tied cottage was threatened as farmers wanted to cash in on the housing boom, increase their rents or sell them outright.

'Lodger' a Wessex saddleback breeding sow, obviously a friend of her cottage owners.

Only a very few were given the opportunity to further themselves through farming itself by working a smallholding, share milking or herding. Two chief handicaps prevented success – lack of capital and the slender margin of profit to be made on a small acreage. A comprehensive study of those who tried to do so in Wiltshire has yet to be tackled.

Until the 1940s, mechanization on Wiltshire farms in the 20th century increased slowly, especially on the dairy farms. Only the large farmer or landowner really had enough capital to become highly mechanized and, particularly for dairy farmers, the habit of hand labour and its comparative cheapness often won the toss when a choice had to be made. Smaller farmers still remained caught between the cycle of cheap imported food and low prices for their products, had little access to capital and were not readily able to increase agricultural wages. That was not to appear until more labour shortages occurred, and even then the effect was still slight. Union activity made jobs a little more secure, but very little else was accomplished by it without enormous effort. Labourers continued to leave the land, especially the unmarried who had less to lose. Some found work nearby created by the expanding needs of Wiltshire military establishments. A few emigrated, and others sought jobs in urban areas. In most cases they earned little more than what they had on the farm, but they had shorter hours, slightly better housing and a more lively social life.

Farmers struggled on. The agricultural depression continued until 1939, except for a break during the WWI years, cheap food prices being made a priority of all governments. Hasbach, writing in 1908 believed that farmers, because of political policies, tended to lose their faith in farming and the land, finding it difficult to retain their love of the soil and their belief in its permanency because of the difficulties of making a profit. But despite the continuing collapse of the old community of interest between employer and labourer running parallel to this loss of faith, Hasbasch's opinion is too strong. Though more tenancies had become shorter, few farmers went out of business, and family farm ownership increased. In 1914 less than 10% of farms were owner-occupied, by 1941 the figure was 37% in Wiltshire, partly due to the sell-off of land from the large Wiltshire estates, the increase being a positive gesture of faith that the land would produce a living.

The tie between farmer and employee began to sever at the start of the 19th century, and continued into the 20th. The premise that a man is a more productive and loyal worker and requires less supervision if he is decently paid and housed was sadly not to be perceptibly realized by farmers until nearly WWII. At the beginning of the 20th century agriculture in Wiltshire had become a business, with a need for skilled management and labour. The lack of formal training for most farmers and their workers began to show without recognition by either, except for a few large farmers who had adapted the tradition of educating their sons, and one or two far-sighted union members who foresaw the need for instructional courses for agricultural workers. Most farmers still shunned a labourer with any education at all, it was felt that a knowledgeable labourer was hard to discipline. These notions, plus more education for farmers' sons, were to change little until the thirties and forties.

Some Wiltshire farmers slowly learnt to cut labour costs by consolidating their farming systems, establishing milking herds in or near the chalk valleys, while increasing milk production on the clays. Due to unprofitability, they cut back on corn and sheep operations on Salisbury Plain, and often modified or abandoned water meadows and other high cost farming operations. As the public demanded more milk, dairy farmers, the new on the chalk and the old on the clays, kept a more balanced equation between profits and labour costs. One result was a further loss of jobs on the chalk.

Another half century dragged on while the labourer who remained on the land endeavoured unsuccessfully to seek a better wage and decent living conditions, with fewer jobs on hand. Despite the Foxham evictions of 1912-13 (see page 297), which were ordered by the WCC, few men were arbitrarily dismissed, partially due to union presence in the county, partly because of labour shortage. Farmers had finally begun to value their men, even if they still thought of them as servants rather than persons. Also between 1900-1914 an increase in government regulations, both local and national, dictated and changed farmer-employee interaction. And farm work still remained a refuge for a person of low mentality if his farmer-employer was patient. My observations in the thirties and forties found the two had often discovered each other, to make a stable relationship.

Village Life

The decline of village populations continued through the first half of the 20th century, labour requirements on Wiltshire farms only stabilizing as full mechanization was achieved. Those who remained in the villages seldom went to bed hungry, though it was still hard to make ends meet. After WWI, the internal combustion engine began to supply opportunities for a little more social life and communication with the outside world. The radio, coming in the 1920s provided an added feature to recreation already supplied in the village.

But for widows, the poor without regular work and the elderly with no families, to make ends meet needed much skill and patience, with a garden or an allotment often a vital factor. Poor Law relief continued to be needed and the hated workhouse still loomed as the last resort. Ralph Whitlock in *Living Village* tells of Pitton paupers in the 1890s, out-patients of the local workhouse, who had an allowance of 5s and two loaves of bread each, brought weekly from Salisbury by a relieving officer. The loaves were described as gray, insipid and guaranteed to kill any appetite. The first universal national coverage of pensions for the elderly came in 1909, giving a weekly allowance of 7s 6d to all over 70 years of age who had an income of less than £31 10s year (1s 4d bought 3 large loaves of bread). It was a start and supposedly alleviated extreme cases of poverty, but the pension eliminated those with a criminal record or those who had ever received Poor Law relief (obviously a punishment for being poor). Not until 1925 was the eligible age lowered to 65. By then weekly allowances had increased marginally, but at the same time the system of old-age pensions came under the umbrella of the National Health and Insurance Act. More increases just kept up with prices and in 1946, retirement pensions came to all, except those who had no work-linked contributions to the NHIA, which meant all women who had never 'gone out to work' or only held a domestic service job.

In some villages life still evolved round the church or the chapel, much depending on the remoteness of the village and the enthusiasm of the minister or local vicar. In some closed villages, the squire still expected villagers to participate in church activities. At Langley Burrell, where Kilvert was once curate, the Ashe family exerted their influence on church attendance until WWI as many of their employees lived in estate cottages. In the opposite corner of the county, Farley enjoyed a thriving social calendar based on the church, the activity enhanced by the fact that Lord Ilchester and his agent, who resided nearby, kept an eye on all village matters.

At nearby Pitton, a nonconformist village, life evolved round the chapel. Prayer meetings during the week were held for adults and the children attended an active and thriving Sunday school. In the early years of the century, the chapel ran Band of Hope meetings. The organization promoted the understanding among young people of nonconformist overseas missionary work, and their gatherings often featured magic lantern shows, a fascination for children of all ages. The Whitsun holiday in many Wiltshire villages saw many festivities being organized on similar patterns. On the Sunday the church and chapels played the most important role in activities. At Pitton, villagers looked forward to a visiting preacher and a special choir presentation complete with local soloists. On the Monday children enjoyed organized games and sports, but the high spots of the day had to be the cricket match against a neighbouring team and its aftermath, the village tea. Those who could afford it wore new clothes and special outfits materialized for the youngsters. But the event of the year was surely the Sunday School summer outing, at first by wagon to a picnic on the downs or in the woods nearby; after WWI by charabanc to further-away places, Bournemouth often being the destination and the first sight of the sea for many

Collecting faggots for baking ovens obtained from a felled tree at Littleton Pannell, circa 1930s.

children. At Christmas time, tradition decreed a decorated tree in the chapel and little presents for all. Everleigh youngsters are reported playing cards at Christmas parties if they could get their hands on a pack and their chapel-going mothers did not catch them at it.

Supposedly few children in Wiltshire worked on farms after compulsory education, except occasionally at harvest or haymaking, but individual stories show this was not always true, especially amongst the boys. They still rook 'starved,' helped with the machine threshing (often handling the chaff and caven – much lighter to work with than the grain), or just lent a hand to their fathers when necessary, all training for their later farm employment. But by 1900, on the whole, they enjoyed a happier childhood than had any of their ancestors in the past two hundred years. Life was safe in the Wiltshire countryside; until the 1950s, a child could wander anywhere at all times, except near military training areas. But this sometimes did happen, despite parental and authority disapproval. The fascination of the banging of the guns and the danger of it all held enormous attraction for both the brave and the not-so-brave! The hazard of gunfire was totally discounted, it was the thrill of disobedience and not being caught that created the excitement of the moment.

Village children knew an uncomplicated existence, they grew up in a set social pattern, in familiar and secure surroundings amongst known people. They had the responsibility of attending school and most had some household chores, but during their first fourteen years, from about 1890-1940, life was carefree. Then came the realization of the limitations of village life and their future, unless they broke away. It was an unique era in the history of the Wiltshire agricultural labourer.

Nothing is ever perfect; to a great extent a happy village childhood depended greatly on loving, caring parents and the child itself. If the parents and the local school teacher did not recognize their potential, life could be frustrating for the thoughtful or intense child, but for most, countryside life was never boring. If their inner resources were nurtured as well, the child gained enough wisdom to understand how to make a life for himself after he or she went into the world. Education and opportunity were out there to find if they could see it through. A few sat and passed their eleven-plus, attended a secondary school, endured five years of journeying to it, usually by bicycle, then left their village to find employment. Some returned defeated, to a job on the land for the man, marriage for the girl, and may or may not have found peace of mind in country living, despite misfortune. But a future with more advantages for the agricultural worker held little hope, even when wages and hours in the 1950s went up, but still did not reach anywhere near the level of other labouring occupations. The Wiltshire farm labourers I knew in the 1940s did not want their sons to go on the land or their daughters to go to domestic service. From the early years of the 20th century, the labourers and their wives had urged their sons and daughters away from village life, not only because of the lack of local employment, but also because of the pervading condemnation of their class by society.

Compulsory education for all children went into effect in 1880, but the village schools could still be very perfunctory, the learning mechanical and limited. In some, slates were not replaced by exercise books until after WWI, and few text books were made available, except perhaps an arithmetic primer. After 1902, local education authorities offered a little more than the 3Rs and Bible studies, but much depended on the teacher, the space and the money forthcoming. Up to 1918, children could leave school at age twelve, then fourteen became the crucial age, to remain until 1973. This system meant that education usually finished early, unless a child showed enough ability to pass into a secondary school. Nationally in 1936 barely a quarter of secondary school pupils were rural, and many of those were farmers' offspring or of persons in rural trades, rather than labourers' children. For Wiltshire this statistic was probably too high, due to lack of transport to remote villages, and that held true until after WWII. I remember fellow students cycling into Chippenham Secondary School from outlying villages as far as six miles away, (and one cycled from North Wraxall, a distance of ten miles with a steep hill to negotiate at Ford coming and going) between 1938-1943, as transport to the school was limited to trains and a bus from the Melksham area.

Ralph Whitlock considered that lack of education did not prevent Pitton people in the early years of the 20th century from learning large chunks of the Bible. What the preacher had said at chapel or church the previous Sunday, he claimed, would be discussed in the fields or the house later on during the week. Sometimes a professional evangelist visited the village, able to transport people into a religious trance. For some it stuck, but there were always backsliders. With no other social distractions until the radio, a bike or the little local public transport that materialized in the 1920s, perhaps Bible studies and congregational activities gave some Wiltshire agricultural labourers a spiritual awareness of their rural life. Religion, with its offer of existence in the hereafter, no doubt helped some village people to accept the harsh way of life they had always known, and to be tolerant of its difficulties; but for others, particularly after WWI, when other interests came to village life, it seemed irrelevant.

Will Staples, carter at Urchfont in 1932.

I do not recall any persons of the countryside or working on a farm remotely interested in religion by the 1940s, except for christenings, marriages and funerals, and the few attending chapel. Because of lack of leisure time, rural life had less attraction for the agricultural labourer than it has for others living in the countryside today, especially if they possess a car. The endless work with little reward and the battle against poor living conditions did not mitigate, for the labourer and his family, what are considered today the advantages of country living, especially as he had no means of transport out of the village until after WWI, and then only a cycle if he was thrifty. The peace and quiet of rural living was not then always considered an asset; the town lights twinkled invitingly.

The falling populations of the Wiltshire villages and their isolation, combined with opposition to any form of education for adults from local farmers and others of the middle class, are likely to have continued to discourage establishment of Workers' Education Association facilities in the early decades of the 20th century, though they existed in the larger towns. Seend village opened a Workmen's reading room in the Cleeve in 1881. From its roots sprang the village Social Club, still in existence in 1980, providing skittles, billiards and quoits for the villagers. Evidence is sparse for the county on such provisions, yet another absorbing topic needing further research and exploration.

All Cannings and Poulshot are two of the few villages in Wiltshire which possessed a large enough local common to hold team sports, matches and other organized games. As football and cricket grew in popularity, by the 20th century or even before, a local landowner would be approached to furnish a field where either sport could be played. From this developed strong support for local teams and matches, giving much pleasure and local rivalry. However, the agricultural labourer, usually working on Saturday afternoons was hard put to participate in such matches. And until WWII the likely rule was 'no play on Sunday', the only day a labourer working on an arable farm had time off to play in practices or any matches, which left him only summer evenings when he could participate.

At the end of the 19th century, some large landowners had made arrangements for village halls to be constructed, while some were provided by parish church trustees. Halls grew in number after WWI, many being built as a memorial to those who died in that conflict. They varied in quality from surplus army huts to brick buildings equipped with canteens, perhaps a stage as well. Some villages shared a hall. Both the British Legion and the Women's Institutes played an active role in the establishment of halls in several Wiltshire villages.

Scout and Girl Guide troops, Brownies, Girls' Friendly Societies, even the Church of England Temperance Society organized in the villages before WWI, and along with other youth organizations, used the amenities offered by the new halls. They in turn created focal points to attract people. Jumble sales, whist drives, games and concerts also lured people to the hall. If the agricultural labourer had the time and energy, with his wife, he could enjoy such gatherings. Whether politically-based clubs or gatherings took place is another subject in need of investigation, as does the fabric of village politics and the agricultural labourer in general, as both he and his wife had the vote after WWI. But for what party? Supposedly the chalk people were conservative in their views and loyalties, dairy country dwellers liberal. But, as with politics, village life varied, some villages interwove different social levels to create a community spirit which in turn led into communal activities, others did little and lacked animation or a lively life style.

Few villages had easy railway or bus connections to towns or other villages, so the life of the labourer's wife was still limited. Often with little time to spare from family cares to participate in events except in her own village, she was sometimes an oddball in another village. The Church of England offered the Mothers' Union to women villagers, but she was yet to be welcomed at Women's Institute meetings until after WWII; as the WI slanted its activities towards farm wives, membership to a labourer's wife was rarely offered. Women seldom went into pubs and little social activity was devised specifically for them. Facilities for

Horse team carrying their own food and water on their way to field work. Despite metalled road, the horses are not shod. Their curved backs indicate a long working life. 15,000 horses worked on Wiltshire farms in 1930, today who knows, but they are being bred again, to give great pleasure to their owners. My experience with them was always good. They were docile, hard-working and companionable.

a restaurant, cafe or pub meal did not exist and if they had, a meal out was seldom affordable; the most a wife would be able to manage was a cup of tea and perhaps a bun in the nearest town when shopping.

When bus services after WWI came to some villages, the routes usually went to the nearest town through other villages, mainly during employment hours or shopping times only. Buses fares were expensive. Many walked or pushed a pram up to three miles or more to shop, some cycled even further. Alison Hartford tells of her mother in the 1920s and early 30s, before bus transport came to her village, cycling to Calne, 5 miles away, for weekly groceries, and one Christmas going ten miles into Swindon on her bicycle to buy and bring back *all* the family's presents, making for a tiring ride home. Grocers and butchers, sometimes a fishmonger, went round to the not-so-remote villages at the beginning of the century with horse and trap, later with a motor van selling their goods, but it was an expensive way of buying items and did not allow for the pleasure of a visit to the town. All in all, village women lived a somewhat restricted existence, with little chance to go farther than her legs or her bike could carry her.

Homemaking, housekeeping and cooking for any labourer's wife remained onerous. Meat and bacon was still short in a household because of its cost, meaty bones boiled up in a large pot with added vegetables and a slice of bread was often a substitute for a roast dinner. Many still depended on the poached rabbit, the odd pigeon, rook or other bird to provide alternatives to costly meat purchases. Faggots also served as a meat substitute.

With the meat items, the butcher also sold and delivered beef fat and lard, to be used in cooking or spread on bread and salted or sugared. In the corn-country poultry were frequently kept, some of the eggs produced being carefully divided as a treat amongst the children for tea once a week, and many used for cake-baking, a very important food item, as sugar and flour had dropped in price. Families made jam from wild berries, and a few kept bees, their honey selling for a 1s lb, contributing to the family's boot money. (Nearly everyone in the family wore still boots, and if a careful budget allowed it, felt slippers in the house.) Vegetables, mainly potatoes, onions, carrots and greens, came from the allotment; seldom is there mention of any fruit except in season, or legumes; a very monotonous diet and still in existence until 1950.

Housing

By the turn of the 20th century tied cottages formed a large portion of the available housing for agricultural labourers. Whether the houses were in or away from a village depended on several factors. On the chalk, it had always been more customary for labourers to live in villages, on the clays, cottages more often sprang up on the farm where a man was employed. When the larger Wiltshire estates built fairly extensively after 1860, they placed their cottages in both situations. Speculative cottages could be built anywhere that suited the land owner who was willing to sell a piece of land; or a farmer commissioned a cottage, usually a double, or even a row, on ground conveniently situated to the farm which, for the worker inhabiting the cottage, often made for a difficult situation, for the nearer the cottage to the farm, the less privacy he had, and the more likely he could be called to the farm at odd hours, particularly a dairy farm. Seldom did any cottage away from an urban area have running water, electricity or sanitation until after WWII.

The tied cottage system locked in both farmer and employee; it secured a roof over his head for the labourer, and provided an employer with definitive labour for a year. Drawbacks of the system for the farmer were the difficulties in finding labour if he was short of accommodation, and the problem of dismissing a bad worker before the end of his contract, usually at Michaelmas, when most job changing took place around the countryside. Workers could not be turned out of their cottages if they were paying the agreed rent, so a poor worker could take advantage of the farmer until the end of his contract. From the employee's point of view he was stuck with the house, whether poor or good, as any other accommodation could seldom be obtained within walking or cycling distance of a job.

The situation for both farmers and labourers was still difficult in 1939. A.G. Street complained of the subsidized rent of 3s a week, exclusive of rates (taxes), for workers' cottages on farms, whatever their condition. He illustrated the unfairness of it by the following example. Three labourers are paid the same wage of 43s per week:

A) gets a new 10s cottage for 3s = 40s wage plus a good cottage
B) gets an old 5s cottage for 3s = 40s wage plus a poor cottage
C) can't find a subsidized cottage, so he rents a non-farm cottage for 10s = 33s week plus a good cottage

At Pitton at the end of the 19th century, land could be leased from the Ilchester estate for three lives. The lessee built a cottage, which at the death of the third life-holder, reverted to the estate. If the family continued living in it, they had to pay rent to the estate. Cottages were usually constructed with cob walls, thatch roof and earthen floor. Certain cottages were allocated to farmers who rented them from the estate. Their employees then rented them as a term of employment or at a nominal rent. Some farmers liked to change employees; others did not. Incomers usually originated from nearby villages. Apparently a few squats continued into the 20th century, Ralph Whitlock describes at Pitton the building of a chalk cob cottage on a piece of land obtained by negotiation, purchase or squatting. It would be interesting to find out if other large Wiltshire estates had similar rental and building activities, or like Bowood and Wilton, financed cottage building on their lands with no ground rents or leases independent of employment with the estate.

Like most other villagers, Pitton residents obtained their water from wells, though a few used running streams close to their houses. Ralph Whitlock mentions the phenomenon of springs erupting every seven years from the village spring line. (Does this still happen today, or has the water table in the area dropped too much for this to occur?) Dairy farmers in the area had to allocate men to draw up water, particularly on Saturdays to make the Sunday work less. Farmyard ponds were filthy, and the ones in fields not much better, though those used only by sheep were cleaner.

Water supplies and sanitation were the perennial problems of Wiltshire villages until the late 1950s. Despite the understanding, since the mid 1800s, of the importance of clean water and disposal of household and human waste, not to mention animal waste, very little changed until the 1930s, when Wiltshire villages slowly began to receive piped water. Before piped water there was no possibility of having flush toilets and in most Wiltshire villages existing sanitation arrangements were ignored as far as possible and never discussed. Farmers were sometimes a little better off than their laborers; the more enterprising pumped water from a well, and with the advent of small motor pumps, the water closet was not unknown on a few farms as early as post-WWI.

A case at Potterne reflected current housing problems at the beginning of the century. Two working men, members of the Parish council in 1912, complained of bad housing in the village. Local government paid no attention to the complaint and finally Whitehall insisted on an official enquiry. Before it took place, some magistrates, the owners of property, went round and warned their tenants of rent rises and evictions if they spoke at the enquiry. So villagers did not come forward, but a solicitor from the National Land and Home League read details of the crowded and unsanitary living conditions of nineteen households in Potterne. The local Sanitary Inspector demonstrated that half the houses in the village had less than 300 cubic feet of space per person, as is required in lodging houses. The average occupation level for the village was 3.6 inhabitants per house. There were ten empty cottages in the village, of which seven were uninhabitable. Other cottages had been allowed to go to ruin in the past few years, for the simple reason that it did not pay private enterprise to build or repair housing that did not yield an economic rent. The cottages, almost without exception, were on the outdoor 'bucket system', one closet being shared by four families, and water was obtained from wells. As a result of the enquiry, the Rural District Council was ordered to build twelve new cottages and make 70 (sic – probably seven) old ones habitable. The new cottages would have commanded rents of 4s 6d or 5s a week, unaffordable to the agricultural bourer, but if necessary, the rents were to be subsidized. Potterne did not receive much new housing, even after WWI, and it had to wait for piped water until 1938.

In the years preceding WWI the WCC had another difficulty regarding rural housing. The 1907 Small Holdings Act had instructed county councils to make efforts to purchase land suitable for use in such projects. Four smallholdings, varying from 21 to 52 acres, were created on the Council's farm in Melksham forest; yearly rents varied, depending on acreage and quality of land held, but in 1913 they averaged £2 an acre. The holders lived in nearby cottages and paid the Council £10 rent a year. But sometimes housing for new smallholders created a problem if the council could not find cottages for them, or it had to use eviction powers to vacate a cottage already purchased. Instances of eviction occurred at Foxham and at Chitterne, due to the Council's efforts to fulfill the demands of the Act.

Laden dung cart , the horse being watered, while the carter takes his refreshment elsewhere. Photo taken outside Keevil village shop in 1934.

In 1912 Lord Lansdowne put 1000 acres of farmland on the market, in and around Foxham. The WCC bought a farm of 193 acres, with eight inhabited cottages. The eight families concerned were given notice to quit. Similar situations occurred on other farms which had changed hands. Out of 47 cottages, 35 changed hands, so many families were looking for cottages. Two members of the Bremhill Parish Council, both farm labourers (the other seven members were farmers), brought an action through the Rural District Council to the government asking for more cottages to be built under the auspices of the recent Housing Act. No action was taken, so the two PC members appealed and the government called for an enquiry. Twenty men testified in Bremhill schoolroom that it was impossible to find a place to live in or around Foxham.

Nothing more happened; meanwhile the WCC had exhausted its patience and on Friday 21 January 1913, with the help of policemen under official supervision, it evicted two of the families. It was a snowy day and the parents and children, along with their furniture and possessions, were soon very wet after a couple of hours in the street. All relevant members of the WCC denied, at a later hearing, that they knew of any need for housing accommodation at Foxham. The families involved in the eviction left the neighbourhood, some supposedly evicted by their farmer landlords.

The 1909 Housing and Town Planning Act made it obligatory for county councils to set up a Public Health and Housing committee, to be run by borough and district councils. By the time they had been organized, WWI had begun, postponing action until 1919. By then the demand for housing had grown and the problems of creating the accompanying necessary infrastructure had multiplied. In addition, the war itself had directed the nation's resources away from social needs, which created difficulties in finding the required financing and slowed the WCC's efforts in putting in place the bureaucracy to provide housing and infrastructure. So the number of houses in the Wiltshire countryside grew slowly between 1919 and the beginning of WWII, when all house-building ceased.

After the 1909 Act, one of the problems that the WCC had to face was finding building land for rural housing, most farmers being reluctant to sell. Rents had to be low for a rural population earning a basic wage of 10 to 16 shillings a week between 1900 and 1912. So speculative builders could not possibly make a decent return on their investment, and the council had no way to raise loans, even if they were enthusiastic in their hunt for building land. When the council finally began to implement the Act because of demand, much of their house-building took place in urban rather than rural areas. But Wiltshire, and indeed, any other county, was never able at any time to satisfy the need for low-cost housing.

In general, the history of housing for agricultural labourers can be read today in any Wiltshire village. Labourers' dwellings built before 1860 have not survived. Houses and cottages erected before that date and still in existence were more substantially-built, generally by farmers, well-to-do craftsmen or middle-class persons. After the 1860s nearby estates and other large landowners continued to add cottages to the villages until 1914. Between 1919 and 1939 council houses supplemented existing dwellings, plus a few labourers' cottages built by nearby farmers, especially on the chalk. A few more council houses appeared after WWII, then village populations began to drop, not to be revived until the 1960s, when the ease of car ownership made living in the countryside an attractive option, and so precipitated the renovation movement, which today has involved most village housing. But a puzzle remains. What is the origin of some small village or rural houses, built between, say, 1790 to 1820? They survive due to reasonably good construction of stone and stone rubble, or timbered with daub or brick panels, or flint walls, depending on their location. Did well-to-do village craftsmen or tradesmen construct them? In all likelihood however, nearby farmers built them to house their laborers and families, or single labourers. Certainly no labourer himself had the means to construct such dwellings in that particular period.

Smallholdings

Agitation in Parliament for smallholdings had begun as far back as 1862 and union activity ten years later contributed to it, but despite the Small Holdings Act of 1892, no provision bill was passed until 1907, when county councils acquired enough authority to proceed with actual land purchases, not only for smallholdings, but for further 'garden' allotments in both towns and villages. Despite the Foxham and Chitterne evictions giving the council a bad name at the time, most of the WCC acquisitions proceeded smoothly,

Bratton shepherd 1912.

though suitable agricultural land at a reasonable price was hard to find. At Pitton, with the purchase of land from a local estate, the council arranged for six smallholdings and allotments; they continued until WWII. The possibilities of the 1907 Act seemed boundless. The WCC accepted applications for smallholdings as required, but in the end, only a few were successful. Aspiring candidates first had to be interviewed and vetted for their abilities to manage a smallholding. In 1908, a total of 807 applicants applied. 161 withdrew, 196 were considered unsuitable and nearly 200 obtained holdings. 44 were to be allocated holdings in the future, 57 received one-acre holdings and 116 holdings of less than 1 acre. Applications dropped the following year to 162, and again in 1910, when, of the 80 applicants who applied, after 8 being found unsuitable and 7 withdrew, the remaining 65 all received varying amounts of land.

The explanations for declining numbers of smallholding applications involved several factors. The strong demand for agricultural land meant enough employment existed for those who still were willing to endure the hard life of working on the land. The straits of the agricultural labourer himself decreased slightly between 1907 and 1912 due to a greater purchasing power, giving him the equivalent of a few shillings wage rise. And the agricultural labourer and his family were fully aware of how difficult it was to make a go of a smallholding. The council's selection process, through which applicants were put, was rigorous. But smaller allotments of land were very much less of an issue, always being taken up with no hesitation, the applicant doubtless a part-time worker.

Despite union expectations, an individual smallholding often did not turn out to be the solution for the agricultural labourer at the time, unless he truly wanted to work for himself and had the backing of his wife and some financial buffer to get started, the latter always the really critical factor. Other factors often proved discouraging, among them the thought of a change and a sudden move away from the familiar. Difficulties of finding suitable housing, sometimes education for children, the impossibility of any future advancement from being a smallholder could also prove problematical; no wonder the percentage of labourers who applied or held holdings in Wiltshire was low. In 1911, 115 smallholding tenants held a total of 2,759 acres, an average of 24 acres each. In Wiltshire, the number of tenants peaked in 1924 at 682, holding 16,616 acres. The average holding size remained at almost the same between 1911 and the 1930s, but by 1952, it had increased to 28.5 acres, and the number of tenants had dropped to 520.

A break during hay-making near All Cannings circa 1930. This scene was repeated in early summer time all over Wiltshire for a thousand years, until mechanisation came to the farms after WWII.

Outlay on smallholdings increased steadily. Exact figures are buried in the council's accounting expense category of 'Small Holdings and other Agricultural Services,' but undoubtedly the purchase of smallholdings and their administration accounted for the bulk of the expenditure in this category. Nearly £400 in 1890, spending increased tenfold by 1914. In 1924, a peak year for smallholdings acreage held by the council, agricultural services totalled near £53,000; ten years later, the outlay figure was £83,000. But these costs were not all borne by the ratepayers, only about 7% of the total. More than 34% was funded by central government, and the remainder provided by rents from the smallholders. Possibly the number of council smallholders through the first half of the 20th century represented between 2-4% of the total males in agricultural occupations.

Medical Services

By the end of the 19th century, as has been shown, medical attention for the labourer and his family depended mainly on doctors representing friendly societies, the Poor Law relief if eligible, or local skilled or unskilled help. Though the government and public authorities had begun to recognize, as early as the 1830s, the need for more doctoring, nursing and hospitals, comprehensive medical services did not begin to reach the Wiltshire agricultural labourer and his family until 1911.

One of the problems was the lack of provision for family members other than the male head of household. The first full-time medical officer, appointed in 1899 by the WCC, faced enormous problems with very few resources. He undoubtedly understood the concepts and advantages of preventative medicine, but the working classes had little access to the basics of good diet, housing and working conditions. Time would prove that due to difficulty and expense all three were not going to be remedied, except by the development of a national social policy. Within his powers under local government acts and with great opposition, the MO for Wiltshire began by appointing visiting health officers.

Childcare was made one of the first priorities. Both illiterate and literate midwives held the responsibility for rural child birth until the 1900s. By 1904 a Miss Stephenson, Chairman of the WCC Health Commission, who strongly supported a rural nursing service, had made improved visiting midwifery services her priority, but the services were hampered by lack of provision to give help to an infant over a year old. Adequate care for children of one to five had to wait until 1929, hence little change was seen in infant mortality rates. Despite an official proviso for maternity beds in 1929, few appeared and delivery at home remained in the Wiltshire countryside until well after WWII.

School medical services began in Wiltshire in 1907. The scheme received little promotion and was often received with much suspicion, especially by parents. In the early days of the services, children had to be checked for vermin, plus any need for spectacles and dental care, but the services were minimal, again due to lack of resources. A visiting nurse examined pupils and gradually access to clinics began. Orthopaedic clinics had arrived by 1924, ear, nose and throat clinics by 1930, heart clinics a year later. I recall the dental care in the 1940s at Chippenham Secondary School. A dentist arrived once a year and set up his chair and a foot-operated drill and went to work on those needing fillings and extractions, no orthodontics in those days! Students avoided a visit to the dentist by any possible means and for some reason, the distrust of parents (particularly of rural pupils) for any kind of dental work was intense.

On the prevention front, 1921 saw the advent of the school meals scheme and the daily 1/3 pint of milk supplied free to those needing it. But it took 25 years for the service to reach all over the county, so many village schools having just a few pupils and hence the cost was too great to include then in the scheme. Diphtheria immunization began in 1940, in 1946 speech therapy was initiated, and soon after chiropody and psychiatric treatments.

But social status played a role in school health services. A note from a middle-class parent relieved a child of examination by the health nurse and the dentist, though not the diphtheria immunization shot; in 1941 all had to receive it, and I remember we girls looked on with great glee and feelings of superiority as several boys fainted at the sight of the jabbing needle! Clinic visits often favoured the urban child; it was hard to get the rural child to necessary treatment. If the parents did not insist on treatment and it was inconvenient, the child could be deprived of it. Services were uneven, for instance, the yearly visitations might be missed by the service's nurses, or absentee children not followed up.

Wiltshire always had had the problem of transporting people to hospitals from rural areas, as except for some workhouse infirmaries, all hospitals were in towns. An exception was Salisbury Infirmary; it opened in 1771 and immediately served a wide network of surrounding villages, and some parish vestries paid an annual subscription which entitled parishioners to receive treatment. (It will be recalled that the badly wounded labourers from the Captain Swing fracas at Pythouse in 1830 were taken to the 'fimary.') By 1862 the greatest number of patients came from the country, mainly labourers and servants, and records show that chronic illnesses brought in more patients than acute injuries and other medical problems. When cottage hospitals came into being, they were largely inaccessible to the rural population until the motorized vehicle became common. Even then, emergencies happened when no ambulance could be commissioned, particularly in wartime. During WWII, a farm worker, while building a rick under an electrical line at Cocklebury, brushed a piece of damp straw with a pitch fork off the overhead wire. An electrical charge went through the metal peak fastener of his cap, burning a hole in his forehead, and immediately rendering him unconscious. Chippenham Cottage Hospital, a mile or so away, had no ambulance available. Neither the doctor brought to the farm, nor Mr Self, wanted to transport the unconscious man by car, for fear of him vomiting, so he was laid on thick straw in the bottom of a farm wagon. I can attest to this, as I harnessed the horse to the wagon for another employee to drive him through the town. The man lived and returned to work two weeks later.

The 1911 National Insurance Act was the first step to universal medicine in Britain. In the beginning it was oriented to adult males with an annual income of less than £160. A fixed weekly contribution, paid for by special stamps purchased at a post office and affixed to a card, had to be kept up to date. The men signed up with a local doctor and became known as 'panel' patients. They also received sickness benefits, but their dependents were still not covered, except by separate local services. A farm worker often had a tedious and tiring journey to reach his doctor's surgery and country practices were rare. The contribution did not cover dental care, unless a tooth problem meant major surgery in a hospital; neither did it cover ophthalmic services. A doctor had the power to refer a patient to a local hospital for care, but charity hospitals still caused controversy when dealing with the NI Act, and adequate hospital care remained scarce in Wiltshire until after WWII. Poor families who could not afford home care for seriously ill and chronic long-term illnesses had to resort to the workhouse infirmaries. The situation eased a little when the county medical services began health visits to house-bound adults.

The government gradually added more services to the 1911 Act. Confidential clinical treatment of VD began in 1916. The Maternity and Child Welfare Act of 1918 admitted women and children to the NI health scheme according to their household income, with free allowances of milk and special foods for expectant and nursing mothers and milk for children under five. Institutional care for TB had commenced by 1921 and the Winsley Sanitarium established for Wiltshire. Not a very practical site, for, despite its exposure to clean air and rigorous weather conditions, for visitors to reach it by public transport from most parts of Wiltshire was a long and tedious journey.

Any form of treatment for the mentally ill always has presented an insolvable problem in any society until the latter half of the 20th century. Two of the largest asylums in England had existed in Salisbury from an early date, at Fisherton and Laverstock. But if the patient was not violent, much of Wiltshire probably depended on family care and Poor Law relief. Devizes asylum opened in 1852, which undoubtedly alleviated some suffering, perhaps more for the carers than for the patients, especially those who were violent. Feeble-mindedness in most villages was usually treated at home, paupers, if manageable went to the workhouses. Gradually, as the 20th century progressed, a place could be found for a mentally deficient person with the help of voluntary associations and mental officers. However, benefits were very uneven and not until the start of the National Health Service in 1948 were solutions found to cope adequately with all those needing mental care.

In general, medical care for the Wiltshire agricultural labourer and his family in the first half of the 20th century was a miscellany of public health and charity. A jaundiced writer of the time considered it 'not the right of the poor, rather the gift of the rich.' Though extreme, it had to be admitted that social status played an important role in who received enough attention and time from a doctor, nurse or other health officers. (I am quite sure that had I been the person to be electrocuted at Cocklebury, I would have gone to hospital in the doctor's car, as he knew me personally.) But for the labourer, it was hard to get to a doctor or dentist. In the 1930s and 40s, a farmer would seldom give time off; if his employee had to go during his working hours, he did not get paid for the time taken. Sickness benefits were patchy and not all labourers belonged to friendly societies. His dependents could be deprived too; the services of the visiting rural nurses in Wiltshire were really stretched, especially during the depression, and then in wartime due to lack of personnel. Other factors entered the equation. The wife, her presence in the home always needed full-time, often avoided seeking treatment until an illness was acute, and in pre-antibiotic days. a mild case of 'flu or a chill, if ignored, could create a serious situation. And most people were still frightened of hospitals, a hangover from the workhouse system. Care for children was not as careful as it is today, often symptoms were ignored, or a child treated at home, when hospital treatment was necessary. So child mortality rates remained high in Wiltshire.

Other forms of deprivation affected the medical services the agricultural labourer received. No teaching hospital existed in Wiltshire, neither did any modern hospital system, so it is likely that his chances of receiving advanced diagnosis, if needed, were very slender. For example, working class people were seldom sent to one of the Bath hospitals for exploratory examination. The expansion of the cottage hospitals, the most common in Wiltshire, during the first half of the century did not help the labourer. Most hospitals were small and inward-looking and still linked to the workhouse system for the poor, who, if a problem, could be easily shunted off to the workhouse infirmary to make room for other cases when needed. The problem intensified after 1929, when Poor Law administration and its hospitals were transferred to local authorities and the cottage hospitals looked further inwards and depended more on voluntary and charitable help for extra services, a thought-mode which would continue until all medical services, whether voluntary, local or centrally governed, were combined into the NHS.

No family planning or contraception services reached the villages, except perhaps a few words from the visiting nurse or midwife if asked, but she had received little if any instruction on the subject. Doctors also avoided discussing contraception, unless specifically requested and only gave information to married patients. By the 1940s, most labourers understood the use of condoms, but probably no rural women had access or the money to any female-form of contraception. Using a large family as a criterion, one in three labourers probably did not use condoms. On record is an oral history of a labourer's wife in the thirties, who, if her husband began to show signs of *amor* during the evening, set up the kitchen table to iron and continued until he had gone to bed and to sleep!

But visiting nurses or midwives were not only deficient in contraception knowledge. They had mainly received their instruction at second class professional levels, usually ending up with very basic and very narrow training. On occasions, this factor must sometimes have affected the health of the households they attended, as they had not been taught to recognize many medical symptoms or understand what to look for.

The Agricultural Scene – 1900-18

By 1900 the agricultural depression had reduced tenant rents on Wiltshire farms, until they could go no lower without economic disaster for landlords. Farmers began to realize that to make a living they had to increase production and at the same time reduce labour and work with less capital. The sheep and corn partnership continued on the chalk and, where possible, the production of milk began, or was increased, in the valleys and on the clays. If the same amount of labour stayed on the farm, this meant that a higher output per man had to be accomplished and maintained. But if less man-hours to run a farm resulted, with consequent loss of jobs, the labour statistics for rural Wiltshire seem to show that if jobs were fewer, less men were seeking them, so the equation of work available versus full employment seemed to balance up to 1914 when WWI broke out.

Despite the awareness of the need to grow more food to replace imported, the government took a long time to set up rules for farmers and to enforce them, and the Wiltshire Agricultural Committee (WAC) was never really successful to a great extent in increasing output. It was able to persuade, occasionally by threatening legal action, the generally conservative Wiltshire farmer to plough up pasture to increase corn output, especially in the last two years of the War. Farmers maintained milk production at pre-war levels, despite difficulties in obtaining milkers. Livestock numbers dropped slightly, root and other animal feed crops varied from year to year. The potato, invariably a good yielder and easily harvested if plenty of casual labour was available, gave farmers bumper harvests, the yearly crops more than doubling by 1918 to some 32,000 tons. Except for 1918, when the corn crops were more bountiful due to good weather, harvests were minimally larger, but wheat prices paid to farmers gradually doubled through the War. About 10% of permanent grassland was ploughed up to grow corn or potatoes. Towards the end of the War, a few of the larger dairy farmers had invested in milking machines, several hundred tractors aided in the yearly ploughing, but aside from the threshing machine, much of the harvesting and almost all other farm work was still done by hand and horsepower in Wiltshire.

Milking team at Bassett Down Farm circa 1926. Jack Cypher, ? Edward Kinch ? Val Kinch ? Tom Cypher, (the young lady is Sabina Loosemore, daughter of the farm baliff)

Agricultural Labour in WWI

Labour proved a problem all through the War. Farm work not being a reserved occupation, as in WWII, meant that until conscription came into force in January 1916, men could quit their job and join the services. In addition, the army steadily requisitioned horses from farms, drastically affecting movement of hay and corn harvests from field to market, and even by 1918 very few small farms in Wiltshire, especially the dairy farms, ever ran a tractor. By 1916, 10% of labourers nationally had left the farms, perhaps a greater percentage in Wiltshire as the army training on the nearby chalklands made it close and familiar, hence easy to join. Young, unmarried men in particular responded to the call of patriotism and a change in life-style. After 1916, although there were no exceptions made for male agricultural workers under age 25, men called up, or their employers, had the right of appeal and did so. On the whole, Wiltshire tribunals supported the appeals, and if not giving a permanent exemption, granted a temporary exemption, which could then be appealed *et al*. Other means of supplementing labour requirements appeared, though not always satisfactory, as most agricultural work needs understanding incorporated with particular skills. First, soldiers were released to Wiltshire farms at ploughing and harvest time. Later, 200 lived in barracks at Devizes and were 'rented' out to farmers at 4s a day, or 2s if lodging was provided. If the farmer had to transport the soldiers, it was quite a costly exercise for them, or so they said. The quality of the labour was another matter, for only a small percentage of the soldiers understood farm work and could be more expensive than

Threshing gang, circa 1919.

they were worth. (I can vouch for this from my observations of some of the voluntary labour at Cocklebury during WWII.) By 1917, agricultural workers who had joined up could apply for release, perhaps a welcome move by some men who were willing to leave their army comrades, especially if serving on the front lines. The number of soldiers helping on the land in Wiltshire at the end of the War is likely to have reached 1,300.

Farmers would not accept conscientious objectors during WWI, and they resisted German prisoner-of-war labour, until the men were split up to work in small groups such as threshing or or ploughing teams.

Despite the protests of educational officers (and even the Bishop of Salisbury) boys age 12 or 13 could apply for farm work and if accepted, terminate their education. Over 1,000 boys did so in Wiltshire. However, perhaps half found jobs in more urban areas, particularly as accommodation for them in the countryside was hard to find. Girls were given permission to absent themselves from school if they were needed at home to mind children, while their mother worked on the land. Only 76 girls applied to do this. Children also helped with haymaking and harvesting in the summer and autumn, especially in the latter years of the war; harvest camps also became popular, to include public school boys.

1027 women in 1914 worked mainly part-time on 590 Wiltshire farms, those being mainly pastoral. During the first year of the War, field workers' pay was so low that in Wiltshire, widows filed through the Poor Law for supplementary relief to their earnings of one shilling a day. By 1916, the WAC instigated a register of village women willing to work on farms. Eighteen months later, 2,590 women, one third full time, the rest part-time, worked on Wiltshire farms. The county also instituted a scheme to train young urban female volunteers, mainly from outside the county, to take three to four week training periods to become milkers and then be billeted on farms. Perhaps the scheme attracted a few hundred girls at the most, and had varying degrees of success, as there was no central authority or *esprit de corps* to help or hold the girls together, as the Womens Land Army did in WWII. However, though some farmers did not seek out village women, considering them unskilled and untrained (a far call from a few generations back), many began to tolerate and later accept trained female labour on their farms, probably making it much easier for females in WWII to ease into jobs at Wiltshire farms, whether on the chalk or the cheese.

The unions offered no effective resistance to these dilutions of conventional labour forces. It was probably considered unpatriotic to protest, wages were reasonable, so an organized objection would likely have gained little support at a time when everyone was pulling together to win the War.

Wages in WWI and After

Up to 1914, an agricultural labourer's wage had fluctuated very little. In 1898 normal wages in Wiltshire, with no reckoning for perks, reached approximately 12s in summer and 11s weekly in winter. A shilling increase was given in 1902, then wages remained static until WWI, with purchasing power going up. However, 1914 saw strikes in many counties. At Chitterne, men protested their wages, demanding 13s instead of 12s a week. By 1917, wages in Wiltshire had improved to £1 a week, by 1918 £1 10s, supposedly to reach £2 6s by 1920; an amazing increase, due mainly to war prices euphoria and labour shortages. (But the new union newspaper, *The Landworker*, disputed these wage level figures.) After agricultural wage controls began in 1916, the NUAW national membership had grown from just over 7,000 to nearly 127,000 in 1919, due in part to the greater wages paid during this period. Farm workers definitely had benefitted from the continuation of controls through the actions of the Wages Board.

The Agricultural Act, passed in 1920, continued control of guaranteed prices on agricultural commodities and workers' wages, which meant protection for farmers from world prices. The Act also carried cultivation controls. By May 1921, the subsidies payments had created problems of budget balancing, as agricultural prices, falling at the time of the Act, continued to drop. The thirteen year old National Farmers Union kept excellent records on this payment of subsidies crisis. While supporting the price controls, it vigorously lobbied behind the scenes for the reduction of controls on actual farming methods. The NFU and the government had struck a secret deal by the end of the month. In acceptance of *laissez faire* prices, the government was to pay the farmers a crop bounty for wheat and oats in 1921. At the same time, the wartime Wages Board would be disbanded, which meant controls would be lifted from the wages of the agricultural worker. And, as part of the deal, the NFU also wanted a reduction in wages to 42s a week for men, and women to be paid 8d an hour, or 32s for a 48 hour work week. A month later, the Lloyd George government repealed the 1920 Act.

Meanwhile, the NUAW felt government attitudes backing them into a corner, as they were doing to coal miners, also in a similar situation. The June 1921 agreement between the Government and the NFU took the officials of the NUAW completely by surprise. They notified their members of the proposed wage reductions and organized protests, meanwhile emphasizing to their MPs the importance of the Wages Board continuing to function as it had in the past. They also insisted on statutory enforcement of minimum wages, rather than voluntary conciliation. One of the problems the NUAW faced at the time was a period of deflation and growing unemployment, when they were asking for wages to remain stable. Not helping their opposition abilities was the loss of union membership from 121,045 in 1920 to 46,695 in 1922, which though unemployment caused some loss, was mostly due to disillusionment by the threats of lower wages. At the same time the NUAW was perfectly aware of the unwritten understanding between the NUF and the Government, that to compensate lowered guaranteed prices, wages could be reduced.

Cartoon: Harvest Home, from The Landworker *(March 1925)*

The NUAW lost its political battle; the forces against it were too great, despite their insistence that they fight openly instead of clandestinely with the Government as the NUF did. Support for the NUAW, though strong in Parliament, could not save the vote from going against them. But they had kept the clause that registration of agreements must continue, which was vital for acknowledgment that the Government stayed involved in wage negotiations between the farmers' and farm workers' representatives.

The farm workers were betrayed. The farmers received £19 million in subsidies in 1921, but the workers lost their Wage Control Board, faced more unemployment and further poor relationships with their employers. And the individual worker himself had to deal with the eternal poor housing, medical services and fewer jobs. Farmers' incomes were to drop and particularly on the chalk they attempted to cut labour needs. The recent large estate sales in Wiltshire also had an effect on the Wiltshire labour market. Amesbury had had to sell its whole estate of 10,000 acres in 1915, Wilton sold some outlying estates two years later, Longleat sold 9,000 acres after 1918, and, in 1929, Savernake sold 25,000 acres. Tenant farmers usually bought up the farms, which sometimes meant consolidation of labour, sometimes of land, often stringent changes in farming the land itself and, of course, added to the statistics of individual farm ownership in Wiltshire.

Eventually, greater economic depression caused the Government in 1930 to reverse its policies again, to implement price and wage supports, but for the worker, what happened besides having to endure the sting of the government's letdown? The Wiltshire branch of the NUAW union worked hard to keep membership up and fought in cases of individual dissent between labourers and their employers. But for the most part, depression times created a balance between the two. Men stayed on the farm, farmers tried to keep their men as the numbers of skilled farm workers had dropped due to alternative employment offered elsewhere, or single men abandoned farm work altogether. In general, the actions of both the farmers' and the employees' unions in the period from 1930-1937 showed changes of attitudes on both sides, alliances made and lessons learnt, which smoothed the way for co-operation after the Depression and into the WWII years.

The actions of the Trade Union movement in Wiltshire between the Wars can be used as a basis to describe the painfully slow movement of the life of the agricultural labourer and his family at this time. Economically it was not a happy period for anyone in the countryside, with the exception of the children, who had a more carefree existence until they left school at fourteen. And even this did not apply to every child, as Benjamin Spreadbury explained in his book *Farmer's Boy*.

During the 1920s and much of the 1930s in the Wiltshire countryside, wages fluctuated very little as the years assumed yet another era of agricultural depression and the countryside became totally dependent on the prices the farmer obtained for his crops. The Government waived any controls in world food markets that might aid British farmers, making England a market place for cheap food. The farmer had lost almost all his political power, as both farmer and labourer now created only a small portion of the Gross National Product. Wiltshire NUAW membership roll was slender, the union's branch activities confined to small meetings, with endless effort expended to find new members and hold onto the old.

Contact between employer and employee was close and not acrimonious; they were both in the same boat in their struggle to make ends meet. The farmer had no need to threaten the worker if he joined a union local chapter, he knew he had control over the worker through his tied cottage, the lack of alternative employment, and he still knew exactly what the labourer did with his time, whether working or not, and with whom he associated. Organisation in the Wiltshire countryside, on the slender funds the union brought in from dues, was hard work, the men were scattered all over the fields during the days and in the farm cottages after work. Few men frequented the pubs, church or other social clubs. They were too poor; the garden or allotment, his family, tobacco, and the infrequent visit to the pub were the only pastimes for the majority of labourers.

This is not to say that the men were unaware of national union activities, they were; but from their vantage point deep in the countryside, with their employers suffering a severe depression in prices (they always knew how much the farmer got for his crops, those prices were never a secret), they also realized little could be done for them, especially nationally. So they 'bided' their time and hoped. By 1943, when I worked with them, the possibility of a better future seemed on the horizon, thanks to socialism and the Beveridge report. They could not move from their jobs while the War was on, but they were actively seeing that their children did not go into farm work. Their awareness of the nation's continual short-changing of them remained; as did the long tradition of differences in rural and urban wages and living conditions propagated by their pre-war wage, unemployment and benefit rates, the latter always so much lower for them. union publications ceaselessly emphasised this realization and the lesson was taken in by the men and frequently their wives too.

Reading through *The Landworker,* a new publication in 1919, created to express the voice of the NUAW, one sees the tremendous dedication just a few men had to the union movement. From the start *The Landworker* made union demands clear, they looked for Benefits Protection under the Workman's Compensation Act of 1897 (WCA) and Legal Aid and sought a 50s weekly salary and better housing . They wanted to set up strike pay of 12s a week, also victimization and lock-out pay at the same rate. Accident disablement was to begin at 7s 6d, a permanent disablement grant of £10, shorter working hours and better compensation from the WCA. The NUAW set the entrance fee for men at 6d, weekly dues at 3d; women and youths were charged 4d and 1½d respectively. Throughout this period, though most of the Wiltshire labourers had secure employment, if he was temporarily laid-off, the laborer's miniscule benefits took often more than a week to come through.

Efforts to establish branches throughout the county started after WWI, showed enthusiasm for the union at first. By January 1921 Wiltshire had 3,044 members of good standing. The main points of the union's platform on the county included the abolition of tied cottages, standard wages, a 48 hour week with a half-day on Saturday. Sunday was now a day off on arable farms, not so on dairy farms, there it was still milking twice daily. Members were asked to pursue seats on local parish and county councils to gain political power.

By July 1921, the purchase of a motor bike for the county representative was suggested, but the 'great betrayal' had just occurred, so this item did not appear again for some time, and bicycles or public transport was to be the order of the day and evening. Six months later a weekly budget appeared for a Somerset agricultural labourer and his family, 6 persons in all; it amounted to almost £2, which on similar Wiltshire wages would leave nothing for emergencies: 10 loaves @ 9d, 7s 6d, 1 lb tea 2s, 4lb sugar 1s 10d, 1 lb butter 2s 3d, 2lb margarine, 1s 1d, 2 lbs cheese, 2s 8d, 4 lbs bacon 5s 4d, 4 lbs meat 5s 4d, 7 qts milk 3s 6d, 2 cwt coal, 4s, rent 4s total £1 19s 6d. (126 meals for 474d or 3.76d per meal). This can be compared with Greene's 1912 Wiltshire budget for a family of 8: bread 6 gallons @ 11d, 5s 6d, butter 2lbs @ 11d, 1s 10d, lard 1lb, 6d, bacon, 1s, tea ½ lb 6d, sugar 4lb, 1s, rice 2lb, 4d, milk 6d, soap 3d, starch 1d, oil 2 qts 6d; 168 meals for 144d, or 1.17d per meal. Both sets of figures show the heavy consumption of bread, the basics much the same with the exception of higher consumption of cheese, meat and tea, and no rice being consumed after WWI.

1922 saw a lack of any national action, as the union tried to plan which way to go. Conciliation wage boards had failed to function. Locally, members continued to be enlisted; a new branch with 30 members opened at Avebury, always a stronghold of protest. By April weekly dues were reduced to 4d and efforts made to recruit new members by leaflets and evening house visits. *The Landworker* created a woman's page, seeking additional support from the men's wives. Towards the end of the year the Trowbridge branch representative at a county committee meeting proposed no alteration to the existing weekly wage rates. At Warminster the Wilts branch of the NFU stated farmers as paying a 30s minimum weekly wage, but the unions claimed 27s for a 50 hour week. The conservatives won the November election and by April 1923 a 25s weekly wage was settled on, the union adding the hope that the weight of sacks would not exceed 112 lbs. (In 1944 at Cocklebury, except for grain sacks, always holding varying weights depending on the grain itself, sacks still held a cwt or 112 lbs.)

In February 1925, the union requested specific wages nationally. Depending on their age, at 21 or older, a man should earn 30s weekly with 8d hour overtime, going down to 10s with 3d an hour for a fourteen year old. One 'short' day of 6 hours was included in this calculation with Sundays off. Milk was to be purchased from the farm at wholesale prices, and cottage rents were not to be over 3s.

Three months later the union requested unemployment insurance for a man thrown out of work because of foot and mouth disease, very pertinent to the Wiltshire farm labourer. A hopeful headline followed in June, 'A living wage must come!' but it did not. Unless a man had overtime (and most of them did) he could not now afford tobacco or beer and a holiday was out of the question. Days off with pay did not exist.

Conditions on the farms and the agricultural economy paralleled the financial state of the national economy. *The Landworker* recommended that men seek employment with the police in 1926, a sad indictment on the lives of the farm workers and farmers. Wages remained at 30s, with overtime on weekdays and Sundays still at 8d an hour.

Three years later, in the November 1929 issue, the Wiltshire union county commissioners reported on 19 branches in Wiltshire, mainly on the chalk. They felt that union power had increased, as when farmers tried to reduce wages and raise cottage rents they were successfully resisted. A few more houses in the villages were also reported, doubtless due to the WCC housing schemes. But the depression continued for both the farmer and worker, very little money about and not much hope for the future either.

The union continued to request a contributory unemployment insurance, 1½d to be paid by the worker, 3d by the Government. Other (somewhat extensive) requests made included the mechanical conveyance of bulls to market, (for safety reasons), more Labour magistrates and that the National Wheat Board and grain markets be re-organized.

The following year the county commission asked for pay days on Fridays within working hours. This was something the men had craved for years, so that the wife could go into the nearest town on a Saturday morning for food shopping; when paid on Saturday, on a dairy farm in particular where work did not finish until after the late afternoon milking, she had to wait for Monday to shop, or depended on credit, if she had the luck to be given it. And for a few wives the Saturday pay night meant a drunken husband and not much to eat for the rest of the week. Nothing came of this request on the dairy farms, though Benjamin Spreadbury records that at Everleigh in the 1920s and 1930s men were paid fortnightly on Fridays. In the dairy country, at Cocklebury in the 1940s, we were paid on Saturdays after finishing our work about 5 pm, this was still the universal custom of the area.

After 1933 in Wiltshire, particularly in the dairying areas where the foundation of the Milk Marketing Board had conferred a steadier market for milk, the financial situation on the farms slowly began to improve. *The Landworker* in the 1930s conveys an assurance that the NUAW was making a difference. In Wiltshire, even if its members were not numerous, it stood up for men's rights, and fought when any wage reductions were proposed. It went to bat for the individual worker if needs be. At the end of 1934 a wage increase was announced, a shilling extra to the prevailing wage of 30s for 50 hours, with 8d for overtime, 9d at harvest overtime. Women's earnings remained at 18s week, with 5d overtime. Not much, but it was a start. During the year, the union had proposed that milkers should have one Sunday off per month, and a clear ½ day a week. By this time, some farmers on the chalk gave their men Saturday afternoons, but shepherds had to work on Sundays to feed their flocks. The Government continued to waffle over a contributory insurance scheme and in October the NFU came out against it.

Unemployment insurance for the agricultural labourer was confirmed by the Government in 1938. The same year the union expressed concern at the number of men leaving the land and more women working in their stead. A 48 hour week and a Saturday half-day were still being sought. Wages had gone up considerably, however. Highworth branch reported wages in the area were generally at 33s 6d for 50 hours, 9½d or 10d for overtime, and a month later they were a shilling per week higher, which meant three extra loaves of bread, 20 cigarettes, or a couple of pints of beer. By the outbreak of WWII in September 1939, the basic wage had reached 38s for a 50 hour week.

Despite history often reporting to the contrary, there were people behind the government scenery who saw the approach of conflict in Europe, especially after the Hitler-Mussolini pact and the latter's invasion of Abyssinia in 1935. Signs of preparation began to appear in Wiltshire, new aerodrome sites, more military activities on Salisbury Plain, and on the agricultural scene, the county War Emergency Agricultural scheme put into place by the Government, to be ready when called. Agricultural policy became incorporated into the country's rearmament process. Besides the goal to produce more food from the farms, it was understood that, unlike during WWI, agricultural work on the whole was to be a reserved occupation and carefully regulated to assure the greatest possible output from each man. And from each woman, as they would soon to recruited for the farms, either privately or through the newly-formed Women's Land Army.

So when Britain declared war on Germany on September 3, 1939, some policies to ensure extra food production to replace food imports were already in place. The county War Agricultural Committee backed by the Ministry of Agriculture immediately concentrated on basic commodities such as grain, milk, potatoes and other vegetables. The biggest effect the Wiltshire WAC had on agriculture in the county was ordering the ploughing up of grasslands for arable crops. On the chalklands this reduced the number of sheep, while in the old Cheese Country, many farmers claimed they were ploughing up grassland that had not seen a plough since the Napoleonic wars, or possibly even further back in history. The national figure for the additional ploughed land by 1945 was 62%.

The agricultural labourer would be affected in many ways. He saw much additional labour on the farms all through the War, but in 1940, little change, due to slack in the local labour supply. Some men left their farm to work in other civilian occupations, such as military construction which had increased tremendously in the county, others joined the army. By the summer of 1940, the government had decided to restrict the movement of labourers from the farms, making farm work a reserved occupation, with a new minimum wage rate.

At this time the relationship between farmer and worker changed somewhat. The new government regulations conveyed a strong message and he became a figure of necessity to his employer, the general public and his country. His job was important and he held his head higher. He gained status and again took a pride in his skills, valuing them far more highly than many 'factory skills.' His employer knew that a comfortable relationship with his employees meant more money in the long run, as the more productive his workers were, the more food he shipped to markets. He also understood not to press his worker too far, and in time, a partnership evolved, with concessions on both sides. The employee played his role, particularly in the dairy country where he was not so fervent a union supporter, by seldom complaining to the NUAW, not wanting to be thought unpatriotic, a troublemaker, or a defeatist. In common, both farmer and worker had the defeat of the enemy always to mind, which smoothed over the extra long hours worked on the farm, the mechanical and supply problems constantly cropping up due

Eleven WLA members from the Mere hostel during their lunch break while hoeing at a local farm

The WLA 'wonder gang' from Corsham hostel. Note open neck shirts, despite the obviously cold weather

to labour and other material shortages. Most dairy farmers worked as hard as their labourers, which added to the strength of the partnership. The labourer still remained aware of every nuance of class consciousness, but accepted the prewar social barriers and quietly went on working. The farmer understood this and so a mutual *modus operandi* developed.

Though some other counties had seen female workers leave the farms for other war work, this did not happen much in Wiltshire, as few women were employed as farm labourers in the first place. Three months before the war had started, the Women's Land Army came into existence and immediately started recruiting, training and sending girls out to farms to work alongside the men. These girls were brave in their ignorance in volunteering and accepting farm jobs, particularly if they were sent to work on a farm in a remote area. Few farm houses after the long depression were comfortable, (if they were, the girl was likely to be billeted elsewhere as another mouth to feed was more work for the farm wife), and if the farmer's wife accepted her, her living circumstances were seldom on a par with what the family enjoyed, especially in food, accommodation, heat and hot water. The girls' wages were officially 28s per week, with up to 14s a week being deducted for room and board. Some wives resented the girls as an au pair girl is objected to at the present time. Often the wife was very protective of her husband and son(s). From my own observations, the girls who stayed, and they were in the majority, were tough and soon settled down to the farm life of endless hard work, more often than not usually in difficult living conditions and dreary weather. By 1944 over 1,500 WLA girls were employed in Wiltshire.

Far better off seemed the Land Army girls who worked in gangs and lived in billets with other girls. They had much more freedom and more fun. The girls who made up the threshing- machine gangs were probably the hardest worked of all; read Hardy's description of Tess of the d'Ubervilles on such work and one gets the picture. I recall after one visit of the threshing machine to Cocklebury, the farmer and the men all agreed how well the girls kept up with the endless pace of the machine; for myself, I couldn't have done it, my teenage muscles not being able to cope. So I took care of the grain emerging from the machine, since the pace was not so frenetic! The forestry girls were a resilient lot, too, but they come outside the scope of this book. No record appears of the Wiltshire agricultural labourer's thoughts on land girls. Based on my own experience, they took all wartime extra labour on the farm as it came, whether male or female. If the work was not properly done, they had to remedy it. Certainly auxiliary labour contributed no threat to the labourer during the war, he being in a reserved occupation; if he really wanted to leave the farm for another reserved occupation, this could sometimes be accomplished if he knew how to twist the official arm, thanks to the extra labour available to the farm.

Prisoners of war supplied a large amount of labour on the farms, either in gangs, or in the case of the Italians, billeted on the farms, as were most of the Land Girls. The Italians were popular, the Germans were not. Both nationalities worked well, but seen from my Cocklebury experiences, the Italians always won the popularity contest. For one reason they had closer contact with people and always conveyed a demeanour of cheerfulness about themselves. They had soul, often a little perturbing to the male labour on the farm, but not to the female! Their appreciation of children (not an outstanding attribute of the Wiltshire country dweller) and their musicality opened many doors to friendship and sometimes love. The Germans struck us labourers on the farm as sullen and uneasy, for which they probably had cause to feel, as we did not exactly show any enthusiasm for them. Other sources of labour, soldiers, school children are fairly well documented, although local conditions and supply varied tremendously. Employment of local females, such as myself, are poorly documented and I suspect very few of them reached official work reports and are hence seldom recorded.

Farm Activities undetaken by Land Girls.

Productivity did not increase much in the first two years of the War, mainly because of lack of machinery and old habits on the farm dying hard. Gradually change came, as the Wiltshire countryside mobilized to grow more food. Certainly workers and farmers could not work any harder, hours were extremely long, and seldom did anyone take time off. Half-days, if previously given on arable farms, ceased, and on the dairy farms there never were any, as the milking had to be done twice daily. On Sundays both milking and feeding took about five hours. Holidays, which by 1944 had been set at ten days per annum, (six days with pay and four public holidays), were seemingly not taken; I cannot recall anyone taking time off from work at Cocklebury, except for medical reasons. Instead we worked for overtime pay.

The numbers of male agricultural workers in Wiltshire during the War dropped slightly from the 1939 figure of 11,000, but much extra labour came from women and prisoners of war, besides members of the public, including children during holiday times. By 1942 corn acreage went up from 77,000 to 155,000, the potato crop covered 10,000 acres, sugar beet was produced on 800 acres, a figure to greatly increase after 1943 when the Government made the subsidy really worthwhile, and the 2,000 acres of flax grown celebrated the return of an ancient frequently-grown crop in the county.

Wages were regulated by district committees, but the Central Wages Board fixed the national minimum wage. The first wartime wage regulations had to be negotiated with the NFU and the workers, with wages related to the guaranteed prices of agricultural products. These were passed in April 1940, 48s being the first weekly wage. Throughout the War all wage increases were balanced by similarly raised increases in products prices. By 1945 the basic agricultural wage totalled 72s, and as wage gains were greater than the increased cost of goods, the farm workers' purchasing power during the war years statistically increased by 50% from 1939.

The war years saw an increase in support by Wiltshire labourers for the NUAW. Both women farm workers and land army girls joined. With wage rises guaranteed throughout the war, the men felt that the end of the war would see the time come when agricultural wages would equal industrial pay levels especially after the promise of the Beveridge report, suggesting that the agricultural worker should have 'a status equal to that of other industries in respect of terms and conditions of service.' Union officials realized that to accomplish that equality, and particularly the wage parity, it was essential for the Government to maintain agricultural prosperity by guaranteed prices, which would lead to stability. The NFU eventually followed this train of thought also. The days of cheap food had to end. This is still a wonderful dream, nowhere in the world on the horizon. Economic subsidies continue today, despite machinations to promote change.

Besides more wages, the agricultural labourer began to receive more status, and his contributions to Britain and the war effort, along with those of the farmer, began to be of interest to the news media at times. The Ministry of Agriculture propaganda plus German U boat attacks on shipping furthered that interest and by 1943, we agricultural labourers were popular indeed! A few months after the outbreak of war, saw the first NUAW member elected to the WCC, a very significant event, dominated as the council was by middle- and upper-class members. During the war, the Government further increased the farm workers' status by acknowledging their special needs with additional rations or allowances; cheese, soap, clothing supplements and extra clothing coupons. In 1944 the union unfavourably compared the meals supplied to industrial workers in factory canteens with farm workers' extra cheese rations. At the time the union, in their course of pursuing helpful little comforts for their member's lives, was seeking a source of glass thermos liner replacements! No doubt we preferred our ration privileges, factory workers performing their monotonous work did not raise our envy. Despite the weather sometimes, we much preferred an outside environment and the comparative freedom of our job.

The union announced in 1941 that the Government would make surplus army clothing available to farm workers, but I never saw one wearing any; perhaps this occurred in the chalk country. The Italian prisoners of war wore them, however. The battledress trousers, jacket and overcoat were all dyed chocolate brown, the jacket then had a large, round, coloured piece of material inserted in the back. They always wore their own much-treasured Italian army cap. When their country surrendered in 1943, the patch was discarded and the prisoners were allowed a limited amount of freedom. The prisoners worked on the farms in gangs mainly, earning up to a shilling a day until they were able to return to Italy after the War in 1945 or 1946, but some 'lived in' on farms. At the end of the War those live-ins, if they so chose, continued working on 'their' farm, a factor which concerned the NUAW greatly, as they feared job losses for English farm workers. Some German prisoners of war were slow to be sent back home and farmers continued to employ them as gang labour.

Specifically in Wiltshire, the concerns of the union centred greatly on small but important issues of interest to the rank and file, the focal issue of wages, insurance and accident compensation being taken care of through the War. Not that the union couldn't criticize. For instance, *The Landworker* in 1941 brought up education, (a need for more access to secondary education for rural children and a higher school-leaving age), child labour regulations and, inevitably, tied cottages. But the union had little influence in the tied cottage sphere. During the War, both the farmer and the employee in a tied cottage were restricted to their employer-employee housing relationship; farmers were not able to dismiss a man from his job except for gross inefficiency and rents were controlled. Tied cottage occupants depended on the goodwill of their employer for repairs, they could not move, as little alternative housing existed in the countryside and council building-schemes stayed on hold. The condition of houses in the Wiltshire countryside deteriorated all through the War, and for the agricultural labourer, would show little improvement until the 1950s.

It went without question that during the War almost no new houses were built, or any social amenities increased. The labourer suffered much, especially as his standard of housing was low to start with, and few cottages had running water, sewage systems or electricity. Repairs were executed at a minimum too, as the labourers' wages still did not allow rents conducive to keeping the house in good order. The war was always an excuse not to do very much. In 1943 the Government gave permission for local authorities to erect 3000 houses in certain selected areas, but few were built in Wiltshire.

Rural schools suffered during the War. The standard of teaching, never high, dropped as men were called to the service, to be replaced by retired teachers or married women, neither often able to carry a full teaching load, due to age or commitments. And evacuees strained the resources of village schools. Billeted on households, child evacuees caused fewer problems than adult evacuees, perhaps because they were soon absorbed into the daily living of the villages. The adults, mainly young mothers, usually became bored with rural life and returned to their home city, invariably London. These women may have caused domestic difficulties in some cases, as most rural houses were small, but the children were more welcomed and their billeting allowance was often considered worth the inconvenience of a stranger in the household. Certainly the villages became more lively, the land army girls and troops stationed in the vicinity opened up a demand for entertainment, besides the pub, and more dances and other get-togethers ensued. But this hardly helped the labourer; if married, he still kept to his usual recreations, and his wife really had none. If single, he was far less desirable as a partner in fun, with little money and much overtime work, especially in the long summer evenings of double daylight saving time.

Post WWII

At the War's end the NUAW continued to watch every government move which affected the welfare of the agricultural labourer. The main aim was still wages and benefits on a par with the industrial worker, which sadly was not going to materialize, despite the actions of the new Labour Government elected in 1945. Other concerns in Wiltshire centred on the availability of rural housing, the need for smallholdings and more minor but important points, such as the danger of insecticides, weekend schools for union members and more national conferences, the latter showing the growing awareness of the power of a united union. And yes, a Friday pay day still appeared on the agenda. Compensation for adequate notice not given by an employer, an off-shoot of the housing problem, provoked a demonstration at Warminster in 1950.

All through the war, J. V. Coe of 10 Meadow Drive, Devizes organized all the union affairs in Wiltshire. A 1950 tribute to him told of his travels around the county in all weathers, first on a motor bike (finally acquired by the union!) and in later years with a car. He knew every member and had seen a great increase in the number of union branches and members in the county.

As had happened in the last twenty years of the 19th century, a drift from agricultural employment began in Wiltshire after WWII. The Labour Party's role in placing the agricultural labourer's status and his wages on a par with urban workers achieved part of its goal as can be shown by the progression of wage rises to 1950 and welfare measures. But agricultural wages did not keep up with other work categories and to reach a reasonable wage standard still meant reliance on overtime. But changes in productivity, more owner-occupier farms, price guarantees creating more business-like ways and more family labour – all these lessened the job prospects for the farm worker. Again the prosperity of the farmer did not reach his worker and training for the job was still scarce. Mechanization continued to eliminate hand work, as did different standards of cultivation and husbandry. But prospects in the urban job markets increased steadily. Unlike any other time in history, those who wanted 'out' could 'out' from the farm labour market without difficulty New reasons for leaving the land joined the old – no formal qualifications, paper or otherwise, to automatically raise wages, no future or promotional prospects. The productivity increase per man on Wiltshire farms represented a catching-up by 1960s to modern times, due to heavy use of capital, chemicals and energy. But his chances of farming for himself by the early 1970s were more slender than those of winning the football pools, land was so scarce and costly. The cumulative result of all these changes was to make the agricultural labourer of this book, in a short span of twenty years, to become an outdated anachronism; a worker left with little other intimate contact with soil or beast than the wheels he rode on or the machine he operated.

Modern technology began to increase the opportunities for work in other occupations. His wife wanted a job outside the home and his children were beginning to receive training

Workers and families of Cocklebury Farm on Peggy Self's wedding day 1951.

in technical aspects of work. Village schools started to close, affordable housing in the Wiltshire countryside in the early 1960s began to lessen and a car started to be a necessity for country life. It became easier to move to the town. And move they did. The phenomenon of the Wiltshire agricultural labourer, his wife and family tied to the land, the village and their cottage, had disappeared by the 1970s, to be frequently replaced by a worker with skills and assets, benefits, better-housed, housed, able to travel a reasonable distance to his work and beholden to no employer.

And so the tradition of the Englishman, always his own individual, well aware of his legal rights through the ages, ready to go to law to preserve them, turned out not to hold true for those at the bottom of the social scale, the labourers, the vagrant and the prisoner. From the beginning of modern times until the end of WWII, to stand up for their rights was nearly always an effort doomed to failure. Protests belonged to the classes above them. In Wiltshire, after land was denied to him, either by law or by cost, the agricultural labourer was left to fend for himself, with minimum work and minimum wages. The social structure had locked him into this position by the 18th century, and only 20th century industrialization, cheaper food or sometimes emigration, released him from being just a source of cheap labour at the bottom of the social scale. Now the farm employee and his wife in Wiltshire today are more likely to live on a similar level to other workers, have the same problems, hopes and aspirations. Two major problems beset him however, reasonably priced housing in the countryside, and the ability of the Wiltshire farmer to employ him, for it is becoming more economical for the farmer to employ contract labour. Now only their grandparents' generation can remember what it was like to be an agricultural labourer, and of those still alive, including myself, I doubt there is one who would ever wish their labouring life on their descendants.

The ethnic identity of the Wiltshire agriculture labourer sprang from his prehistoric roots. Undoubtedly with them is blended some Roman blood and his Anglo-Saxon heritage. With perhaps a dash of Normandy blood, his racial identity was completed, and later developed by the English language and culture. These, in turn, shaped his attitudes to marriage and family, work, common rights, personal freedom, property ownership, food and drink. If he ceased to become an agricultural labourer, he took these attitudes with him; if he remained, they became part of his descendants' heritage. These common links were shared by all landworkers in Wiltshire's past. I wrote this book to share their heritage with my reader and with the hope that they will always be remembered.

A reaper in operation at Etchilhampton 1927. The machine cut and bundled the grain crop, the resulting sheaves were then stooked by hand to dry. The author stooked for several summers at Cocklebury in the 1940s.

Chapter 8 Bibliography

Much material for this chapter came from my own memories and my work as an agricultural labourer during WWII. An enquiring child, my questions were invariably patiently answered, and unusually for a middle-class youngster, I was fortunate to mix with the many layers of society strongly in place at the time. Other source material, besides that mentioned in the text and the general bibliography proved to be:

ARMSTRONG, A., 1988, *Farmworkers in England and Wales: a social and economic history 1770-1980.* Aimes: Iowa State University Press

FUSSELL, G., 1948, *Tolpuddle to T.U.C.* Slough: Windsor Press

GREENE, F., 1913, *The Tyranny of the Countryside,* T. Fisher Unwin

SLOCOMBE, I., 2002. Agriculture in Wiltshire in World war I. *Wiltshire Studies* 95, 69-88

BRACEY, H., 1952, *Social Provision in Rural Wiltshire.* Methuen

PENNINGTON-ROWSELL, E., 1997. Who 'Betrayed' Whom? Power and Politics in the 1920/ 1921 Agricultural Crisis. *AHR* 45.2, 176-194

Eviction at Foxham, 1913.

The author riding after milking one Sunday morning, 1943 (no time to change into riding gear).

Glossary

CARBON DATING: The decay of carbon in a previously living organism or plant measured by radio-active means to produce a date the organism died, i.e. a measure of time.

CAUSEWAYED CAMP: Areas enclosed by one or more lines of earthworks, often ditches, made up of elongated pits separate by narrow causeways, their function unexplained. Windmill Hill is Wiltshires's best example.

CHARTER: A grant of privilege, perhaps land, but a land grant does not necessarily confer privilege except to the land.

CHURCHSCOT: A tax developed from Heriot, a claim from landlord after death of a tenant, usually for the best beast, and by the 14th century, generally had been commuted into money. Here is the origin of getting off *scot-free.*

CLOD-HOPPER: A clumsy person, originally applied to a person or labourer 'who hopped from clod to clod in the fields'.

COB: A mixture of mud and straw or mud and lime (derived from chalk) built up in layers and left to dry (*see also daub and wattle*).

COPPICE: An area of undergrowth and small trees, periodically cut to stimulate new growth.

COUCHING: The work of collecting creeping couch grass, piling it into heaps and burning it.

DAUB AND WATTLE: Daub is in-fill for a wall, similar to cob, with the addition of dung and cow hair. Wattle consists of a network of split wood holding the daub in place.

DEMESNE: Land held by a manor lord as his own, close by the main estate building, by late medieval times invariably rented out to tenants.

FAGGOT: Bundle of sticks for firewood. In 19th and 20th century Wiltshire, a faggot also referred to a mixture of pig's innards, onions and herbs chopped and fried, sold by butchers.

FARM: Originated from *ferme*, a lease, rented land or the rent itself. A collection of animals, buildings and persons assembled to cultivate a particular piece of land.

GILDAS: A British cleric circa AD 475-550. Wrote the tract *On the Ruin of Britain,* containing current history of his time, not always considered accurate.

HARROW: A horse or tractor drawn large rake, consisting of spikes fifteen cms apart on a rectangular frame, used to break up soil after ploughing and before planting.

HERIOT: Heriot, a feudal obligation to a lord on the death of a tenant, is derived from Churchscot, the portion of a dead man's goods 'donated' to the church by his family.

INQUISITIONS POST MORTEM (IPMS): Inquests made on the death of a tenant holding royal land. Can be of great interest to local historians and genealogists as they contain lists of both landholders and tenants, commencing from the 13th century.

KNAPP: *(Verb)* The Prehistoric art of chipping a stone or flint to produce a useful tool.

LIMING: The process of treating soil with burnt lime (calcium oxide) to increase fertility. Marling is a similar process.

LONGHOUSE: A rectangular farm building constructed to house both family and large animals.

MOONRAKER: A native of Wiltshire. The name is derived from the legend concerning smugglers in the late 1700s who hid a contraband keg of brandy in a pond near Bishop's Cannings. On a moonlit night, they went back to retrieve it, taking wooden rakes with them. Unfortunately excise men sighted them and asked what they were doing. 'We be trying to get that ther' cheese we do see in the pond' they replied, indicating the reflection of the moon on the pond's surface. The excise men laughed, commented on the stupidity of people thereabouts and went off. The men recovered their keg of brandy and laughed at the stupidity of the excise men to believe such a tale, priding themselves on their canny sagaciousness, characteristic of a Wiltshire native.

PROBATE INVENTORIES (PIs): A list of goods belonging to a deceased person who has left goods to the value of £5 or more, the inventory made by a reputable person.

SALISBURY PLAIN TRAINING AREA: Located due north of Salisbury, approximately 39,000 hectares taken over by the military from the end of the 19th century, the area stretches 38 kms east to west and 14 kms north to south.

SARSEN STONES or GREY WETHERS: From saracen, a stranger, or from the likeness of the stones to a recumbent sheep. Moved by erosion to the surface from Tertiary deposits 100 million years ago, cracked by frost, then transferred by glacial and water action, mainly in Wiltshire, to Marlborough Downs area. These are the stones that are likely to have given prehistoric man the preliminary idea for monument building, supplying him with the major material for his monuments, while giving agriculturists throughout history the problem of their removal to make cultivation easier

SKIMMINGTON: Derivation unknown. Generally a ceremony performed on an unpopular person, but in Wiltshire in the 19th century, according to the *English Dialect Dictionary*, more specifically confined to the rough music performed to accompany the shaming of a scandalous or immoral person.

TOFT: A house or small group of farm buildings, used or abandoned.

VILL: Originally a basic unit or framework wherein an agricultural society exploited an area; later a unit of government, often becoming part of a parish unit with field system rights delineated.

General Index

Index of Place-Names